Bertram Windle, the Honan Bequest and the
Modernisation of University College Cork,
1904–1919

Dr Madoline O'Connell, granddaughter of Bertram Windle, 30 August 2010.
Photo: Clare Keogh

Bertram Windle, the Honan Bequest and the Modernisation of University College Cork, 1904–1919

ANN KEOGH
and
DERMOT KEOGH
with Patrick Kiely

CORK UNIVERSITY PRESS

First published in 2010 by
Cork University Press
Youngline Industrial Estate
Pouladuff Road, Togher
Cork, Ireland

© Ann Keogh and Dermot Keogh

British Library Cataloguing in Publication Data

A CIP catalogue record for this book is available from the British Library.

ISBN-13: 978-185918-473-8

Published with the support of the National University of Ireland

Printed in the UK by J.F. Print
Typeset by Tower Books, Ballincollig, Co. Cork
www.corkuniversitypress.com

 An Roinn Fiontar, Trádála agus Nuálaíochta
Department of Enterprise, Trade and Innovation

 European Union
European Regional
Development Fund
Investing in your future

 HEA

Higher Education Authority
An tÚdarás um Ard-Oideachas

 Ireland's EU Structural Funds
Programmes 2007 - 2013

Co-funded by the Irish Government
and the European Union

Dedicated to
Madoline O'Connell,
to Loretta and Lewis Glucksman,
to the late Fr Gearoid O'Sullivan,
to Madelaine and Matthew MacNamara,
to Abi, Luke, David, Aisling and Darragh,
and to
Eoin, Caroline, Niall, Elizabeth, Aoife,
Marco, Clare and Barry

Contents

Illustrations

Acknowledgements

The publication of this book owes much to the persistence of two women, and to the initiative of a former president of University College Cork, Professor Gerard Wrixon, who, nearly six years ago, asked me as head of the Department of History to find a graduate student willing to write a biography of Bertram Windle, president of QCC/UCC between 1904 and 1919. The proposal, Professor Wrixon said, had come from the daughter of Windle's eldest daughter Mary, Dr Madoline O'Connell; born in 1915, she has had a lifelong curiosity about a grandfather she never really knew in person. Madoline wanted to support the writing of a scholarly academic study which would review comprehensively his life and times. She made a generous donation towards the publication costs of the monograph.

At the time Professor Wrixon approached me, I was in a position to tell him that a thesis was being completed in the Department of History on a topic close to the subject he had in mind. In 2004, Ann Keogh – and here was the third force behind the biography project – had completed an MA entitled 'A Study in Philanthropy: Sir Bertram Windle, Sir John O'Connell, Isabella Honan and the Building of the Honan Chapel, University College Cork'. As I am married to the author of that work, I had received many tutorials on the life and times of Windle as the thesis was being researched and written. After considering the suggestion of Madoline and Professor Wrixon, we decided to join forces and to work together on a biography.

This handsomely produced monograph, a tribute to the consistently high production standards of Cork University Press, was written substantially between 2008 and 2010. As a Professor of History who has taught for thirty years at UCC, I found the research a pleasure and a refuge from the ever intensifying professional challenges posed by the changing administrative culture and ethos in the university. Turning adversity into opportunity, this biography is the by-product of the three most difficult years of my three decades of service to higher education in Cork. We are very grateful to the former Vice-President for Planning, Communications and Development, Mr Michael O'Sullivan, who helped guide this project through those difficult times. Retiring at the age of fifty in 2009, it is our personal belief that UCC is impoverished by his absence.

Ms Virginia Teehan, a joint editor of the beautifully produced Cork University Press book *The Honan Chapel – A Golden Vision*, helped to stimulate our interest in the subject of Bertram Windle and the Honan Chapel. We are thankful for all the help and support that she gave this project.

Madelaine and Matthew MacNamara, our close friends, worked with us to decipher the handwriting in Windle's diaries. Their combined scholarship, particularly their knowledge of the classics and modern languages, helped unlock many of the secrets of a personal archive of great historical richness. That work took persistence, tenacity and detective work. Dr Niall Keogh helped us locate a number of important sources in Dublin and London. Niall, who is our second son, located the will of Sir John O'Connell, 8 November 1944 [died 28 December 1943]. He also helped establish that the will of Matthew Honan had been destroyed during the Irish civil war. He located the wills of Robert and Isabella Honan. In London, he conducted research on our behalf in the British National Archives, Kew, and in the Cardinal Francis Bourne papers in the archives of the Archdiocese of Westminster. Aoife and Clare, our two daughters, helped at different stages in the writing of the book. Aoife checked the text of different drafts. Clare helped edit old photos reproduced in the book and took others which are also included. We are grateful to Angela Cahill.

We are very grateful to Patrick Kiely who brought alive for us the multiple possibilities of digitisation as a research tool. He digitised almost the entire Windle collection, including diaries from 1908 to 1920, letters, scrapbooks and manuscripts. That made it possible to access the entire Windle collection at home. As mentioned earlier, much time was needed to pore over the diaries and letters in an effort to break 'the code'. We are grateful to Patrick also for reading the final draft, eliminating unnecessary duplications and standardising the footnotes. Patrick also digitised photographs and illustrations for the volume together with other cognate collections of papers. He leads the international field in the application of these new techniques of remote capture. His skills will help keep the School of History in UCC in the van of the pioneering of new digital research techniques.

Patrick's work could not have been completed without the coopera-tion of the staff of Special Collections, University of Birmingham. We are thankful to the Senior Archivist, Ms Philippa Bassett, Ms Jenny Childs, Mr Martin Kineally and to the Director of Special Collections and University Archivist, Ms Susan Morrall, for their help and assis-tance. Their progressive policies greatly facilitated the completion of this biography.

Fr John Sharp, Archivist, Birmingham Archdiocesan Archives, Cathedral House, Birmingham, helped us source a valuable collection of letters in the Mgr John Parkinson collection. We are also grateful to the library staff of St Mary's College, Oscott, Birmingham, for helping us track down a variety of sources. We thank Sr Jean Bunn, Sister of Notre Dame, for her letter and enclosures on 29 December 2004. We are also grateful to Ms Clare Walsh, Archivist, British Province, Sisters of Notre Dame, England and Wales, for supplying us with information on Windle's first biographer, Sr Monica Taylor.

In the UCC School of History, we have many friends who were of great help at different times during the research of this manuscript. In particular, we thank Gabriel Doherty who supervised the original thesis and has been a major help. Andrew McCarthy located a number of letters in the Cloyne Diocesan Archives and provided other important refer-ences. We thank the following colleagues in the School of History: Damian Bracken, Diarmuid Scully, Hiram Morgan, Donal O' Driscoll, Mervyn O'Driscoll, Larry Geary, the late Diarmuid Whelan, Finola Doyle O'Neill, Jerome aan der Wiel, Paul Loftus and John O'Donovan. Ms Sheila Cunneen, another colleague, worked very closely with us deci-phering Windle's writing and that of his more impenetrable correspondents. She also read and edited a number of the drafts. We thank Charlotte Holland, Deirdre O'Sullivan, Geraldine McAllister and Maeve Barry of the School of History for all their help and support. Our thanks to three other members of staff who are retired: Norma Buckley, Margaret Clayton and Veronica Fraser.

Many colleagues in other departments in UCC, too numerous to name, helped our research in different ways. We must, however, single out for special thanks the University Archivist, Ms Catriona Mulcahy, and the UCC Heritage officer, Mr Michael Holland. They were infinitely patient and handled our requests with great efficiency. We are grateful to have gained access to the very rich collection of college archives for our period of study. Ms Mulcahy also tracked down and scanned photo-graphs which we have used in this volume.

Thanks also to the University College Cork librarian, Mr John Fitz-Gerald, and to the Head of Special Collections, Crónán Ó Doibhlin, and its staff, Mary Lombard, Peadar Cranitch, Elaine Harrington, Sheyeda Allen and Elaine Charwat for making available for consultation papers relating to the presidency of Bertram Windle, the Honan Hostel Minute Books, the William O'Brien papers and publications on the history of the college.

Our thanks to the former Finance Secretary, Mr Michael Kelleher, and his staff for locating two files relevant to the history of the Honan scholarships. We also thank Professor Seán Ó Coileáin and Dr Neil Buttimer for supplying us with a number of articles on the history of the professorship of Irish at UCC. Professor David Gwynn Morgan, School of Law, helped us with queries regarding the identification of legal advisers to the college. We are grateful to James Cronin, Art History, School of History, UCC, for putting us in touch with the Sisters of Mercy, Oaklea, Tunstall Road, Sunderland. Sr Wilfred conducted research on our behalf, sending on information and photographs.

The chaplaincy team at UCC have been most helpful and encouraging of this project. We will continue our study in the coming years of the history of the Honan Chapel; our thanks to Fr Tom Riordan, Fr Michael Regan, Fr Seosamh A. Ó Cochláin, Canon George Hilliard, Fr Dave McAuliffe, Ms Gertie O'Donoghue and Ms Bernadette Twomey.

The Local Studies section of Cork City Library provides researchers with an outstanding service. The specialist knowledge of its Director, Kieran Burke, and the other staff helped us answer many queries and kindly supplied copies of newspaper articles and helped check references. We are thankful to Brian McGee, Archivist, Cork City and County Archives, Seamus Murphy Building, Blackpool, for his help. The late Sr Cabrini, Archivist, Diocese of Cloyne, helped identify a number of letters from Windle in the Bishop Robert Browne collection. We also acknowledge the support that we received from Bishop John Buckley and the staff of the Diocese of Cork.

We thank Joe and Anne Lee, friends for many years, for their help and support while writing this volume. In NUI Galway, Professor Gearóid Ó Tuathaigh and Dr Mary Harris drew our attention to a number of important references. Our thanks also to Professor George Boyce.

Many individuals and institutions in Dublin helped locate valuable material. The Registrar of the National University of Ireland, Dr Attracta Halpin, Ms Ann Milner and NUI staff copied sections from the minute books and correspondence at our request. Fr Ignatius, Franciscan Archives, Dun Mhuire, Killiney, provided access to archives relevant to Saint Anthony's Hall of Residence. The former Dublin Archdiocesan Archivist, Mr David Sheehy, located Archbishop William Walsh–Windle correspondence. His successor, Ms Noelle Dowling, kindly copied a number of letters at our request.

We are grateful to Catriona Crowe, Michael Kennedy and the staff of the National Archives of Ireland, to the staff of the manuscript room, National Library of Ireland, for their assistance and to the staff of the reading room in Trinity College. Anne-Marie Ryan, Researcher/Exhibition Assistant, Pearse Museum located a number of documents relating to Windle's links with Patrick Pearse and St Enda's School. Ms Teresa Whitington, librarian, Central Catholic Library, Dublin, gave us every assistance especially in locating journals. The librarians, National College of Art and Design, Dublin, gave access to files on Harry Clarke.

The historian Michelle O'Driscoll helped us locate material on the death of Canon Magner, who was shot by a member of the British forces in West Cork in 1920.

We thank the architect Michael Hurley, who was responsible for over-seeing restoration of the Honan chapel during the 1990s. He kindly loaned us a copy of Sir John O'Connell's book on the Honan and helped us make contact with Mr Ken Ryan, The Abbey Stained Glass Studio, 18 Old Kilmainham, Dublin. The latter kindly gave an interview during which he explained the history of his company which has a direct link with the Clarke studios. He gave us access to the Joshua Clarke Studio Order Book. This was part of the submission Mr Ken Ryan made on behalf of the Abbey Stained Glass Studio in the 1990s to the then rector of the Honan, Fr Gearoid O'Sullivan CM to win the contract for the restoration of the stained glass windows.

In Rome, we consulted the papers of two rectors of the Pontifical Irish College, Michael O'Riordan and John Hagan. We are grateful to the Rector, Mgr Liam Bergin, Vice Rector, Albert McDonnell, Fr Billy Swan and Fr Chris Hayden. Vera Orschel, who catalogued the John Hagan papers, was of great help on our many visits to the Pontifical Irish College as was her fellow archivist, Martin Fagan.

In the United States, we are thankful to Scott S. Taylor, who made working on the Shane Leslie papers in Special Collections, Joseph Mark Lauinger Memorial Library, Georgetown University, a real pleasure. We are also grateful to the staff of the Library of Congress and the US National Archives. A former colleague in the Woodrow Wilson Center for Scholars, Ms Susan Nugent, read a late draft of the manuscript. Both Susan and her husband Paul provided hospitality on our visits to the United States as did Mike and Kath Lacey. Our thanks also to Ms Connie Lewis, John M. Kelly Library, University of St Michael's College, Toronto, for helping draw our attention to three box files on Bertram Windle containing mostly offprints of his work.

Joseph P. Cunningham and Ruth Fleischmann's *Aloys Fleischmann 1880–1964: Immigrant Musician in Ireland*, which had not been published before our study was completed, should serve as important and invaluable complementary reading to the study of Windle. That work sketches in very well the cultural and musical life of Cork during the period that Windle was president of QCC/UCC. It is a very lively and scholarly narrative and has added greatly to our understanding, albeit after the writing of Windle, knowledge of the period. It serves as an important survey of cultural life in Cork from the latter decades of the nineteenth century until the middle of the twentieth century. There are frequent references to Mary and John Horgan who were close friends of Aloys and Tilly Fleischmanns and of their children. We thank Ruth and Maeve Fleischmann for also providing us with a number of photographs of Professor Wally Swertz.

We thank Eibhear Walshe, Maeve McDonagh and other members of the Cork University Press (CUP) committee for supporting the publication of this work; also the CUP staff: Mike Collins, Maria O'Donovan, Mary O'Mahony and Mary White-Fitzpatrick. Part of the funding which helped support the researching and publication of this volume came from a number of sources. We thank the following: Professor Geoffrey Roberts and the History Department Research Fund; Professors David Cox and Caroline Fennell and the Publication Fund of the College of Arts, Celtic Studies and Social Science; Dr Hiram Morgan and PRTLI4; Dr Attracta Halpin and the National University of Ireland Publication Fund; and Dr Madoline O'Connell who helped set the research project in motion, gave a generous donation to Cork University Press towards publications costs and allowed the authors access to her family photographic collection for inclusion in this volume. This work is dedicated to her.

Our thanks to Kay and Rebecca Harte, to Mirco, Ewa and Liam of the Farmgate Café, English Market, Cork. We have had many fruitful discussions there on the content of this book.

Finally our thanks to Eoin, Caroline, Niall, Elizabeth, Aoife, Marco, Clare, Barry and to the new generation, Abigale, Luke, David, Aisling and Darragh for giving us both joy and a sense of continuity.

Ann and Dermot Keogh
Rome, 22 May 2010

Introduction

This two-volume project developed out of an MA completed in 2004 in Local History, entitled 'A Study in Philanthropy: Sir Bertram Windle, Sir John O'Connell, Isabella Honan and the building of the Honan Chapel, University College Cork'.[1] The study posed many questions about the philosophy and character of Sir Bertram Coghill Alan Windle – the president of Queen's College, Cork/University College Cork (QCC/UCC) from 1904 to 1919 – which went beyond the scope of the thesis. What was Windle's family background and education at Trinity College Dublin? What were the details of his early professional career as a professor of anatomy in Birmingham? Why did he become a convert to Catholicism in the early 1880s? How did he reconcile his scientific and religious beliefs? What was his attitude to land reform in Ireland and to home rule? What was he like as a father and a family man? Why did he come to Ireland in 1904 to take up a position as president of Queen's College, Cork, giving up his comfortable post as Dean of the Medical Faculty at Birmingham University? What role did he play in the resolution of the Irish 'university question' and in the subsequent governance of University College Cork? What part did his Catholicism play in the modernisation of UCC? How did he respond to the rise of radical nationalism and revolutionary unionism in Ireland? What was his reaction to the First World War and the Easter Rising in 1916? How did he view the emergence of Éamon de Valera and the ascendancy of Sinn Féin over the Irish Parliamentary Party (IPP)? What were his views on Irish Catholicism? How did he judge the bishops and the clergy? Why did he leave Ireland to take up an academic position in Canada or, put another way, why did he resign from the UCC presidency in 1919?

In an effort to answer the questions posed above, we combined forces over the past six years to complete this study of Bertram Windle. We

1

continue to collaborate on another volume on the Honan bequest and the building of the Honan Chapel. Our task in starting this study of Windle has been helped by the existing scholarly literature on UCC.[2] Studies on the Honan Chapel were also of major assistance. Sir John O'Connell, one of the people most responsible for the building of the Honan, had published a study in 1916.[3] Professor Michael J. Kelly wrote in 1946 an excellent sixteen-page guide with sixteen pages of plates.[4] In 1992, Dr Paul Larmour published an important book on the Irish arts and crafts movement, containing important information on the Honan Chapel and its furnishings.[5] A conference entitled 'The Craftsman's Honoured Hand' was held at UCC on 29 January 2000 on the Honan Chapel and the legacy of Irish arts and crafts from the beginning of the twentieth century. Edited by Virginia Teehan and Elizabeth Wincott Heckett, a handsome, scholarly volume was published in 2004 entitled *The Honan Chapel: A Golden Vision.*[6]

Dr Madoline O'Connell, Windle's granddaughter, was both the initiator of the idea for this book and a strong source of support and information for both of us as we worked through the sources. She, too, was also of great help to her nephew, John Horgan, when he researched his introduction for the new edition [2009] of her father, John J. Horgan's *Parnell to Pearse.*[7] This latter volume, which first appeared in 1949, may be read at two levels. Firstly, it is a much undervalued source for the study of the history of Ireland between the 1880s and 1918. Secondly, *Parnell to Pearse* is also a very important source for an analysis of Windle and QCC/UCC. Horgan's nephew, John Horgan, has written an important introduction to a new edition which draws together various sources to craft a very strong, chiselled and controlled portrait of his uncle. Besides reading *Parnell to Pearse* and speaking to Madoline, we also read *Sir Bertram Windle: A Memoir*, which was published in 1932 – less than three years after its subject's death. Its author, Sr Monica Taylor, was a member of the Sisters of Notre Dame.[8] Besides being a biographer, she was a scientist of international repute and a role model for women in higher education in the early part of the twentieth century. Born on 1 November 1877 in St Helens, Lancashire, her parents were Joseph Taylor and Agnes Pickton. She entered the Notre Dame order on 8 December 1900 and took final vows on 2 September 1903. Her intelligence and academic ability were evident to her superiors. But the conservative religious culture of the time did not encourage a sister to attend university to study science. However, permission was sought from the superior general of the order and she was allowed to go to Glasgow University to study science in 1908. She went as a private student and was always accompanied by a 'chaperon'. Sr Monica overcame the many obstacles which were placed in the way of a woman religious pursuing an academic career. She won the Steel-Strang Scholarship in Zoology, an award no woman student had ever won. In 1917, she was awarded the degree of DSc. She became a member of the Scottish Marine Biological Station. Her work on amoeba gained her international fame. In 1953, Glasgow University conferred her with an honorary degree of LLD in recognition of her eminence in science.[9] Sr Monica spent her professional life, from 1901 to 1946, teaching at the Notre-Dame-run teacher training college, Dowanhill, Glasgow. She moved to Birkdale, Southport, in 1946, returning to Dowanhill in 1947 where she remained until her death in 1968.[10]

How and when did Windle come to know and befriend this formidable international woman of science? Perhaps he first read her papers while he was an external examiner in the Department of Anatomy at the University of Glasgow before taking up his duties at UCC in 1904? More than likely he would have heard talk of a brilliant young nun scientist while doing the rounds of the universities. We know that the two met in March 1914 when Windle was invited to give an address to the Catholic Institute in Glasgow as the guest of Professor Phillimore. He visited Dowanhill Convent to meet Anne Hardman, the daughter of his close friend, John B. Hardman. (Her name in religion was Sr Anne.) Windle met the superior of the convent and principal of the training college, Sr Mary of St Wilfrid (Mary Adela Lescher). His diary also makes reference to meeting 'other nuns including the biologists'. That was probably the first occasion on which he met Sr Monica.[11] He dined that evening with Judge Lord Skerrington and Prof. Phillimore. He gave his address on 'The Argument from Design', noting in his diary: 'It went very well.' Out of the chance meeting between Sr Monica and Windle flowered a prolonged intellectual relationship. An exchange of letters began in 1914. The first letter from Windle is dated 30 October 1914, acknowledging receipt of her 'excellent piece of work' which he was sending the Professor of Zoology in UCC.

The first letter from Sr Monica to Windle in the Birmingham collection is dated 25 July 1920.[12] But it is evident that they corresponded frequently between 1914 and 1919. The proof of that is that Windle's letters to her are in his personal papers at Birmingham. Sr Monica may, however, have destroyed her early letters to Windle. More than likely she destroyed each letter sent by him soon after she had received it during those early years. It would not be unusual for a nun in those austere times to be prevented from carrying on a regular correspondence with a layman. However, her superiors were quite enlightened to have allowed such a development.

Windle met Sr Monica a second time in early December 1919 (see final chapter) when he came to lecture at Glasgow University and at the Notre Dame Training College, Dowanhill. It was a very brief visit as he was catching a boat to Canada within days. He made a trip back to England in 1921, visiting Glasgow and Sr Monica and the community at Dowanhill. That turned out to be his last visit across the Atlantic to Europe.

The correspondence between Windle and Sr Monica is quite remarkable in many ways. Windle began in the role of a senior professor writing encouragingly to a brilliant science student who also happened to be a nun. Windle observed the religious conventions of the day, writing as if he were a priest or a religious, seeking the prayers of Sr Monica and her community. He was very careful to acknowledge the nature of the relationship on more than one occasion. It was, he was at pains to demonstrate, completely platonic and open. Sr Monica's superior reading their correspondence – and it is certain that that would have been the case – would have discerned the help which the president of UCC was deriving from the prayers of the Notre Dame community. As the years progressed, Windle grew to trust Sr Monica implicitly, treating her as a confidant to whom, as time progressed, he revealed his innermost thoughts and fears. He articulated, in a most uninhibited way, his feelings and emotions, his religious doubts and fears, his family secrets and his political views, to a highly intelligent, wise and holy woman who wrote reassuringly to him for fifteen years. Sr Monica, privileged and burdened by the exchanges, came to know him better than anyone other than his wife, Edith.

There was one development which changed the nature of the relationship; on 7 March 1923, Windle wrote to his future biographer: 'Do you know I have been turning over in my mind a kind of wild thought for some time. I have a vast lot of cuttings, diaries etc affording a picture of my not very wonderful career. I cannot think of anyone who would be more interested in them than you or whom I would rather have put together any account – if any – which might appear about me since you know more of various sides of me than anyone else. I do not intend to die for some time to come please God but what would you say to this or do you think it too wild to be contemplated. Let me know.'[13]

On 31 March 1923, having received an encouraging reply, he wrote: 'I sort of felt that you would like to have the papers and books and if your Superior does not say no, you shall when I am done with them. Not yet – you will say. Well – sometimes I wish it could be but there is my wife and who would look after her? Also things to be done and I like doing them.'[14] Sr Monica wrote on 20 July 1923: 'Yes, I have asked Sister Superior and she says "Yes". I am so glad in one way but you know what I have said before about my incapacity. However you want me to have the records. No one will value them more than I do – that I can say – and no one more appreciates the delicacy of the feeling that prompts you to bestow upon me this heritage and thus give me such a mark of your trust.'[15] On 23 August 1923, Windle typed a note regarding the future disposal of his papers. It read as follows: 'The Papers in this box together with all my cuttings, books and diaries are to be sent to Sister Monica D.Sc. S.N.D. at Notre Dame Convent, Dowanhill, Glasgow, Scotland. After she has done with them they can be given to Nora if she cares to have them. John Humphreys has all my letters to him and Sister Monica had better be told this so that she can apply to him if she survives me.'[16]

The designation of Sr Monica as his biographer changes, for the historian, the way in which letters after that date should be read. Windle was, from that point, not simply writing to a friend. He was putting down his thoughts for posterity. He knew that those innermost thoughts would be published soon after his demise. In 1929, upon Windle's death, it fell to his widow, Edith, to act upon the instructions of her late husband. But between Edith Windle's letter of 17 February 1929 in which she wrote 'that my darling has left me' and her letter of 5 November, the box of diaries, correspondence and files – left to her by arrangement – was sent on to Dowanhill. It cannot be entirely ruled out that Windle had sent the archive to her sooner or edited his correspondence with a blue pencil. However, the surviving correspondence between Edith and Sr Monica, two letters of 5 November and 31 December 1929, contain detailed answers to biographical questions. Although it is not clear whether Sr Monica had started to work on the biography before the death of Windle, it is virtually certain that she had done so. Her superiors, it seems likely, gave her help to type out large sections from the letters which were marked out with a blue pencil.

Bearing in mind that Sr Monica was publishing a memoir less than three years after the death of Windle, it is not surprising that she used the content of the archives selectively in her text, leaving out many of her subject's more forthright passages in his diaries and references in his letters that would have caused hurt to people who were still alive. Windle's only brother, Colonel Reginald Jocelyn, is a case in point. Although he was quite helpful to Sr Monica, he remained distant and reserved. He did not like Bertram who, he felt, had used his home in Dublin as a hotel when need arose. He claimed his brother used to turn up at short – or no – notice and expect meals and lodging to be provided. The relationship between the two broke down for a number of years. Reginald, or Reggie, did go to Cork at least once during the war to meet his brother. The former was serving as a surgeon in the army and ran a hospital with over 1,000 beds for most of the war. He told Sr Monica bluntly that he did not want to be credited in the memoir with having been a source of information, dictating the references to himself he would like to see included. Sr Monica respected his wishes scrupulously. Edith Windle may also have helped in that regard. Writing to Sr Monica on 1 May 1931, she had before her either a typescript of the memoir or proofs of the book. She had suggested a minor change: 'First let me thank you for corrections about Reggie. I was glad to have them, though you need not have been agitated or troubled in your conscience. I just imagined the words in brackets in Reggie's letter were those he wished taken out, not included, as was evidently the case. It is very comforting to think that he may have repented just a little of his unbrotherly attitude. I could tell you so much if we were face to face that would make you understand the family misunderstandings, though of course Bertie and Reggie never had much in common with one another . . .'

Sr Monica yielded to Reginald's wishes. She had little choice but to do so. However, she was not writing hagiography; her unrivalled knowledge of Windle informed her text throughout. She handled the most sensitive issues in a delicate and nuanced way, leaving it to the discerning reader to interpret her meaning and read between the lines. It is a fundamental mistake to view her volume as uncritical, reverential and pious.

Sr Monica, who died on 12 June 1968, was buried at Dalbeth cemetery, Glasgow. We, the authors of this volume, are deeply indebted to this woman of science. Sr Monica could not have used the diaries to reconstruct the troubled relationship that Windle had with his two daughters, Mary and Nora. The breakdown of his relationship with Mary at the time of her marriage in 1908 to John J. Horgan was a very sad, if not a tragic episode in the life of the president of UCC. Sr Monica treats Windle's intransigence towards the marriage of Mary and John Horgan in a subtle but perceptive way – in a well-chosen sentence. We deduced from her treatment that Windle was an obstinate man, inflexible and unyielding, and that his daughter inherited many of his characteristics.

Edith helped Sr Monica in every way to complete her research, retaining contact with her throughout the writing of the book. She was brutally frank, providing the unvarnished truth as she saw it. In the same letter – as quoted above – 1 May 1931 – she spoke of retrieving her husband's letters from a publishing house: 'I enclose those she [the editor of *Commonweal*] sent me a couple of days ago. Is it too late to have them, or parts of them included? They are so very characteristic and full of interesting things that rather emphasise his more literary than scientific side – to me far more interesting than many of the letters you have. There are just a couple of things I have pencilled as better left out, otherwise they could be inserted as they stand unless you see reasons otherwise . . . How I do appreciate your practical vision of things and contempt for anything that savours of unreality, or insincerity.' Edith also wrote a short commentary on the final draft of the manuscript offering minor suggestions. There was one line in her notes with which we fully empathise: 'I know how difficult Bertie's small writing is to decipher'. In particular, that held true for the diaries, a rich and wonderful source, but very difficult to 'decode'. They survive for 1906 to 1920.

Besides Edith and Reginald and the large archive, Sr Monica had access to Sir Bertram Windle's wide circle of friends. For example, she corresponded with John Humphreys, a close friend from their days together in Birmingham University. He provided her with access to a lifelong correspondence between Windle and himself. She must have returned to Humphreys all the letters quoted in the book. There is no trace of any of those letters in the Windle Papers or in the Humphreys Papers. Neither have we found any letters from Windle to Humphreys in the Birmingham archives.[17] Sr Monica also used letters from the Jesuit psychologist Fr Michael Maher, who remained a close friend to Windle until his death in the early part of the First World War. But we have not had access to the originals and have had to rely on the excerpts in the biography. We were fortunate to gain access to what survives of the extensive correspondence between Windle and Mgr Henry Parkinson (died 1924), a long-time president of the seminary at Oscott. Windle had known him since the 1880s. Alas, there is a large gap in the collection, with but two letters from 1909 and half a dozen from 1919.

Nora Thomas, Windle's surviving daughter, was another source for Sr Monica. She died in 1962. Edith Somerville, Admiral Boyle Somerville and Violet Coghill were also very important sources for his biographer.

Why have Windle's papers remained unused by scholars since Sr Monica first worked on them? In keeping with the terms of Windle's note, it is probable that the papers were first offered to Nora, his only surviving daughter. It is not known whether she took possession of them for a time, but that is improbable. The route by which the papers found their way to the Special Collections in Birmingham University is not very clear. One possibility is that the archive was deposited for a time in the Oscott Library, Birmingham. Windle had had a long-standing personal association with that seminary and with its staff, particularly with Mgr Henry Parkinson, who had known him from the time of his conversion to Catholicism in the early 1880s. In June 2004, the Windle archives were transferred from Oscott to Birmingham University medical school library and then to the Special Collections there.[18]

Sr Monica's *Windle* also relied heavily on the diaries which have survived for the years 1906 to 1920. The contents are frank, very often brutally frank, accounts of his professional life, his musings on public events and personalities, and they chronicle his political opinions on

British and Irish politics, the Irish Catholic Church and the life and times of UCC. When writing this book, we did not have to labour under any of Sr Monica's self-imposed constraints. Legibility was the only drawback in determining the use of the contents of the diary. His script even defied Sr Monica in some instances. Where possible, we have filled out the abbreviations in order to make the entries more accessible to the reader.

The use of the diaries presented a number of serious methodological and stylistic challenges. This book is not a transcription of diary entries in their totality. We have, of necessity, had to be selective. Historians of weather and climate change might find Windle's opening lines in every entry of particular interest. He hardly ever failed to comment on the day's weather. Neither have we reproduced the final lines in each entry which refer to the book/s he is reading. That, too, would make an interesting study. We have interwoven the diary entries into the text usually in chronological order. But sometimes it has been important to cluster certain entries to provide the full impact of his private thoughts. We have not footnoted each diary entry as that source is readily identifiable in the text.

Windle's candour when describing politicians, prelates and professors may shock readers. Outwardly, he was an Edwardian gentleman who lived a very controlled life. But the diaries reveal an alter ego; privately, he was willing to articulate his feelings of despair and despondency with 'vile man'. Windle may have derived a psychic release by daily putting down on paper his anxieties, his dislikes, his fears and his hopes. His private persona was certainly not that of a self-controlled and self-contained man. It is worth speculating about why the diaries survive only for the years 1906 to 1920. Did he keep a daily record of his life in Trinity and Birmingham before coming to Ireland? Did he continue on his diary for the years he was living in Canada? It is not possible to answer these questions. But what may be said of the diaries that survive is that Windle made absolutely no effort to interfere with any of the entries at a later date. He did not change and editorialise. Even the account of his worst days – such as the day of his daughter Mary's wedding in 1908 – were not altered in any way. What he wrote on the day generally remained the record on the page.

Besides the rich Windle archive, this book has also drawn upon a wide range of personal papers which are listed in the bibliography. We also relied heavily on the UCC college archives, the minutes of the Academic Council and the governing body, and on the files relating to the Honan Hostel and the building of the Honan Chapel. We have had access to the papers of William O'Brien MP at UCC and in Dublin. We have also reviewed the papers of his wife, Sophie Raffalovich. We have examined the Archbishop William Walsh Papers in the Dublin Archdiocesan Archive and the Cardinal Francis Bourne Papers in the Westminster

Archdiocesan Archive. We have also consulted the archives of the Irish Franciscans in Killiney, County Dublin. In the National Library, we have examined the George Wyndham, John J. Horgan and William O'Brien Papers. The Michael O'Riordan Papers, at the Pontifical Irish College, Rome, were valuable as were the Shane Leslie Papers at Georgetown University, Washington, DC.

The book is divided into nine chapters structured chronologically and thematically. Windle's early life, his university studies at Trinity College, his early professional career in Birmingham and his decision to move to Cork are covered in the first chapter. Chapter 2 examines his early years in QCC/UCC, his efforts to establish a University of Munster and his role in the setting up of the National University of Ireland (NUI). The third chapter examines Windle's approach to the reform of the university and to the building of links with the wider community. This chapter also reconstructs his role as a father and family man. It charts his relationship with the British government, with the Irish Parliamentary Party and with a new radical nationalist movement with which he had no sympathy.

Chapter 4 analyses Windle's part in helping to normalise relations with the Catholic Church and with the building up of support for a Catholic community in UCC. His use of the Isabella Honan bequest to found and fund the Honan Hostel and Chapel are examined.[19] The fifth chapter evaluates the impact of the First World War on UCC. Windle's commitment to the winning of the war is analysed, showing his enthusiasm for John Redmond and the stance of the Irish Parliamentary Party in support of recruitment to the British army. It also reviews his role as a leading Catholic intellectual and polemicist. This chapter concludes with an evaluation of Windle's day-by-day reaction to the 1916 rising, to the British government's handling of its aftermath, and to the rise of Sinn Féin under the leadership of Éamon de Valera. Chapter 6 traces Windle's reaction to the British government's handling of Anglo-Irish relations from late 1916, his role in the Irish Convention and the decline of the Irish Parliamentary Party without its leader, John Redmond, who had died in March 1918.

Chapter 7 reviews the analyses of the conscription crisis and of the 'German plot' in 1918. It analyses Windle's growing despair over the 'mistakes' made by the British government, the Irish Parliamentary Party and the leadership of the Catholic Church when confronting the rise of Sinn Féin and radical nationalism. Chapter 8, entitled 'Windle's Last Hurrah', details his campaign to establish a University of Munster in 1918 and 1919. The chapter also shows the divisions within the National University of Ireland and the British government's lack of will to force through change in the structures of the NUI. The final chapter examines the background to Windle's decision to leave Ireland for Toronto in 1919, his subsequent academic career and how he viewed Ireland during the final decade of his life.

This study provides an unusual view of Irish history during the first two decades of the twentieth century. Windle was a home ruler who, at the same time, admired the constructive unionism of George Wyndham. He was a nationalist who was never a separatist, and a Gaelic Leaguer who eschewed the movement's later radicalism. He was a university reformer who helped transform and professionalise UCC during his fifteen-year stay. He was a Catholic who helped redefine the college's relationship with the Catholic Church and provide a welcoming atmosphere for Catholic students in what was formerly regarded as being a 'Godless college'. Windle was one of the architects of the NUI settlement in 1908 who soon came to regard it as a disaster and an impediment to university reform. His solution was to press, unsuccessfully as it turned out, for autonomy for UCC, first soon after his arrival and later in 1918 and 1919. He failed in that objective. As a devout Catholic, Windle wrestled with what he saw as being the defects of Irish Catholicism. Disillusioned by the poverty of Irish episcopal leadership, he left the country in late 1919 disheartened and defeated, fearing for his life and the very survival of his own Catholic faith. He never returned, dying in Canada in 1929.

This study of Windle crosses many historical fields, providing a unique view of Irish history in the first two decades of the twentieth century. His life and work as a president of QCC/UCC are offered in this biographical study as an invitation to scholars to devote more time to researching the complexities of the early part of the twentieth century. Sir Bertram Windle deserves to form a more prominent part of a more inclusive Irish history narrative.

Chapter 1

The Early Years,
1858–1904

Bertram Coghill Alan Windle was among the leading medical professors in Great Britain and Ireland in the last two decades of the nineteenth century. His list of scientific publications by the 1890s was as impressive as it was extensive. He also wrote on archaeology, anthropology, ethnology and literary topography. Why did this foremost scientist and man of letters forgo a distinguished academic career at Birmingham University to become in 1904 the president of Queen's College, Cork, and remain in that post for fifteen years? The answer lies partly in his family background, education and religion.

Bertram Coghill Alan Windle's father, Samuel Allen, was descended from the Windles of Claverley, Shropshire, nine miles from Wolverhampton. The family goes back to 1684. There is a Windle Chapel, taking its name from the benefactor Thomas Hattam Windle.[1] A grandson, William Hattam, became a dyer in Wolverhampton and, according to Sr Monica, 'amassed a considerable fortune'. He was a religious zealot and was believed to have become a lay preacher sent out by John Wesley. He married Anne Allen in 1781 and their eldest surviving son, William, who lived between 1790 and 1851, owned a private school in Wolverhampton. He had a reputation for being 'highly esteemed and reserved'. He and his wife, Martha Smith, had a large family. Their third son, Samuel Allen, was born in Birmingham in 1827. On his mother's side, he was related to the Cadbury family,[2] Allen being his grandmother's maiden name. Samuel Allen Windle was a Church of England clergyman. In early 1854, he met Sydney Coghill at the Manor of Mayfield, Staffordshire. They were married on 18 October 1854 in the parish church of Bray, County Wicklow, by Rev. W. Windle, the eldest brother of the bridegroom. 'Samuel Allen was by nature inclined to at times be almost melancholic and subject to periods of deep depression,' Sr Monica wrote.[3] Edith Nazer, Bertram

Windle's second wife, wrote in 1929: 'I have heard him [Samuel] spoken of as a dour and rather depressing person – I suppose that was how he would strike the gay and witty element on his wife's side. Undoubtedly he was a somewhat remarkable preacher and greatly adored by his parishioners.'[4] Bertram Windle's mother was very different to her new husband in social class and background. She was the fifth daughter of Vice-Admiral Sir Josiah Coghill, who had served with Admiral Nelson at the Battle of the Nile. He had three daughters by his first wife, Sophia Dodson.[5] When she died in 1817, he remarried in 1822 Anna Maria, the eldest daughter of Charles Kendal Bushe. The latter, born in 1767, was a Chief Justice of Ireland who had voted consistently against the Union. He was reputed to be 'incorruptible'.[6] He died in 1843.[7]

Sydney, Bertram Windle's mother, was a child of Coghill's second wife.[8] She had three step sisters and seven sisters. When the Coghill sisters visited Dublin they had a base at 49 St Stephen's Green. That was the home of another sister, Sylvia, who had married Thomas Greene, secretary general of the Church of Ireland.[9] The second youngest, Adelaide, married Thomas Henry Somerville of Drishane, Castletownshend, County Cork, in 1857. The novelist Edith Oenone Somerville was born in 1858. Her works included the very popular *Some Experiences of an Irish RM.*[10] Edith had seven brothers and sisters. Boyle (born 1863) and Hildegarde (1867) became very close friends of Bertram Windle.[11]

Sydney and Samuel Allen Windle's first child, a daughter, was stillborn on 11 August 1855. Bertram Coghill Alan Windle was born at 5.47 a.m. on 8 May 1858, at Mayfield, Staffordshire. His father had been appointed to that parish by the Bishop of Lichfield on 19 December 1852. His baptismal certificate, no. 276, describes his father as a 'clerk in orders and Vicar of Mayfield'.[12] His father performed the baptismal ceremony on 4 June 1858. The infant was given the names Bertram Coghill Alan.[13] His biographer, Sr Monica, wrote that he changed the order of his initials in later life in order to avoid being known as 'Alphabet' Windle. In reality, his baptismal certificate gave the former B.A.C. which, no doubt, would not have prevented him from being known as 'A.B.C.' in the school yard.[14] A second son, Reginald Jocelyn, was born on 18 August 1860 at Mayfield Vicarage.

When Bertram Windle was four, his father became the vicar of the Trustee Mariners' Episcopal Church in Kingstown (now Dun Laoghaire), County Dublin. They lived at 17 Adelaide Street. On 20 May 1866, Wilfred Theodore Sydney was born. He was baptised by his father in his church on 14 June. He died on 12 October 1866 in a cholera epidemic.[15] According to Reginald Jocelyn, his father 'was a remarkably eloquent preacher and in the summer season he would hold a fashionable congregation of some 1,500 spellbound during his 45 minute sermon'.[16] Reginald also recorded that there was a left chancel window, illustrating the parable of the sower, to the memory of his father – together with a photographic portrait of him – in the vestry in the Mariners' Church, Dun Laoghaire.[17] Rev. Samuel Allen Windle served in Kingstown from 1862 until June 1873, raising his family by the sea which gave Bertram Windle a lifelong love of boats. Edith, Windle's second wife, wrote to Sr Monica in 1930: 'Bertie did want to go to sea when he was a boy and he wept salt tears in the garden because his parents refused on account of what appeared to be his delicate health. Right up to his last days he kept that love and craving for the sea – always he regretted having to live so far from it. He would sit for hours watching the waves on shore or from the deck of a ship, while I turned my back because it made me giddy! There is no doubt about it a fine admiral was lost to the British navy when the way was barred to Bertie but had he realized his boyish wish the probability is that the Church would have had one great champion the fewer.'[18]

Life in the Windle household was strict if not puritanical. Bertram had a strained relationship with his father and he did not get on too well with his brother, Reginald Jocelyn. Edith explained: 'I could tell you so much if we were face to face that would make you understand the family misunderstandings, though of course Bertie and Reggie never had much in common with one another and Reggie was always his mother's darling, accentuated in later years when Bertie became a Catholic. You see Reggie was always the good little boy who handed cakes politely to ladies who called at the Vicarage while Bertie either glared in another corner of the room or disapproved altogether. He never had any parlour tricks and was too honest and perhaps a little too self centred to pretend or disguise his feelings. It is so silly to look for perfection – young or old and sinners can be so very loveable – don't you think so?'[19] In a letter on 11 May 1930, Edith contrasted the personalities of both brothers: 'I think Reggie is more Windle than Coghill. He has a sense of humour but not Bertie's sparkling wit. Both inherited from the Windle father a wonderful capacity for organization. In Poona [India] when the plague was so bad there years ago Reggie did great work as army doctor and again during the war at Staples in France. He lost his only child – aged 4 – when he was in Poona – one of only two white children who died of it. A great sorrow to him – his selfish wife would never have another.'[20]

Resentment developed between the brothers as they grew older. In a letter to Sr Monica dated 4 April 1930, Reginald Jocelyn described Bertram as 'a typical cold unemotional Englishman. He never cared for his parents or me and during the last some years of our lives he and I agreed to cut communications.' He also revealed that 'as boys we always fought and in consequence were sent to different schools and later on we disregarded one another till about the year 1905–6 when he transferred to Cork and finding that I had a very comfortable house and an excellent cook he made the fullest use of me and mine never showing any gratitude or offering any thanks, he generally managed to arrive by telegram on a *jour maigre* and grumbled much at having to eat soles and salmon backed up by tempting egg dishes. That is Bertram as he was to me however for the sake of the family and especially my very old mother, whom I adored, I suffered and put up with him.'[21] (Their mother died in 1910.)

While Reginald Jocelyn's recording of events about his family tree is quite useful, he ought not to be regarded as anything other than a partisan judge of his brother's personality and character. Writing on 20 September 1930, he told Sr Monica in blunt military fashion: 'Now to refer to something unpleasant but, from my point of view, unavoidable – I know, *from your kind thanks*, that you recognise that I have done all I could to assist you with any information that I thought might be useful to you in compiling the Biography.' I have always recognised my brother's quite exceptional 'Brain,' but I have no admiration for him or his heart, *quite the contrary,* in his personal relations to his family by whom I mean his Father, Mother and myself and I should most strongly object to be in any way associated with him in this Biography.'[22] He gave Sr Monica very clear directions: 'If it is necessary to mention me at all – and for sake of accuracy as Military matters are technical, may I suggest – "His only surviving brother was commissioned as a Surgeon in the Army Medical Staff July 28.1886, was promoted Major in the newly formed Royal Army Medical Corps July 28, 1898, being finally promoted as Colonel in the Army March 1, 1915. He survives"'.[23] Sr Monica took him at his word, making reference to Reginald Jocelyn on four pages of her 428-page biography. On page 6, the text read: 'In 1860, another son, Reginald Jocelyn, blessed the union.' A footnote repeated verbatim the dictated paragraph in the letter quoted immediately above.[24] He is also mentioned on page 9, quoted very briefly on page 22 and is referred to by Bertram in a letter on page 246. His brother, therefore, got his wish. Discretion, and the fear of wounding those still alive, prevented Sr Monica from quoting what can be read above.

Bertram Windle did not show early scholarly promise. He went to Dame's School run by a Miss Peake in George's Street, Kingstown (now Dun Laoghaire). At ten, he moved to a school run by Rev. Dr William Church Stackpoole. The school, according to Reginald Jocelyn, 'was celebrated·. . . in those days. Most of the Irish boys who entered Navy, Army or Civil Service had been at "Stacks".'[25] His time there was not a

particularly happy experience. He learned Latin and Greek but his performance was far from distinguished. According to his brother's
recollections, Bertram 'was not an industrious pupil or inclined to work
at his lessons but the Dr. who was very fond of my Father made the best
of it in the "Term Reports". But in those days it was a case of "eyes but
ye see Not" and from the age of 10 years, I can well remember how
"B.C.A." made collections of fossils and botanical specimens and was
interested generally (as a child) in Natural Science – Nobody appreciated that either then or for years afterwards.'[26]

In 1868, Windle senior was ordered by his doctors to spend the
winter in the south of England. He remained at St Cuthbert's, Wells, for
six months where Bertram developed a strong interest in archaeology
and in medieval architecture and history. By the age of fourteen, he also
had a strong interest in science. He was given no encouragement at
home to consider a life in the navy. In 1871, Bertram was sent to Repton
in Derbyshire where Rev. S.A. Pears was the headmaster. Repton was
noted for its strongly religious ethos, and Bertram studied the classics
and developed a love of literature. But his application was not reflected
in his report cards. His brother records: '"B.C.A." did no good at Repton
and there was always turbulation in the home when his Term Reports
arrived saying "Plenty of brains, no industry, no application etc. etc.",
the fault lying with the incompetent school masters who knew nothing
and taught nothing but Latin Verse and Prose plus Greek.'[27] There he
developed a strong dislike for Calvinism – a strand of religion he
claimed that had made him think of God as a policeman instead of a
tender loving father.

In 1873, Rev. Samuel Allen Windle moved to St Bride's, Percy Street,
Liverpool, where he remained until June 1878.[28] At Christmas 1873,
father and son had 'a heart to heart talk'.[29] As a result, Bertram was sent
to Ryle, Isle of Wight, to work with a private tutor, Rev. Mr Spear. He was
given permission by his father to go on a walking tour of the island. His
father received a full account of the visit in a text which showed that his
son was not without talent or intelligence. Quite the contrary. In 1878,
Windle's father moved to Market Rasen, Lincolnshire, dying in that
parish on 21 January 1882. He was buried in Mount Jerome Cemetery,
Dublin. Windle's widowed mother moved back to Dublin to take care of
her sons. She died there in 1910.

Bertram had entered Trinity College Dublin on 1 November 1875. He
had lodgings on the Front Square, sharing a room with a distant cousin,
George Greene. The latter was a bright and industrious student who was
a Senior Moderator, first place, and the winner of a gold medal in English
literature and modern languages. Windle followed in his footsteps, his

name appearing thrice a year at Hilary, Trinity and Michaelmas terms with first class honours in English literature. He either headed the list or was very near to the top.[30] He also carried off other prizes, 'the Early-English Prize' and the 'Shakespeare Prize'.[31] His brother recalled: 'The only time I ever knew him to fail was when he essayed a prize in "the theory of music and double bass" that floored him and no wonder – he had no more music in him than a tin can.'[32]

During his last two years as a 'Sophister' at Trinity, he was in the first class honours lists three times a year – in Natural Science. He graduated as a Senior Moderator and gold medallist in that subject. His achievement was all the more remarkable because, as his brother recalled, he could not read for four to six weeks before his finals.[33] Because of his blond hair and looks, Windle earned the nickname 'cherub' during his undergraduate years. His brother wrote: 'socially he was a popular undergraduate and had many friends tho' he was very shy.'[34] He was also an office holder in the Philosophical Society in 1877–8. He played hockey 'but no other game'. He was a member of the university rowing club 'and won several pots'. Windle was devoted to bell ringing and helped to found a branch of 'the Society of College youths' in Dublin – an ancient society for campanology. Every Sunday the group rang the peal of eight bells at St Patrick's Cathedral, Dublin. Windle always rang the tenor bell.[35]

Windle's time in Ireland honed his nationalist feelings.[36] His brother wrote that Windle had been deeply influenced by a neighbour, Fanny Smith, who 'adored Bertie' when he was between the ages of four and fourteen. She had 'an extraordinary influence over him and was the only woman (except his two wives) that I ever knew him to be really fond of'. According to the same source: 'this Fanny Smith in addition to being a very holy woman who spent her life doing good, especially in reforming drunkards, was a most *intense Irish Patriot* and my mother always said that Fanny "bit Bertie and infected him with an enthusiasm for Ireland and things Irish" – Her sister Jane had a great affection for me and inculcated into my mind that the Irish were a lazy, dirty, drunken lot as a rule, a scheming hypocritical lot.'[37] Sr Monica commented: 'If the measure of the interest he took in Ireland, an interest which materialized in service entailing very hard work and copious self-sacrifice rather than in much talking, be the criterion on which he is judged, then his claim to be Irish is much more strongly substantiated than that of many a so-called patriot.'[38] By the 1880s, Windle was a home ruler and a supporter of the Irish Parliamentary Party. He was in university a contemporary and close friend of a founder of the Gaelic League and future president of Ireland, Douglas Hyde.

Reginald Jocelyn Windle entered Trinity in June 1878. He had been educated at the Rev. Thomas Cornish Pratt's School on the Eltham Road, Blackheath, and later at the Royal Institution, Liverpool. Bertram entered the Trinity Medical School the same year as Reginald began his studies in the college, 1878. Their mother moved to Dublin to make a home for her two boys. Both gave up their rooms in Trinity. Bertram had also roomed with H.D. Conner, who later became a judge. They now lived with their mother.[39]

Qualifying as a doctor, he was awarded an MA (first class Natural Science honours at BA), MD, BCh and DSc. His medical studies earned him outstanding marks. Windle had gained a mark 10 per cent higher than any other student on the list. He also got the highest marks of any student during the previous twelve years. Sr Monica received a letter on 1 April 1930 from the Registrar of the School of Physics, stating: 'With reference to your letter of 26th March, the marks shown on the attached sheet are those awarded at the Final Medical degree Examination held on February 6th, 1882 and following days; those obtained by Sir Bertram Windle indicate that he was a student of outstanding ability.'[40] He was top of his class, receiving an overall mark of 77, which was the highest percentage grade awarded for twelve years. The second student in the class received a grade of 68. Paradoxically, Windle received his lowest mark for Anatomy at 4.5. The highest mark awarded that year was 7.5. It was necessary to present two theses for the medical degree at TCD. He was awarded an MD in 1883.

Windle, according to his biographer, worked in Dublin for a short time after qualifying: 'He now became Demonstrator of Anatomy and Histology in the school of the Royal College of Surgeons. He was House Physician and afterwards Surgical Registrar to Adelaide Hospital, Resident Obstetric Assistant to the Coombe Hospital and Medical officer to the Dublin Throat and Ear Hospital. He was also engaged in research in Embryology and Anatomy under Professor Macalister.'[41] Windle moved to Birmingham to work as resident pathologist to the General Hospital, Birmingham. According to his brother, 'about this time he published a paper on the development of the muscles of the manus and pes (mainly the result of work on cats shot by him with an air gun in our "catwalk" garden in Dublin). For this paper (I believe) he was made an F.R.S.'[42]

In January 1884, he was appointed Medical Officer with the supervision of all the 'medical beds'. In July of that year, he was appointed to the chair of Anatomy at Queen's College, Birmingham, a medical school at the time affiliated to the Anglican theological seminary of Queen's College. According to his brother, 'this was a divinity college with a moribund medical school of perhaps 60 students. In a few years time he had 150 students.'[43] Windle approached the Mason Science College in Birmingham and was instrumental in having the medical school transferred to that un-denominational institution. He persuaded the college to spend £13,000 on building a medical school. Windle drew up the plans with the help of the school of architecture. According to his brother, 'one of the features of this school was that it had a Female Side and its first professor of anatomy was his cousin, Miss Violet Coghill, youngest sister of the late Sir Egerton Coghill Bart'.[44] Windle proved to be an outstanding academic success as a researcher, teacher and administrator.

Conversion to Catholicism

Windle, who came from a very strict Protestant household, had become an agnostic in his secondary school days, according to John J. Horgan: 'His father was strictly evangelical and severe, and it was probably a natural revulsion from the home atmosphere that caused him to be noted at this period for his agnostic views.'[45] Reginald Jocelyn held the view that the young Windle had no religion 'and was a professed atheist – Early in his undergraduate life he became a sworn 'Orange Brother'. 'To H. with the Pope' was music in his ears. He hated the Papists and ran a sporting sweepsteak [*sic*] on the election of a new Pope when one died [Pius IX] in 1878. A list of the Cardinals was hung on his 'Oak' and the buyer of the successful cardinal scooped the pool.'[46] This view is not substantiated by any other source.

Soon after his return to England, religion, according to his brother, became 'the main spring of his life – How this remarkable change took place I have not the slightest idea.'[47] There are a number of fragments in his personal papers which help throw partial light on his conversion. After returning to Birmingham at the end of 1882, he came into contact with Mgr Henry Parkinson at Oscott, the seminary for the archdiocese. He also visited St Chad's Cathedral, hearing one Sunday a sermon on the 'Immaculate Conception'. He began his quest, reading Cardinal Newman's *Apologia*. But, he wrote, 'the book which was largely instrumental in making a Catholic of me was Richard Frederick Littledale's *Plain Reasons against joining the Church of Rome*'. He found by accident another book: Henry Ignatius Dudley Ryder's *Catholic Controversy: A Reply to Dr Littledale's Plain Reasons*. Published in 1880, the author was a friend of John Henry Newman and was elected superior of the Birmingham oratory after the cardinal's death. Windle, having read the book, wrote: 'I remember marking some dozen passages where each author contradicted the other, and thus provided, I hunted up the references which I wanted in a great library and of course speedily learnt which the truthful witness was. In a sort of way, Littledale made a Catholic of me – a thing I am quite sure he never intended to do for any man.'[48] A close friend from his University of Toronto days in the 1920s, Fr Henry Carr, wrote about Windle's struggle to achieve objectivity; Littledale had given a quotation from St Augustine which his opponent claimed was mangled and proved the very opposite to what was being claimed. Windle went to London, found a text of St Augustine and satisfied himself that Ryder was correct.[49] Edith told another version to Sr Monica on 11 May 1930:

> You speak of two stories that led Bertie to the church and wonder which is the correct. He *may* have taken refuge in a Catholic Church out of the rain but I never heard him mention the incident, whereas often I heard him tell the story of Sunday morning at the general hospital in Birmingham where he had to wait for an unpunctual surgeon (I think) and while he was kicking his heels he would wander across the road through the open doors of St Chad's Cathedral just to listen to the Gregorian music which was one of the few kinds of music he appreciated. Incidentally he heard part, or perhaps, the whole of a sermon which may have been on the Immaculate Conception. He then bought Dr Littledale in order to hear both sides of the question. Not satisfied with that he sought further enlightenment . . . There was a Canon Greenery [*sic*] who – I believe – at that time was living at the Cathedral or close by and I seem to remember it was to him he went first of all for help. I know he always spoke with great affection of him and the help he had given when he was seeking light. I cannot remember ever hearing him say that communion under one kind had been a stumbling block to him but the fact may have slipped from my very bad memory. I imagine you have the article Father Carr [see below] wrote for the Catholic World. You can rely on anything he says as being accurate and coming to him from Bertie. Their friendship was a very intimate one.[50]

On 24 January 1883, this son of a Church of England rector was received by an elderly Irish priest and founder of the Scott Museum, Canon William John Greaney, into the Catholic Church at St Chad's Cathedral, Birmingham. Fr Carr wrote: 'The old Irish priest who received him into the Church always retained a high place in the convert's admiration and esteem. Even then the young medical professor stood high in scientific circles. The priest was a sensible old fellow without much up-to-date scientific lore. When a difficulty was presented to him, he would say, "I cannot answer that. It does not mean there is no answer. Give me time and I will see what I can do by study. Even if in the end it is over my head, it does not follow that there is no answer. Remember that there always is an answer." His catechumen took that as one of the guiding principles of his life.'[51]

Becoming a Catholic in England of the 1880s carried with it a very high professional cost. Conversion, in a predominantly Protestant culture, was not a particularly prudent career move. Institutionalised sectarianism was one of the reasons why Windle quickly felt the chill wind of prejudice after he had followed the path to Rome. While there is no direct evidence of how Windle's mother and brother reacted to the news, it is likely that neither was best pleased. He told Sr Monica of how he had returned to Dublin soon after his conversion. He called to Trinity to see one of his tutors 'who had been especially fond of him and proud of his success. The tutor refused to see him.' Sr Monica adds: 'It is hard for us at this date to realize what a disgrace to an old Irish Protestant family his reception into the Catholic Church must have been considered by those living at the time, and, indeed, for long afterwards.'[52]

Windle became a strong and lifelong admirer of Franciscan spirituality. He was a member of the Third Order of St Francis – a devotional branch of the order run for laymen. He was also an admirer of Cardinal John Henry Newman and the Oxford Movement. He records a meeting with Cardinal Newman in Birmingham in 1890 – the year of the cardinal's death:

> It was my fortune to have a few interviews with him and to hear him preach on the last occasion that he ever ascended the stairs of a pulpit. He then delivered the series of short discourses on the Stations of the Cross which were afterwards published in the volume 'Meditations and Devotion.' He was a man in whose face it was impossible not to see the deep lines which had been engraved not merely by prolonged study, but also by great disappointments. The last time that I saw him, in company with Bishop (afterward Cardinal) [Herbert Alfred] Vaughan was one month before his death. He was so feeble that he was wheeled into the room in a chair and could not even lift his hand to raise his little scarlet skull-cap when etiquette required it, so that the action had to be performed by a young Oratorian father who stood beside him. His voice was a mere whisper, though his mind was perfectly clear. I went, almost from his side, to Oberammergau to the Passion Play, and on my way home heard a lady say to her companion in the coach which was taking us to the station, 'Cardinal Newman is dead.' His reception of our deputation was the last public act in the life of the founder and leader of the Oxford Movement.[53]

The oratory at Birmingham remained a strong focal point for Windle throughout his life. (He compiled a 'who's who' of the Oxford Movement in the 1920s.)

Politics formed another important part of Windle's identity. But where Church authority and politics came into conflict – as will be seen in the Irish land war struggle – he followed the teachings of his newly espoused Church. Windle had worked very hard in the 1880s to establish branches of the Irish National League of Great Britain in Birmingham. In one letter to the press, he wrote about the attitude of English Catholics towards Ireland: 'We Irish cannot forget that but for the fearless action of our race and our hierarchy, English Catholics would be either still striving for emancipation, or what is more probable, writhing under the intolerable burden of the "Veto".[54] To one who loves the faith and desires its spread, no fact can be more grievous, no reason more cogent, for desiring an early and satisfactory settlement of the Irish question.'[55] However, Windle grew in his lifetime to develop a deep mistrust of politicians *per se*. According to Edith, 'Bertie mistrusted all Churchills and descendants of the Dukes of Marlborough. He had some very violent prejudices. Churchill was one of them. I can't exactly remember why – something political no doubt.'[56] However, even in politics, Windle's loyalty to the teaching of the Catholic Church was unquestioning. There is a good example of his rejection of *à la carte* Catholicism in 1888 when Pope Leo XIII issued a rescript condemning the tactics used in the Plan of Campaign land agitation in Ireland. Tenants boycotted landlords by withholding their rent, which was paid into a common pool and saved. Windle, having spoken strongly in favour of the campaign in Birmingham, was due to give a public lecture the very night news of the contents of the rescript was published. The news reached his friends shortly before the lecture was to begin; John B. Hardman ordered a hansom cab and got to him as he was about to go on to the podium. Windle gave his lecture, beginning by mentioning the number of times he had spoken in favour of the boycott in Ireland: 'But there is another question that I am much more keenly interested in, about which you probably know nothing – that subject is the teaching of the Catholic Church. I have recently had the honour of being received into that Church. Now, Leo XIII, Her visible Head on earth, has declared that boycotting is against Christian charity, and therefore as a loyal son of the Catholic Church I withdraw anything I may have said against Her teaching and the lecture will not be given tonight.' Sr Monica noted: 'There occurred one of those moments of stupor when the silence is so intense, as to have the effect, of a sharp cry. A moment later the audience had broken into thunderous applause.' Canon Greaney, when asked about the effect of the rescript on Windle, replied: 'He was stunned but received it as a good Catholic should have done.'[57]

Marriage and Family Life

Windle, while working hard and building his academic career in the 1880s, showed that he had a lighter side to his character. He joined the Kyle Society which put on light entertainment for the poor and raised funds to improve the living conditions of those living in slums. Windle played the role of Wellington Wells in Gilbert and Sullivan's *The Sorcerer*. While working on different productions, he met Madoline, the daughter of William and Emma Hudson of Birmingham. In the company of his friends, Dr and Mrs Harvey, Windle planned a holiday and invited Miss Hudson to join them on a tour of the Eifel district of Germany. They fell in love and married on 4 May 1886 in St Chad's Cathedral, Birmingham. Canon Greaney, who had continued to play an important part in his life, was the celebrant.

According to Sr Monica, his wife 'possessed a very cultivated mind with a more than ordinary knowledge of English literature. She was a fine pianist, an interest which Dr Windle was never able to share because he was tone deaf. In the local society of her day, she shone by the brilliancy of her wit and repartee, holding a room full of guests in conversation with the utmost ease. To those who knew her intimately she was a very sincere friend, though never outwardly demonstrative in her affections.'[58] Windle's wife was not a Catholic at the time of their marriage. She later took instruction and converted. She, like her husband, became a zealous and devout member of the Church.[59]

For most of his twenty-two years in Birmingham, Windle enjoyed a happy family and social life. He was surrounded by friends, amongst his closest being John Humphreys. They met in 1883 and remained steadfast friends while Windle was at Birmingham and when he was in Ireland and Canada. Humphreys was, like Windle, a founder of Birmingham University. He was secretary to the dental school in the 1880s. The correspondence between both men, some of which is reproduced by Sr Monica, shows how much Windle valued Humphreys and respected his judgement.[60] (He dedicated *The Malvern Country* to him when it was published in 1901.) From the 1880s, Windle was also a regular visitor to the home of John B. Hardman, where Dr Whitcombe and Canon Greaney used to be present.

The couple had two daughters; Mary Madoline was born on 18 March 1887 and Nora was born on 6 March 1889. Windle was very anxious to have a son, and his wishes were granted when Laurence Alan Ignatius was born on 20 August 1896. But the proud father's happiness was, as his biographer points out, short-lived. On 13 November, the child died after a brief illness. Sr Monica writes: 'The father's grief was inconsolable, and he was thoroughly unmanned for the time being.' Mrs Ellen Pinsent, who was a regular visitor to their home, was a source of great strength for the couple at that time. She would play an important role in the life of their daughter Mary. Four years later, on 22 January 1900, Madoline herself died and was buried with her son in a secluded graveyard near the Passionist Fathers at Harborne.[61]

Ellen Pinsent, one of the people who helped Windle out in the immediate aftermath of his wife's death, was a very good influence on both girls, and developed a close bond of friendship with Mary in particular. Edith Mary Nazer, his late wife's cousin, had taken over the running of the house during Madoline's final illness. They were very close friends. Madoline encouraged Edith to become a Catholic, which she did. After Madoline's death, she came to look after the two girls on a permanent basis. A relationship developed and, in February 1901, Windle married Edith in the Church of St Catherine of Siena.[62] After his death in 1929, Edith wrote to Sr Monica: 'I knew Bertie years before we were married. I liked his wife and I liked him and saw quite plainly the shortcomings of both and realized why that first marriage failed to make either quite happy.'[63] Edith also told Sr Monica: 'I suppose I have always been an energetic person – my perpetual motion did rather worry Bertie at times. I explained it to him as the law of compensation – his was the brain that was unceasingly active – mine the body – that was why we married – at least where nature's part of the arrangement came in – we did not take those things into consideration ourselves! . . . I knew I always had to be on the alert to keep the tracks clear for him . . .'[64] The second marriage did not produce any children. It was a very happy union. Edith was a good mother to his two daughters, Mary and Nora, and that not always in the easiest of circumstances. Windle was a strict father who sought to over-direct the lives of his children. That would lead to serious complications and unhappiness, not least for Windle himself.

Edith was an accomplished artist who painstakingly illustrated Windle's *Remains of the Prehistoric Age in England*. Published in 1904, there are 307 drawings in the book – many if not most of which were done by his wife. That involved sharing her husband's passion for archaeology and travelling around the country to different museums and sites over a number of years. The book reveals her gifts as an artist. She was also very good at embroidery and needlework. Edith, who left only a few letters, reveals in them her strong personality, her good judgment and her love of her husband. John J. Horgan, who married Mary Windle in 1908 against her father's wishes, wrote that Edith 'remained his devoted companion and helper to the end'.[65] He had good reason to appreciate the peacemaking skills of his mother-in-law.

Windle's Inner Circle

Retaining a very close association with a number of prominent clergymen throughout his life, he recruited them as his spiritual and intellectual directors. He knew Mgr Henry Parkinson, who later became the president of Oscott Seminary, since the 1880s. Both men were often to be seen walking through the grounds deep in conversation in the 1880s and 1890s. When the monsignor died suddenly in 1924, Windle wrote: 'With him goes the last of my real old friends. I shed bitter tears over his death, for it takes away the last priest to whom I could write with perfect freedom, and who was always willing (and how able!) to help me with a philosophical problem. Please say a prayer for his soul, though I cannot think he needs it, for he was a most holy, simple priest.'[66]

Windle was also very friendly with the Jesuit academic and psychologist Fr Michael Maher. He acted as his spiritual director for many years – an onerous task for a man like Windle who was so scrupulous about his religion. The word 'scrupulous' might also be applied to him in the more direct psychological sense. He appeared to be wracked throughout his life by feelings of his own inadequacy. He set himself impossibly high spiritual standards. Windle needed the authoritative and sober voice of a Parkinson, a Maher, and a Canon Patrick Roche in Cork to prevent him from becoming enveloped by feelings of failure and spiritual inadequacy. While he was prone to depression, Windle often found himself in what spiritual writers call 'the dark night of the soul'. Although a convert to Catholicism, Windle felt that he was never quite able to shake off the dour influences of Calvinism.

Windle enjoyed a long friendship with Cardinal Francis Aidan Gasquet, a leading Benedictine historian, archivist of the Vatican Secret Archives and later Vatican librarian. They exchanged letters for over twenty years.[67] As a prominent Roman Catholic scientist, Windle wrote extensively throughout his lifetime on religion and science. One of his first studies in that area, *Catholics and Evolution,* was published by the Catholic Truth Society of Ireland in 1900.[68] He corresponded with the distinguished biologist and Catholic convert St George Jackson Mivart in the 1880s and 1890s.[69] He spent a lifetime immersed in that debate which, according to Sr Monica, was 'the ostensible reason for so many shipwrecks of faith at the time of his conversion'. He spent a good part of nearly thirty years, she wrote, trying to disabuse '"the man in the street" of the fallacy that evolution and religion are necessarily antagonistic; nay, more, he would have corroborated, had he heard it, the statement made by an extreme evolutionist of the Natural Selection school of thought, who is a member of no external Church, that it is not only unreasonable, it is well nigh impossible, to be an evolutionist and an atheist. Disbelief in God and belief in the theory of organic evolution are allelomorphic.'

Teacher, Researcher, Writer and Administrator

Windle, by the end of the 1890s, was a respected Professor of Anatomy with a very strong publication record. He had an international reputation in his field, publishing a text book and a large number of scientific articles.[70] We make no attempt to evaluate Windle's academic standing as an anatomist. That task lies outside the scope of this volume. But the following illustrates his standing in his profession. In June 1899, he became a fellow of the Royal Society. He was an external examiner for the Natural Sciences Tripos in the University of Cambridge, and was also an extern for the medical degrees at Durham, Glasgow and Aberdeen. He was visitor of examinations in chemistry, physics and biology for the conjoint boards of the Royal College of Physicians of London and the Royal College of Surgeons of England and he gave extended service on the Council of the British Medical Association. He was given an honorary doctorate in science by his *alma mater*, Trinity, in 1891.

Parallel to his life as a Professor of Anatomy, Windle also indulged a passion for the study of pre-history. He published a study of prehistoric Britain in 1897. His 320-page study, *Remains of the Prehistoric Age in England*, was published in 1904. It was, as mentioned above, beautifully illustrated by his wife Edith.[71] Windle also published a series of carefully observed studies covering a range of different areas. These works cross the academic frontiers of literature, history, art history and archaeology.[72] He also brought his academic acumen to the task of producing a series of important works on *Shakespeare's Country* in 1899 which was followed in 1902 by *The Wessex of Thomas Hardy*.[73]

Windle brought his enthusiasm for learning into the classroom. Dr R. Allan Bennett, one of his former students in Birmingham, wrote on hearing of his death in 1929:

> Sir Bertram Windle's death will carry many an old Birmingham man back in spirit to the prehistoric dissecting rooms of the Queen's College, and to the dark and dangerous stone stairs that deviously led to them. Now, nearly forty years after, I can see Dr Windle's tall figure dash into the lecture room; I feel again the hush that used to fall upon the most turbulent as his grey apocalyptic eye ranged over the class; and I can remember, as though it were but yesterday, the patience, the brilliance, the vividness of his enthralling lectures. He never appeared to bother much about our personalities. He rarely

spoke to us, and hardly ever had a word of encouragement or of praise; but in after years one awoke to the fact that he had always taken the keenest interest in the performance of his men, and the realization dawned that behind that singularly undemonstrative manner lay innumerable springs of kindness and of loyalty. He was just, and fierce, and self-sufficing, and was the greatest teacher I ever knew.[74]

John J. Horgan, his future son-in-law, left the following pen-picture of a students' view of their professor: 'A students' magazine of his Birmingham days once depicted him dressed in skins as a prehistoric man, grasping a stout club and a volume of anatomy, and glancing fiercely before him, whilst underneath was written, "He fixed me with his glittering eye", a quotation from "The Ancient Mariner" which admirably suggested an aspect of appearance with which his students were familiar. This fierceness of demeanour and abruptness of manner were really the protective covering of a warm and affectionate nature, which, unfortunately, seldom escaped from this cloak of shyness and reserve.'[75] Horgan offered his own view from within the family circle of this complex human being: 'at his best, and in congenial company, no one could be more pleasant and entertaining, and in his private conversations and intimate letters he revealed a quaint sense of humour, and a whimsical turn of phrase and idea . . . His large and almost encyclopaedic knowledge of anatomy, anthropology, science and religion, was combined with a simplicity of mind and intellectual humility which, at the very height of the attack upon revealed religion in the name of evolutionary science, had caused him to decide for religion and most conservative form of spiritual authority.'[76]

Windle took, according to J.J. Horgan, 'an interest in the wider aspects of education, having served on the Birmingham School Board, and also as a member of the Consultative Committee to the English Board of Education.'[77] In 1899, the Duke of Devonshire, who was lord president of the Council, appointed Windle as one of a Consultative Committee to the Board of Education. Assisted by Joseph Chamberlain, he 'brought off his pet scheme and the Mason College received its Charter, becoming the University of Birmingham [in] 1900'.[78] Fr Henry Carr explained: 'Up to that time Oxford and Cambridge were the only universities in England and they were a type *sui generis* and only for the upper classes. Birmingham was the first of the new English universities which are more after the American plan. Dr Windle was Professor of Anatomy and Dean of Medicine. In the words of one who was in a position to know and competent to appraise, "Birmingham University was his creation. He had the vision and the driving power to bring it, the first provincial university, into existence – the pattern of all the other universities which followed in his lead."'[79] Windle was given the position of Dean of the Medical Faculty, a post he held between 1900 and 1904.[80] *The Lancet* stated: 'In any case, the medical profession may congratulate itself upon the election of so distinguished a teacher as Dr. Windle to the responsible post which he holds.' After he had moved in 1904 to Cork, Joseph Chamberlain said in a speech that Windle had brought to him the proposal for creating Birmingham University, and he went on to stress how much the same university owed to his devoted and disinterested services.[81] Those were the features which the chief secretary of Ireland, George Wyndham, sought to recruit in order to help solve the Irish university question. The manoeuvrings to get Windle to come to Cork were orchestrated at a very high level.

George Wyndham, Windle and the Presidency of Queen's College, Cork

George Wyndham, newly appointed as chief secretary of Ireland, wrote on 25 November 1900 to his sister Madeline: 'In this country you must never be tired and never in a hurry.' [82] He would have good reason to understand the profundity of his comment by the end of his tour in Ireland in 1905. A descendant of Lord Edward Fitzgerald, Wyndham was born in 1863 and was elected as a Conservative MP for Dover in 1889. His five-year posting resulted in the passage of the Land Purchase (Ireland) Act in 1903. He devoted much time to the resolution of the Irish 'university question'. To that end, he was instrumental in bringing Windle to Ireland in late 1904 to take up the position of president of Queen's College, Cork. The inspiration for the invitation may also have come from Wyndham's able assistant, the Catholic Sir Antony MacDonnell.[83] Windle turned down the invitation at least once, as may be gathered from an undated letter Wyndham wrote to the Principal of Birmingham University, the noted physicist Sir Oliver Lodge: 'To my great regret I received a wire yesterday from my Under-Secretary to the effect that Professor Windle declines consideration for Presidency of Queen's College Cork owing to insufficiency of salary. I am very sorry as I am pretty sure it would be impossible to get a better man. The emoluments are £800 a year on the consolidated fund, a residence, and the salary of any chair he chose to occupy. Living is cheap in Ireland and there the chance of helping her where she needs it most i.e. in university Education. It is disappointing. If, and when, we make progress with Irish Higher Education a man such as Windle, Irish, Catholic, graduate of Trinity, distinguished, scientific and literary, would be invaluable.'[84] That combination of attributes was difficult to find in a single individual. Windle would provide a bridge to the Irish Catholic hierarchy and open up the possibility for progress in the hitherto intractable area of third-level education. The correspondence between the two men reveals the lengths to which Wyndham was prepared to go to secure Windle's appointment. Not entirely unrelated to the question of money, Windle wished, as a condition of going to Cork, to continue teaching in the new position as Professor of Anatomy. On 28 September 1904, Wyndham wrote to Windle from the chief secretary's lodge:

> I must go to Ireland tomorrow and shall at once investigate the ques-
> tion of a 'chair'. My information is that the President can occupy a
> chair. It may be, however, that any of the curriculum which you would
> care to undertake in addition to y[our] Presidential duties is already
> subserved [?]. Of this I know nothing. So soon as I have this matter I
> will communicate with you. But, in any case, it would give much
> pleasure to Lady Grosvenor and myself, to welcome you at the Chief
> Secretary's lodge on any day from Saturday next onward, the earlier,
> the better. The question of emoluments must, of course, be carefully
> examined on its merits. But, should the result of examination be sat-
> isfactory, I must not disguise my own hope that you will permit your
> name to be considered.

Before making up his mind, Windle crossed to Cork in early October 1904 to investigate personally, 'and almost anonymously', what he might be taking on. His visit must have convinced him that he was making the right decision even if he was certain that the new post would be 'by no means a bed of roses'. While travelling by train back to Dublin on 7 October, he met John J. Horgan, a 21-year-old solicitor and member of a leading Cork pro-Parnellite family who would become his son-in-law.[85] After seeing that Horgan was reading *An Claidheamh Soluis*, the paper of the Gaelic League, the 'fair-haired, clean shaven man of middle age, whose character was indicated by his firm mouth and the alert, piercing, blue eyes behind his gold-rimmed spectacles' asked him did he speak Irish.[86] They fell into conversation about the general position of education in Ireland and discussed the ban on Catholics attending the college: 'I was able to tell him that this was more apparent than real and that, at least so far as "bread and butter" studies were concerned, there was no difficulty in obtaining permission from one's confessor to enter the College.'[87] Discussion then turned to the vacancy for the presidency of the university left by the retirement of Sir Rowland Blennerhassett (1897–1904), who never allowed his presidential duties to weigh him down. He was reputed to have made two annual two-week visits to the campus – one in October and the other in May, and was remembered for his appearances on horseback in the main quadrangle where he held court with professors while still in the saddle.[88] Horgan, in his book *Parnell to Pearse*, described him as 'a Kerry baronet, who had been mixed up in the rather unsavoury intrigues which culminated in the publication of the forged Pigott letters by *The Times*'. He knew that the discharge of his duties were of 'a perfunctory kind, with disastrous results for the College'.[89] He had been given the job of president, despite not having the qualification, 'no doubt [as] a reward for this and other services to the Unionist Party'. At the end of the journey, Horgan was given his travelling companion's business card: 'Professor Bertram C.A. Windle, M.D. F.R.S., Dean of the Medical Faculty at Birmingham University'.[90]

Upon his return to Birmingham, Windle informed Wyndham of his acceptance of the post. The latter wrote on 10 October 1904: 'I wired to London and herewith enclose the Prime Minister's "hearty approval". So *"alia jacta est"* [The die is cast]. If, by any chance, unforeseen, the lectureship, or the new plan, falls through, I shall, of course, revert to the other arrangement of which I spoke confidentially.' But the securing of the professorship Windle sought proved more difficult than either man anticipated.

Despite accepting the post, Windle remained very nervous about how his appointment would be received in Cork. On 14 October, his close friend, Douglas Hyde, wrote to reassure him: 'I am indeed greatly delighted at the good news in your letter and I congratulate you heartily on coming to Ireland. I cannot tell you how delighted I am at it. You will be of untold good to us, and I feel sure you will find almost every one quite willing to respond to any attempt on your part to rationalize Irish education. This is becoming a most interesting country to live in, with all its new-born efforts in different directions and I think and hope you will be glad you have come to it from Birmingham. You may be quite sure I shall defend you *à outrance* if any attack (but that is inconceivable) be made on you from the nationalist side. I shall let people know what a blessing it is to have you here. But what about the Unionists? . . . I'll be here for the next fortnight if you pass through Dublin.'[91]

Windle's letter of appointment from King Edward VII was dated 21 October 1904:

> Know Ye that we reposing great trust and confidence in your knowledge discretion and ability do hereby in pursuance of the powers vested in Us appoint you the said Bertram Coghill Alan Windle to be President of the Queen's College, Cork, during our Will and Pleasure, in the room of Sir Rowland Blennerhassett, Baronet, resigned; with all Fees, Salaries, Rights, Profits and Privileges thereunto belonging or in anywise appertaining. Provided always that it is Our will and

Pleasure that if you the said Bertram Coghill Alan Windle shall during your full [??] tenure of the said office of President of the Queen's College, Cork, attain the age of seventy years, you shall then cease to hold such office, unless His Excellency the Lord Lieutenant of Ireland for the time being shall be satisfied that an extension of your tenure of the said office for not more than five years would be for the interest of the public service, in which event only you may continue to hold the office of President of the said College during Our Will and Pleasure for any period that We may determine in that behalf not exceeding five years from your so attaining the age of seventy.[92]

News quickly reached Cork that Windle had accepted the position as president. Horgan sent him a letter of congratulation, and, in reply on 25 October, Windle set out his rationale for taking the post: 'After a great deal of consideration and after having once refused to consider the appointment I was led by representations as to the possible use that I might be to the cause of Higher Education in my own country to accept the appointment. I do not for a moment suppose that it will be a bed of roses at first but I have lain on thorns before and managed to turn them into down and I will try what I can do in Cork. I hope I may not be too badly received there but I am happy to think that there is one person who knows that I am of Irish heart as well as of Irish race. I suspend any further remarks until we meet, which I hope will be before long, but this I will say that I hope to take as active a part in the work of the Gaelic League as is permitted to me.'[93] However, the *Freeman's Journal* took a critical view of the appointment, but true to his word, Hyde jumped to his public defence: 'I know that for many years he has kept closely in touch with Irish thought and Irish literary movements. He *believes* in the *creation* of an Irish Ireland with ideals of its own and not those of any other country. He is a member of two different branches of the Gaelic League, and I have heard him express himself strongly on the necessity for Irish education following Irish lines. I think that a man holding these (to my mind) absolutely sound views on Irish education should be set free to practise at home.'[94]

A Dr M.G. McElligott, a Munster man and a Catholic practising in Wigan, strongly defended Windle, describing him as 'a thorough Irishman, and a Catholic of the most devoted type, [and] a scientist covered with the highest possible distinction'. He had 'converted a minor school of medicine into the great Birmingham University School of today – one of the most militantly progressive schools of medicine in the whole of the Empire'. McElligott concluded that Ireland had 'few sons like Professor Windle. Does it not behove her, therefore, to cherish them, to honour them, and to receive them with all the warmth of which she alone of nations is capable?'[95]

On 25 October, Windle sent in his letter of resignation to the university. The distinguished chemist, Percy Faraday Frankland, wrote to him:

> I only heard last night that you had accepted the Cork Presidency, and whilst congratulating you most cordially on this appointment, I confess that I am even more concerned with what your removal means to the medical side of the University. It seems to me a most unfortunate moment for severing your connection, and I deeply regret on all grounds that you could not be persuaded to remain for at any rate some years longer. I am sure that this feeling will be shared by all your colleagues. I should like to take this opportunity of expressing to you, if you will allow me, my admiration of the single-minded and conscientious manner in which you have administered and guided the affairs of the Medical Faculty, and to thank you for the tact and courtesy which you have invariably displayed in all matters in which I have been brought into relationships with you. Trusting that the move you are making will fulfil your anticipations and that a career of great usefulness is still before you.[96]

On the 26th, the University Council, on the motion of the Principal and seconded by the vice-chancellor, passed the following resolution: 'that the Council receives the resignation of Dr Windle with regret and while congratulating him on his important Educational and Administrative appointment in Ireland under the Crown, takes the opportunity of thanking him for his long and distinguished services to the School of Medicine in Mason College and to the Medical Faculty of this University, both as Dean and as Professor, as well as to the general cause of Higher Education in the Midlands'.[97]

The *British Medical Journal*, on 29 October 1904, wrote: 'This appointment, by which Cork gains a distinguished President, deprives Birmingham of one who has been for twenty years the corner stone of the Medical School.' But it was to be to 'no bed of roses that Windle was going', as his biographer pointed out.[98] The Journal of the Birmingham School of Medicine, *Queen's Medical Magazine*, stated: 'Never since the foundation of the *Queen's Medical Magazine*, or indeed, for many years before, has such a momentous change in the staff of the Medical Faculty taken place as that on which the thoughts of the whole school are now centred.' His successor in his two important offices (dean and Professor of Anatomy), 'if they are still to be conjoined – will find to a great extent that the success of the school is his personal responsibility'. The writer was most struck by Windle's versatility: 'When, far away from the restrictions of academic life', it stated, '– as, for instance, on an excursion – sights and surroundings, familiar to him from many vacation cycle tours, would call forth a stream of anecdote and history'.

There was also a reference to his role as a dean meeting the students returning to the university: 'Who does not remember the swift passage from the chattering, impatient crowd without to the calm *sanctum sanctorum* where the searching eye of the Dean and the extreme brevity of his remarks made the chill comfort of the arm-chair by his desk peculiarly unattractive?'

Triumphal Entry into Cork

Bertram and Edith Windle, on 8 November 1904, made a ceremonial entry into Cork. Some 300 students assembled in the quadrangle and walked in procession to the railway station 'bearing an immense banner of the college colours, adorned with the familiar skull and crossbones'. Just after 11 a.m. 'the train arrived amid a scene of unbounded enthusiasm, the ringing cheers of the students alternating with the strains of "He's a jolly good fellow".' The Windles were given 'a reception probably unequalled in the history of the office'.[99] John J. Horgan led the receiving committee and introduced the couple to the student leaders. Interrupted by repeated bursts of cheering, D.L. Kelleher read an address signed by students of the faculties of Medicine, Engineering and Arts. The Windles then got into an awaiting carriage and were escorted to the quadrangle where, at the archway, women students presented a bouquet to Edith. The carriage was surrounded by students who gave 'round after round of ringing cheers'. Windle rose to reply: 'It gives me great pleasure to come amongst you, but I come not altogether as a stranger to Ireland. I should say it was a little over twenty years since I left this country as a young medical man, and during those twenty years of absence I can honestly say I have never forgotten the country to which I belong. I have always tried to keep up an acquaintance with the country, and to maintain an interest in her history and in her literature, and I have never once relinquished the hope of coming back. It is with very great pleasure I find myself amongst you. I shall never look back upon my action with any regret.'[100]

In Dublin, Wyndham viewed the reports of the reception with great pleasure. He wrote on 12 November: 'I read of your enthusiastic reception by the students with such pleasure. I am glad, though not surprised, to find that they appreciate their good fortune. I enclose a cheque of £200 for the purpose on which we agreed. I shall look forward to seeing you early in the new year and trust that you will stay a day or two with Lady Grosvenor and myself at the lodge on your way to Cork. (Many thanks for copy of "Prehistoric Age" which duly arrived.)'[101]

Windle returned to Birmingham to complete his round of farewells. The Catholics of the city organised, on 14 November, a banquet in his honour. He was present at a dinner on 26 November given to Sir

William Turner, who was the outgoing president of the General Medical Council. A presentation was made to him at the annual dinner of the medical students of Birmingham.[102] Windle also received testimonials from the Medical Faculty. On 8 December, the university gave a dinner at which the Principal, Sir Oliver Lodge, presided, and at which many tributes were paid. However, beneath the surface, Windle was less than fulfilled at Birmingham University. Perhaps Horgan furnishes part of the answer: 'There can be little doubt that if he had remained a Protestant the very highest position in English academic and scientific life would have been open to him, and these things he sacrificed willingly for his religious convictions.'[103] Windle himself gave part of the reason for his leaving in a letter to Sr Monica, albeit in 1927: Birmingham University had been created by men 'with the Birmingham corporation spirit burnt into them. They were always polite but the Board was the Corporation; the Principal was the Town Clerk and the Professors were the officers like the Medical Officer of health and so on – not altogether a pleasant position for them. . . . All the same I never got a great deal of recognition there and when I left they sent me a vote of thanks (literally) typed on a half sheet of ordinary note paper.'[104]

Windle had hardly settled in Cork when his patron, George Wyndham, resigned on 12 March 1905.[105] In his diary, on 5 March, he wrote: 'news of Wyndham's resignation, great blow – wrote to him.'[106] Despite his departure from Ireland, he continued to take a keen interest in the work of his protégé. On 1 November 1905, Wyndham wrote in appreciation of all that Windle was doing at the college:

> . . . I also read with pleasure and relief that you 'find plenty to do and never have an idle moment'. That reconciles me to having lured you into such troublous seas. . . . . In the long run it may prove that my failure to secure support in Ireland and financial assistance from Parliament is not to be regretted . . . If Irishmen come to understand how little English politicians – Conservatives, Liberals, Free-Traders, Protectionists and labour men – know or care about Irish interests, they will discover that they cannot afford to imitate the worst features in our Party system . . . So, as a private individual without any political *arrière-pensée*, who merely cares for the well-being of Ireland, your Conference [All-Ireland Industrial Conference] and your attempts to improve the opportunities for higher education have my heartfelt good wishes.[107]

Wyndham remained Windle's strong supporter, as will be seen in Chapter 3. He died at fifty in June 1913. Windle entered in his diary on 9 June: 'George Wyndham's death reported. An extraordinarily brilliant man and the most fascinating conversationalist I ever met. No man worse treated by the Nationalist Party, and no man ever loved this country more.'[108]

Queen's College, Cork, 1904

But what challenges faced Windle in his new posting? The Professor of Midwifery, Henry Corby, was likely to have succeeded to the presidency of QCC had the chief secretary not intervened and invited Windle to apply for the position. But that was a transitory problem, if not the least of his worries; he could overcome professorial opposition in time. But the state of the college was a disgrace. Professor Denis Gwynn described Queen's College, Cork, in 1904 as being 'almost moribund' and having 'sunk almost to its lowest level, both in prestige and in the number of its students.'[109] John J. Horgan, an *alumnus* of the college, wrote: 'At that time [1904] Queen's College, Cork was little more than an excellent medical school, which manufactured doctors for export. It had little or no interest in or connection with the life of the country or the community amongst which it was situated, and it was tolerated rather than approved by the Church. Outside the football field its students had hardly any opportunity for social intercourse. In addition to all this it was poorly endowed, and was neglected both by the Government of the day and, with the exception of one great President (William K. Sullivan), by those more directly responsible for its management.'[110] Professor John A. Murphy wrote that the entire student body numbered 171 in 1900–1, and it grew by about fifteen a year in those very early years of the twentieth century.[111]

Denis Patrick ('Dinny Pa') Fitzgerald, Professor of Anatomy between 1909 and 1942, had left the following description of the relationship between 'town and gown': 'The College almost gloried in its well-merited title of the "Godless College", and in that aloofness and divorce from public sympathies and aspiration that made us, as boys strolling past its forbidden portals, gaze with awe at the cold stern buildings high up behind the trees. The legend – "None may Enter"– seemed to be cut deeply into the keystone of the archway under the grim lodge that sentinelled the main entrance . . . The College and the medical students were synonymous terms in those days . . . And no city brawl of any decent proportion was complete unless the "College students" turned up to impart some finishing touches . . . But there were many things the small boy did not know, and one was that this hero before entering the college had to leave his religion at the gate.'[112]

Windle faced a series of major tasks. He was a Catholic and the president of a college in an overwhelmingly Catholic city and region where Catholics were technically 'forbidden' by the hierarchy to attend. One of his first challenges was to help restore good relations with the local clergy and religious, demonstrate a welcoming attitude to all Catholic men and women, provide the necessary structures to support their growth in the faith, build bridges with the local bishops, and persuade the Holy See to lift the rescript which had been there since the Synod of Thurles in 1850 (see Chapter 4). A second challenge was to win university status for QCC and to make it autonomous and self-governing, based on the Birmingham model. The establishment of a University of Munster was the focus of his attentions between 1905 and 1908 and 1918 and 1919 (see Chapters 2 and 8). Thirdly, and related to the second challenge, Windle sought to have a major influence over the content of the settlement of the Irish university question. Fourthly, Windle had the objective of overhauling QCC from top to bottom. He needed to strengthen its academic performance, hire new professorial and lecturing staff, broaden the curriculum, build better facilities and increase the number of students.

CHAPTER 2

The 'University of Munster' and the Founding of the National University of Ireland

George Wyndham, the chief secretary of Ireland between 1900 and 1905, had very clear policy ideas about how to solve 'the Irish question'. His constructive unionist policy approach laid great emphasis on the resolution of the Irish university question. The Royal University, founded in 1879, served as an examination body[1] for Catholic students. It was not an ideal system. In 1900, the British government, under growing pressure from the Irish Catholic hierarchy and the leaders of the Irish Parliamentary Party, had established a Royal Commission on University Education in Ireland under the chairmanship of Lord Robertson. Trinity College Dublin was not included in its terms of reference.[2] The Archbishop of Dublin, William Walsh, refused to give evidence before Robertson. The prelate was a major force in the intellectual and pastoral life of the country. He favoured the establishment of a Catholic College within Trinity College. There was little prospect, in such a divided climate, of achieving a consensus. The Jesuit president of the Royal College, Fr William Delany, sought an extension of his college. The influential Bishop of Limerick, Edward Thomas O'Dwyer, argued publicly in favour of the establishment of a Catholic university. The report, published in 1903, proposed that the Royal University should be reorganised and established as a federal teaching and examining university. The Queen's Colleges of Belfast, Cork and Galway were to be constituent colleges. That did not satisfy any of the major figures in Irish Catholic education. The report met with failure.

The chief secretary, George Wyndham, and his under-secretary, Antony MacDonnell, published a new scheme in 1904. The Fourth Earl of Dunraven, a unionist with a family seat in Adare, County Limerick, and former under-secretary for the Colonies (1885–7) in the Salisbury government, produced a more advanced draft. It favoured the establishment of two new colleges within the University of Dublin; The Queen's College, Belfast; and a King's College in Dublin. The King's College would give Catholics a college comparable to Trinity. That might have satisfied Archbishop Walsh. Bishop O'Dwyer was opposed and there followed a public argument between Limerick and Dublin.[3] The matter of higher education in Ireland remained unresolved in 1904.

Wyndham, as seen in the last chapter, was instrumental in coaxing Windle to Ireland to take up the presidency of QCC. He also had a much wider role in mind for his protégé, friend and admirer. Wyndham wanted Windle, who had played a central role in the establishment of the University of Birmingham and demonstrated his worth as a university administrator and reformer, to take a lead role in breaking the logjam in Ireland. Wyndham's untimely resignation as chief secretary in March 1905 – literally within weeks of Windle's arrival – was a terrible personal blow for the new QCC president. Undaunted, Windle continued to take a leading role in university reform. He petitioned Wyndham's successor, Walter Long (12 March 1905–4 December 1905), to continue the constructive policies for the reform of higher education in Ireland. But Windle had lost his patron. What his subsequent career might have been had Wyndham remained in Dublin and the Conservatives in power is a matter of mere conjecture. The Liberals took office in 1906. The new chief secretary, the historian James Bryce, was a man of the highest ability. Born in Belfast, he had spent most of his youth in Scotland.[4] Bryce had chaired a Commission on Secondary Education in 1894–5. That had not met with success.[5] But it helped raise a sense of misplaced confidence in his ability to resolve the university problem.[6] Official attention again turned to the question of the University of Dublin and Trinity College. A Royal Commission, under the Lord Justice of Appeal, Sir Edward Fry, was set up. Wyndham, out of office nearly a year, wrote to Windle on 25 January 1906 that he was writing to Bryce to request an interview at an early date. He felt that the Liberals had 'a chance that I never enjoyed. I hope that they will use it for Irish Education. It is the *only* Irish question they can advance. I have suffered in that cause and am ready to suffer again. But they must drop "step by step to constitutional Home Rule." That spells ruin to all practical measures. I am fighting our "lost cause" *de nocte in noctem*. But I have time for the things that I care about; and Irish Education is one of them.' Earlier in the letter, Wyndham wrote: 'I can enjoy no *public* peace of mind until something is done to get rid of the disparity in respect of opportunities for Education under which Ireland suffers'.[7]

Wyndham continued to press behind the scenes – in support of Windle – to make two professorships of the chair of Anatomy and Physiology at UCC. On 27 January 1906, Windle wrote a long letter of thanks to Wyndham in that regard, confessing that he had been influenced greatly by Wyndham's reforming policies. But while Windle had confidence in Wyndham, he wondered whether the Conservative Party would ever shake itself loose from 'Orange domination'. If the Tories did not break that link, Windle saw nothing 'for it but Home Rule with all its uncertainties and difficulties'. He admitted that he had been a very strong home ruler at one time' [in the 1880s] and had spoken 'in many places [in England] on that platform'. But he had never been a 'separatist', he wrote. By Wyndham's policy, he had been converted to the belief that English politicians might provide 'fair treatment for my country'. But there followed Wyndham's 'betrayal' and nine months of Long as chief secretary, leaving Windle not knowing where that left him.[8] The Tory–Orange alliance, growing in strength during the succeeding years, left Windle with no option but to remain a strong home ruler.

Denied the central role in Irish university reform which Wyndham would have ensured, Windle expended his energies trying to bring into being an autonomous University of Munster. He turned for help to William O'Brien MP, the leader of the All-for-Ireland-League. In correspondence since early 1905, both men were on close terms by that summer. Both were agreed on the need to establish an independent university in the south and worked together towards that end. On 17 January 1906, Windle wrote to O'Brien that things were moving rapidly. He had made preliminary contact with Sir Antony MacDonnell advising him that he wanted to take a delegation to Dublin to discuss with the chief secretary his future plans for QCC. At this point, it appears that O'Brien had already made an offer of a large donation to the college. Michael Murphy, the legal adviser to the college, had written to the MP 'respecting the pecuniary proposals involved and it seems to me that it is very important that the deputation should have these clearly in their minds in order that they may state them to Mr Bryce'. Windle also told O'Brien that he had had a successful meeting with the editor of the *Cork Examiner*, George Crosbie. He was seeking the support of the paper for a public campaign in support of the University of Munster idea.[9]

On 20 January 1906, Windle held a meeting of likely supporters of the autonomy proposal. They were as follows: Clery (chair), M. Healy, C.J. Dunne, Stanley Harrington, M. Murphy, Dr MacDonnell, J.J. Horgan, Macnamara (secretary), Dr Cotter and one or two others. Windle suggested that they should write to Bryce stating that they were a committee formed for the purpose of looking after the interests of higher education for Catholics in the south. He was to be informed that they had held several meetings to consider whether they should ask to be received by Bryce. They were to forward a resolution passed in 1904 at a large public meeting in Cork, calling for autonomy for Queen's College, Cork. They did not want Bryce to reach any decision on the university question without first hearing the views of the delegation.

Windle and Healy were given the immediate task to draft a letter. That was done and signed that night, 19 January, and sent to Dublin Castle. Windle told O'Brien: 'Bryce knows now that there is an organised body of opinion behind any claim for the college and can ask for the views of the Committee when he is ready to hear them. There is no doubt that there is a good spirit rising about the College, but – Well I needn't tell you that it will take time. However there is much more fire in the movement than I had dared to hope for.'[10]

Windle next drew up a proposal for a University of Munster and sent it to the Archbishop of Tuam. He also distributed the scheme to the bishops of Wexford, Waterford and Cork. William O'Brien MP received a copy too.[11] Windle wrote on 11 February to O'Brien giving him details of a long conversation with Michael Murphy: 'By the way you were quite right as to his being a first-rate man.' He outlined his thinking thus: 'I began by saying that I want here, if possible, an entirely independent University, but that if I can begin by getting the substance – fully and completely, the substance – I shall not quarrel about names. Now it has been suggested that the easiest thing to get would be this: Three (or four) Colleges, or they might even be called Universities – here is the name I would not fight over – each entirely independent of each other or of any outside dictation, drawing up their own courses, making their own regulations, engaging their own examiners, conducting their own examinations, giving their own degrees. In a word absolutely autonomous.'[12] In such a scheme, Windle sought to provide for a co-ordinating and inspecting body which would have the power of visiting the examinations of all the colleges, including Trinity College, and warning them if they let down their standards. Based on his experience on the General Medical Council, he would give that body no power other than seeing that the examinations had been properly conducted. He sought O'Brien's views on such a scheme.[13]

Windle also told the MP that a delegation was going to the bishop in Cork. Windle hoped that it would really speak the mind of the laity: 'Did they tell you that the Bishop has warned all the Catholic girls here that they will be refused absolution if they do not leave? One of them saw me yesterday, heartbroken, telling me that her career was ruined. Another was being instructed solely by Catholic Professors. There will have to be some means of guarding against this kind of thing if we are to have a proper University, but with democratic control I suppose such a thing would hardly happen,' he wrote to O'Brien.[14]

On 15 March 1906, Windle told the MP that several meetings of the university committee had been held and 'you will be glad to hear that their spirit and determination is rising every time. Mr Murphy is a tower of strength and Mr Forde, who has now begun to attend, seems likely to be a strong man. Mr Healy also very valuable. Mr Forde suggested that I should see Mr Redmond, when in London on behalf of the Committee. I asked whether this would be in any way displeasing to your feeling and Mr Forde said it would not, so I am to see him.' Windle intended going to the House of Commons for the meeting, where he would also hope to see O'Brien.[15] Windle told the MP that he had also been promised an interview with Bryce. On his return from London, he was going to stay with Lord Dunraven: 'If you could drop a word in the right quarter Dunraven is the man who should be made Chancellor of the R.U.I. now that we have got rid of Meath – for which Heaven be praised. D. might be *most* useful to us all in that position. Try what you can do.'[16]

Windle saw the chief secretary on 23 March and told him of his opposition to what he was proposing. He found him to be most kind and courteous, but only committing himself to statements as to what he thought might be attainable in the House of Commons. Windle reported that Bryce was thinking seriously about the university question. He found that he was not committed to the Dublin university scheme, 'tho' in some ways he likes it'. Neither the Catholic hierarchy nor the presidents of the colleges in Cork, Galway, and Dublin reacted with much confidence to the Bryce commission hearings. Windle was pessimistic about the outcome of the discussions.

Windle told Bryce of his objections to the chief secretary's proposals. The latter, doubtful about the Windle scheme, said he thought that the existing House of Commons would pass a bill allowing – as suggested in Windle's scheme – ex officio ministers of religion in the governing body or a board of visitors. The question was whether the bishops would accept the Bryce scheme. Windle wrote again to O'Brien on 29 March urging him to come to talk with the committee on the university question: 'The one danger is that we have some very talkative people on our Committee and I hope when you meet them that you will give them a good strong injunction to hold their tongues.'

Windle told O'Brien that there were some points in his talk with Bryce which gratified him: 'He evidently feels Cork's claims strongly. In fact he said that the position of things here was what most strongly impelled him to try and settle the University question and he further added that he would not enter into any scheme unless it was clearly understood that the ban was to be taken off the place if the arrangement was carried out. This shows that we hold a very strong card in the whole settlement and some day we may have to expose it.' Windle told O'Brien that he had invited Bryce to visit the college, promising in reply that he would go there 'either at Easter or Whitsuntide and stay a night with me and see the place'. Windle, who could not speak too warmly of the way in which he received him, felt that his visit would make him 'still more anxious to put things right'. Windle also reported to O'Brien that he had had a long and most satisfactory talk with Wyndham and 'feel certain that we can fully count on him to back Mr Bryce in anything which he may feel inclined to take up'. Windle wanted to try to bring about a conference of the Catholic bishops in a round table with a few other persons. He was heart and soul of the view that that was the way forward. He concluded: 'If we do not get a settlement next year no man can say when we shall get one. But to get a settlement next year we must be prepared to accept such a scheme as Mr Bryce thinks that he can carry through the House. He is evidently anxious to do something and in him we have a man more conversant with such matters than we have ever had before in such a position. It seems to me that we should try and get this view laid before the Bishops and endeavour to get them to see the urgency of trying to arrange a settlement now, for this is an opportunity which may not arise again for a long time.' Bryce was willing to receive a delegation 'though he did not think that he could learn more from them than he had from me or say very much to them'.[17]

Windle wrote to O'Brien on 10 May 1906 that he had satisfied himself that there was no chance of a Cork-style movement on the university question emerging in Dublin: 'The respectable shoneens want a T.C.D. settlement and are constantly proclaiming this. The mass of the people know nothing about the matter and care less. Those who do know and care – of the democratic side – do not want a T.C.D. settlement but are unvoiced and ununited. There is no M.P. there to set things going as you have done in Cork, perhaps none in Dublin who really cares or thinks much about the matter.' Windle said that Delany had strongly urged 'that we should go ahead here as hard as we can. He thinks that this will stir up a general interest in the matter and do general good and I have made it quite clear to him that we are in no way antagonistic to him or his College.' Windle had come around to O'Brien's idea that 'we should go ahead for a Cork settlement saying that we want one for the whole country but are not going to presume to offer any advice as to how that could be done save to say how we think it should be done here and that moreover we are determined to have it settled here and at once.' Windle felt that would force the Dublin people to come forward with a scheme, on the lines Cork had suggested, 'but if it is on the T.C.D. lines, then we must make it clear that that involves a separate University for Cork and another for Belfast for we here are not going under Trinity without a desperate fight'. He wanted O'Brien to arrange for a Cork delegation to be received by Bryce in Dublin: 'I am clear now from what I have heard in Dublin that we must fight our own battle in our own way and the sooner we begin the better.' He felt that the educational horizon – from a Catholic point of view – looked a little brighter 'as far as I can judge'. He again asked O'Brien to contact Lord Dunraven over the university question. He was a Munster man and was very broad-minded.[18]

O'Brien replied on 11 May indicating that he had not been asleep on the university question. He had spoken to Bryce who was willing to receive a deputation from Cork but 'he says at present he would have nothing to say that would be worth the while of the deputation to come to hear'. O'Brien found Bryce somewhat pessimistic. All he would say was that 'he does not despair'. He thought that he would have most trouble with his own party: 'He seems to have made up his mind to concentrate his energies on his Devolution measure of next session and trust to its working for a settlement of the University question.' O'Brien had taken a contrary view: 'unless he first proposed some settlement of the University question the cry that the Protestants were to be handed over to a Catholic University would be one of the most powerful grounds of opposition for any scheme of local self government he may propose.'[19]

Windle kept the campaign for autonomy going throughout the summer – but at a slower pace. On 11 September, he sent a letter to the *Cork Examiner* entitled 'A Call to Action'. He wrote to O'Brien on 15 September that the MP had been the 'originator of this movement as every body knows and, though we have carried it to a certain point, it is now time for you to step in and take your proper place in the matter'. He told O'Brien that he had asked the lord mayor and a number of aldermen about the holding of a public meeting on the issue: 'I do not know whether you would be willing to make a public announcement as to the sum of money which you proposed to give if a University or Autonomous College were established, but, if you felt that you could do so, I have no hesitation in saying that it would raise the current of feeling, now beginning to run very high, to a bank-full stream and one that no Government could afford to neglect. It seems like the psychological moment to me, but of course, it is a matter entirely to be decided by yourself.' He wanted O'Brien now to 'publicly identify yourself with a movement which you have so long fostered in private'.[20]

On 17 September – two days later – O'Brien wrote that he would be glad to take a public part in the campaign, suggesting 18 October as a convenient date for a meeting. He had no objection to the other MPs for the province being present. He wondered whether it should be confined

to Catholic laymen. But he thought that the presence of southern unionists, like Lord Bandon, would 'give immense éclat to our demands'. On
the other hand, he felt that the presence of Protestants might make the
bishop uneasy. He asked Windle to consider whether he should
announce the gift of £50,000 to the university from both himself and his
wife.[21]

In 1890, O'Brien had married Sophie Raffalovich (1860–1960), sister
of the poet Mark André Sebastian. Raised in Paris, she was the daughter
of a Russian Jewish banker from Odessa, Hermann Raffalovich, who
had moved to the French capital in 1863. She brought a sizeable fortune
to the marriage which enabled her husband to take an independent
political path and to edit his own newspaper. Sophie died in poverty in
the south of France in 1960. The Irish government had granted her a
small pension for her work on behalf of Irish nationalism. She was a
source of great strength and intellectual support to her husband, who
died in 1928.

The willingness of William and Sophie O'Brien to fund an
autonomous university in Cork was an early example of the philanthropy
which Windle sought to encourage in the region. The president, supported by the promise of a large cash donation, used the annual report to
the king to raise the question of autonomy for the university. He suggested that the university should become a college for the Catholic
people of Cork and Munster, without prejudice to either class or creed.
Cork Corporation took up the central message, passing a resolution cordially endorsing the Windle proposal which was sent on to the king, as
were similar resolutions from Waterford and Limerick.[22]

Windle wrote on 14 October in the *Cork Examiner* that Cork 'would
fight it to the death', indicating to Delany and the presidents of the other
two Queen's Colleges that a statement was to be sent to the commission
in the following terms: 'We understand that one solution is this federal
university. We desire to say we think this the worst possible solution to
the difficulty.' Windle argued that the colleges brought into the scheme
would be of different standings in age, equipment and income. The
interests of the respective colleges would be vastly different. That would
result in constant friction and in increasing struggle for supremacy on
the part of each constituent college. Windle had talked the matter over
with Bishop O'Dwyer of Limerick, who, too, pressed for a statement
from the Royal University. Windle left the matter to Delany, as he was 'a
far better hand at these things'. Windle concluded: 'let us act, for before
we know where we are we shall be improved off the face of the earth.'[23]

Bryce, it was widely believed in autumn 1906, was seeking a federal
University of Ireland. Windle regarded that as the worst 'of all abominable

ideas'.[24] Windle and Delany were of one mind – the federal solution was neither in the interests of education nor those of the Catholic popula-tion. There was a fear that Catholic influence would be diluted within a Trinity-College-dominated federation. Therefore, on 23 October, the Senate of the Royal University passed a unanimous resolution stating that it would be disastrous to the interest of education in the country to concentrate the control of higher education in one university.[25]

On 26 October, a government commission had begun taking evidence on the Irish university question. Windle had been asked to give evidence on 'the question of the desirability or otherwise of introducing the Queen's College Cork into the University of Dublin, or of connecting it in some manner with that University'. Windle was in no doubt about the dangers to Cork of such a scheme: 'This means tying up our college in Egyptian bondage,' he wrote to O'Brien: 'It would be disastrous to higher education in the country; it would be most vehemently resisted by T.C.D.; it would be unpopular – as I know for a fact – with all the Bishops but one, and he is hesitating; and I need not say that it would be most unpopular here.'[26]

In his evidence, Delany, according to his biographer, laid emphasis on the intensity of national feeling among the great mass of Irish Catholics. The British policy on higher education appeared to be: 'Refuse Irishmen what they ask even though it seems reasonable enough; but give them something else they do not want and then complain to the world how unreasonable and ungrateful they are.'[27]

As the commission was meeting in London from 7 to 14 November, Windle stepped up his campaign for a public meeting in Cork as soon as possible to 'speak our minds'. Windle told O'Brien that 17 November had been suggested. The campaign, he wrote, had already secured a large amount of important Protestant support and the lord mayor would be able 'to present a list of names of men as agreeing to our resolution such as perhaps never before in Cork agreed to any one proposition'. Windle, having kept O'Brien's name to the front of the campaign, felt it was the time for him to take his place at the head of the movement.[28]

The Lord Mayor of Cork, Alderman J. Barrett, and the chairman of the county council, William McDonald, convened a large public meeting for Saturday 17 November, at noon in city hall. The *Cork Examiner* carried the positive headline: 'Munster University – Great Meeting'.[29] The attendance list stretched to over half a column. Letters of support were then read out from MPs, public figures and chairmen of organisa-tions who wished to be associated with the university project but who were unable to be in attendance. William Redmond MP sent 'his sym-pathies and good wishes'.[30]

The lord mayor said that the large turnout 'from all corners of Munster' showed 'by your presence and by your resolution, to the powers that be that you are united in your demand that justice be done to the people of this province, and that no settlement of the University question will satisfy us unless our claim is considered. If the Munster boy must still go to Dublin, the Government may as well ask him to go to London or Edinburgh, for his parents will not be able to send him to either of them, (hear, hear), and I may tell you, gentlemen, that was the text of my evidence when I was under examination before the Royal Commission in London on the 9th of this month.' The lord mayor added: 'We want University education for all creeds and classes in the community, for the poor boy as well as for the clever rich boy; and I do hope that you will to-day let the Government in power know that we only want justice, and that Munster will fight – and Munster will be right – to achieve the objective.'[31]

William O'Brien MP, who was the featured speaker, was received with great cordiality. His long speech was very strong and pointed: 'No rational person can blame the people of the South, or say that you are acting too precipitously, if you take up the position to-day that the people of Munster have interests and views of their own, which must not be denied a hearing, and which in fact as some us believe, open a way to the settlement of the entire Irish University Question.' He wanted an autonomous university for Cork, feeling it would 'take the edge off all the old sectarian difficulties and controversies'. O'Brien said that 'on St Finbarr's rock, we have got University buildings ready made which are worthy of expansion into a majestic seat of learning hereafter'. What they proposed was simply to do in Cork what had been done in Birmingham and to do it by means of the very man – Windle – who had done it already in Birmingham. He felt it was as necessary to overcome English prejudice in that regard as it was important to challenge the view that Catholic laymen had no interest in the university question.[32]

O'Brien argued that 'John Bull is incorrigibly addicted to measuring the extent of one's feelings by the pounds, shillings and pence standard'. He did not know whether or not it would make a difference if London was aware that the people of Cork and of the fair and generous province of Munster were determined to stand to their guns, 'without, of course, for one moment surrendering the unanswerable case of Ireland as to her ill-treatment and over-taxation by England, in the department of education, as well as in every other department'. O'Brien, on behalf of his wife and himself, said that 'as we have an attachment to Cork which perhaps all the world will understand, and have hitherto had no substantial opportunity of proving it, and as we cannot imagine any object that is likely to fructify in such a multiplicity of blessings for the people of Cork

and of the province, as to the success of the movement we are inaugu-
rating to-day, we have made up our minds, if you will allow us, to
[bequeath] on our demise practically all that we are worth in the world as
a contribution towards the endowment of a Cork University.'[33] He mentioned the sum of £50,000, offering £10,000 a year for five years 'if the
borough and county councils would undertake to put a burden of half a
farthing in the pound on the people, every penny of which would be
repaid at the death of his wife and himself'. This, Mr O'Brien said, in
addition to the £10,000 which the college had, and private benefactions
which he hoped would be made, rendered it possible 'to start the
University at once, even if the State contributed nothing more'. The generosity of Sophie and William O'Brien was cheered warmly. The meeting
resolved in conclusion that the constituted college in Cork should
possess the largest measure of autonomy.[34]

The campaign for the University of Munster had been launched with
great fanfare. On 27 November, Windle told O'Brien in a letter that a
friend at Dublin Castle had told him 'that a deputation to the C[hief]
S[ecretary] is the first thing'. He had also heard from the chief secretary,
'expressing the greatest interest in what is going on, his admiration for
your munificent gift and his hope that it may lead up to a satisfactory ter-
mination of the present dispute'. He wanted Bryce to make a sufficient
change in the government of the college 'as would enable the Bishop to
write to Rome and to get a change made in the attitude towards this
place'. Windle told O'Brien, 'strictly entre nous', that Bryce's attitude
towards Cork had 'entirely changed' and that he was considering 'steps on
his own account of a startling character and that – as he himself puts it –
"a little good will on both sides will settle the matter"'. Windle wanted to
press the initiative but felt that Bryce would not draft a charter for Cork
'but I suppose he can't do it until the whole matter comes up for settlement'.[35] Windle felt that the chief secretary and the prime minister should
be asked jointly to meet a deputation and to meet it in London shortly.
He urged O'Brien to speak to Bryce if he got the chance on the Munster
university idea: 'Again I would say that everybody here knows that you are
the man who has urged on this movement and everybody looks to you to
give it the impetus which no one else can give it in Cork.'[36]

On 30 November, Windle wrote again to O'Brien briefing him on
developments. He had sent a strong statement to Bryce together with a
detailed account of the meeting in Cork. He would not press forward
with the idea of getting the prime minister to see a deputation 'until
Bryce has quite made up his mind what he is going to do; and I will
advise the committee to hold their hands until they see the result of the
enquiries which you will be able to make in London'. He did not want

O'Brien to reveal the position of the Bishop of Cork. It was 'no good showing our hand at present', as there were 'strong influences working against us'.[37] Bishop O'Callaghan had been actively trying to remove the papal rescript forbidding Catholics from attending.[38]

On 7 December, Windle wrote despondently to Bishop O'Dwyer of Limerick: 'If Winston Churchill comes here, as it seems certain that he will before long, anything on earth may happen. Does it not sometimes seem to you that nothing but separation from England can save this country as a Christian country?' As expected, the members of the commission were divided in their views. But that did not remove the threat of the one-university solution.[39] Delany was very alarmed. He felt that there was a proposal on the table that would 'establish Protestant ascendancy in education for an indefinite time to come'. He urged Windle and others to reiterate their opposition 'in the very strongest manner'. The former was very combative but wary of the fact that the bishops were suspicious of him. He asked Delany to tell them that he was disinterested and that Cork would fight its way into complete independence before long. The proposal before them was to give Ireland 'a university with a permanent Protestant majority in its governing body'. He urged active leadership from Dublin. There was, wrote Windle, no graduate association in Cork, and the men were 'so supine' that he could get them 'to do nothing except earn their living and sail boats and hunt'. It was, he said, the work of Sisyphus. But he would continue to try to stir up the people of Cork to insist on a university, force the pace and complete the settlement through Dublin.[40]

On 22 December, Windle heard the news that Bryce was being sent to New York as British consul. He wrote exasperatedly in his diary: 'Four Chief Secretaries in two years I shall have seen – all quite ignorant when they came, all having to be taught, all going when they know a little. Is it any wonder that every honest Irishman curses every time he hears the name of England?'[41] [Bryce, in fact, went to Washington as ambassador where he served from 1907 to 1913.] On 28 January, Windle wrote: 'To Dublin by 12.55 to Club . . . full of talk about Bryce scheme. Told them of the article in the *Cork Examiner*, and said people much annoyed that Bryce had not seen a deputation. Said my own view was that it was neither the best, nor the second best, but being an improvement on the thing we had – I would take it rather than nothing.'[42]

The university commission, presided over by Sir Edward Fry, reported on 12 January 1907, having been meeting since 2 June in London and in Dublin.[43] As anticipated, the report was inconclusive and revealed irreconcilable differences between the various parties. The first group favoured the expansion of the Dunraven-like solution – an expanded Royal University of Dublin. Three others supported the model of an expanded Royal University. A representative from Trinity College opposed the implementation of both models. A submission by 500 Catholic laymen had favoured an acceptance of Trinity on condition that there would be a Catholic chapel, a Catholic Theology Faculty and the duplication of the chairs of Philosophy and Modern History.[44] Fry, Sir Arthur Rucker and Mr Butcher felt 'very strongly that to introduce a Roman Catholic College side by side with Trinity, the stronghold of Irish Protestantism, would work for discord and not peace, and we drew up a full statement of our views on the matter, which may be read by whomsoever will in the Blue Book.'[45]

Within four days of the report being published, Bryce, who was leaving his post, sought to introduce his own bill into the House of Commons, telling his fellow MPs on 25 January that the plan was to create a single new university for the island. It would contain Trinity, a new Catholic college in Dublin and the Queen's Colleges at Belfast and Cork. Magee College, Derry, Queen's College Galway and Maynooth would become affiliated colleges. All sides attacked the blueprint, Trinity being both well organised and vociferous.[46] Bryce was incorrect to state that the Catholic bishops were in agreement with the scheme, although a few favoured the idea of a Catholic college in Trinity.[47] Windle made very clear his disapproval of the proposed scheme. He wrote in the *Cork Examiner*:

> I have urged, and perhaps may again be allowed to urge, that this is essentially a matter to be taken in hand by Munster people. I wish those in Dublin and elsewhere every possible success in settling their educational affairs upon lines satisfactory to themselves and beneficial to the higher education of this country, which is so much in need of amendment. But whatever settlement, as indeed the Commissioners recognize, is made in Dublin will not settle the affairs of the south. Here we have our own problem to solve, and I do not think that its solution is one which presents any insuperable difficulties. Given a little goodwill, I believe it is quite possible to create a university there which will deal fairly by all classes of the community, and which will be acceptable to all: and I would earnestly call upon the people of Munster to join in making an effort to secure a local settlement of the question which is of such importance to the rising generations of this part of Ireland.[48]

Augustine Birrell was sworn in as chief secretary on 27 January 1907. He took over his portfolio in what F.S.L. Lyons has called 'unpromising circumstances', inheriting the unresolved third-level educational question from his 'ineffectual predecessor' who had left 'a legacy of frustration and annoyance . . . among the Irish parliamentary party leaders'. As may be seen above, Bryce had also alienated the Catholic hierarchy and the senior officers of the Queen's College in Cork, Galway and Belfast.

Windle, bruised by his experience with Bryce, wrote on 1 February to O'Brien that a university scheme might be forced on the country which had been repudiated by 'every person of every kind of denomination and politics who has the slightest knowledge of university affairs'. He said that the proposal 'largely destroys my interest in the matter and leads me to regret that I was ever tempted back to this country'. Windle, expecting more from the new Liberal government, had received a letter on the matter from the under-secretary, Sir Antony MacDonnell, which had 'filled him with dismay'. Writing to O'Brien on 14 February, he said that MacDonnell told him that Cork would be 'independent of outside control in the administration of its business and management of its funds. It will conduct its own examinations for scholarships and prizes.' Windle pointed out that the college was doing all those things at that time, 'so where are we to be benefited by the change'. Windle continued in his letter to O'Brien: 'then he produces: "But the conferring of degrees is the function of the University; and therefore all tests of knowledge must be applied by the University. But I conceive that each constituent College would be represented on the University Examining Boards."'[49]

Windle commented that that was

> simply the system which now curses Ireland. And, as far as we are concerned we should be worse off under it in a University dominated by Trinity than in the Royal. If we have to send our students to Dublin to be examined by a Board there we might as well be as we are. It does not matter a brass farthing whether the Board is labelled 'Royal' or 'Dublin' or anything else. I have written to Sir Antony explaining this point and have written very plainly. Possibly I have misunder-stood him for his words are quite opposed to the suggestions of the Commission which are as good as can be made for a Federated University. But if the Victorian system and worse is going to be set in operation here good-bye to any chance of improvement in Irish edu-cation. I hope I have misunderstood him, but I must confess that I find it a little hard not to have the opportunity of even expressing my views on a subject concerning which I do after all know something and which affects this place fundamentally.

Windle said he did not want O'Brien to do anything 'at this moment' but 'I think it right that you should know how things are and that it may be necessary to declare bitter war on this scheme.'[50]

The following day, 15 February, he wrote again to O'Brien about how disheartened he felt over Sir Antony MacDonnell's letter: 'The kind of monster there foreshadowed is a thing which it would not be worth while taking any trouble about and about which I would not myself take the slightest trouble. It is not the kind of thing for which you offered your money nor to which you would be disposed to give it. It is a thing tied up and strangled from its birth and with no chance of developing or making any advances in accordance with local needs. And this is the kind of thing which Sir Antony supposes we shall welcome.'[51] Windle wondered 'what on earth is the good of telling us that we can examine for [our] own scholarships when we are to be tied up by University courses set by an outside body. Is the man so incredibly ignorant of educational affairs as to suppose that you can get students to read one course for scholarships and another for degrees. Of course scholarships have to be more or less on the lines of the ordinary courses and so we come back again to our crippled, tied-up state. And this is what a Liberal Government is going to give us.' Windle wanted O'Brien to get better terms for Cork: 'As for me I will fight this plan for all I am worth and as far as I can fight it, for it would be absolutely destructive of educational progress in the South of Ireland.'[52]

Birrell had his faults as an administrator but he was not ineffective. He had a better feel for Irish politics than his immediate predecessor. He changed tack and sought to govern Ireland 'on a light rein rather than to bear down heavily in the traditional manner'. Like many of his predecessors, he spent more time in London than in Dublin. But that was not a cause for local resentment provided he did his job well. Birrell, with tongue firmly in cheek, once said that 'he took his evidence of public opinion as much from the programmes of the Abbey Theatre as from the reports of the R.I.C.' If he had an identifiable fault it may have been his 'uncalled-for levity'.

Windle, in concluding his letter to O'Brien on 15 February, said he had written to MacDonnell pointing out the defects in his thinking on university restructuring. He also wrote to Birrell, appealing 'that the details may not be finally settled without my having the opportunity of saying a word on them'.[53] On 1 March, Birrell replied to Windle, accepting his invitation to visit the college. He arrived on the 30th. Windle's diary recorded: 'Birrell came in morning and went all over place. Said that he would fight for it and would fix Anatomy thing as soon as he got to Dublin. No University Bill this year: hoped there would be next. Dublin University must be left out. Bryce hypnotized by Sir Antony who strong-willed and ignorant and no chance of parliament passing his Bill. Explained position of those who supported Bryce, and those who hadn't opposed him, and why. Discussed this matter at great length and also question getting religious difficulty brought to an end. Did not refuse to consider possibility of settling this thing. Also discussed question of buying Berkeley Hall.

Seemed inclined to do this. Then lunch, and walked with him to his hotel, talking of Newman, Manning etc.'[54] That evening, Windle gave a dinner for Mr and Mrs Birrell. His cousin Hildegarde was also present together with Stanley Harrington, General and Mrs Parsons and Admiral and Mrs King Hall.

There was more substance to the new chief secretary than his critics believed. He resolved the issue of the chair of Anatomy with despatch. At a debate on the universities question in the House of Commons on 5 July, according to Windle's diary entry, 'Birrell makes a great discourse about Cork and me. Gwynn and Butcher also spoke of me in glowing terms.' In a letter to O'Brien on 4 August, Windle agreed that 'Mr Birrell is not unfriendly to our Cork project'. He said he was hesitant about approaching the bishops as they did not understand 'that I am most anxious to help in a settlement in which they will fully concur, but so it is, and hence I am afraid that if I were to open up negotiations, and particularly by letter, the result would be failure'. He told O'Brien in strict confidence that the government would have settled the question on the Robertson lines had TCD and the bishops publicly committed themselves to accept such a settlement. Windle had attempted to get movement on the matter but 'the whole thing collapsed! With this failure fresh upon me I hesitate to make any further attempts.' He mentioned that 'Mr Birrell was most friendly to me and to the college and – as you will have seen – he spoke of Cork in the highest terms in the House – it must have surprised a good many people that he should do so.'[55]

Windle, having spent a good deal of the summer in England, wrote on 3 September to O'Brien, enclosing a copy of his QCC report to the king which had just been published. There had been a short report in the *Cork Examiner*. He had asked George Crosbie not to have any leader on it until he had come back 'when I would write a couple myself (this strictly *entre nous*)'. He said he could not 'trust anyone else in Cork to write on this delicate matter and I think the thing can wait till October and had better wait till then for most people are now away'.[56] He thought that 'with a little pressure Mr B. might be induced to give us a new Charter, if we could get that, you would see the University Question very rapidly settled'. Windle continued: 'My own fear is the so-called Irish Parliamentary Party which would I fear offer their resistance to such a change. It must be prepared for me by arranging – as can be arranged – an outburst of public opinion as soon as the Letters are placed on the tables of the Houses, I will work up to this in the "Examiner".'[57]

He was very critical of the English press which, he said, 'simply pick and choose the things [to report] which will irritate English opinion against Ireland', adding that 'if Dante were now writing his Inferno he would certainly have to invent some new kind of hell for the English jour-nalist and the job of the same would be reserved for the "Times"'.[58]

Back in Ireland in October, Windle urged O'Brien to encourage Birrell to take up the university question. Windle urged him to see Lord Castletown while in Cork or at Mallow: 'He is full of ideas and plans and has recently seen Birrell.'[59] He wrote again on 10 October stating that 'at any rate *I* can do nothing in the matter which has now become one for politicians and that makes it less vilesome for me to be held by the leg here than it would otherwise be'.[60]

In a letter to his friend Humphreys shortly before Christmas 1907, Windle expressed confidence in the chief secretary: 'Birrell seems to be going to make a supreme effort to get this Bill through. I am in constant correspondence with him over it, and find him a very frank, honest man to deal with. But I must own that the intrigues and dirty tricks of politics are enough to make any honest man sick when you see them from the inside, as I begin to do since I came to Ireland. Also the despicable lying of the English papers does make one positively sick. However these are not Christmas subjects, and I will drop them'[61]

Windle wrote to Humphreys again on 14 January: 'I hope that Birrell is going to give us a good University Bill and I think that he will, and is in good heart about passing it.' He explained how the chief secretary had sent down a non-conformist minister to Cork to discuss the issue with Windle who hoped, after a long talk, he had put some sound sense into him. He wondered what the reaction of an Irish Catholic priest would be had he been sent over to England for a week to study the intricacies of the Tariff question: 'Yet our University Question is just as tangled a web. However, we haven't long to wait now to see how things will go.'[62]

Forced prematurely to handle the unsuccessful Irish Council Bill,[63] Birrell did not make a similar mistake with the Irish Universities Bill which – in his own good time – he introduced in March 1908. Writing to O'Brien on 13 March, Windle wanted them both to remain in close touch during the progress of the bill. He had received a 'confidential' letter the previous day containing a list of the names of those who were to form the Senate of the new university and asking him whether he would serve in that capacity. Windle accepted the position but he wanted to point out to O'Brien that 'this list is altogether too Dubliny and too University Collegy also'. There were twenty-seven names 'and of those three only belong to Cork and three to Galway. There are two Bishops, so that there are nineteen others, nearly all of whom are connected with Dublin and either ten or eleven of these are connected with the Catholic University College.' Windle did not think that was 'a fair or a workable arrangement, for Dublin is placed in such a position that it can outvote all the rest of the country and determine things just as it desires – which you may be very certain will not be the way that Cork wants things'. He thought that the number of Cork representatives ought to be materially increased 'unless it is understood that Cork is only to be a miserable appendage to a great Dublin establishment and I'm sure you will never permit that. I would rather see the whole Bill smashed than see Cork made subservient to a Dublin institution which will do everything in its power to ruin it.'[64]

Windle wrote to O'Brien that there had been a number of rumours as to the probability of his being offered the presidency of the new Dublin college. He had heard of a letter from a priest to the Archbishop of Dublin, William Walsh, in which it was stated that 'I was doing everything in my power to get this place and that they feared I would be successful but hoped I might not be.' Windle stated that he was aware that 'the Archbishop of Dublin is an *acharné* [unrelenting] enemy of mine and has been for years because I happen to have been educated at T.C.D. and born a Protestant and I am well aware that he would do his utmost to keep me out of this place and to put Dr Cox, who wants it, I am told, into it.'[65] Windle claimed that he had not raised a finger in the matter and had even refused to allow others to raise a finger in it, though they had asked him leave to do so: 'so much for the lie contained in the letter in question.' He said he would wait for the post to be offered to him – an offer he had no earthly reason to expect to be made – and decide whether to take it or not: 'In many ways I would rather stay in Cork but I would not stay and will not stay a day longer than I can help if the place is going to be made a mere appendage to a Dublin College which can crush all the life out of it.'[66] As things stood, if the Senate had the power to appoint professors, 'it means that Dublin can fill Cork and Galway with men of its own choice irrespective of the views of the South and in a host of other ways Dublin can – and I am sure would – hamper our action'. Windle felt that if Cork did not get autonomy 'the college had better be closed'. He wanted O'Brien to lobby hard on the matter.[67]

Birrell, sensitive to the opposition in Cork, had sought to address local disquiet when introducing the Universities Bill: 'I say frankly I would much sooner that Cork and Galway, great and important places, were strong and powerful enough to run Universities of their own – I hope that Cork may yet be.'[68] O'Brien and Butcher, on 31 March, made strong speeches on behalf of Cork. Windle wrote on 1 April to O'Brien that the sum being voted to Cork was not ungenerous and a good deal could be done with it. He hoped that the considerable sum would not be less than £30,000. Windle said that he was writing all the articles on the matter in the *Cork Examiner*. He was convinced that the bill was 'quite certain' to pass and with 'a very few modifications'. He thought that it was 'one which will prove of enormous benefit to the country'.[69] On 5 April, Windle told his friend Humphreys: 'The University Bill promises, I think, well. It does not give us all we want here, but is a decided advance, and will put me in a position to make a really big thing of this place, as I hope to do if I live and remain here.'[70] Windle sent two letters to the *Cork Examiner* on 12 and 13 April making the case for an autonomous University of Munster.

Birrell sent a copy of the Cork charter to Windle on 17 April and came later to discuss it with him. A big public meeting was held on 25 April. Windle's diary for that day recorded: 'O'Brien called and we went fully over the situation being in entire consent on all points. He is very hopeful about the Bill passing.' Windle again used the *Cork Examiner* to explain the bill to the public. He spent the following days sending out copies of the charter to various persons and bodies. Behind his mask of enthusiasm for the bill lingered a great disappointment over not having secured autonomy for Cork. But he determined to continue the fight to secure that objective.[71]

The draft legislation bore the hallmarks of good planning. The proposal was to establish two new universities on the island – Queen's University, Belfast, and the National University of Ireland. The recommendation was to make both state-funded and non-denominational in character. The Royal University was to be abolished. There were to be three constituent colleges of the NUI, Cork, Galway and Dublin – the latter being a reconstituted University College Dublin. Maynooth had, under the bill, the opportunity to become an affiliated college. The proposals were simple and overcame many of the dilemmas on which previous plans had foundered. While the universities were secular in character, and there was protection against interference in religious beliefs, there was the strong likelihood of Cork, Galway and Dublin recruiting a large number of Catholic staff to teach a predominantly Catholic student body.

On 12 May 1908, the bill received a second reading and was carried by a huge majority. But the charter was non-denominational and the teaching of religion was explicitly prevented. There was no religious test for appointments and all professorial staff signed, upon appointment, a declaration that they would respect the different religious opinions of the students. Bishop O'Dwyer was the most vociferous among the bishops in opposing the bill, expressing his concerns over the inadequacy of Catholic representation in the Senate. He did not feel that there was sufficient protection of religion or adequate control over the religious orthodoxy of the teaching staff. It was a 'Birrelligious university', according to contemporary wags.

Bishop O'Callaghan, as the details of the bill became clearer, had taken a more acquiescent line, as had the majority of the other bishops. The structure of the new NUI governing bodies of the constituent colleges meant that the Churches were well represented. The Catholic bishops, not entirely satisfied with the solution, sought to use the structures of the NUI and to 'baptise it and make it Christian'. [72] The Cardinal Archbishop of Armagh, Michael Logue, was grudging in his acceptance of the compromise settlement. Like all concessions from their friends in England, he told an audience in Belfast in June 1909 that it 'bore the brand of slavery impressed upon it'. [73] He also described the settlement as a pagan bantling dropped in the midst of us, 'but please God if we can, we will baptise it and make it Christian'. [74]

Archbishop Walsh had threatened not to take his seat on the Dublin commission if the title was to be the King's University of Ireland. The title of 'National University of Ireland' was adopted and met with general approval. [75] The Dublin commissioners were named as follows: [76] Right Honourable Christopher Palles, Bertram Windle, Archbishop William Walsh, John J. Boland, Alexander Anderson, Denis J. Coffey, Stephen Gwynn, General Sir William F. Butler, Sir John Rhys and Henry Jackson. Windle was very active. On 2 December, the charter of the NUI was published. [77]

Windle recorded details of the first meeting of the NUI Senate on 17 December, seconding the nomination for chancellor of Archbishop William Walsh. This was carried unanimously [78] and he held that post until his death in 1921. The vice-chancellor was Christopher Nixon. He was succeeded in 1914 by the president of University College Galway, Alexander Anderson. Windle became vice-chancellor in 1916 and held the position until 1918 when he was succeeded by Denis Coffey. The latter had become the first head of University College Dublin in 1908, Delany taking a seat in the Senate. [79] Joseph McGrath was registrar of the NUI from 1908 until 1923. [80]

St Patrick's College, Maynooth, applied for affiliation as a recognised college. This was granted for the faculties of Arts, Celtic Studies and Philosophy. After a period of four years, affiliation was granted in perpetuity. Right Rev. Daniel Mannix, president of St Patrick's College, Maynooth, was also appointed to the Senate in 1908. He was replaced upon his resignation in 1913 by Right Rev. John F. Hogan.

The NUI was nobody's idea of an ideal solution. Professor Donal McCartney, the author of the history of University College Dublin, saw it as the offspring of 'political compromise'. At one level, Windle found the post-1908 situation much more desirable than what he had first begun with in 1904. To borrow two phrases from the early 1920s, the act was a stepping stone, and freedom to achieve freedom and full autonomy. He outlined the benefits as follows: half a loaf or even quarter of a loaf was better when it was not possible to get the entire article. The act had given each of the constituent universities a representative governing body in touch with the interests of the area. It provided that all students would be examined in Cork by UCC teachers, with the assistance of an external examiner system. Thus was ended the system of Cork students having to go to Dublin to be examined. Control was given over the subjects that were going to be taught, subject to the approval of the NUI Senate. Windle, post 1908, was much freer to pursue his wide scheme of reforms in, and on behalf of, University College Cork. He also, despite having helped bring the NUI into being, clung to the idea of establishing an independent University of Munster in Cork.

In Cork, the news of the setting up of the NUI structure was not greeted with enthusiasm. At a public meeting in city hall, William O'Brien had a motion passed, which was seconded by Alderman Dale and supported by Windle, expressing 'deep regret and disappointment that it has not been thought fit to provide Cork with that separate University which has been so often and so long asked for, and demands that nothing shall be included in the present Bill which will prevent or even place obstacles in the way of an early attainment of the only settlement which can be regarded as final by the people of the South of Ireland'.[81]

Windle found that the federal system was weighted entirely in favour of Dublin. For example, excluding the chancellor and the registrar, the NUI Senate consisted of thirty-five members. Dublin had seventeen. The Crown nominated four (usually from Dublin). Cork had seven members and Galway five. That meant that neither Cork nor Galway, nor both together, could change anything in the university unless with the consent of Dublin. The reverse was also the case. Dublin, if unanimous, could – in spite of Cork and Galway – 'do exactly what she pleases'. UCC found that to be 'an unfair, even humiliating, position'.

The UCC governing body formulated the position thus in 1918: 'It robs those connected with College of freedom, and hampers their initiative, since in considering progressive operations this College has always to take into account not merely their educational advantages but at least as much how far they might be tolerated by, or inconvenient to, another Institution. With differing interests on both sides such a situation cannot but lead to grievous friction and does lead to a lamentable delay in educational progress.'[82]

Although Windle used the 1908 settlement to the full, his life as president of UCC was scarred by his failure to uncouple Cork from the federation. Writing from Toronto on 23 January 1927 to Sr Monica, he gave vent to his feelings:

> As to Cork and N.U.I., which I helped to hatch, the less said the better. The N.U. I. was, I suppose is, the most utterly detestable thing that man ever had to do with. Of course Birrell, that master of cynical opportunism, was responsible for that but I never went to any of its meetings without coming away pining for a moral carbolic bath. I had one happy moment in connection with that fifteen years – it was the last when I stepped on the steamer and said good-bye to the whole abominable, concatenation. Then Toronto – well, a prophet – if I may venture so far – not without honour save in his own country and here I have had nothing but kindness and generous appreciation from the moment I started work down to this day. No vile intrigues and mephitic lies such as formed the Irish atmosphere and no civic patronage as in Birmingham.[83]

Those words were written after Windle had been beaten down by a lifetime of struggle in Cork. However, in 1908, he set out in a very different frame of mind, with reforming zeal and a plan to change the reality of UCC from being a glorified medical school into a modern university.

CHAPTER 3

The Modernisation of
QCC/UCC 1905–1913

Windle forged ahead with the modernisation of UCC, taking full advantage of the opportunities which the university settlement had provided. Quickly, he emerged as a significant figure at a national level and appeared destined for greater things in the evolving national university administration. He combined great energy with a talent for administration and a commitment to reform. During his fifteen years in Cork, he left his mark on an institution which had languished under his predecessor in a state of near paralysis. His record as a builder of a modern university in Cork must also be seen in the context of his holding professorial chairs in two different disciplines while remaining active as a scholar in a number of diverse disciplines.[1]

Windle's extraordinary work rate is part of the reason for the transformation of UCC during his tenure. His first biographer compiled the following table of letters written, books read and meetings attended for the period 1905–19 from the information provided at the back of his diaries.[2]

TABLE 3.1: RECORD OF WINDLE'S WORKLOAD 1905–1919

Year	Letters	Books	Meetings	Dublin
1905	3090	218	118	–
1906	2826	309	106	–
1907	2354	387	82	53
1908	2646	273	57	57
1909	3706	269	153	112
1910	4845	240	175	52
1911	4727	284	177	44
1912	4699	217	186	39

1913	3770	300	111	36
1914	4051	306	119	36
1915	3629	301	147	32
1916	3456	329	158	20
1917	3494	328	204	60
1918	3175	303	153	42
1919	3140	313	113	23

Many of Windle's early visits to the capital were to attend to his duties in the drafting of statutes for the NUI, accounting – in part – for the 112 visits in 1909. He had many other reasons for being in Dublin. As a member of the NUI Senate, he had to make the trip regularly to the headquarters of that new organisation. It was not long before he experienced the shortcomings of the new federal university structure. UCD could outvote UCC and UCG on every occasion. The president of UCD between 1908 and 1940, Denis J. Coffey, was not slow to take full advantage of the position of hegemony enjoyed by his university.[3] Both Windle and Coffey were medical doctors, but that was where similarities ended. Windle wrote regularly and disparagingly of the UCD president. In contrast, his relationship with the president of UCG, Alexander Anderson, was cordial. Windle came to admire the NUI registrar, Joseph McGrath, and to consider both himself and his wife amongst his close personal friends. There are scores of letters in the NUI archives over his time as president. Much of the time they dealt with routine matters. But throughout, Windle displayed a warm affection for McGrath. The closeness of their relationship meant that Windle felt quite free to describe his symptoms of poor health in many of those letters which also dealt with routine college business. For example, he wrote on 22 April 1913: 'It is a very unlucky thing for me that I have developed a most infernal cold and my usually silvery voice resembles the strains of a worn-out bicycle horn. I am inhaling, stopping-in, taking various things with the object of getting up to Dublin tomorrow. The following day he wrote: 'Although I am better I am still as hoarse as a crow and a coughing simulacrum of a man.' The same day, he wrote again: 'I wish I could get my accursed bronchi clear: when I try to talk I appear to be like a child's doll stuffed with saw-dust.' On 23 May, he told him: 'I do not know whether it was your baneful influence or the effects of Dublin but I developed an attack of gout in my left arm which has kept me in bed for the past three days and it is from that exhilarating place of refuge that I am now dictating this letter.' On 30 September 1913, Windle condoled with the McGraths over an unspecified loss – probably of a child: 'I once had a small boy – he died, a lasting grief to me – for while he lived I said a prayer every night that he might grow up to be a S.J. [Jesuit]. His lot is a better one . . .'

The UCC president, from the very outset, did not conceal his dislike for the NUI. He ended a long letter to the former on 26 November 1909: 'There has never been any concealment of our intention here to get out of the National University at the first possible moment and to that task I intend to devote all my energies which are left over from the necessary business of the University and College. Meantime my own desire is that when we part, we may part with unbroken friendship.'[4] That personal friendship did not mean that Windle spared McGrath when it came to a professional disagreement. For example, on 6 May 1914, he wrote scathingly: 'I have long believed that the arrangements regarding the University are the most amazing the world contains. One of these amazing conditions is that the Registrar of the University apparently does not read the regulations of the Colleges. If you will turn to our calendar for 1910–11, page 151, you will find that in the very first group of courses presented to the University and approved by them a Diploma in Commerce at the end of two years was included.' Windle had urged on McGrath that a digest of the degrees and diplomas offered by the various colleges should appear in the university calendar: 'Had that been done from the beginning, it would not have been possible for the Registrar of the University to speak of a Diploma, which has been in existence as long as the University itself, as an innovation.'[5]

Windle, in fighting for the autonomy of UCC, sought to make sure that the NUI did not deepen its roots by assuming any direct internal role in the constituent colleges. There was a proposal in the autumn of 1912 to have the NUI registar, Joseph McGrath, as a member of the governing bodies of each of the colleges – an idea he gave up when confronted by local opposition. On 13 October 1912, Windle wrote to him 'for yours eyes only', saying that he would have supported the proposal 'but I should have had great difficulty in carrying my colleagues with me. We all of us loathe the N.U.I., and that loathing increases every year. It will be intensified by the Dublin policy of grab as again exemplified by the Vice-Chancellorship business on which I mean to speak out pretty freely.' Windle viewed the exclusion of the presidents of the constituent colleges from holding that position in rotation as part of the Dublin-based control of the NUI. He further told McGrath on 13 October 1912: 'I personally am bitterly affronted by the attitude of some at least of the dominant majority and their obvious intention of working everything in the interests of Dublin and Dublin alone and like all my colleagues I would do nothing which would in any way tend to glorify or exalt what is called the University. Quite the contrary. That is a plain statement of facts which cannot have escaped your notice.'Windle then went on to state to McGrath that he could differentiate 'between a man whom I esteem and the damnable institution which it is his misfortune to be connected with and I would have welcomed you on our Governing Body as J. McG. but <u>not</u> as Registrar N.U.I. But I very much doubt if others would have done so though <u>there is not one of us</u> [underlining in pen and may have been done by recipient of letter] who has not a personal regard for you.' Windle stressed that held for himself and his colleagues. But not in the event of such a state of affairs arising in the future. He was, however, pleased that McGrath had not persisted with the idea as it would have involved him 'in very awkward quandaries by virtue of your dual positions. . . . However *cadit quaetio.*'

Windle, in the same letter, explicitly bemoaned the absence of 'any competent Vice-Chancellor'. Sir Christopher Nixon held that position between 11 November 1909 and July 1914. He had little regard for him, and less for Lord Christopher Palles – also a member of the senate – 'whom I think a most wrongheaded and ill-advised little man and one thoroughly dangerous to education in this country'.[6] Windle explained to McGrath on 13 October 1912 that it was impossible for both himself and the registrar, Molohan, to be away together at that time of year. He had to return swiftly to Cork to attend a funeral. But he had 'to waste a whole day and a half over rotten details which any competent Vice-Chancellor would settle, so far as concerns two-thirds of them, with you and without troubling any Committee'. He thanked McGrath for 'trying to convenience us uitlanders'. If all others in the NUI 'gave us the same consideration we should not feel our position so much as we do and should entertain very different feelings towards that accursed institution whose speedy destruction forms the object of my sincerest prayers. Yours always sincerely, Bertram C.A. Windle, ps Kindest regards to Lady McGrath.'[7])

The needless trips to Dublin, together with the acrimony and length of meetings, were a regular feature of Windle's diary entries and correspondence with the NUI. Writing on 3 December 1913 to McGrath, Windle complained about the impositions he faced having to travel to Dublin to attend meetings which imposed upon him unnecessary strains: 'The fact of the matter is that I find the system of coming up by the Mail on one day, attending a meeting on the next, hastily bolting some lunch and then catching the awful 3 train in order to arrive home by 9 p.m. knocks me up altogether. I got home last night feeling perfectly fagged out and have not got over it yet. This is the usual history of such attempts.' As an alternative, Windle proposed coming up and staying two nights: 'I needn't tell you that I have no desire to spend any more time in Dublin than I can possibly manage but I see no other way out of my present difficulty.' Supporting his argument, he further told McGrath: 'You will understand that it is no small strain to get into a train – smoker almost always crowded – at 3 and not get to one's home until 9. No dining-bar, nothing but a tea bar – that consumed on one's knee.' McGrath acceded to the request.[8]

Two days later in another letter, Windle suggested on 5 December that the NUI would hold occasional meetings 'of university bodies in the outlying Colleges.' That would be, in his view, 'an enormous advantage for the University and hold it together more than anything else could.' But he was convinced that he would get no support for such a proposal: 'Is it not obvious that, generally speaking, it is enough for me to propose anything to have it slated.' Windle said that he did not wish to become engaged in controversy. He did not see why he should fret over things with which he was not likely to be bothered for many years. Moreover, he could now 'see a pension with a telescope'.[9]

Windle was among those who pressed for change in the method of selecting a vice-chancellor of the NUI. On 10 December 1914, the NUI senate decided that each of the presidents of the constituent colleges should hold the position for two years in rotation. The president of UCG, Alexander Anderson, held the position between 10 December 1914 and 10 December 1916. He was succeeded by Windle who held the position of vice-chancellor until 6 December 1918. Denis J. Coffey of UCD held the position for the following two years until 6 December 1920.

On another matter, Windle strongly supported the idea of the NUI having its own accommodation. When established, it set up headquarters in the buildings of the former Royal College, on Earlsford Tce, Stephen's Green, Dublin. Belonging to UCD, the NUI moved in 1912 to 48/9 Merrion Square. But there was a move in early 1913 to have the NUI transfer permanently to the Earlsford Terrace Skating Rink, an idea with which Windle strongly disagreed: 'It ties the U. up to U.C.D. in a most undesirable manner. You may say that, if we get clear, this don't matter to us. Well, tho' I put a bold face on it and have good hopes, I am quite clear that we are not yet in part and may not get there till goodness knows when, perhaps not till you are out of Purgatory and I too and that won't be to-morrow. We must legislate on the status quo. I should oppose E. Terrance for all I am worth. The U. there would be a mere trifling appendage of U.C.D.' Windle thought that the NUI should occupy a building in a more prominent part of the city 'and not tucked away into a corner'. But he was aware that McGrath and himself were part of a 'minority and that sufferance is the badge of all our tribe and that if the dominant Dublin majority decree it we have got to meet in the sewer station at Ringsend. All the same I hope this will not come off nor the Skating-Rink either. These are the sentiments of B.C.A.W.'[10]

Elaborate plans were drawn up to move the NUI into a new building. An architectural competition was held and a winner was chosen. But with the intervention of the war and the establishment of Irish independence, the original plans were scrapped. Purchasing 49 Merrion Square in 1927, the building became the permanent home of the NUI. Windle's worst fears of the physical integration of the NUI with UCD never came to pass.[11] But his life as president of UCC was – as he saw it – complicated by a federal structure which worked to the disadvantage of his university. It was, however, the framework within which he had, with great reluctance, to work for ten years.

Reforming UCC

Under the new act which came into law on 1 August 1908, the governing body of the college was to be reconstructed. Ceasing to consist entirely of academic members, it added to its ranks representatives of publicly elected bodies; of the graduates; of the Crown and of the co-opted members. The Catholic and Protestant bishops of Cork were members. UCC's newly composed governing body would thus give the college a strong connection to the life of the city. In 1919, the governing body reviewed itself: 'No more harmonious body has ever been in existence, nor during the ten years of its existence has there been any serious difference of opinion amongst the members. All members, elected and *ex officio*, have worked strenuously together for the good of the College, and with a success which may be alluded to not without permissible pride.'[12] Not everyone would agree with that assessment.

Windle worked with four registrars during his fifteen years in Cork: the Professor of Civil Engineering, Alexander Jack (1876–1906), the Professor of Modern Languages, William F. Butler (1906–9), the Professor of Latin, John P. Molohan (1910–15), and the Professor of History, Patrick J. Merriman (1915–19). Windle's administrative difficulties in his early years at QCC/UCC were linked to the quality and standard of professionalism of his secretary/bursar. His diaries contain critical references to three who came in quick succession. They were: Denis C. Newsom (1902–8), Samuel Hollins (1909–10) and H.C. Clifton (1910–12). The briefness of their terms of office reflected, in part, that they were not really up to Windle's expectations. He was an exacting task master. Ill-health also accounted in certain instances for the lacklustre professional performance. However, Windle's prayers were literally answered when he recruited Joseph Downey in 1912.[13] He turned out to be a highly capable secretary/bursar, a close collaborator and friend of Windle, and a man who enjoyed longevity of service to the college, holding his position until his death in the early 1940s. The diaries show very clearly how strong the professional relationship was between Windle and Downey. The president relied upon him implicitly. He was a man of good judgment and calm demeanour. Downey had local knowledge and was in a position to advise a headstrong Windle against certain courses of action likely to bring him into confrontation with the academic council and leaders of the local community. Downey retired in 1944. An obituary in *Cork University Record* spoke of 'his untiring devotion' and his competence and vision which had won for him the unstinting admiration of his colleagues. His death meant the university had suffered 'an irreparable loss'.[14]

While his closest collaborator in the running of the college was Downey, the solicitor Michael Murphy, who served as a legal adviser to UCC, was frequently seen in his diaries as being a confidant. Windle also had a small number of members of the governing body with whom he worked closely, Sir Stanley Harrington and Sir John O'Connell in particular. At the first conferring ceremony in the college on 25 May 1910, Windle took the opportunity to show that the college had entered a new and more open and progressive phase in its history. He invited all the leading notables of the region – 'all the bishops of Munster – both Catholic and Protestant, as well as all the mayors and members of parliament, the peers and principal landowners, the county councillors and representatives of every important interest group'. He had printed and distributed a full programme of the ceremonies, giving details of protocol and the order of procession to and from the hall. All the professors, two by two, processed. The college silver mace, of Irish design and workmanship, led the procession. Windle brought up the rear preceded by the deans of the faculties. This ceremony was to confer degrees on six newly qualified doctors. A higher degree was conferred on J.J. Kearney, Professor of Midwifery and Gynaecology from 1926 to 1948.[15]

In his presidential address, Windle stressed that before the establishment of the NUI, the college had agitated for a 'free and independent university' in Munster. They had soon realised that that would not be granted. They then asked that 'they might at least be given a fully autonomous college, and we defined that as a college which drew up its own courses and conducted its own examinations, both subject to the approval of the university; and in my opinion certainly I further postulated a college in which the degrees conferred on its students would be conferred locally. All these things we have got.'

However, Windle said he would never rest content until Cork had a completely independent university.[16]

He then demanded that Munster must send its sons and daughters to be educated at UCC. He noted with satisfaction that the number of students was rising rapidly. He then asked his distinguished audience for monetary aid. He wanted the region to take pride in the college: '. . . and you must do so. There is an abominable habit too prevalent in some parts of this country of depreciating everything Irish. Let us have none of that in connection with our college. At any rate, it is a very Irish institution; for all its students are Irish, and almost without exception every Professor, Lecturer and Demonstrator has had the main portion of his education in Ireland. And yet, in spite of this fact – as some people would say, though not I – we have shown an excellent record in comparison with other institutions on this or the other side of the water.'[17]

Windle took the opportunity to show the recent remarkable successes of the college faculties. Engineering, under Professor Alexander, had 'leaped to a position of absolutely untouched eminence in this country'. Taking the years 1907, 1908 and 1909, he said that Cork had received twenty-one honours of various kinds, and the other three colleges thirty. He extolled the successes of UCC doctors in the examinations for the Indian Medical Service – 'long been considered the prize among the public medical services'. There had been thirty-four candidates for thirteen vacancies and first place had gone to UCC's Edward G. Kennedy. In Law, a Cork student had won the Brooke scholarship. Windle felt sure that once the Arts faculty had a chance to overcome its former handicaps, it also would soon produce more striking results.[18] During Windle's early years in Cork, the college had 261 students, Galway 111 and Queen's College, Belfast 390. In 1908, Birrell gave the numbers as follows: Cork 327, Belfast 508 and Galway 208. In 1918, UCC had a student population of 566.[19]

Chair of Anatomy

But statistics tell only a small part of the story. The rebuilding of the college required great patience and negotiating skills. Prior to the university settlement in 1908, the path to reform was slow. The reasons for this were firmly rooted in the structures which made the top-down relationship between the government and the college very cumbersome. For example, the splitting of the chair of Anatomy and Physiology, which was one of Windle's earliest objectives, provides an interesting case study.[20]

Windle, as a pre-condition of taking the presidency, wished to take over a chair of Anatomy at QCC. The incumbent, John James Charles, was due to retire in 1907. In order to give Windle what he wanted, it was necessary to split the chair of Anatomy and Physiology and that was a decision which had to be taken at government level. His teaching was to be done in tandem with his role as president. Wyndham wrote to Windle on 18 November 1905: 'Your letter of yesterday suggests a solution to the problem created by my resignation which I should be glad to see adopted. I may say that I wrote very fully to Mr Walter Long on the 1st November giving the circumstances under which you accepted the Presidentship and the nature of my Pledge. I sent at the same time a formal memorandum, embodying the same points, and asked, in the covering letter that, in the event of finding himself unable to deal with the matter, the memorandum should be filed and left upon record in the Irish Office.'

Long, who served as chief secretary for Ireland from 12 March 1905 to 23 January 1907, replied to Wyndham that he was anxiously considering the matter and would write again later. Wyndham, returning to the issue of the chair, wrote to Windle on 18 November 1905:

> I propose, now, to communicate to him Prof. Charles' willingness to resign on certain conditions and offering . . . to meet the Chancellor of the Exchequer with him. I trust that there may be no difficulty in carrying out Prof Charles' suggestion. I cannot express a confident opinion on that point in the absence of precise information on the circumstances of Prof Charles's tenure and the application of the Statute – for it is not merely a Treasury Rule to these circumstances. Speaking broadly, and from memory, the highest terms can only be given – I believe – on abolition of a post. It would, therefore, probably be necessary to abolish the dual chairs of Physiology and Anatomy on public ground; a very sound proceeding, in my judgment. There is only one sentence in your letter which does not quite tally with my recollection: or, rather, which is not free from ambiguity. You write: 'you promised me . . . that I should have £100 per annum until a chair fell vacant which I could accept, and . . . you *also* promised me to make an arrangement whereby the anatomical work should be removed from the Physiological and placed in my hands.' My only observation – made solely for the sake of clearness – is that the £100 was to continue until either of two things happened: viz: (a) a chair falling vacant which you could take or (b) a division and transfer to you of the anatomical work at a suitable remuneration. Let me put it in this way: the division and transfer to you was an object to be effected on its own merits. But, when it had been effected the £100 would have ceased. If it was not effected – a contingency which I considered remote – the £100 would have continued until a suitable chair fell vacant, or for five years, if no chair fell vacant in that period. I think that the sentence I have quoted means this but I should like to avoid any ambiguity.[21]

Wyndham received a reassuring letter from Windle, and he replied to the new president of Queen's College, Cork, on 25 November 1905: 'Your letter puts the other matter in complete harmony with my own recollection. I trust that it will soon be concluded. Mr Walter Long in a letter which I received ten days ago tells me that he has it in hand and will accept my assistance with the Treasury if it should be needed. He gives no details, but leaves the impression that he expects to proceed without further aid from me. I have supplied him with all the facts and arguments.'[22]

However, the matter dragged on and on. A Liberal government was returned to office in the general election of January 1906. Wyndham, returned for the constituency of Dover, continued after the change of government to try to redeem his promise to Windle. James Bryce was the new chief secretary. Wyndham wrote to Windle on 25 January 1906: 'It is always a pleasure to see your hand-writing. I appreciated your kind letter of congratulations on Dover above almost all that reached me, and now, we come to a business which I long to see concluded. I am writing a brief note to Mr Bryce by this post, directing his attention to the *formal* memo which I sent to Mr Long and asking for an interview at an early date. I wish we could both of us meet him soon. The *personal* obligation on my part to you is the only outstanding Irish question which vexes me. But apart from, and beyond, that I can enjoy no *public* peace of mind until something is done to get rid of the disparity in respect of opportunities for Education under which Ireland suffers.'[23] Windle replied on 27 January 1906 thanking Wyndham for his concern and telling him of his anxiety to have the matter of the separation of the chairs resolved. He did not quite know where he stood.[24] On the political question, he wondered whether the Conservative party would ever shake itself loose from 'Orange domination'. If not there was nothing 'for it but Home Rule with all its uncertainties and difficulties'. Windle confessed that he had been 'a very strong home ruler at one time' and that he had spoken 'in many places on that platform'. But he had never been a 'separatist', he wrote. However, he admitted that Wyndham's policy had converted him to the belief that English politicians might provide 'fair treatment for my country'. But that was followed by his 'betrayal' and nine months of Long as chief secretary. Windle did not know where that left him.[25]

It took another year before the matter of the chair was resolved. Wyndham was dealing with a new chief secretary, Augustine Birrell. He had been appointed in January 1907, having served as president of the Board of Trade. On 4 March 1907, Wyndham wrote from the House of Commons to Windle: 'I had a full, pleasant and I trust satisfactory talk with Mr Birrell this afternoon. I gather that you will be offered the chair when a vacancy occurs. In any case Mr Birrell tells me that he hopes to see you shortly at Cork. I hope that the vacancy *is* a certainty. Is it Professor Charles? I have not a book of reference by me but understood from the Chief Secretary that his was the resignation in question. It will be an immense relief to my mind to learn that the matter is settled and my promise at last redeemed. In the end Cork will – I am certain – float off as a separate University.'[26] Thus, even out of office, Wyndham had redeemed his long-standing promise to Windle.

Birrell visited the college on 30 March 1907 and, soon afterwards, the chair was at last divided, 'and for a time the President subserved the Chair of Anatomy'. He was paid a nominal salary, devoting the other 99 per cent of the money to the creation of a new chair of Physiology which was given to D.T. Barry.[27] Professor Denis J. O'Sullivan explained what had happened: 'The President held the chair of Anatomy for two years. He lectured four times a week – more than his full-time predecessor.'[28] Windle's friend, the Professor of Zoology, Dr Marcus Hartog, wrote in 1919: 'At this period he lectured (around 1910) for a short time on Anatomy as later he did on the new subjects here of Anthropology and Archaeology, and also on the practice and technique of Journalism. He also arranged the Archaeological and Ethnological Museum which he enriched by personal gifts.'[29] Professor O'Sullivan eloquently summarised Windle's contribution to the building up of UCC: 'Bertram Windle was undoubtedly an outstanding president. His contribution to the medical school, while very significant, was of much less import than his overall impact on the college. At the time of his appointment, the outstanding medical dean and, more importantly, cultured and far-seeing polymath, found in Cork a medical school that needed some improvements and a college which required immediate and drastic reform and[30] Windle built large physiological laboratories, fully equipped with power, electricity, gas and water, for teaching and research. He also added a Pathology Department and an Operative Surgery Department with a museum of instruments. Within a few years of his arrival, the medical school in Cork had undergone a root-and-branch transformation. Windle got his priorities right across the university.[31]

New Professorial Appointments

After the university settlement, Windle sought to increase the number of professors in the college. Maria (Wally) Walburga Swertz was appointed as Professor of German in 1910. She was the third woman professor to be appointed under Windle in UCC. She was born in Cork *c*.1880, and was the daughter of Hans Conrad Swertz, organist, St

Mary's Cathedral, Cork. Her sister Tilly married Aloys Fleischmann senior. She attended St Angela's High School in Cork and graduated in 1904 from the Royal University of Ireland. She was conferred in 1908 with an MA in German and French. She studied for a fellowship and was awarded a prize of £100 which enabled her to study in the University of Bonn where she also taught in two secondary schools. She returned to Cork in autumn 1910 and was appointed to the first chair of German at UCC, according to President's Report 1910–11. She proved to be a good appointment and a strong asset to the language teaching staff. At the outbreak of the First World War, she was on holidays with relatives in Crefeld, Germany. Unable to return to Ireland, she remained in Germany. Professor Wally Walburga Swertz fell seriously ill in 1917. She died in January 1918.[32] Elizabeth M. O'Sullivan got the chair of Education in 1910. Dr Mary Ryan, who was already on the staff, was appointed Professor of Romance Languages in 1909, becoming the first woman professor in Ireland and the United Kingdom.[33] Her brother, Finbarr, was a Dominican and Archbishop of Port of Spain (Trinidad). Another brother, Sir Andrew, was a British diplomat in the Levant. Ryan, a graduate of QCC, held that chair for over thirty years. During her first year substituting for Professor William F. Butler, she did fourteen hours of lectures in French and German, 'Italian being for the moment mercifully in abeyance'. She described in an article in 1945 a UCC that had few women students and staff accommodation that was crowded: 'The years before 1914 were halcyon years; fresh zest for work, a large proportion of keen students, pleasant friends. It is true, we were rather packed in our various Private Rooms, though the council Room could be used as a Common Room – Professor Hartog was often to be met there – and had a fire and a good supply of current periodicals . . . But those were the leisurely days of old.'[34] Ryan did a great deal to foster the recruitment of women students to the college. She also played a leading role in looking after the welfare of those women who entered that patriarchy. In 1904, the college had four women students.[35] There were seventeen women in the student body in 1906–7. That number rose to 113 in 1917–18. Ryan retired in 1939, having enriched student life and forged ever closer links with France and French culture.[36]

The Professor of Zoology, Marcus M. Hartog (1851–1924), was not a Windle appointment. But he was one of the president's friends and supporters. He was of French Jewish descent, the second son of the Professor of French at the London Royal Academy of Music, Alphonse Hartog. Graduating from Cambridge in 1874, he got the chair of Natural History in Cork in 1882, involving the teaching of geology, botany and zoology.

He had the habit of reading while walking or cycling and was supposed to have apologised on colliding with a gas-lamp on the side of the road. He dressed habitually in a special cycling costume, a grey Norfolk jacket and knickers.[37] His carelessness in dress gave him 'an exaggerated reputation for eccentricity', according to the Professor of Chemistry in Galway, T. Dillon, who got to know him quite well but 'when I showed up against the Empire during the last war [First World War], he would not speak to me again, proving that when it comes to politics even scientists cannot always take the broad view'.[38]

While Hartog remained a strong empire man, that was not the political coloration of a number of the new appointments. William F.P. Stockley, who became Professor of English in 1909, is a case in point. Originally, in 1905, Windle thought that Douglas Hyde might fill that job. He was not interested and suggested Stockley, a Trinity graduate and a convert to Catholicism. He had also been a contemporary of both Hyde and Windle in Trinity.[39] Horgan describes him as having been a happy choice as he had 'a real love for great literature and the ability to communicate his ardour and knowledge to his students'.[40] He was English on his father's side and Irish on his mother's, she being related to the revolutionary leader William Smith O'Brien of 1848. Stockley became a strong supporter of Sinn Féin, and was an alderman for Cork Corporation between 1920 and 1925. He voted against the Treaty in December 1921. Although he refused to accept the legitimacy of the Irish Free State, he was a TD for the National University of Ireland constituency from 1921 until his defeat in the 1923 general election. In 1929, Windle wrote to Sr Monica: '*Entre nous*, I never got over Stockley's disloyal actions during the war – he would have been interned but for my intervention. I told him that it was a dishonourable thing for a man holding his post under the King's warrant to behave treasonably as he did. We had little to do with one another after that and as I cannot like anyone whom I can't respect I hope never to see him again unless we meet in heaven by which time he will have been well cleaned up. Any way he is God's own ass and perhaps that fact may intercede for him.'[41]

Since coming to Cork, Windle had sought to advance the teaching of Irish in the curriculum. On 12 April 1906, he wrote to Douglas Hyde: 'I have been slowly and cautiously working Irish into our curriculum here and hope in a year or two to make real strides in that direction.'[42] Three years later, Fr R.H. Henebry was appointed Professor of Irish, a post he held until his death in 1916. His appointment gave Windle an ally against the more strident elements in the Gaelic League which had won a victory at the NUI Senate on 5 May 1910 to make Irish compulsory for matriculation. He was an outstanding scholar and very well liked by Windle, who grew to dislike intensely the new radicals in the Gaelic League.[43] Henebry did not belong to the latter category.[44]

Timothy A. Smiddy was appointed to Economics in 1909, and, the same year, Rev. T.E. Fitzgibbon got the new chair of Philosophy, principally scholastic philosophy. The latter chair was, *de facto*, in the gift of the local Catholic bishop. That remained the case until the 1970s and was also the same for the chair of Education. Windle did not resent Church influence on appointments in both areas. He made other important appointments. History was separated from English Literature in 1909, P.J. Merriman becoming the first to hold the chair. Born in 1877, he was a Dubliner who was educated by the Christian Brothers in North Richmond Street. Entering University College Dublin in 1895, he graduated in 1898 with first place and first class honours in Modern Languages and Literature. He received an MA the following year in Modern History, Political Economy and Political Philosophy, being awarded a studentship and a junior fellowship. He taught at Maynooth and served for a time as registrar and bursar at his *alma mater*. After his appointment to UCC, he quickly built up 'a high reputation, attracting a large number of students to history by the clarity and brilliance of his lectures'.[45] Frederick St John Lacy was appointed to the chair of Music between 1909 and 1934. At the time of the Irish Universities Bill in 1908, there were in the college seventeen professors, ten lecturers and a handful of demonstrators. In 1917, there were thirty-two professors, twenty-three lecturers and ten demonstrators.

Two new departments – Commerce and Dentistry – were also opened by Windle. In addition, an almost new department had been established in connection with the Crawford Municipal Technical School, providing instruction in mechanical and electrical engineering. That widened the choice in that subject beyond civil engineering. Windle also secured a large increase in the number of staff in Engineering. That subject had, prior to 1908, been taught by a professor. By 1918, that department had a professor, three lecturers, a demonstrator and a research student. Chemistry also increased its staff to a professor, a lecturer and two demonstrators.

UCC facilities were used under Windle to help support the Workers' Education Association. A three-year course in sociology was set up and, in addition, monthly lectures on scientific and literary subjects. That meant that the educational advantages of the college had been placed at the disposal of the working men of Cork.

Windle, as future research will show, transformed the system of providing external examiners. His academic contacts enabled him to attract important English professors to serve in that capacity, one being the Jesuit psychologist, Fr Michael Maher.

Besides increasing the number of staff and broadening the curriculum, Windle doubled the accommodation for teaching on campus. He quickly discovered soon after arriving that there had been little done to improve the plant of the college since the death of Dr William K. Sullivan who had been president of QCC between 1873 and 1890. Windle's two immediate predecessors, James W. Slattery (1890–6) and Sir Rowland Blennerhassett (1897–1904) had worn their presidential duties lightly. There was no Physics laboratory. The Chemistry laboratory was 'ridiculously small and inadequate'. The 1918 governing body statement argued: 'There is now a separate building for these two subjects, the accommodation in which will compare favourably with that of any other institution of its kind.' In 1904, the Engineering laboratories 'can scarcely be said to have existed'. There were in 1918 the 'most complete laboratories for testing materials, scarcely surpassed in their own particular lines even on the other side of the Channel; and, without any desire to deprecate other institutions, in advance of anything else in Ireland'.[46] Windle also improved the size and equipment in the Biological laboratory. By the year before he resigned, there was 'a well equipped and self contained building for Botany, Geology and Zoology'. Windle built administrative offices and enlarged the Council Room. Windle laid great emphasis on the setting up of student clubs and societies. Clubs had been built for men and women students and fifteen acres of playing grounds acquired by the college.[47]

Under Windle, the college developed a stronger research reputation, staff having published 15 books, 114 scientific papers, 248 literary, historical and archaeological papers, and 8 musical publications. Professor Hartog's work on Mitosis was singled out for mention, as were Professor Dixon's numerous papers on Thiocarbamides. Added to that were, of course, the publications of Windle himself. The reputation of the medical school was also emphasised. Of the eighteen professors of medicine of the college, fourteen were past students. Of the eighteen medical officers of the two large public infirmaries in Cork City, fourteen were alumni of UCC. Over 80 per cent of the doctors of Munster were graduates of the college. UCC doctors had served in large numbers in the Indian Medical Service, a number getting first place in the examination. In his report for the session 1905/6, Windle wrote that Sir T. Gallwey, who was then surgeon-general of the Knight Comander of St Michael and St George (KCMG), had served as head of the Medical Department in India. Col. Magill had just retired from the chief position in the Medical Service of Egypt and was succeeded by Col. Allport. Both were Cork students. The report went on to list a large number of doctors who had held distinguished positions in the British medical services at home and abroad.

The Engineering Faculty was equally distinguished. Its graduates worked in all parts of the world. A large number of graduates were serving as county engineers and surveyors. There were sixteen former students serving in the Public Works Department of India, and many were engaged with private firms of contractors in all parts of the world. Other graduates of UCC were listed for their scientific work. One had been master of the Mint in Calcutta, another, imperial mycologist for India, and a third, a cryptogamic botanist to the Malay States, and afterwards their director of the Department of Agriculture. There was a Surgeon Haines R.N. who was medical officer to the *Basilisk* expedition, and had left to the college a valuable collection of objects from the South Seas. J.C. Johnson was Professor of General Biology, Auckland University, New Zealand. J.A. Pollock was head assistant, Astronomical Observatory, Melbourne.

In the world of education, the late Stephen Kelleher was mentioned for his distinguished role as Professor of Mathematics in the University of Dublin as well as Professor O. Bergin, who was Professor of Early Irish Language and Literature, University College Dublin. Moreover, three UCC alumni were appointed as senior inspectors to control the inspection of the whole of the island under the National Board of Education.

In the legal world, UCC graduates had also distinguished themselves. The record showed that by 1918 Stephen Ronan was Lord Justice of Appeal, Matthew Burke was the Recorder of Cork, Justice Wall was a judge of the High Court of Bombay, and Justice J.M. Busteed was a judge of the Small Causes Court, Madras. In the field of local politics and local government, T.C. Butterfield was Lord Mayor of Cork. UCC had also provided a mayor for Waterford and a Lord Mayor of Cardiff. Among the people who gained distinction in other fields, Sir John Pope Hennessy was governor of Mauritius; M. Finucane had been a distinguished member of the Indian Civil Service and was land commissioner in Ireland; E.D.J. Wilson was a leader writer for *The Times* and in whose memory the Wilson Fund for Historical Books had been established; and Sir Stanley Harrington was a director of the Munster and Leinster Bank, chairman of the Cork and Passage Railway and of other industrial undertakings. He was also Commissioner of National Education and had been knighted.

Women graduates, although small in number, had, by the end of Windle's time in Ireland, distinguished themselves in different fields. Female graduates were assistant medical officers of health for Birmingham and Plymouth, headmistress, Cork High School, welfare superior in large state-controlled works at Coventry and a medical superintendent of a tuberculosis sanatorium at Rossclare.[48] The governing body statement, in setting out the successes of UCC, directly and indirectly, praised Windle's fifteen-year tenure as president as the most significant in terms of reform in the history of the college.

More Irish than the Irish Themselves

Windle had found the professional adjustment to working in Queen's College, Cork something of a culture shock. The move for himself and his family from Birmingham to an Irish city was quite a challenge. Neither his wife, Edith, nor his two daughters, Mary and Nora, shared his feeling of coming home to the country of his early childhood and university years. Moreover, west Cork was also the world of his mother's extended family – his cousins, the Coghills and the Somervilles of Castletownshend. He frequently employed 'we' when referring to what was both good and not so laudable in Irish politics, religion, culture and society. English by birth and Irish by choice, he nevertheless remained a quintessential Edwardian English gentleman. He was upper middle class, something of a snob and hostile to Protestants. But, upon his arrival in Cork, Windle had every reason to feel that he was coming home. His first cousins in Castletownshend included Admiral Boyle Somerville and his sister, the novelist, Edith.[49] The latter lived at Drishane – nearly sixty-five miles from Cork City. Boyle Somerville lived at Cosheen which he changed back to the old name, 'The Point House'.[50]

The Windles – both converts – observed the religious divisions in Ireland at the time of their arrival. Edith wrote in 1929:

> Castletownshend has one little street with a post office, a public house and a few not too clean little shops – some cottages inhabited by people who work almost entirely for Somervilles, Coghills and Townshends – there are a few fisher folk besides . . . It is almost impossible for anyone not born in Ireland, or never having lived there, to appreciate the great gulf there is fixed between the gentry and – the rest – for that is what it really amounts to. Socially they never mix and as the gentry are – Imagine – 90 per cent Protestant they of course have nothing to do with Catholics. This condition arose in the days when no Catholic gentleman could live in Ireland – the Protestants simply regarded the rest of the people as serfs and dependants. In the last century a large professional class has grown up of both religions – even so they do not mingle socially with the country people. There is nothing to correspond with the 'squire class' in England that served as a bridge to unite to some extent the country and professions.[51]

Given his family background, Edith argued that her husband had many advantages when he moved to work in Ireland: 'My husband's position was unique – born of an old Irish family he was accepted as such and greatly loved latterly by his own kinsfolk. Nevertheless on account of his being a Catholic we were conscious of a barrier between us and the Protestant upstarts who had crept under the fringe of the gentry – mostly because they were brewers or Army or navy. As President of University College we were very much in contact with all professions and we constantly had people staying in our house who would not have been entertained in the homes of the country folk.'[52]

Religion in Ireland did not necessarily predetermine political allegiance. According to Edith Somerville's biographer, Gifford Lewis, the letters of Edith and Boyle 'are of serous interest in showing how two pro-Irish Big House inhabitants first perceived and then adapted to revolutionary ideas'.[53] David Gray, the US wartime envoy in Dublin, knew him well: 'It was from his lips that, as an American student of Ireland, I first heard details of the barbarities of Cromwell's captains in West Cork, recounted with an indignation so passionate that old Irish wrongs became to me living things.'[54]

The Windles maintained a close friendship with both Edith and Boyle throughout their time in Ireland.[55] Windle's wife, Edith, regarded the admiral as 'a very charming man and full of similar interests as my husband. They did quite a lot of exploring of prehistoric monuments in Ireland together – I often went with them – in Donegal – Lough Gur, Donaghmore and in West Cork around Skibbereen. The Admiral has published a number of papers on archaeological subjects – at sea he was a hydrographer (I hope that is the right word) – something to do with measuring deep seas and coast lines.[56] On land his chief interest was in proving the connection between the arrangement of stone circles, alignments, standing stones and with the positions of certain planets and stars. When Boyle and Bertie were about together there was always a lot to be done with compasses and measurements.'[57]

Boyle Somerville was indeed a very interesting and accomplished man. He was a chart-maker and a linguist. He had studied the languages of Polynesia and published a dictionary. He was a student of the Irish language and of Irish history, a most enlightened and well-published man.[58] In one of his better-known works, *The Chart-Makers*, published in 1928, he described a difficult passage from Auckland to Sydney on HMS *Dart* where, after two weeks, the ship and all aboard were presumed lost: 'One monster, however, took her unawares on the starboard side, and as she lifted to it, hurled its foaming crest on the deck, carrying away to leeward, sweeping in a wash of icy waters coils of rope and the men standing by them, over against the berthing at the ship's side, where, fortunately, they were brought up.'[59] His description of the storm continued: 'a tremendous sea rolled in on us over the starboard quarter, deep and green, and poured down the companion-way.' When they reached Sydney and the safety of Farm Cove, they were greeted with 'cheers and flag-waving, not only from the boats, but from crowds of people gathered on the end of the pleasant wooded points'. A boat came alongside and told them that they had been reported in the papers for two weeks as having been lost. 'It was quite an embarrassing resurrection,' he wrote.[60]

Meanwhile, in Castletownshend, 'anxiety was settling down into despair' as the 'hoped-for news came not'. With hope gone, his family had written him off and were 'even into the wearing of "mourning"'. But news of Boyle's survival came by telegram. The postmaster, an ex-naval petty officer, did not wait to write out the message. He rushed to his house to tell his mother: 'Ma'am, Ma'am, the *Dart* is safely in Sydney! Glory be to God.'[61]

Despite Boyle Somerville's distinguished commitment to Irish culture and language, he was assassinated in 1936; on 24 March, the admiral, an Irish nationalist, was shot by the Irish Republican Army (IRA) on his own doorstep. His killers left a placard in the hallway with words made out of cut-outs from newspapers. It read: 'This English Agent sent 52 Irishmen into the British army in the last seven weeks.' According to his daughter, 'the village reaction to it [the murder] was terrific, and when we arrived the next day all the curtains in the village were drawn. At my father's funeral it was a long step from our house to the CT [St Barrahane's Church, Castletownshend] church and then up very steep stone steps but the village men insisted six of them in turn to carry the coffin all down the village street. They were Roman Catholics of course and they all stood outside during the service.'[62]

Windle, Patrick Pearse and St Enda's

Irish political and cultural divisions remained very fluid during Windle's early years in Ireland. His household in Cork became a very active social centre with a constant stream of visitors and guests. The couple entertained, among others, Lord and Lady Aberdeen, Augustine Birrell, Douglas Hyde and Horace Plunkett. Bishops and senior clergy, staff and students, were invited frequently to the president's home.[63] Mindful of the fate of Patrick Pearse for his role as a leader of the 1916 rising, it may appear difficult to see what both men might ever have had in common. Yet, Windle and Pearse shared a common cultural background in the Gaelic League. Both were home rulers and had deserved reputations as educational innovators. A combination of those factors brought both men into contact in May 1910 on the question of the funding of Pearse's school, St Enda's, then at Cullenswood House, Rathmines. Founded in 1908, it later moved to the Hermitage, Rathfarnham.[64] On 10 May 1910,

Pearse sent out a general letter looking for subscriptions. Windle was one of the recipients and he sent a positive reply. Pearse responded on the 15th: 'A thousand thanks for your kindly letter and for its promise. I shall be delighted to show you the school at work.' He welcomed Windle's offer of a subscription of £5.5s: 'Since I sent you the circular the V. Rev. Canon Arthur Ryan, P.P., Tipperary, has consented to join my Board of Governors. Would there be any chance of *your* joining it, now or later? There is no one in Ireland whose name would be more valuable. Indeed, with the addition of you and Canon Ryan I should consider the Board an ideal one. Its chief practical function will be to exercise a veto on expense. Of course details of financial management must be left to the working heads of the school. With many thanks, and looking forward to your visit.'[65] It is probable that Windle did visit St Enda's, although this is not certain. Pearse wrote on 23 November to him, and to others who had subscribed or promised to do so, inviting them to attend a meeting at St Enda's on 3 December to discuss plans for the school and the funding of the new premises, the Hermitage, at Rathfarnham. He wanted Windle to attend or to give his views in writing.[66] It is evident from Pearse's next letter, dated 20 December, that Windle did not attend, as was the case for many others outside Dublin who had subscribed: 'In the first place I must thank you very sincerely for your generous promise of further help,' Pearse told Windle. He would like to see the UCC president the next time he was in Dublin. The meeting had agreed that a company or incorporated body model for St Enda's was 'undesirable and unwieldy'. Instead, the executive control and financial liability for the college would rest in Pearse's hands. A body of subscribers would be formed; those giving £1 and upwards would be eligible to be present and to vote at the annual meeting. An advisory council would be elected to meet quarterly or monthly. Pearse told Windle that the meeting was also in favour of the issuing of an immediate appeal for financial support.[67] Soon afterwards, Windle accepted the invitation to sit on the advisory council. His name is first under the heading 'council' on an appeal letter, dated 15 October 1912, under the signature of Patrick Pearse. Windle was in distinguished company: Mary Hayden,[68] Professor of Modern Irish History, UCD; Seaghan P. MacEnri, Professor of Modern Irish, UCG; Canon Arthur Ryan, PP of Tipperary and former president of Thurles College; Fr Matthew Maguire, PP of Kilskeery; Joseph T. Dolan; William Gibson; Seamus MacManus; Edward Martyn; and Shane Leslie. In the appeal, Pearse wrote: 'I firmly believe that in appealing on behalf of St. Enda's I am appealing on behalf of the most important thing in Ireland. *Our work is radical: it strikes at the root of Anglicisation*. Infinitely the most vital duty of the hour here is to train the young in an Irish way for the service of Ireland. It is to this we have set our hands.'[69]

It is not clear quite how long Windle remained an active member of the council for St Enda's. While both men diverged politically, particularly after 1913, Windle and Pearse shared sufficient common educational ideals for the UCC president to sit on the council at St Enda's and lend his name to public appeals for funding. Declan Kiberd writes that 'Pearse's theory of education was a protest against the fact that everyone was made to read the same books, think the same thoughts, be decidable in an instant'.[70] British procrastination over the implementation of home rule helped radicalise him and orientate him to membership of the Irish Republican Brotherhood and the espousal of revolutionary nationalism.[71] The growing stridency of the Gaelic League and the cultural nationalist movement alienated Windle, driving a wedge between himself and the radical sections of that movement which most closely identified with Pearse rather than Douglas Hyde. In Cork, the Gaelic League had divided as early as 1905 with the establishment of the O'Growney branch in Fr Matthew Street. The branch secretary was Seán O'Hegarty.[72] His brother, P.S. (Patrick Sarsfield), was also involved. In that circle, cultural politics and ideas of Sinn Féin and radical republicanism commingled.[73] Windle was, and would remain, a loyal follower of John Redmond and the Irish Parliamentary Party through thick and thin. His life would be complicated, as may be seen later in this chapter, by the growing local opposition to a mere home rule solution.

Loyalty to the British Crown

How was it possible for Windle to be actively involved with Patrick Pearse and his school and, at the same time, be respectful of the British monarchy? Quite simply, there was no contradiction to such a relationship in 1910. Pearse was, like Windle, a home ruler and a constitutional nationalist. When King Edward VII died on 6 May 1910 Windle noted: 'An excellent sovereign and a good friend to Ireland.' On the occasion of the royal visit to Ireland in 1911, Windle wrote on 5 July to 'Their Majesties, King George [V] and Queen Mary, making reference to the securing in 1908 of a new royal charter for the college from King Edward VII that had placed the college in a position of nearer relationship to the people.' He wrote: 'Your Majesties will be graciously pleased to accept our respectful assurance that the powers thus granted to us will be used to the best of our abilities in forwarding the educational welfare of the Province of Munster, of which we are the University College. We recall with gratification, Most Gracious Sovereign, that Your Majesty is the Visitor of our College, and we venture, with great respect, to express the fervent hope that in Your Majesty's next progress through this Kingdom you may deign to visit our City and its College.'[74]

Windle went to Dublin with Edith and Nora to witness the arrival in person. He wrote on 8 July 1911 of the 'fearsome excitement' in the capital and about seeing the 'fleet illuminated, a beautiful sight'. He wrote of 'crowds of well-behaved people everywhere and very little drink. . . . What a people we are – pretending to be not loyal and then carrying on like this.' He recorded an account of his visit to Maynooth on Sunday, 9 July, with Edith and Nora. There he learned from a friend who was to be decorated that Windle's name had been on the original list. But his informant was told that 'difficulties had arisen'. His source did not think the problem was in Ireland as 'everybody would have liked it'. Windle speculated: 'Then who was it? Birrell.' His entry concluded: 'The King and Queen came to Maynooth. Splendid reception.' Edith was presented to the royal couple, according to the diary entry, on 10 July. That evening the Windles went out to the east pier at Kingstown: 'Thousands there. No illumination but fleet looked very fine.'

On 11 July, they went to the royal garden party and later they attended the official banquet. Windle noted: 'Illumination of Dublin very fine – great enthusiasm every where and scarcely a sign of drink except a few sailors.' He wrote to a friend on 24 July 1911, making the latter point more forcefully: 'My visit was delayed by the King's affair in Dublin. Never anywhere did I see greater enthusiasm or finer decorations. It was amazing. I was at the Maynooth Garden Party, presented an address before the levée in full canonicals, was at the Royal Garden Party, and also at the Drawing Room, where Edith was presented – all very gorgeous but very tiring.[75]

There were illuminations of a different kind when, immediately after the royal visit, Windle attended three days of NUI meetings. His entry for 12 July focused on how 'Coffey took his beating very badly. Even the Dublin men did not stand with Coffey,' he added for emphasis. In his letter, quoted earlier, he ended: 'Then three days of university meetings – very wearisome in the heat.'[76] Lady Aberdeen wrote on 22 August noting that he was passing through Dublin going directly to Cork: 'otherwise I would have asked you to endeavour to keep a few minutes for me as you passed through, so that we might discuss the arrangements for my visit to Cork later in the year.' She thought that she would be in a position to go down at the end of October. She was delighted to fall in with the arrangements that he might suggest 'as to my giving the Address under your kind and congenial Presidency'. She approved of the people he was preparing to invite 'and I should be very glad to place myself in your hands if you wish me to meet personally any who have special influence in the matter, or whom you think I could be of use in winning over'. If he thought that the offer of any medal, 'or anything of that kind from myself would be of use, I should be delighted to offer such on any conditions which you might suggest'. Lady Aberdeen hoped that he would return from his stay at Harrogate 'feeling strong, and able for your busy Winter'.[77]

The Windles returned to Cork on 30 August: 'Dear dogs so pleased to see us.' He found the new term particularly difficult but he had a new source of amusement – a motor car. The Windles lived in Ireland but, having most of their close personal friends in England, continued to holiday there until the outbreak of war in 1914. Harrogate, with its exotic spa, was the favoured spot for the annual break from the tedium of Cork. Windle had other reasons for being in England frequently. He was a member of the British Medical Council. He was also an external examiner for Cambridge, Glasgow and a number of other universities. He was much sought after as a speaker in the English Catholic world. He also needed to lobby the British government.

On 31 October 1911, Windle presided at conferrings: 'The students behaved splendidly, keeping their promise to behave. After it was over there was a photo taken of the lot.' After lunch, he set out to meet Lady Aberdeen. She gave an excellent discourse to women students and others on the study of the domestic economy. He then took Lady Aberdeen over to another venue to speak to women: 'Was much impressed by the lying-down room.' At five o'clock, Lady Aberdeen went off to Bandon.[78] The lord lieutenant, it seems, had been disappointed that Windle had not been made a privy councillor during the royal visit to Dublin, but good news came in the new year honours list – Windle was to receive a knighthood. He wrote on 25 December that he had received 'a most kind' letter – enclosing one from Prime Minister Asquith – asking him to accept a knighthood: 'Considering the beasts that have been given it I hesitated but (a) Aberdeen so very kind about it and (b) such snub for some who have elevated the nose at Edith to have her "Lady" and also (c) an advantage for the place. I accepted and wrote to Asquith and Aberdeen thanking the latter very warmly.'[79]

The news of his honour was published in the press on 1 January 1912. He received many letters and telegrams of congratulations on his knighthood. He noted that there was 'no one from any other college in Ireland' in the honours list: 'I'm afraid that's rather a relief to me,' he commented. He was at the conferring on 3 January of the freedom of the city on Redmond Barry, the new lord chancellor, 'a very good fellow'. He found Dicky Beamish, the owner of the local brewery, 'very sulky at not having been awarded a knighthood. Palpably did not congratulate me though everybody else did.' Afterwards, he went to a lunch in the Imperial Hotel where the lord mayor, to Windle's great surprise, toasted him in a very graceful little speech – to which he responded. He had a meeting in the afternoon with a director of *The Times*: 'a very interesting man and a very interesting talk. He thinks as long as N.E. Ulster [stays] out, Home Rule is impossible and so do I. A broad-minded man.'

On 24 January 1912, he wrote that he had gone in the evening 'to college dance that damnable function – Far too many there and hardly any professors – came away after supper and having had 2 hours sleep was waked up by bell. The others being locked out by some ass of a servant.' He raged round the house but none of the servants were down: 'So waited till morning when I gave them all beans. No more sleep till I got up.'[80]

On 5 February, Windle hosted the first official visit on behalf of the NUI to Cork. The vice-chancellor, Sir Christopher Nixon, was introduced to the governing body. The Archbishop of Cashel took the chair while the following motion was being proposed: 'That we, the members of the Governing Body of University College Cork, view with the utmost satis-faction the distinction which has been recently conferred by His Majesty the King on our President Sir Bertram Windle. The settlement of the Irish University Question was largely due to his experience, foresight, and labour which have also contributed in no small measure to the success of the College.' Nixon, on behalf of the NUI Senate, expressed 'the thorough concurrence of the University in paying this tribute to the President and suggested that the name of Lady Windle should be included with that of the President in the congratulations'.[81]

On 6 March 1912, Windle went to Buckingham Palace where he was knighted by the king. His diary entry read: 'Lovely day . . . to Dorchester where got into levée dress and to Buckingham Palace where knighted by king. Back to Dorchester, changed and lunch with Bond who was R.M.O. [in] Birmingham. Had not seen him since 1884.'[82] Windle returned to Cork and continued with his duties at UCC. On 24 May 1912, he went to England where he gave an address to 2,000 people. The audience was made up primarily of young Catholics. He spoke on the subject: 'Reason for the Faith that is in us.' He had some leisure time on Monday which he spent 'on the water and in the dockyard'. He spent the evening until 11.30 'talking with the bishop – a most inter-esting man'. Windle outlined his programme to his friend Humphreys for the rest of the week: 'College sports on Wednesday – Inter-Varsity to-morrow – Technical Congress, at which I reside, Tuesday, Wednesday, Thursday of next week – dinners and all kinds of activities – by June 24th I'm done, and shall want a holiday. I'm having hay-fever injections like last year and, so far, am free . . . I enclose a set of papers on

Darwinism which I hope will interest you. They are going to form part of a book. My Lough Gur paper is nearly finished.'[83]

On 3 June 1912, Gasquet wrote thanking Windle for his Darwin articles from the *Catholic World*: 'Dear me! Are we ever to meet again in this world? I had hoped that you might have been coming out to Rome this past winter . . . Do you never come to this benighted land now? If so do let me know, it would be such a pleasure to grasp your hand once more.'[84] The two men dined together on 16 July. The cardinal was 'looking very well'. The following day, the Windles went to London and attended a garden party given by the Duchess of Northumberland at Syon House, meeting many old friends there. They went to a reception in the evening at the Royal Society rooms. He wrote: 'I suppose the most wonderful assembly of scientific men I have seen anywhere.' He told his friend Humphreys: 'For once women had to play second fiddle in dress, for their frocks were thrown in the shade by the gowns of every description there to be seen on men's shoulders. My black and gold confection was much admired by both sexes.'[85] On 18 July 1912, the Windles attended the royal garden party at Windsor. He told Humphreys: 'That was a wonderful show – ten thousand asked, and I suppose eight to nine thousand there. It rained at first, and looked very bad, but afterwards cleared up. It was worth seeing, even by one who does not take much stock of garden parties.'[86]

The Windles went back to their hotel, packed and returned to Dublin the following day in order to attend on the 19th a party being given by the Aberdeens at the Vice Regal Lodge. The British prime minister, Asquith, was present at lunch. Afterwards, Windle 'had a few words with Birrell who says he will do what he can. Also spoke to Dogherty [?] about going.' (Windle was in crisis over whether or not he should remain in UCC.) Lady Aberdeen took Windle over to meet Asquith. 'Let us go on to the lawn, for it is hot here,' he said to Windle. Both men sat and talked for about ten minutes, according to his diary: 'all eyes directed on me and no doubt everybody wondering what it meant.'[87] He commented to Humphreys: 'As I was the only person thus distinguished you may imagine how the eyes of all beholders protruded from their heads . . . anybody might have heard our conversation, but I'm sure the people thought he was conferring with me as to whether I would be the first Home Rule Lord Lieutenant. So, if you hear of my being elevated to the Peerage, you will understand.'[88]

Sr Monica wrote about Windle feeling unable to help UCC: 'Never yet was I in such a sea of troubles. Sanctify these to me, O God.'[89] He continued with his plans of expansion, hoping to bring a school of dentistry to Cork.[90] Windle decided on 25 January to try to worry less about the college, and 'to slack off and amuse myself a bit more – and generally let things slide a bit. Must try to keep this up.' His on-going troubles with his youngest daughter, Nora, were a cause for concern. He wrote on 6 March: 'Trouble with Nora who is discontented and fractious. Wants to go away and earn her living – perhaps best thing she can do but a pity that she can't content herself. Nora should get a husband.' Later in the month, on 21 March, he was delighted to meet his friend John Humphreys and his daughter, Winny, who came to Ireland on a holiday. He took them on a motoring tour of the south of the country. He drove to Dingle on the scenic route where the 'view magnificent' but they had a 'fearful descent'. After the return of his friends to England, Windle again settled down to the daily grind of running the university in a land which he thought he knew but he knew it not. Windle had, by his own reckoning, adapted to his new home. Yet, no matter how hard he tried, he remained very uncomfortable in an Ireland that he thought he knew so well. His discomfort and sense of alienation had intensified because of domestic family 'troubles' of which he was the main architect.

Windle – the Family Man

Windle was an Edwardian father who, despite his many accomplishments, made a very poor job of his role as a parent. His unreasonable behaviour towards his daughter, Mary, resembled more the behaviour of a character in a Gustave Flaubert novel than that of a refined and rational human being. An explanation for his actions may be set in the following context. The death of his first wife, and the loss of his only son soon after childbirth, scarred Windle emotionally. He never felt that the birth of two daughters in the same marriage – Mary Madoline (b. 18 March 1887) and Nora (b. 6 March 1889) – adequately compensated for those losses. Mary, according Sr Monica, inherited her mother's musical ability. Windle, in contrast, was practically tone deaf and had no interest in music other than in plain chant. Nora inherited her father's love of the plastic arts and became very skilful at enamelling.[91] In Birmingham, both girls had a strong friend in Mrs Ellen Pinsent who helped out when Windle's first wife died. A sister of the judge and scientist, Lord Parker, she was the wife of a distinguished Birmingham solicitor. John Humphreys described her to Sr Monica as 'a very remarkable woman and a devoted admirer of his [Windle], and sincere friend of his and his first wife. She was most good in looking after the children [Mary and Nora] after his wife's death. I have never seen anything in Ellen Pinsent which I did not admire. She had 3 children, two boys who both died during the war, and one daughter, married to a Cambridge Professor.'[92] Sr Monica wrote enigmatically that Pinsent bestowed 'a more than motherly interest on Mary and Nora, long after their first grief and loneliness had been somewhat softened over the years'.[93] In time, Edith filled the emotional vacuum left by the death of their mother and provided a good home for the girls. Mary was independent-minded and high-spirited. She had completed school by the time she had come to Cork. Her sister, Nora, who was fourteen in 1904, was sent to the local Ursuline convent. Windle mistakenly thought that he could regulate the lives of his daughters in all spheres, including matters of the heart.

John J. Horgan was invited to dinner on 24 January 1905 where he met Mary for the first time: 'She was nearly eighteen and I was only twenty-three, yet at that first meeting we both knew that we were clearly destined for each other. I can still remember, as if it were yesterday, every detail of that evening – the President's drawing room with Gothic windows, Mary standing there as I came in, fresh, young and graceful in her simple evening frock before the great fireplace.'[94] A relationship developed: 'We entered at once that enchanted land where youth and love conspire to create the most perfect happiness possible in an imperfect world. For us both mean streets became noble, little things great, all things wonderful. Thus began a true union of minds and hearts which surmounted all obstacles and survived all tests, constant and faithful to the end.'[95] The love affair, which went on under Windle's very eyes, went unnoticed by him for a time. 'Like most self-centred men of action,' wrote Horgan, 'Windle was oblivious of domestic affairs that did not directly cross his path, and he remained entirely blind to the now obvious relationship which existed between his daughter and myself.'[96] In June 1905, Douglas Hyde returned again to Cork to visit Windle. Horgan and Mary were both 'inspired by his enthusiasm'. At a garden party in the college, Horgan recalled the shock caused by the arrival of a kilted pipers' band: 'Such native revivals were then hardly considered good form.'[97] Hyde, Horgan, Mary and another charming young lady fled 'to a secluded portion of the grounds where we spent the afternoon in pleasant conversation whilst emissaries were vainly seeking for him to do the honours elsewhere.'[98] And so the relationship between Mary and Horgan deepened.

When Windle discovered the relationship which had developed behind his back, as he construed it, he sent Mary travelling on the conti-nent, as he explained on 15 June 1906 to John Humphreys: 'Strictly *entre nous* I have been having a bit of bother about Mary, who had attracted an estimable young man . . . She is much too young and immature for any-thing of the kind, so I stamped on it and sent Mary off for a couple of months' rambling. It did not come to a declaration thank goodness . . .'[99] According to Edith: 'Horgan had many most excellent qualities but he wasn't absolutely honest with Bertie – a thing he could never forgive'. Edith then gave the real reason for Windle's opposition: 'There was a man in England who proposed to Mary – one whom Bertie would greatly liked to have had for a son-in-law. But Mary had given her heart to the other when she was about 18 and she never went back on her first choice.' Windle, according to Horgan, refused his consent to her marrying anyone until she came of age, 'but he also clearly intimated that even then he would continue, for reasons which seemed good to him but which naturally did not appeal to his daughter or myself, to oppose her marriage'.[100]

Mary returned to Cork in September 1906. She had turned nineteen in March. Horgan proposed to her 'and, while in deference to her father's views, she refused to pledge herself, she left me in no doubt of her real feelings which indeed, I had long known'. But, as Sr Monica perceptively wrote: 'Indeed she [Mary] was too much her father's daughter to alter her mind easily in any decision she might make.'[101] There followed two years of separation. Mary went as a governess to St-Jean-de-Luz, south of France, returning to England to become the secretary and companion of Mrs Ellen Pinsent, who had become her virtual 'guardian'. Horgan wrote that Pinsent's 'advice and sympathy never failed us in a time of great delicacy and difficulty'. On 18 March 1908 – Mary's twenty-first birthday – they announced their engagement in the Pinsent household. Edith explained:

> The friendship [with Pinsent] broke down later at the time of Mary's engagement. My husband felt that she had encouraged it against his wishes for the engagement was announced from her home in Birmingham where Mary was staying at the time. I believe a woman, and an English woman at that, would have gone on the lines of least resistance and resigned myself without protest to Mary's choice but Bertie never compromised and he was too honest to pretend he didn't mind and make the best of a bad business. In the home women have to do so much to smooth out rough places and keep one difficult temperament from bulling against another they can never be quite as honest as men – at least they must intrigue a bit and appear to like what in their hearts they resent.

What was the basis of Windle's objection to Horgan? He was a perfectly decent suitor. Born on 26 April 1881, he was educated at Presentation College, Cork, and the Jesuit-run Clongowes Wood where he made friends with Tom Kettle and Oliver St John Gogarty. He came from a highly respected family which had played a leading role in the legal profession in Cork. His father, Michael Joseph, was a solicitor and coroner for Cork County. He had served as election agent in Cork for Charles Stewart Parnell and was a legal adviser to the Irish Parliamentary Party. Parnell had been best man at their marriage in Clapham on 7 August 1880. His mother, Mary Bowring, from Jersey, passed her bilingual skills in English and French on to her son. John J. Horgan recalls growing up in a house which was frequently visited by Parnell and by nationalist MPs. Horgan studied law at QCC and entered his father's legal practice, completing his legal studies in Dublin during the year 1902. Horgan had, in 1908, published his first book, *Great Catholic Laymen*, which was a series of profiles of Daniel O'Connell, Louis Pasteur and Frederick Ozanam. He succeeded his father as coroner in December 1914, having become a member of the Cork Harbour Commissioners in 1912 – an attachment he preserved throughout his life. He was very active in the Irish Parliamentary Party and a long-standing member of the United Irish League (UIL). He had joined the Gaelic League early in the century, becoming vice-president of the Cork branch. He was a close friend of Douglas Hyde, Edward Martyn and Eoin MacNeill. In 1909, Redmond asked him to stand for the IPP, but his father's ill-health necessitated that he remain in the family firm. He was a strong supporter of the IPP until his resignation from the UIL in 1919.[102]

Horgan was, objectively speaking, a very appealing prospective son-in-law. He was a man of talent and creativity and not, in any sense, a bounder. Windle's disproportionate reaction to news of the engagement was recorded in his diary on 20 March 1908: 'Letter from Mary and J.J.H. saying they had become engaged on her 21st birthday. Nice kind thing of Mrs Pinsent to arrange for that and of them to take absolutely the first minute she could to do it. Wrote and told them a part of what I thought of them and then decided to shut as soon [?] possible Mary out of my mind. 21 years ago I was distraught at having a daughter. I should have been ten times as much so if I had known the kind of thing she would grow into. Told the Horgan person that she neither had nor would have any money from me.'[103]

John Horgan and Mary Windle set the date of their marriage as 16 September 1908. Windle did not mellow in the intervening weeks. The day before the wedding Windle wrote: 'Much unpleasantness over Mary's affair. Spoke to her in evening and explained to some extent my position. Also wished her happiness etc. She agreed that if I came to her house – as I said I would – I was not to be brought in contact with the Horgan gang . . . and if N[ora] goes to any entertainment there, [a] list of those present is to be previously submitted to Edith.'[104] His diary entry for the wedding day reads: 'wet all day. On the whole the bitterest experience of my life, Mary being married to a man with whom I can have little or nothing to do. Went to Holy Communion and offered it up, with all the good-will I could command, for their happiness, but a poor job altogether. Exit Mary to make out her own life. Would that it could be in some other town or country but this!' With double underlining, Windle scored into his diary the words: '*Exit Mary*'.[105]

| 260 | ♍ | **SEPTEMBER.** | 9th Month |

16th. WEDNESDAY.

Ember Day.

Sunrise 5.8.
Sunset 6.13.
H.W. London 1.13 a.m. 04
Lighting up 7.12

PLANETS.	Constells. on Meridian at 9 p.m.	Moon Sets 11.58 p.m.
☿ S. 6.41 p.m. ♀ R. 1.26 a.m. ♂ R. 4.46 a.m. ♃ R. 3.27 a.m. ♄ R. 6.44 p.m.	*Cepheus, Cygnus, Delphinus.*	Rises 3.27 p.m.

Max. Temp.	Min. Temp.	Bar.	Wind.	Rain.	Remarks.
Highest, 85·3° ('55) Lowest, 57·2° ('76) Mean, 67·6°	Highest, 61·4° ('84) Lowest, 38·5° ('70) Mean, 49·3°		Cm.	in.	

Wet all day

on the whole the bitterest of scenes
of my life. Mary being married to
a man with whom I can have
little or nothing to do – coram to
H. C. suffers it only, with all
the good-will I could command,
for their happiness. But a poor
job altogether – Exit Mary from
us her own life. Would this it
could be in some other known
country but this –

Exit Mary.

Mr. afterw. Hildegarde (dear woman) being
sole if by this came will look to
me. An excellent pressure to
the Com. Michael at times. Neither I
us sick nor any of the Hildegards

Windle's diary entry, 16 September 1908 – the day his daughter
got married to Cork solicitor, John Horgan, against his wishes.

A marriage notice appeared in the *Cork Examiner* on 17 September 1908: 'Horgan–Windle – On Wednesday, Sept. 16th 1908 at St Finn Barr's West, Cork by the Very Rev. Dean Shinkwin P.P.V.G., assisted by the Rev. P. O'Leary C.C., John Joseph, eldest son of Michael Joseph Horgan, Clanloughlin, Cork, to Mary Katherine older daughter of B.C.A. Windle, M.D. F.R.S., President, Queen's College, Cork.'[106] That Windle attended the marriage service is confirmed by a reference in his diary to taking Holy Communion that day. There was almost certainly a reception at 'Clanloughlin', the home of Mary's new father-in-law. But the father of the bride refused to socialise with 'the Horgan gang'. His diary entry for the afternoon of 16 September records that 'in afternoon Hildegarde [Coghill] (dear woman) and boys and all off by Inniscara with Edith and me. An excellent passage though the colt kicked at times. Neither of us sick nor any of the Hildegardes.' There is not a single mention of a wedding reception in the day's entry.

Windle lost control when writing from England on 21 September to his friend William O'Brien: 'The marriage to which you refer is one which I have always strenuously opposed and which has been carried through without my consent and in direct opposition to my wishes – The approach of this event has poisoned existence for me for two years past and often taken all heart for work out of me. It was this domestic trouble to which I alluded when I said in my last letter (I think) to you that I might not be long in Cork.'[107] Windle continued:

> I came away here to stay with my sister-in-law as soon as the unpleasant business was over and have been devoting a great deal of thought to the question of making an effort to get some other post out of Cork and indeed out of the British Isles if possible. I have not come to a final decision and I am bound to say that my wife and my friends in Cork – the few to whom I have spoken on this matter, which is, naturally one I don't care to discuss with everybody – all urge me to carry on my work in connection with the college and try to steer it into full University powers [?]. No doubt there is a good deal in this but, on the other hand, there will be a thousand unpleasantnesses in being resident in a small place with a daughter married under such circumstances and I own that the occurrence itself and way in which it has been carried out has knocked the spirit out of me a good deal, perhaps, indeed I hope, only for a time – I would not trouble you with my domestic worries and I feel ashamed to do so, but you have been so exceptionally kind to me that I think it right to explain this matter to you. You will I am sure regard it as confidential (except so far as Mrs O'Brien is concerned).[108]

Regaining his composure towards the end of the letter, Windle spoke of returning to Cork by the 27th and of meeting O'Brien for a discussion before he met with Birrell, 'and must by that time have made up my mind what my own future action is to be'.[109]

The newly-weds set out for Italy on their honeymoon. Horgan wrote: 'there followed days of wonder and delight as we went from Venice to Florence and so on to Rome. We were both young, filled with great happiness, and ready to absorb the beauty and culture which surrounded us.'[110] There they met the rector of the Irish College, Mgr Michael O'Riordan, who arranged for the couple to be received in private audience by Pope Pius X.

After an idyllic few weeks, the couple returned to make their new life together in Cork. Michael Joseph Horgan and his wife received Mary with enthusiasm into their family. They built 'Lacaduv' for the couple as a wedding gift – a fine house on the Lee Road – next door to their own home. Whatever about Horgan senior, who was used to the rough and tumble of politics and public life, his wife was permanently scarred by the ignorance and insensitivity of their oh-so-cultured in-law.[111] Windle, unyielding and unrelenting, wrote on 31 December – at the end of a year of considerable professional achievement with the passage of the Irish Universities Act – the following: 'End of the worst year I have ever had. God grant 1909 may be less painful and anyway God will, I hope, accept my imperfect efforts to do my duty under most difficult circumstances. Lost – a daughter and a friend. Gained a university settlement for the public. Gain hardly makes up for private loss.'

During the months that followed, the estrangement from Mary and her husband took its toll on Edith's health. She remained poorly in early 1909. Windle wrote on 12 February, after his wife had a particularly bad few days and was under medical care, that her doctor said the 'whole of this thing is due to Mary and her cow-boy. How grateful I ought to be to them – as [?] I am to old Horgan who has forbidden his oaf to come to my house'. The following day, he went to see his close friend, Fr Roche, 'with whom I discussed the whole question of Mary and her husband. He says I have done everything that man or a Christian could be expected to and that the conduct of the old man in first inducing his son to bluff it out with and defy me and then trying to stare me out so to speak is detestable.' Separation was the way Windle, according to his diary, planned to manage his relationship with his daughter, adding: 'Let her [Mary] lie in the dung-heap she has deliberately chosen and see how she likes it.' Such a brutish attitude stands in stark contrast to his feelings for Edith. He wrote on 14 February: 'Dear darling, I love her more every year we have been together, for a better or more delightful woman never trod this earth.' The cold war with Mary and her husband continued for a number of years without respite.

The couple did not allow the disapproval of Windle to undermine their happiness. A photo album, assembled by John Horgan after Mary's death in 1920, shows a very happy couple, Mary looking quite radiant in the snaps.[112] Their first child, John Ivor, was born on 5 September 1909; a second boy, Joe, was born a year later. Madoline Mary, who was born on 26 May 1915, reminisced in 2008: 'Life in those days was more leisurely and they [her parents] entertained many interesting people at their beautiful home, Lacaduv.'[113] It was a full life. Besides politics, the Horgans were interested in the arts, painting and photography. Many of the most distinguished politicians of the day – Douglas Hyde, John and William Redmond, Tom Kettle, Eoin MacNeill, Patrick Pearse, Roger Casement, etc. – were guests in their home. According to Horgan, Windle 'continued unsympathetic and our friendship remained in abeyance for six years, as much I think to his loss as to our'.[114] There is no evidence that he made any contact with Mary when either of the boys were born. But we surmise, and it is only surmise, that Edith may have done so. The unnecessary hurt which Windle caused Mary during the early years of her marriage was simply unpardonable. Moreover, his other daughter, Nora, was the most serious casualty of his unreasonableness. Cut off from being able to see her sister, whom she adored, Nora had a very difficult life in a strict household where Edith protected her husband and always took his side. Nora eventually escaped to London in the early years of the First World War but not before she had suffered greatly. Windle, too, was a casualty of his own obduracy. He wrote petulantly on 15 April 1912: 'It appears Verity has been up to stay with Mr John J. Horgan for a month and is then to come here for a few days – pretty sickening business – What a gang and how I wish I could clear out of this place and beyond their ambit.'[115]

Windle's final diary entry for 1912 shows his egotistical character and his unsettled and troubled state of mind: 'Prepared lecture for Literary and Scientific Society and did other work – walked about place – not out otherwise. Very dyspeptic and awfully upset about Edith whose condition I can't understand and hope most fervently it is not the menopause. Nora's frivolity and utter idleness and obvious intention of doing nothing but amuse herself and get her own pleasure also very disturbing. Must give her a good talking to. What with worries of one kind and another and foul weather 1912 has certainly not been a good year.'

Two further years elapsed before Windle and Horgan senior saw the light. It took a family tragedy – and the intervention of his close friend Canon Roche – to bring about a fragile reconciliation. Mary wrote unexpectedly on 16 August: 'Letter from Mary! To Edith suggesting that I should write to old Horgan (which I shall certainly not do) on death of his wife [Mary] – unintentionally most impudent in its tone.'The same entry records that he had a difference of opinion with his other daughter, Nora: 'concocting [?] to Nora with whom I must have a settlement. My children have certainly given me but little comfort.' On 20 August 1914, he noted: 'Walked to end of Penrose Quay . . . and melancholy to see the soldiers going off in thousands to this diabolical war. Letter from Mary to whom replied after visit from P. T. [unidentified] who told me the fearful tragedy of Mrs H's death.'

On 21 August, he wrote: 'Letter from J.J. H and M – and talked it over with Canon Roche who wants me to write and make it up which I suppose I must do though much against the grain. Nothing I like less but it would be unchristian not to and there need be and can be no great intimacy.' On 22 August 1914, he wrote: 'Made up my mind and wrote to old Horgan – the hardest thing I ever did and I wonder if anything will come of it. I could never love Mary and her lot nor be on intimate terms with them, but things may be better than they are.' On 23 August, he wrote: 'Long letter to John Horgan.' His entry on 25 August noted: 'Mary wants me to write to old Horgan to say I am sorry for having wounded his wife – This I cannot possibly do since my only wounding act was objecting to a marriage to which I still object.' Relations were patched up sufficiently between himself and his eldest daughter for him to write on 31 August: 'Mary to tea first time for five years. Less embarrassing event than might have been expected.' On 11 September, he noted: 'Went to see Mary and saw her two little boys who do not interest me but seemed good and obedient. A job I did not like and was glad to get over.'

On 3 September, he went to see Canon Roche who had been responsible for guiding him towards accepting the path to reconciliation. Although he mentions nothing about the breakthrough in the relationship with his daughter, he may have received further advice from his friend on the need to reconcile with his daughter. He saw Canon Roche again on the 12th. Finally, on 16 September 1914, he recorded: 'Met John Horgan and shook hands with him and so have done my part in this reconciliation.' Windle could ill-afford to be without the sage advice of Horgan and of his father. The 'cold war' between himself and the 'Horgan gang', as he termed them, left him bereft of the support of a very powerful and politically well-connected local family. The mere absence of their support would have been trouble enough without also having the 'Horgan gang' actively against you. On 17 September, he commented 'John Redmond's magnificent manifesto appeared today. A splendid piece of writing.' He then added laconically: 'Mary and children to tea'. Things were never the same again between Windle and his daughter. But, at least, he was behaving in a more mature fashion towards her. The Horgan couple began to be included in social events at Windle's home; On 22 November, he wrote: 'Afterward Mary and husband – Col. [Maurice] Moore and William Redmond [MP] to tea and took them over College (also P.T.) W[illiam]R[Edmond] going to front at 52 – a fine patriotic action.' On 30 December, he wrote: 'Mary and husband to tea. Dreaded it but got over better than expected.' At ninety-five, Madoline recalled in 2010 meeting her grandfather on but the one occasion; she was taken by Mary, her mother, to Windle's home, remembering 'the lovely wood-panelled rooms, darkened as my grandfather suffered from hay-fever, a condition we all inherited'.[116]

The Radicalisation of Irish Politics

Windle could ill-afford to be without the friendship and professional counsel of his son-in-law, Horgan, and his father. Through pig-headedness and obduracy, he had denied himself the services of canny guides to Cork society and political life.[117] His early friendship with William O'Brien, whose faction did so well in the 1910 general election, melted away after the MP failed to deliver the generous endowment he had promised in 1908. It was a dangerous time to be without a guide to the rapidly changing landscape of Irish politics.

Although Windle's cherished ambition of home rule had been passed in the British parliament on 11 April 1912, by the following year its implementation appeared further away than ever. The British government, from Windle's perspective, had buckled under opposition pressure; Andrew Bonar Law, leader of the Conservative Party, had, on 9 April 1912, pledged the support of British unionists to resist home rule. While the prime minister, Henry Asquith, visited Dublin between 18 and 20 July, he appeared unable to calm emotions and restore public confidence in the Irish policies of his government. On 28 September, many thousands of northern unionists had signed the Solemn League and Covenant pledging resistance to home rule. The Trinity-educated Edward Carson, born in Dublin on 9 February 1854, had accepted an invitation in 1911 to become their leader. His legacy provokes divided opinion among historians: 'He has no country, only a caste,' was the taunt of one of his critics. A.T.Q. Stewart concluded: 'The Union was his lodestar, and when it set he plumbed depths of bitterness and defeat which even his followers could not measure.'[118] Windle, as will be seen throughout the remaining chapters of this book, reserved his most extreme language in his diaries for Carson and for a weak British government.

On 16 January 1913, the Third Home Rule Bill was carried in the House of Commons by 367 votes to 257 but defeated on 30 January in the House of Lords. With the Ulster Volunteer Force formed on 31

January, there was every possibility that northern unionists would defy the rule of law in their opposition to the implementation of home rule. On 7 July 1913, the Home Rule Bill finally passed in the House of Commons by 352 votes to 243. It was again rejected by the House of Lords. But that could only now be a delaying tactic. Windle had little confidence in Asquith but he never lost personal faith in the political leadership of John Redmond while being witheringly critical of other prominent members of the Irish Parliamentary Party, particularly John Dillon.[119] By 1913, Windle had doubts about the inevitability of home rule. He knew that a nationalist consensus – bound together by the expectation of devolved government – was in danger of breaking down.

Despite being well connected in Dublin Castle, and with leading members of the Irish Parliamentary Party and the Gaelic League, Windle was very much at sea. Being close to the upper echelons of Irish society in the Catholic Church, nationalist and cultural politics and government meant that he all too easily shared the received wisdom of those circles. He suffered from all the disadvantages of being an 'insider'. What he failed to realise was that the Gaelic League was now synonymous with Douglas Hyde, the IPP and nationalist politics with John Dillon and British government policy with Birrell. Radical changes were taking place and he was both innocent and ignorant of the profundity of the transformation of the Irish political landscape.

Éamon de Valera, Irish Nationalism and UCC

The filling of professorships had gone very smoothly during Windle's early years at QCC/UCC. In early 1913, the mood within the college had become less compliant. He encountered minor difficulties with the filling of the chair of mathematics and an unprecedented problem with the filling of a chair of mathematical physics for which Éamon (or Edward as he was then known) de Valera was a candidate. In the first case, Windle was not an admirer of Arthur H. Anglin, the professor of mathematics. Holding the chair since 1887, he retired in early 1913. On 12 January 1913, Windle wrote to McGrath: 'Rejoice with me that at long last I have got Anglin's resignation. It was like extracting a back molar and one with twisted roots, but it came at last. Of course until it is accepted by my G.B. it can't be reported to you formally. Observe, young man, [Matthew] Conran, is to have this job and no one else, so discourage any other person from thinking of it.' In the same letter, Windle told McGrath that his registrar was not well: 'I don't at all like the looks of Molohan. I wish I could see him in better health for he is a pillar of strength to me.'[120]

The academic council met on 10 March. It was reported that there had been one applicant for the chair of mathematics. Professor Hartog proposed, seconded by Professor Henebry, that Conran be awarded the chair. The motion was passed unanimously and the proposal was sent forward to the governing body. In relation to a cognate professorship, the same meeting also advised the governing body that no change was necessary in the provisions concerning the chair of mathematical physics. The governing body, on 14 March, endorsed the recommendation of Conran for the position of professor of mathematics. But the resolution to the senate also pointed out that he was the only candidate to present for the position. Furthermore, the governing body told the senate that they did not desire to make any change in the conditions of the chair of mathematical physics. Windle wrote to McGrath on 27 March 1913 that until Conran's election to the chair had been made by the senate of the university his present position could not fall vacant and could not be advertised. He told McGrath that it would be 'a matter of the greatest possible convenience to this College if a special meeting of the Senate could be held about the middle of next month for the purpose of electing a Professor of Mathematics in University College, Cork, and I venture to apply, through you, to the Chancellor that such a meeting may be held'. He pointed out, in support of his application, that the circumstances of the case were 'very peculiar. There was only one candidate for the chair and that candidate is the person whom everybody concerned desired to see appointed. It was owing to the fact that this appointment was regarded as an absolutely foregone conclusion that there were no other candidates.' Windle felt further that the convenience to UCC of 'getting this appointment made early in order that the consecutive steps may be taken would be immense'. He said he alone would come to Dublin from Cork for the meeting. There was no need for anyone to travel from Galway and 'a bare quorum of Dublin members with myself could settle the whole question in the space of about two minutes'.[121] Windle ran into unforeseen difficulties with the timing of the meeting: 'I am very much obliged to you for your letter. Being a sober, righteous and godly person I know nothing about your infernal races and could not, therefore, have in mind the fact that Punchestown – which I suppose belongs to that class – was on the 23 April. However, the 24th will suit me very well.' He proposed to come up himself and had advised Anderson that there was no need for anyone to come from Galway: '[Henry] McWeeney will second Conran and I have asked him to bring a few of his men and I have also written to Coffey on similar lines'.[122] As it turned out, Windle did not travel to Dublin for the senate meeting on 24 April. McGrath proposed Conran, seconded by McWeeney. However, William Crawford, seconded by Mary Hayden, proposed an amendment: 'That the question of appointing a Professor of Mathematics at University College, Cork, be postponed until the Governing Body of that College has

33 Morehampton Rce
Donnybrook, Dublin
May 21, 1913

Sir,

I beg to apply for the Professorship of Mathematical Physics now vacant in University College.

I trust that my Postgraduate Studies in Mathematical and Physical Science and my long Experience and Success as a University Teacher, of which I send testimony, will convince your President, the Academic Council and the Governing Body of the College of my fitness for the position

Faithfully Yours
Edward de Valera

Joseph Downey Esq.
Secretary and Bursar
University College, Cork.

Letter from Edward de Valera to the secretary of UCC, Joseph Downey, 21 May 1913, applying for the post of professor of mathematical physics.

taken such further steps as it shall think fit to secure additional suitable candidates'. The original motion was put by the chair and adopted. Conran was duly appointed.

In contrast, there was no shortage of candidate for the chair of mathematical physics. A future commandant of the 1916 rising and later taoiseach and president of Ireland, Éamon de Valera at the age of thirty-seven applied on 21 May 1913 for the chair of Mathematical Physics, signing himself Edward. He wrote in an elegant hand: 'I beg to apply for the professorship of Mathematical Physics now vacant in University College. I trust that my Postgraduate Studies in mathematical and Physical Science and my long experience and success as a University Teacher, of which I send testimony, will convince your President, the Academic Council and the Governing Body of the College of my fitness for the position. Faithfully yours, Edward de Valera.'[123]

He sent a second letter on 27 May 1913: 'As a matter of convenience I asked the Printers to forward copies of testimonials etc to you direct. I expected that they would prepay cost of carriage and charge it up to me. I enclose p.o. for amount and regret that you have been troubled.' [signed, E. de Valera][124] The post paid £250 per annum.

As the mechanism for acquiring a chair in those days required a vigorous canvass of the voters at all levels in the decision-making process, de Valera would prove to be a formidable candidate at a political level. He was a promising young politician with the strong backing of the Gaelic League. Windle, once a member and an activist, had, by 1913, come to regard that organisation as less than honest. His diary on 27 February spoke of 'disgraceful jobbery of Gaelic League', and referred to it as 'a centre of corruption, jobbery and vindictiveness beyond conception. It will kill it in time and would do so to-morrow if there were any public opinion in this unhappy island.' De Valera was a Gaelic League activist.

Horgan left this profile of de Valera after he had come to his home to win his support for the professorship; he was 'a tall, lanky young man' with dark hair and a sallow complexion which 'suggested a foreign origin which his name justified but his rich Limerick accent seemed to belie'. De Valera had a letter of introduction from Horgan's old Clongowes Wood master, Fr Timothy Corcoran SJ, Professor of Education at UCD. Their conversation confirmed for Horgan the accuracy of Corcoran's eulogy of the candidate: 'My visitor, whose modesty was only equalled by his charm of manner, was equally acceptable on other grounds, for it appeared that he was not only an active member of the Gaelic League but also, like most young Irishmen at that time, a supporter of John Redmond's Home Rule policy.'[125] Horgan set to work mobilising support

Bertram and his Aunt Florence.

Portrait of Bertram Windle.

Windle's first cousin, Admiral Boyle Somerville, who was shot by the IRA on 24 March 1936. Windle, a close friend of Boyle and his sister, the writer Edith Somerville, was a regular visitor to their home in Castletownshend.

Windle's first wife, Madoline Mary Hudson. They married in Birmingham on 4 May 1886 and had two children, Mary and Nora. She died in 1900 and Windle married Edith Nazer on St Valentine's day, 1901.

Cartoon of Windle while Professor of Anatomy at Birmingham University. The book under his arm, entitled *Anatomy of Stonehenge*, is meant to reflect his passion for archaeology and pre-history.

Edith Windle in Toronto in the 1930s.

Windle's mother, Sydney, who died in Dublin on 12 February 1910 .
His diary entry read: 'Telegram in afternoon from [his brother] to say that mother died peacefully at 2.30. Deo Gratias! There is an end to her misery. She was a splendid woman up to a few months ago and wish she could have gone then – one must try to forget her last days – Poor soul. We did what we could to make her happy or, at least, comfortable.'

Mary Windle.

Mary Windle, as governess, in St-Jean-de-Luz, 1907.

Mary Windle in 1906.

Douglas Hyde and Mary Windle
at the Oireachtas, Killarney,
26 July 1914.

Mary Windle and John Horgan shortly after
their wedding on 16 September 1908.

Mary and her daughter, Madoline, who
was born in 1915.

Mary Windle with her son, Joe,
and daughter, Madoline.

Mary Windle with her three children, Ivor, Joe and Madoline.

from his friends and supporters of the Irish Parliamentary Party for de Valera, the Redmondite. As proof of his future successful political career, de Valera built up a strong local campaign for his candidature. Windle, not yet reconciled to his son-in-law, experienced the cold wind of opposition from a usually supportive IPP. He now faced unexpected support for de Valera inside UCC.

There were four candidates deemed eligible for the post. Dr Edgar Henry Harper, James R. Riddell, John E. Bowen and Edward de Valera. Edgar H. Harper was thirty-two. He had attended the Royal School, Dungannon, and Trinity College, Dublin between October 1897 and 1902 when he graduated in pure and applied mathematics, gaining a large number of distinctions. Those included the gold medal in mathematics at the degree examination and the McCullagh Prize in an advanced course in applied mathematics in 1903. His entire undergraduate career was marked by straight firsts. He graduated in the Royal University of Ireland, obtaining first of first class honours in mathematics and mathematical physics at both the BA and MA degree examinations in 1904 and 1905 respectively. He was awarded a studentship on the basis of the latter examination. In 1908, he was awarded a special prize of £50 for highly distinguished answering in mathematics. From August to December 1908, he was a teacher at his old school before taking up his post at university.

In summer 1907 and again at the beginning of 1909 he was an assistant lecturer in pure and applied mathematics at the University College of North Wales, Bangor. He was appointed permanently to the post in October 1909. He had a distinguished teaching career, according to his testimonials. He received glowing references from Professors Harry R. Reichel, and G.H. Bryan, Bangor. He also was given references from Trinity by Robert Russell, fellow and tutor, the professor of natural philosophy, M.W.J. Fry and the professor of natural philosophy, Frederick Purser. He had a testimonial from the Royal Astronomer of Ireland and Andrews Professor of Astronomy in Trinity, C.J. Joly.

Reichel described him as 'a man of amiable and sterling character much liked by his colleagues and students. Though quiet in manner, he is by no means a recluse, being fond of games and having always interested himself in the social side of college life. His conduct has always evinced unselfish public spirit.' Harper had proven himself 'an admirable teacher for students of all grades, and a thoroughly competent examiner'. Bangor had recently appointed him internal examiner in applied mathematics for the degree examinations of the University of Wales, 'a responsible post which is hardly ever conferred upon assistant lecturers'.

Bryan spoke of Harper's 'conspicuous success' over four years 'both in class teaching and in the performance of research and original work in Pure and Applied Mathematics'. He praised Harper's work in applied mathematics on the stability of aeroplanes – 'I venture to express the opinion that there are not many lines of investigation at the present time in which it is so difficult to see a few steps ahead as it was in this particular case'. Harper's research had been published in Bryan's book, *Stability in Aviation*. Bryan also stressed that the candidate played a prominent part in the social life of the college, taking a leading role in open air games, and had been secretary of the staff tennis club and a member of the common room committee. He laid emphasis on his role as an examiner and concluded that Harper was 'eminently qualified to discharge the duties attaching to the Chair at University College, Cork, and if the electors appoint him, they will never regret their choice'.[126]

Edward de Valera, in contrast, had a far less impressive academic curriculum vitae. He did, however, have more experience than Harper as a teacher. His application recorded that he had gained distinctions at secondary school. It stated that he was a recognised teacher of the National University in mathematical physics and mathematics, St Patrick's College, Maynooth. De Valera stated that he was a university honourman and graduate (BA) in mathematical physics and mathematics (RUI). He was a scholar of the Royal University in mathematical science and was recognised as a science teacher by the Board of Agriculture and Technical Instruction, 'after courses of Experimental Physics with Professor Morton, Queen's University, Belfast, and Professor Brown, Royal College of Science'. He had a higher diploma in education, NUI and a chief diploma in Irish, Leinster College. He also listed himself as being an assistant examiner in natural philosophy and physics in the NUI, an examiner in mathematics for the Intermediate Education Board and an examiner in Irish for the Royal College of Physicians and Surgeons. In parenthesis, the files of the NUI provided the following additional information on the candidate. On 5 July 1912, de Valera wrote to the NUI: 'Sir, Would you be good enough to particularise the points in which my returns of marks have been "most unsatisfactory" as complained of in your note this morning per "F.H.W."'. This note is in reference to his examining for the NUI. But no context or explanation is given. On 4 October 1912, de Valera wrote to the NUI: 'Will you please register me amongst those who have obtained the "Higher" Diploma in Education NUI, faithfully yrs, Edward de Valera.'[127]

Returning again to de Valera's application, he listed that he had taken courses with Professor A.W. Conway of UCD for four years. He had also taken courses with H.C. McWeeney for three years and with Professor E.T. Whittaker for two years. His teaching experience consisted of thirteen years in St Patrick's College, Maynooth, and, since 1906, professor of mathematics in Carysfort Teacher Training College, Blackrock. Prior to the disestablishment of the Royal University, he was a lecturer in Rockwell College, Cashel, the Dominican College, Eccles Street, and Holy Cross College, Clonliffe, Dublin. De Valera listed the distinctions of his students and supplied references from the presidents of St Patrick's College, Maynooth, and of Blackrock College, Dublin. He also had a reference from the principal of Carysfort and from Professors Conway and McWeeney, of UCD, and from Professor Whittaker, University of Edinburgh.

President J.F. Hogan of Maynooth said that de Valera had 'discharged his duties here with undoubted zeal and capacity'. He had 'high qualifications', was 'assiduous and diligent at his work, and was a "very efficient teacher"'. Professor Conway wrote that his student of several years 'ought to make an inspiring and lucid teacher'. He had over the past few years 'gone deeply into the subject of Quaternions', and was 'at present prosecuting an important original research in them which promises to be of considerable interest. His mathematical abilities are of a high order, and he is possessed of great brilliancy and originality.' In his view, de Valera was 'adapted to excel in Research work rather than to do himself justice in examinations.'

Professor Edmund Whittaker wrote that he had been 'very impressed by the intellectual vigour with which he has interested himself in the most difficult problems of Natural Philosophy. His knowledge is both broad and deep, and I am confident that in any educational position he will exercise the best of influences over those with whom he is brought into contact.' Professor McWeeney wrote that de Valera had had a distinguished career in the late Royal University, 'especially in Mathematics, in which subject he got Honours at several Examinations'. De Valera was 'an able student and an energetic worker' who had 'for many years engaged in teaching work with conspicuous success'. He was sure that the candidate would 'discharge the duties of any educational position to which he may be appointed conscientiously and efficiently'.

The professor of education at UCD, Revd T. Corcoran SJ, knew him from his taking his course in 1909–10 in theory, history and practice of education, gaining in 1910 the post-graduate diploma in education established under the National University: 'Both from my experience of him in the year 1909–10, and from subsequent knowledge, I can with confidence testify to the intellectual interest and energy – joined with marked ability – which he brings to bear on his work as a Lecturer in Mathematics, and to the knowledge he has acquired of the problems connected with that and other branches of educational work.'[128]

A third candidate, James R. Riddell MA had his qualifications from the Royal University and Cambridge. He had gained a first class honours degree from the RUI in 1903 and won a major scholarship, to Trinity College, Cambridge in 1905. He got first class in mathematical tripos in 1906 and 1907. Between 1908 and 1913, he had taught at Queen's, Belfast. His specialisation was to combine pure mathematics with that of the recent developments of experimental sciences. He had studied the modern theories of electricity at Cambridge. He was very strongly refereed by the professor of mathematics, Queen's University, A.C. Dixon, by A.N. Whitehead, fellow and senior lecturer in mathematics at Trinity College, Cambridge. He also had a short reference from R.A. Herman from the same Cambridge college and from J.G. Leathem, a university lecturer in mathematics, Cambridge.[129]

A fourth short-listed candidate, John E. Bowen, studied at Galway and at Cambridge. He entered Galway in 1903 and took his MA in 1910. He had held the senior scholarship in mathematics in 1906–07 and in mathematical and experimental physics in 1907–08. In 1911, he was awarded the 1851 Exhibition Scholarship in Experimental Physics and during 1911–12 did research work at the Cavendish Laboratory, Cambridge, under Sir J.J. Thomson. He had a reference from Alexander Anderson, President of UCG, from Professor W.A. Houston of Galway and T.J. I'a. Bromwich of St John's, Cambridge.

Windle called a joint meeting of the faculties of Arts, Engineering and Science on 4 June. Professor Hartog proposed, seconded by Professor Alexander – both Windle supporters – to set up a committee of the president, the registrar, and Professors Alexander, Anglin, Bergin and Conran to examine the applications and report to the faculties. On the motion being put to the meeting, the vote was tied at eight each side, and 'consequently the motion was lost'. It was decided that the faculties involved in the appointment should, that same day, meet separately and report to the Academic Council on 6 June 1913.[130] The Faculty of Arts duly met on 4 June. Professor Conran was asked by the president to state his views on each of the candidates. He gave his opinion on the four, placing them in the following order: first, Harper, second, Riddell, third, de Valera and fourth, Bowen. Professor Anglin agreed but placed Bowen third and de Valera in fourth and last place. On the motion of Conran, seconded by Stockley, the faculty recommended to academic council that Harper, as 'incomparably the best candidate', be placed first. Riddell was placed second 'as being highly qualified'. De Valera, 'whose qualifications were not so good', was placed third. The report, which was signed by J.P. Molohan as registrar, did not mention Bowen.[131] The Science Faculty met on 4 June 1913. They ranked Harper first and Riddell second. They put

Bowen third. The Engineering Faculty met the same day and gave the same ranking. There were three reports before the academic council when it met on 6 June. Merriman questioned the accuracy of the report from the Faculty of Arts, stating the words 'incomparably the best candidate' for Harper 'were not in his recollection'. The registrar replied that those words had been jotted down by him as 'rough minutes'. Stockley, who had seconded the report, supported the registrar's wording. Conran then provided his rationale for placing de Valera above Bowen. At that point, according to the minutes, Windle intervened and asked that the question of ranking third and fourth be postponed for discussion for the present and that the Academic Council should decide the nomination for the first and second places. Professor Bergin, seconded by Professor Conran, proposed Harper first as 'being in all ways the best qualified candidate' and Riddell second as 'being a well qualified candidate but not so well qualified as Mr Harper'. Professor Dunlea proposed, and Professor Corby Sr seconded, that Bowen and de Valera be sent forward bracketed. This was rejected on a show of hands.[132] A motion was then proposed by Professor Bergin, seconded by Professor Hartog, that Bowen's name be placed third on the list. A motion was also proposed by Professor Conran, seconded by Professor Dunlea, that de Valera's name go third on the list being sent forward to governing body. On a show of hands, the latter motion was lost and it was resolved that Bowen's name would be sent forward as being third on the list.[133]

That evening, 6 June, a deeply traumatised Windle recorded the motion had succeeded, 'but anything like the indecent dishonesty of the Gaelic gang I never saw – However they were defeated. N.B. no more women professors for me. Those we have, have in ordinary affairs, no more sense than canaries.' No woman is named in his diary as having taken part in the debate in the Academic Council. A likely explanation for the 'canaries' remark was that the Professor of Romance Languages, Mary Ryan, or the Professor of Education, Elizabeth M. O'Sullivan, or the Professor of German, Wally Swertz, had voted against Windle.

Between the Academic Council on the 6th and the meeting of the governing body on 13 June, intense canvassing took place on behalf of de Valera. Windle's diary for 12 June 1913 stated: 'The intrigue . . . by Fitzgerald and Merriman goes gaily on and a serious canvass on their part means probably that de Valera will head the poll tomorrow – a most discreditable thing. What to do with these people I know not and I see no chance of escape but I will write again to Birrell – a shocking night in consequence not getting any sleep till 4 am.' Windle – with very little sleep – faced the governing body the following day. Those in attendance were as follows: Professor Alexander; Professor Molohan;

Professor Hartog; the Bishop of Cork, Dr O'Callaghan; Sir Stanley Harrington; Br J.P. Noonan; James M. Burke; the Lord Mayor of Cork, Alderman O'Shea; Rev. E.G. Seale MA; Francis Heffernan; Professor Mary Ryan; Dr J.J. O'Connor; Br E.J. Connolly; William McDonald; Mayor of Waterford, Thomas Power; B. O'Flynn; Canon Barrett; Professor Pearson; and Bishop of Cork, Cloyne and Ross, Charles Benjamin Dowse, Dr J. Cotter and the college secretary.[134]

The report from the Academic Council stated that Harper was incomparably the best candidate, having reached distinction in two universities. The same report placed Riddell second, as his academic record was also excellent but he was not as highly qualified as Harper. Bowen was placed third with a credible academic record, but his qualities were much inferior to those of the other two. De Valera was not even mentioned in the Academic Council report sent to the governing body.[135] Windle introduced the vacancy for the chair of Mathematical Physics as one of a number of vacancies being filled. He explained the procedure in connection with the appointment. Before a decision was reached, Sir Stanley Harrington proposed, and Brother P. Noonan seconded, that the voting should be by ballot. Windle would – in the light of the heavy canvassing – have encouraged the adoption of such a procedure. Anonymity would work in his favour, or so he thought. The individual applicants for the chair were then considered.[136] A preliminary vote was called and the president declared the vote as follows: Mr de Valera 11; Mr Harper 9; and Mr Bowen 2. Riddell received no votes. A second vote was taken and Windle declared the vote as follows: Mr Harper 10; Mr de Valera 10; Mr Bowen 1; and Mr Ridde (*sic*) 1. A number of the members of the governing body felt that no recommendation should be made to the Senate of the NUI. In the end, it was decided to send forward the result of the final vote.[137]

The outcome was a real slap in the face for the hyper-sensitive Windle. The night of the governing body meeting – 13 June – Windle wrote: 'The intrigue at Governing Body came to a head. The worst liars [J.] Cotter and [B.] O'Flynn – the Bishop [not identified] a blackguard. I cannot put down what they did helped by half drunk [James M.] Burke. But the College is lost under these tactics. Afterwards I had a bad attack of some kind – high tension and feeling very bad. Sent for doctor who came and got [?]. Sent to bed with sedative draft.' On 14 June, he recorded: 'Bad – in bed most of day. Staying in bed until the afternoon.' He wrote on 16 June: 'feeing very ill – all the staff worrying me about this infernal thing – wrote to Wright – Birrell – Cardinal – regarding possibility of leaving.' On 17 June, he commented: 'Only out to examinations. Constant bother about these appointments and reduced to great weakness by ill-health and inability to get out. Slept badly.' On

17 June, he wrote to McGrath complaining of his poor health: 'I have had an awful upset over the appointments here'. He was suffering from flu, gout, stomach upsets and hay fever. On Wednesday 18 June, he wrote: 'walked about a good bit with Edith – without eye trouble – still worrying over this affair and worried about it – and a shocking bad night.'

Birrell sent a telegram fixing Wednesday 25 June, 'at 4 in House of Commons for [their] interview'. Early the next week, he travelled to England. On 24 June, he met an old friend who asked: 'Why had we left Cork? Something must be wrong?' Windle noted in response: 'quite true – Try and get away as much as possible – and stick it out.' On 25 June, he saw Cardinal Bourne and told him about all the affairs in Cork: 'Promises to do anything in his power for me.' Windle went to the House of Commons for his appointment with Birrell. Windle told 'him all about the jobbery; one man who could keep college together and that it would fall to pieces if I left'. Windle spent a few more days in England, travelling to Dover, Plymouth and, on 28 June, taking the boat to Ireland. The president and his supporters must have canvassed strongly to win the vote on the professorship. The NUI Senate met on 4 July 1913. The chancellor, William Walsh, was not present. The UCC appointment to the chair of mathematical physics was placed before the meeting. The minutes record that the registrar reported that he had received that morning a letter 'in reference to certain occurrences connected with the filling of the vacancies in University College, Cork, and asked whether this letter should be read to the Meeting or not. The Senate decided that, having regard to the date of its receipt, the letter should not be read.' Upon the motion of Sir Bertram Windle, seconded by Sir Stanley Harrington, Edgar H. Harper, MA, was appointed professor of mathematical physics in University College, Cork, as from 1 October 1913.[138] Windle noted in his diary: 'To our amazement the other side funked [?] it or were better advised and Harper was selected *unanimously* . . . and so ends this dirty intrigue *for the present*. A deal of thanks to [John A.] McClelland [UCD] who travelled all night to the meeting. [Rev. William] Delany [SJ] a dodging [?] little liar – What a gang most of the clergy are.' He added without explanation: '[Rev. John F.] Horgan's speech on Maynooth out-Bourbons the Bourbons.' Having got his man appointed, Windle went to England on 5 July and remained there until early September, touring abbeys, cathedrals, including York, and different archaeological sites. Returning to Cork to prepare for a new term in autumn 1913, he found that he had 'piles of letters' awaiting him. On 11 September, he wrote: 'Letters and all sorts in morning. Wrote to Birrell re [Sir John] O'Connell proposals.' [This related to the Honan Fund.] He 'sat in garden in afternoon and walked about after a prolonged Plombière'. On 12 September, he recorded: 'Town and long talk with Canon Patrick Roche. He thinks I am acting rightly to not hide light under bushel' – a reference to his internal struggle over whether he would go or stay. Birrell replied on 20 September 1913: '. . . You are evidently one of those men who are worth their weight in Gold. I think your well-to-do friend shows his good sense in the conditions he imposed . . . May good come of this bequest to Cork and all concerned! I always regarded your threatened departure as a great blow to a still nascent plan of Education.' Windle's departure, wrote Birrell, would have been 'a catastrophe,' adding: 'These are very critical years in Cork.' For the time being at least, Windle chose to stay. For Éamon de Valera, the defeat had not come as a particular surprise. He had been unsuccessful in his earlier effort to be appointed to the staff of UCG. However, he had come very close to winning in Cork. His strong performance at the governing body may have surprised him, demon-strating that political canvassing for a professional post still might carry the day. Despite being in every way better qualified than de Valera, Harper, his main rival, had a background which provided ample scope for local political manoeuvring and the trading on 'nod and wink' cam-paigning; he was a Presbyterian from Dungannon who had been educated in Queen's University and Trinity College. In the end, Windle gained a victory for 'professional standards over local influence', as Owen Dudley Edwards has phrased it. While 1913 proved a very busy year for de Valera, he did not take defeat in Cork as the death knell of his academic career. In November 1913, de Valera wrote to the NUI requesting that he be admitted to the degree of BSc of the university in accordance with Statute 11 Section 4 as set down in Calendar for 1913 on page 141. He said he was pursuing a course of studies in UCD with a view to proceeding to a higher degree in the faculty of science. He said that Dr [Arthur] Conway's certificate to that effect would follow. A minute on the letter read: 'Pass in Mathematical Science in Honours Course, Autumn 1904.' Later in the month, he again wrote: 'Dear Sir, Please attach enclosed certificate to my recent application to be admitted to BSc Degree under Stat 11.' Dated 13 November, the note from Conway duly arrived stating that de Valera was taking a course in 'math-ematical science' leading to a MSc degree. He did not complete the work for that higher qualification.

Windle was dismayed to the core by the speed with which the cul-tural and radical nationalist lobby in Cork had combined to attempt to railroad through an appointment which was, in his eyes, not profession-ally defensible. At the same time as he fought successfully to preserve professional academic standards, he was shocked at the level of defiance exhibited by governors and by some of his professorial colleagues in UCC. While Edward de Valera had – to Windle – the profile of a trouble-maker, he was no ordinary applicant. He was a very able politician and future revolutionary leader who, paradoxically, became in 1921 chancellor of the NUI.[139]

As the opening of the new term loomed, the tempo of Windle's life intensified. On Monday 29th, he had a long day of meetings. On 2 October, he wrote: 'Stockley makes a holy ass of himself by writing wrong paper for scholarship.' On 6 October 1913, he sent a rebuke: 'Wrote a homily to Stockley on his shortcomings – also a diplomatic letter to the double faced swine Sexton.' Stockley sent a 'humble letter' by return (7th). With an abrasive attitude of that kind, it was little wonder that Windle found his popularity among professors was waning. But that autumn, he found himself in the eye of a public controversy. The debate may have been about best practice in archaeology, but at another level Windle confronted the rise of a form of radical cultural politics with which he had no sympathy.

Windle in the Public Eye – the Ogham Stone Controversy

Windle, very much the strong Edwardian antiquarian, had made it a priority to build a collection of artefacts at UCC. As Professor of Archaeology between 1910 and 1913, he spent a good deal of his leisure time in the company of another amateur archaeologist, his first cousin, Boyle Somerville. Windle was also a friend of the Professor of Celtic Archaeology at UCD, Robert Alexander Stewart Macalister, who was the author of *Studies in Irish Epigraphy* and *Corpus Inscriptionum Insularum*. Both Macalister and Windle were close friends of Douglas Hyde.[140] With the approval of Macalister, Windle believed that collecting 'endangered' ogham stones from the surrounding region was best professional practice. He merely wished to preserve material culture which was in danger of being damaged or destroyed. Macalister supported Windle's plans to build a fine collection of artefacts in the college, but there were other scholars who wished to conserve material culture in the place where it had stood for thousands of years. The idea of destroying a rath to 'rescue' ogham stones was not to their liking. Members of the Gaelic League were to the fore in upholding that school of thought. Little did Windle realise the public controversy his well-intentioned actions of transporting 'endangered' ogham stones to UCC would cause at a local and national level in autumn 1913.

The rath of Knock-shan-a-wee (meaning Old Yellow Hill) is situated on the summit of a hill in the parish of Aglish, three miles from Crookstown, County Cork. The name may be a contraction from *Cnoc*

Sean Mnaoi or Hill of the Old Women. The site, which was surrounded by a *fosse*, or trench, about 20 feet deep and 50 feet wide, was first excavated in September 1910 by two local archaeologists, Cremin and Murphy. The inner rampart was connected to the mound by two short ditches running north and south. The summit of the mound from crest to crest was about 100 feet. The area covered by the structure was 300 square feet. There were also traces of a further rampart. The chamber was about 9 feet square by 7 feet high. The roofing flags were 9 feet and about 18 inches wide. The supporting pillars were 7 feet high by 12 inches wide and 9 inches thick. Dr Phillip G. Lee visited the site with Murphy after Cremin had done his initial work. He found it hard to get rubbings of the ogham stones, noting that the characters were cut in a finer and more careful manner on the upright stone. The carvings were on the local sandstone of the district. Lee speculated that the builders may have used the ogham stones 'as readily shaped for their purpose' or, on the other hand, 'we may have here a real cemetery enclosure'. He felt that further excavation might show that 'the rath to be in itself a cemetery proper, and used for a similar purpose as were the chambered cairns on Slieve-na-Calliaghe and at Brugh-na-Boinne'.[141] On 27 November, in a letter to the *Cork Examiner*, Cremin explained that he had, following his discovery of the site, visited the rath a number of times with Patrick Murphy. He had brought the site to the attention of the relevant committee of Cork County Council who considered it worthy of being preserved. The secretary of the county council, who attended that meeting, promised to have a notice put on the site. 'Such a notice was never put there as far as I am aware or anywhere else,' Cremin wrote, and again: 'That such an Ogham chamber existed in the rath no one can deny, be its dimensions what they may; the stones now at the College, both roofing and upright, can be measured by anyone so minded.' The entrance had been made by C. O'Connor, as no other entrance could be found at the side. Cremin described how the rath had suffered from the many openings and closings. He described that what had once been a flagstone floor was now covered by a foot of earth. The entrances from that area to other parts of the rath had become inaccessible since Cremin's first visit.[142]

Windle has only sketchily laid out in his diary the sequence of events leading to the controversy over his removal of six ogham stones from the rath described above.[143] On 11 October 1913, he wrote: 'fine all day. off at 9 am to [?] and M. Murphy to Knockshanawee and there found 6 oghams which I can have for College – lunched with Fr Coakley [curate, Farran] and home by 6 p.m. cold steadily getting worse.' [Coakley, too, had been at the site.] The first Professor of Celtic at Oxford, Sir John Rhuys (more commonly spelled Rhys) was also present as was Macalister.

Locals Michael Murphy and Rev. M.J. Murphy were also in the party. They were joined by Mr Cremin. On Monday the 13th, Windle returned to the site with Coakley, Rhuys and Macalister.[144] He was 'not home until 6.p.m'.[145] Windle and Professor Alexander set out by car on 18 October for the site 'picking up Fr Corkery, a most admirable man, on the way'. His diary also recorded: 'We got the oghams loaded on to carts and away by 12.15 and were bowling home when the left front spring broke.' Windle 'had to risk it and crawled home in safety'. He noted: 'Stones arrived 6.30 p.m. safely.' On 23 October 1913, he spent 'all morning getting oghams into hall.'[146]

Windle left for London on 31 October. He parted with Edith at Cardiff and went on to Wolverhampton to deliver to an audience of 1,200 people his presidential address to the Literary and Scientific Society. He then took 'a splendid train' to Plymouth where he stayed with his friend the bishop. Windle lectured in Penzance 'to a packed audience' on 'Megaliths.' He took the train to Birmingham and gave the same lecture to another large audience in the Drill Hall. He returned with Edith on 9 November, experiencing a 'fairly rough passage, more pitching than rolling and an hour late . . . got 10 Mass at Saint Peter and Pauls and home'. Having enjoyed public acclaim at each of his lectures on his English tour, Windle woke up the next morning to find himself in the eye of a very public storm. The removal of the oghham stones from the rath was denounced in the press. William O'Brien's *Free Press*, once a staunch supporter of Windle, mounted a vigorous and robust campaign against the removal of the stones. The Gaelic League joined in, sending a delegation to petition Cork County Council.[147] Windle, in a number of diary entries, displayed shock, hurt and outrage at the widespread criticisms of his actions. On Monday 10 November 1913, he wrote: 'Disgraceful attacks in *Free Press* as to which I wrote to William O'Brien – But the man is swollen with vanity and lives in a circle of adoring (and paid) parasites – Hopeless state of affairs.' The following day, he wrote: 'Most impudent letter from William O'Brien,' noting that there had been further attacks in the *Free Press*. A friend advised him to 'take no notice' of O'Brien's article. The next day, 12 November, Windle spent the whole morning with M. Murphy, solicitor, and the officers of the college over the 'wretched Free Press' which 'is the worst thing I have yet come across. They know all about the circumstances and deliberately want to work up a scandal – lying rogues. It seems *Free Press* has about 1,000 subscribers and is dying – Decided that I was to say nothing and Dr Cohalan, whom I saw, was to state facts plainly in *all* the papers and leave it there.' On the 13th, he wrote: 'Cohalan's letter seems to have settled things.' But that was not the case. The O'Growney branch of the Gaelic League passed a resolution of condemnation and sent a deputation to 'stir up' the county council.[148] 'This is indeed a God forsaken country,' he wrote on the 14th. Windle wrote on 15 November that he had 'wasted a whole morning over this damnable Gaelic League worrying with M. Murphy. A few irresponsible people in this God forsaken country owing to total lack of healthy public opinion can do anything they like.' Arthur Griffith's newspaper, *Sinn Féin*, joined the attack. On 17 November, Windle wrote: 'M. Murphy in morning and he subsequently saw Crosbies [*Cork Examiner*] and they will do anything they can to stop this nonsense.'[149] On 20 November, Macalister published a long letter in the *Cork Examiner*, responding to the Gaelic League and to 'a paragraph full of misstatements in *Sinn Féin*'. He did not know what had gone before in terms of public comment in Cork 'though I can guess something of it; and I can see that the whole agitation rests on a complete ignorance of the true facts of the case, which I ask your courtesy to put before your reader.'[150] He had 'greater experience in deciphering Ogham monuments than any other man in Ireland'. There were, he wrote, nearly 300 monuments of that kind in the country and he had personally examined and copied all of those except about a dozen which he had not as yet visited. He had examined all the County Cork examples but two, and had discovered eight of them, besides having been the first to obtain satisfactory copies of a number of others. Macalister greatly disliked talking like that about himself but it was necessary to demonstrate that he was an authority on ogham decipherment which came from long practice. He had also examined scores of souterrains. He was able, based on his wide professional experience, to speak with authority about that particular cave.[151] He had never examined oghams under more adverse conditions than when he had visited the cave in April 1913. He said that his description had been reproduced in an article by his friend, Dr Lee, in the *Journal of the Cork Archaeological Society*. The illustrations clearly showed how difficult it was to read the stones in their fixed positions, he wrote, and in those circumstances, 'we [Windle and himself] decided that the stones must be removed from the cave'.[152] Macalister added: 'No one regrets more than I do that the cave should require to be dismantled, but there are hundreds of such caves in the country, and we can endure the loss of one of them if we can thereby obtain accurate copies of the oldest existing monuments of the Irish language . . . To smash up such a cave for road-metal or roofing stone would be an outrage; to remove the inscription for philosophical purposes is a scientific necessity. In the process of opening the cave three new inscriptions, the existence of which could never have been suspected, were unearthed, all of which add considerably to our knowledge of early forms of the Irish language.' Macalister said it would be an act of folly to bury them again or leave them for 'any bodoch who wanted to dig them up to roof a pigsty with'. Therefore, there was no alternative but to bring them to a public place where they could be seen by everyone.[153] Macalister believed that Windle deserved the thanks of every Corkman for developing a national collection of antiquities in UCC which was open to everyone to see and to study. He felt that there was nobody foolish enough to believe that Sir John Rhuys and himself had taken away some of the stones. He gave an assurance that all were still in Cork. Macalister felt that it was necessary for the sake of scholarship to put a stop to the 'absurd tales' circulating in Cork.[154]

Professor Eoin MacNeill, Macalister's colleague in UCD, wrote to the *Cork Examiner* on 19 November in support of Windle and Macalister. He argued that the debate on the question of the removal of the ogham stones was a 'healthy symptom – a sign that something like a strong sentiment is at last beginning to take root in the country, in favour of the preservation of the precious monuments of our national past'. He concluded by suggesting that it was 'a splendid thing to see public opinion stirring, even in a small beginning, to preserve sacredly the relics of our national past; and we may rest secure that those who have protested against the removal of ogham stones . . . will be generous and enlightened enough to perceive that their aim, and the aim of Windle and Macalister, are identical and that in the special case of ogham inscriptions these men have been doing the very thing that true reverence for antiquity demands.'[155]

Two prominent nationalists, brothers Seán and Patrick Sarsfield (P.S.) Ó hÉigeartaigh, strongly supported the other side of the argument.[156] Ó hÉigeartaigh, who dated his letter the 20th and gave his address as Cobh, wrote stingingly in the *Cork Examiner* on 22 November that the ogham stones should have been left in place as those stones were in a definite location and in a definite relation with other monuments of antiquity. He wanted ancient monuments that had 'escaped the ignorant and the English' to be left *in situ*. The function of professors was to remove ignorance, he wrote, but they themselves were now 'destroying an ancient rath'. He asked: 'Were the Oghams made for the rath or was the rath made for the oghams?' adding: 'Any of these little things may come to have an immense significance when some future generation tries to stamp finality upon the origin and purpose of the oghams and raths. And a true scientific spirit would have remembered this, and not committed the atrocious vandalism. An ogham in University College is merely an inscribed stone, but an ogham in a rath may be an illuminatory document on early Irish mentality . . . The proper place for ogham stones is where the builders placed them; they knew what they were about, and we do not.'[157]

On 21 November, Windle wrote: 'Saw M. Murphy about correspondence – Home very tired after bad night and not sleeping again.' Windle replied to Ó hÉagartaigh in the *Cork Examiner* on the 22nd, agreeing with the contribution by Macalister and Michael Murphy.[158] Fr C. Coakley CC, Farran, County Cork, wrote a letter on the 22nd refuting the arguments in favour of leaving the location intact and the stones *in situ*. He had been present at the excavation on 11 October, together with Windle, Professor Stewart Macalister, Sir John Rhuys and Michael Murphy. He was also there on the 13th. He helped Windle and Professor Alexander on the 18th when the stones were removed to UCC.[159] On 25 November, Windle wrote: 'Long letter Fr Coakley and an excellent one – a scurrilous attack by one of the Hegartys which roused me to reply but advised not . . . a disaster I think rightly. This creature is a minor post office clerk who bosses what passes for Gaelic League in this district – God help us what a country.'[160] The controversy, which eventually faded away, scarred Windle, an intensely private man, and left him in an unsettled frame of mind.

Taken together, the ogham stones and de Valera episodes reflected the emergence of a more assertive nationalism in the region. A worryingly large number of members of the Academic Council and the governing body had differed with, and defied, Windle over the de Valera vote. Did that indicate a mere threat to his authority and leadership on academic grounds and the end of his honeymoon period in the college? That was a partial explanation. But another reason for such a defiance of presidential authority was linked, in part, to a growing sympathy for a more radical strand of cultural nationalism within UCC itself. The de Valera episode was directly connected to the ogham stone controversy, although Windle himself may not have connected both in his own mind. At one level, the ogham stone controversy displayed the extent to which the radical, dissident Gaelic League members in the south were prepared to challenge the Windle *doxa* on best practice in archaeology. Windle was inclined to be dismissive of the challenge, surrounded as he was by the archaeological establishment of his day. Who was a mere 'minor post office clerk' to challenge the president of UCC? What Windle did not know was that that post office clerk would go on to become a senior civil servant in an independent Ireland and that another clerk in the post office, Michael Collins, would help to bring a new independent Irish state into being in 1922. Windle, an establishment insider, was a mere spectator to the radical nationalist circle of power which was emerging, albeit in inchoate form, in 1913.

CHAPTER 4

The Catholic Church and
the Honan Bequest

Windle came to Cork with the ambition to create equal education for Catholics at third level. As a Catholic convert in Birmingham, he had personal experience of religious prejudice in his professional life. He had reached a certain height in the hierarchy of that university but felt he hit the glass ceiling for Catholics in British higher education. This was part of the reason for his leaving for a post where he thought that he could make a difference. Windle came to a country where Protestants were over-represented in the upper echelons of business, the professions, the administration, the police and the army. There were subtle and not-so-subtle barriers preventing Catholic upward mobility in different sectors in the country.[1] The British government had passed the Queen's Colleges (Ireland) Act in 1845 which set up the Queen's Colleges of Belfast, Cork and Galway to 'afford a university education to members of all religious denominations' in the country. However, that did not come to pass. Protestant ascendancy in Ireland was partially perpetuated and reinforced by the policy of the Irish Catholic bishops to stop members of their Church from going to the 'Godless Colleges', being – unlike Trinity College Dublin – not permitted to teach theology. The three colleges were incorporated on 30 December 1845 and opened in 1849. Queen's College, Cork received its first students (115) on 7 November 1849. The Queen's University of Ireland was established by royal charter on 3 September 1850 as the degree-awarding body.

Dating from the Synod of Thurles in 1850, the bishops had, by a narrow majority, forbidden Catholics attending the new colleges. Their words at the time were that the colleges were: '. . . an evil of a formidable kind against which it is our imperative duty to warn you with all the energy of our zeal and all the weight of our authority. In pointing out the dangers of such a system we only repeat the instructions that have been

111

given to us by the Vicar of Jesus Christ . . . [who] has pronounced this system of education to be fraught with "grievous and intrinsic dangers" to faith and morals . . . The successor of Peter has pronounced his final judgement on the subject. All controversy is now at an end – the judge has spoken – the question is decided.'[2] Pope Pius IX, in an official condemnation, said the three colleges of Belfast, Galway and Cork were 'detrimental to religion'.

The 'Godless Colleges' were perceived to be under the control of Dublin-Castle-appointed Protestant staff. Although necessity had forced many Catholics in Munster to ignore the rescript and register for courses at QCC, Windle found upon his arrival in Cork in 1904 that the official Church policy remained consistent with the pronouncement of the Synod of Thurles and the subsequent papal condemnation. The Bishop of Cork, Thomas Alphonsus O'Callaghan, was stand-offish with the new QCC president during those early years. Although obliged to be officially cool towards him and his institution, the bishop quickly recognised the new president to be an ally. But the Catholic Church, caught in the time warp of the Synod of Thurles, was compelled to place a barrier before any Catholic wishing to study at the college.

In late summer 1908, Fr William Delany SJ, University College Dublin, sent a report to the Holy See pointing out the advantages for Catholics of the new legislation. The new scheme was 'the best for Catholic interests'. It avoided a common university in which Catholics and Protestants would be joined together 'and the Catholic students would be enticed to attend the lectures of the Trinity professors, many of whom are known to be agnostics'. In the new university, he added, the three constituent colleges were to be controlled by a body of thirty-five to thirty-six members, twenty-eight of whom were to be Catholic, including the archbishops of Dublin and Tuam, a Limerick priest, Fr Andrew Murphy, and himself. There were eight Protestants but nearly all were friendly to Catholic education.[3] There was a similarly favourable arrangement for Catholics on the respective governing bodies of the three constituent colleges.

As final agreement neared on the Irish university question, Windle's diary entry on 6 June 1908 showed that he had won over the Bishop of Cork to the side of the college: 'Long talk with Fr Roche who confirms the statement that Bishop has acceptance of the College in his pocket and will use it if the Bill fails. This is great intelligence. He thinks everything would go to smash if I left, for the Bishop has only gone this length on my account.' On 22 June 1908, Windle dined in London with his friend, Gasquet: 'Told him of Bishop of Cork; he capped the story by telling me he had settled things with the Pope before the Bishop came.

Had dined and spent afternoon with the Bishop, and put him on proper lines. The Bishop said he could not stand having to treat me as had to.'[4]

However, even before the change in Church policy on the universities, Bishop O'Callaghan proved within permitted limits to be supportive of the new QCC president. From the time of his arrival in Cork, Windle attempted to build bridges with the bishops, clergy and nuns in the city and in the Munster region. He was soon on very friendly terms with Denis Kelly, the Bishop of Ross – an adjacent diocese in west Cork. The latter became one of his closest friends in the Irish hierarchy and the person on whom he most relied to make sense of the changing face of Irish Catholicism. Windle made it a practice to make contact with the principals of schools in the city to encourage enrolment in his college. For example, a diary entry for 16 January 1905 read: 'Fr O'Sullivan called. Nice old man. Thinks everyone would like to utilize Q.C. more and that Episcopacy made error in very beginning in not taking over the thing.'[5] Windle was invited to go on a committee for organising a bazaar to wipe off 'debt on Brother Burke's college Christian Bros., Burke a fine man. Consented.'[6] On 11 February 1905, he wrote: 'Fr Augustine (O.S.F.C.) called. Very interesting man, great Gaelic Leaguer and Irish Scholar. Down to meet Douglas Hyde & various Leaguers there. Up to College & after he had some lunch to see the 2nd half of the Ireland v. England Match. Ireland triumphantly victorious.'[7] On 1 March, he wrote: 'To see Sr M. Gertrude, a remarkable nun at St Mary of Isles, remembered famine and had seen a man die with grass in his mouth of starvation with two children dead in hut close by. Terrible tales of souperism.'[8] On 6 March, he wrote: 'Bishop's Pastoral in Papers. Called on Protestant Bishop, nice old man, solicitous about College. News of Wyndham's resignation, great blow – wrote to him. To dine with Dr P.T.O'S. Pleasant dinner. Took in Mrs O'S. Also there Canon Hegarty, delightful man. Fr O'S. (O.S.A.), Fr T. Barrett, Fraser, Crichtons.'[9] Windle made his way with ease in the local Catholic clerical world. He was readily accepted and his sincerity recognised. An example of this is provided in a letter on 20 October 1905 from the novelist, Canon Patrick Augustine Sheehan, from Doneraile: 'I do most sincerely hope that you will never allow yourself to feel the slightest depression or uneasiness about your work. Personally, you have the goodwill and esteem of everyone, clerical and lay, in Ireland; and you have leaped, at one bound, into a position never reached by any of your predecessors, not even Dr Sullivan. I think you are destined to accomplish incalculable good for the young men of Ireland. The field is wide, and alas! untilled as yet. And you commence with all the sympathies of the country on your side. At least, so I judge by everything I have heard, and by everything the Press reports.'[10] He encouraged Windle to visit him: 'But I should like you to understand that at all times I shall be most happy to see you here. There are many subjects haunting my mind, on which I have never had an opportunity of exchanging an idea with a sympathetic mind. And, therefore, if you could cycle down here in an informal manner, and accept our rural hospitality from time to time, you could considerably brighten our existence.'[11]

At the end of 1905, Bishop O'Callaghan gave his permission for the formation of a Catholic Students' Association at the college. He appointed two Catholic priests as chaplains. That was, according to Windle's biographer, 'a most consoling piece of news for Dr Windle.' It was a significant and historical breakthrough. The thaw had begun. But he missed his close friends in England. On 22 December 1905, he wrote to John Humphreys: 'I shall never have another friend as you are, and I am sure our friendship will last through this life, and I hope into the next. I never omit to pray for you every night of my life, and to hope that some day we may see eye to eye in the most important thing in the world.'[12]

Writing to Douglas Hyde on 12 April 1906, he said '. . . and if we could overcome the opposition of the Church we might do anything here [reference to Irish in curriculum] in that direction. I am not without hopes that we may do even that for great things are afloat and I have a splendid committee of laymen working here, as fine a committee as man could wish, and their spirit is certainly rising.'[13]

In autumn 1906, the bishop gave permission for the students of the college to attend a retreat given by a Jesuit, Fr Fegan. Windle's biographer wrote: 'No greater gesture of friendliness and sympathy with his work could have been given by the Bishop than permission to the students to follow the Spiritual Exercises of St Ignatius as a corporate body.' Windle's friend, Fr O'Sullivan, and a group of students greeted the retreat master in the president's house. Sr Monica wrote: 'Dr Windle and many of the professors took the opportunity of refreshing their spiritual life, at the same time identifying themselves with a cause so dear to their hearts, the moral and spiritual education of the undergraduates.'[14] On 4 February 1907, his biographer points out that Windle 'continued to watch over the Students' Union with a paternal interest, noting with great satisfaction that Fr O'Sullivan gave an excellent and eloquent sermon on February 15th and that Fr Gerard, S.J., addressed the Union on the 27th.'[15] In November 1907 the president of the college arranged a triduum for the students. That became an established annual event. Fr Robert Kane SJ was invited to preach in the college.[16]

Windle recorded in his diary on 9 June 1908: 'Meeting of Temporary Governing Body of the College to consider Charter. Wonderful day in the history of the College and most amicable. I put down the names of those here, it was so remarkable. Archbishop of Cashel, Bishop of Cork, Bishop C. Cloyne and Ross (Protestant Bishop), Dr Barrett, Mr Butler, M. (Christian Brothers), C. (Presentation Brother), Lord Mayor, Chairman County Council, Cork, Maurice Healy, Stanley Harrington, Hill, Dale, Townshend, M. Murphy, Butler, Hartog, Bergin, Corby, Pearson.'[17] The new act put an end to the official 'frigidity' of the relationship between Windle and the hierarchy of the Munster Province. Windle, using his considerable influence at the Holy See, helped in the wake of the NUI settlement in 1908 to hasten the decision to lift the ban. The new chancellor of the National University of Ireland was Archbishop William Walsh of Dublin.

Professor John A. Murphy, in his wide-ranging history of the college, argues that the Catholicising process in the college, associated with Windle's two successors, 'was already underway during Windle's presidency'.[18] This linear historical construct has its intellectual attractions. But, in our view, it is reductionist and fails to come to terms with the complex and evolving nature of Irish society in the first two decades of the twentieth century. Windle sought to break down barriers and literally build bridges and open up the front gates to Catholics. The hierarchy's confidence grew as they saw the life of the college reflect a Catholic ethos – an ethos that was not being developed to the exclusion of Protestants.

If the college were to grow from a student body of about 251 in 1904/5, logically Catholics would have to enrol in far greater numbers. That is what happened. In 1904/5, there were 168 Catholic students, 66 Church of Ireland and England, 5 Presbyterians, 9 Wesleyans and 3 other denominations [possibly Jewish]. In 1905/6, there were 175 Catholics, 55 Church of Ireland and England, 4 Presbyterians, 11 Wesleyans and 1 'other', probably Jewish. The total number of students was 246. The numbers of Catholics had increased to 179 in 1906/7. There were 62 Church of Ireland and England, 6 Presbyterians, 12 Wesleyans and 2 other denominations, for a student body of 261. In 1908/9, the total student body had risen to 264. There were 170 Catholics, 74 Church of Ireland and England, 3 Presbyterians, 16 Wesleyans and 1 other denomination.[19]

St Anthony's Hall

Since his arrival in Ireland in 1904, Windle had made the opening of a Catholic male hall of residence a priority, as a very obvious way to attract greater numbers of Catholics to study at the college. With the help and support of his Franciscan friend, Fr Cornelius Francis Maher of the Liberty Street Friary, that became a reality. The Province of the Irish Franciscans had sought to establish a house of studies in Ireland in the first decade of the twentieth century. The Archbishop of Dublin, William

Walsh, turned down the Franciscan request to open such a residence in his archdiocese. One of his reasons for refusal was that the friars were proposing to wear their habits in public. That was, he felt, a violation of the civil law and a departure from established religious practice.

The Franciscans next approached Bishop O'Callaghan. The latter gave permission in 1906 for the building of a house of studies in the city on condition that the order would not build a public church. A suitable site was not found. In 1908 the Franciscan provincial, Fr Benignus Gannon, received a further instruction from his superiors to open a house of studies in Ireland.[20] Cork was again chosen to be the site. The order wanted all its clerics to graduate from UCC. Windle suggested that the Franciscans might consider buying the now disused Church of Ireland hall of residence, Berkeley Hall.[21]

Berkeley Hall had been designed around 1860 as a residential hall for the Church of Ireland. William Bence-Jones had commissioned the building and the architect was James St Aubyn. Built at Fernhurst Avenue, its completion had been delayed by labour problems. Depleted funding meant that the finished hall had not lived up to the original expectations, and never really succeeded as a hall of residence.[22] In 1908, the Franciscans discovered that the new owner of the property was a builder and the Lord Mayor of Cork, Thomas Donovan. On 24 November 1908, Windle wrote to Maher: 'I have seen Tom Donovan and told him I should not buy Berkeley Hall. I also strongly advised him to sell to you and he is since writing to you. Of course you have now got to agree on a price and that won't be an easy job. But I hope it will be made easier by my interview with him. I trust you will be able to bring the negotiations to a suitable end.'[23]

On 16 December 1908, Windle received the good news that the Franciscans had bought the premises.[24] After all the legal procedures were undertaken, the hall became the property of the order on 11 January 1909. The Franciscans spent a further £1,673 on furniture and fittings. Windle wrote on 16 January to Fr Francis Maher, suggesting that the hall be renamed St Anthony's Hall; the order readily agreed.[25] Berkeley Hall, derelict when the Franciscans took over, was quickly refurbished by a local builder, John Delaney, working under the direction of the architect J.F. McMullen. While the friars felt that the property and refurbishing were dear at £6,000, there was a general feeling of satisfaction that a once Protestant hall of residence was about to become a Catholic one.[26]

On 16 February 1909, Windle held an 'at home' for the UCC governing body. The inauguration of St Anthony's Hall took place the following day. Mass was celebrated in the chapel attached to the hall by the Archbishop of Cashel, Thomas Fennelly. On 18 February, the Franciscan provincial said Mass. Windle's biographer commented: 'the future looked bright with promise, and Windle's medieval tastes must have found solace in the anticipation of the might-be.'[27]

St Anthony's Hall was officially opened on 6 October 1909. Those present included the Franciscan provincial, the Lord Mayor of Cork, Councillor Thomas Donovan, Alderman Peter Sheridan, Maurice Healy MP, David Fleming, former vicar general, Osmund Cooney, the English provincial, Thomas A. Fitzgerald OFM., Edward B. Fitzmaurice OFM, Philip D. Kehoe OFM and Fr Matthew OFM Cap. Numerous other clergy and public figures were also present, as was Fr Francis Maher OFM.[28]

In his speech, the Franciscan provincial gave credit to Windle and the Archbishop of Cashel for encouraging his order to take the initiative. Originally, he explained, the hall was to serve as a residence for Franciscans attending the college but under the guidance of Windle and the Archbishop of Cashel, the order decided to open it up to lay students. Windle, in his speech, said that the opening was a matter of primary importance for UCC and for the Catholic community of Munster. The hall was one of many means by which the college would attract more students to UCC, he said. Windle also emphasised the importance of a residence for the social formation of Catholic students. Praising the settlement of the university question in 1908, the president 'considered it bad policy to so fashion their university as to drive away from it any Irish man or woman and still more any Irish Catholic man or woman'. Windle expressed his gratitude to the Franciscans and hoped for the success of St Anthony's Hall.[29]

A letter from the cardinal secretary of state, Merry del Val, dated 16 September 1909, was read to the congregation: 'I gladly hasten to make known to you that the very pleasing news has reached His Holiness that the school for young Franciscans, and the hostel for Catholic students recently acquired by you, will be solemnly opened in October. The Supreme Pontiff is confident that the best and highest results will be achieved by this, your enterprise, and with that hope in view he is graciously pleased to impart the Apostolic Blessing.'[30]

Bishop O'Callaghan, in the absence of the Archbishop of Cashel, Thomas Fennelly, officiated at those ceremonies. The secretary of the college, H.C. Clifton, read a letter of congratulation from the staff and from his friends. An article in *The Tablet*, in mid-October 1909, captures the mood and the historical importance of the occasion. The writer celebrated the importance of the 1908 act:

> Dr Windle, the President of University College, was naturally anxious
> as an Irishman and a Catholic that the fullest use should be made by
> his Catholic countrymen of the College over which he presides. But

his hands were tied. The College could set up no hostel of its own with opportunities for the practice of religion such as Catholics would desire . . . [The opening of a] Catholic house of studies in connexion with what used to be regarded as one of the 'Godless Colleges' was an event of prime importance in the history of Catholic education in Munster. For it marks a departure which, it is hoped, is but a beginning of similar efforts on the part of Catholics in response to whose demands for a National University the present settlement has been enacted. [Windle's papal knighthood] is as well deserved as the moment of its giving is timely. It comes when for the first time the name of a Catholic priest appears amongst those of the Deans of Residence in Cork, and when a Catholic hall opens in connexion with University College, over which a man of acknowledged eminence and a Catholic presides. So far, then, as the province of Munster is concerned, the new Act is started on its way under the happiest auspices, and we can heartily join in wishing Hall, College, and President *Ad multos annos.*[31]

Pope Pius X made Windle a Knight of St Gregory in 1909 in recognition of his zeal for Catholic truth and his labours for the higher education of Catholic youth. The citation also contained 'very complimentary allusions' to his work for Queen's College, Cork.[32] Bishop O'Callaghan conferred the honour in a ceremony – the same day as the opening of St Anthony's Hall – stressing that the president had opened the way for Catholics to participate in third-level education.[33] Archbishop William Walsh wrote to him on 16 July: 'I must begin by congratulating you on the well-deserved honour you have received from the Holy See. I only wish that such Knighthoods were always as well deserved, as nobly earned.'[34]

Fr Francis Maher had been told on 7 October 1910 that the UCC governing body had 'agreed to recognise St Anthony's Hall as a licensed hostel and to appoint you as Dean of Residence'.[35] In reply to a note of condolence from Fr Maher on the death of his mother [12 February 1910], Windle wrote: 'I am not happy in my mind about St Anthony's Hall. This is strictly *entre nous.*'[36] The hall had its limitations; it did not provide accommodation for a sufficient number of lay students, nor was it large enough to cope with the needs of the student body. But, even if not ideal, Windle recognised the importance of the precedent that had been set. For the first time in the history of the college, on 15 November 1910, a votive Mass of the Holy Ghost was celebrated in St Anthony's Hall. This became popularly known as the Red Mass because of the colour of the vestments worn; it became an annual event. An eminent guest preacher was asked to give the sermon. In 1911, the 'Red Mass' was again celebrated in the same small chapel.

But in 1912, the Red Mass had to be moved to SS Peter and Paul's church, in the centre of Cork. The *Cork Examiner*, on 9 November 1912, quoted the Bishop of Ross, Denis Kelly – who became Windle's closest friend in the hierarchy – as saying that the National University and its colleges were the seed-bed and nursery of the spirit of Gaelic and Catholic Ireland. The paper said that the students in Cork were leaving nothing undone to make the occasion a success, an occasion which is both a celebration and 'a protest against the false notion that there is any opposition between true science and the religion of Jesus Christ'. The *Cork Examiner* reported on 12 November that the success of the occasion was largely due to the students of the college who, from the very start, 'entered whole-heartedly into the occasion. Nor were young lady students behind in their interest in it.'[37]

But this general policy, while wholeheartedly welcomed in Catholic circles, provoked suspicion in Protestant circles. Windle wrote on 24 March 1912 to the chancellor of the National University of Ireland, William Walsh, thanking him for the copy of his timely pamphlet on the Quantavis: 'It will do much good amongst reasonable men but how many of the Protestants in Ireland are not! I am often horrified at the malignity of some of them towards myself and this college. Me they will never forgive because I abandoned the fields of Protestantism for the church pastures, as many of them – how ludicrous a supposition – suppose for the sake of gain, though as a matter of fact I do not doubt that I should have been far better off in this world had I remained a Nothingarian as I was. But it is too bad that they should crab the College.'[38] Windle then added the following statement, understandable perhaps in the context in which it was written: 'The fact is that many of them [Protestants] would not let a Catholic be anything more than a hewer of wood if they could help it. On the other side we are attacked by the Agnostic band . . .'

Windle changed to the subject of Trinity College at the end of his letter: 'May I again say that I am positively aghast at the way in which Catholics & good ones at that are wholesale sending their children to Trinity as if there was no sort of reason why they should not do so. This is a terrible blow to our University & really it seems as if it were hardly worth the trouble of creating it if T.C.D. is available for any Catholic who likes to go there.'[39]

When facing the possible closure of St Anthony's Hall, Windle wrote to the Irish hierarchy sometime in 1912 that there was unqualified admiration at the success of the residence. County councils awarding scholarships, he wrote, had expressed a desire that the recipients should live in the hostel. Every room was taken and filled with a lay student:

His Lordship the Bishop of Cork has allowed students, professors and their families and in fact the personnel of the College to fulfil their obligations of Mass there on Sunday and to make their Easter Communion there. There is a daily Mass at 8.30 during term and the chapel is open all and every day for visits by the students who can go to confession there. As a regular attendant myself I can vouch for the good attendance of the students, for the frequentation of the sacraments and for the excellent order and conduct observed. It is well known that the College cannot itself set up a chapel or take any cognisance of religion. The chapel of St Anthony's Hall serves as a College Chapel in every way and the grounds of the hall, being next door to the college with a direct gate of entry between the two; the chapel though small is well adapted for the purpose. It is a centre of Catholic work for the students, lectures on Catholic subjects being given there from time to time and other religious observances taking place in connection with it. I may mention that the sermon especially intended for students every Sunday morning at Mass alone would make it worthwhile to have such a chapel and that at daily Mass, said at 8.30, there are always a few students as well as others connected with the college. I can testify to this from my own personal observation.[40]

The *Tablet* carried an informative article on the religious practices at the college. It made reference to the recent lectures delivered by Paschal Robinson, an Irish-American Franciscan historian, a high point in the short history of St Anthony's Hall. The Cardinal Archbishop of Armagh, Michael Logue, had spoken of the necessity to introduce a Christian element into the working of the NUI colleges. The writer concluded: 'the process of suiting the institution to its religious environment has been carried on with considerable success.'[41] With reference to Cork, it was noted that the Red Mass, or votive Mass of the Holy Ghost, had been celebrated for two years to inaugurate the new academic year. The *Tablet* article referred to the confraternity for male students that met in St Marie's of the Isle. The chapel at St Anthony's had become too small for the numbers. The lectures were given by different preachers and were 'so designed as to be of special interest to young men and of special service to them on their entry on the independent life of manhood'.[42] During Lent, there was a triduum with morning and evening exercises. It ended with a general communion by special permission of the bishop, serving as Easter communion for students and staff. There was always a special priest, who was assisted by the chaplain, for the triduum. The *Tablet* recorded: 'Very large numbers of both students and staff attend these exercises and participate in the General Communion which terminates them.'[43]

At UCC, women students also had a woman professor, Mary Ryan, who acted as officer of residence. They had their own sodality and special chaplain provided by the bishop. *The Tablet* article added: 'They, therefore, enjoy all the advantages which can be wished for.' The article concluded: 'great advances have been made in Cork, at any rate, in the direction desired by his Eminence [Cardinal Logue].'[44]

The combination of the change of provincial in Ireland and of a new father general in Rome resulted in the closure of St Anthony's Hall. The precipitous withdrawal of the friars from St Anthony's Hall was due mainly to a complex dispute within the Franciscan order regarding the university education of their seminarians. The new father general was opposed 'to students being sent to a University College even such as Cork, in a Catholic city'.[45] Fr Bartholomew Egan strains to be objective when he writes of the forced departure of the friars from St Anthony's Hall to Ennis in County Clare: 'That such a Minister General should object to Irish Franciscan clerics attending a university approved by the Hierarchy for *all* Catholics, and whose President was himself a fervent tertiary of St Francis, is surprising. This was all the more astonishing when one recalls that amongst the chief architects of the new system of higher education now acceptable to the Irish Hierarchy, were John Dillon, M.P., brother of the Irish Provincial, and the Archbishop of Dublin, Dr Walsh, who became the first Chancellor of the New National University of Ireland'.[46] Egan also refers to Windle's very low opinion of the new Franciscan provincial, Fr Nicholas Dillon, who had been a lawyer and a late vocation. Windle, according to Egan, was not impressed either with his knowledge of theology or canon law. With regard to his skill or ability in administration, Egan writes damningly, 'he was quite incapable of making a balanced judgement'.

Windle was 'wild' at the sudden reversal of Franciscan policy. He appealed to Rome, where influential friends, such as Gasquet, were mobilised on behalf of a lost cause. The initiatives had the major effect of preventing Dillon being able to dispose of St Anthony's Hall without first consulting Windle.[47] Bishop O'Callaghan of Cork was petitioned by Irish Franciscans in disagreement with their new provincial's decision to sell the property as instructed, in turn, by his superiors in Rome. A Franciscan Latin scholar, Fr Gregory Cleary, was requested on 10 October 1912 to draft a memorandum to be sent by Windle to the Holy Father. Windle also sent a memorandum to the bishops of Munster, sketching out his views on the sad affair. He sought their active support to keep the hall of residence open for Catholic students.[48] Windle produced another strong argument for the bishops of the region: 'Further, any such abandonment of a scheme inaugurated with so much *éclat* and commenced with the direct blessing of the Holy Father himself would lay us open to the taunt that we were no better able to carry on a hostel for Catholic students than the Protestants had been for the adherents of their denomination for whom the Hall (as Berkeley Hall) was originally built.'[49] Windle concluded his argument with a reference to UCC being a college for the region of Munster. He believed that 'at least to some extent the future of Catholicity in the South of Ireland and, may I add elsewhere, is bound up with its success and more especially with the manner in which it is carried on from a religious point of view'. Windle stated further that from the students of the college 'will come in the future the leading professional and even business men of Munster, together with the future Members of Parliament and of the County Councils, and how much will depend on these men I need not linger to point out'. UCC students would go out to all quarters of the world 'either to be a credit and a support or the reverse to their religion'. He appealed to the bishops 'for advice and assistance in a matter so gravely affecting the interest of our religion'.[50] But despite his efforts which extended into 1913, Windle did not succeed in keeping St Anthony's Hall open.

Inter-faith Polemics

Windle's Catholicism provoked adverse criticism on a number of occasions from Protestant clergymen. Invited to lecture in Limerick in St Michael's Temperance Hall in January 1911, he chose as his subject 'The Life and Death of Blessed Father [John] Wall, O.S.F.; Martyred 1679'.[51] Windle spoke of penal times and the penal laws. There were many relics still in existence of that terrible period, and there were still to be seen numerous penal altars about the country on which their Catholic priests celebrated Mass while at the same time carrying their lives in their hands. He regretted that the old memorials of bygone days, which marked the terrible happenings in those times, were not kept in better order than they were in at the present day. The object of the penal laws was to stamp out Catholicity from the British Isles and the methods adopted were to eliminate and massacre all the priests caught saying Mass. That method, he said, was successful in some parts of the British Isles.[52]

Windle said that the faith died out in Wales not because the people were anxious to lose their religion but because priests could not be got to keep the religion before their minds. That did not happen in Ireland, he said, because the priests and people would not give up their religion at the sacrifice of even their own lives. As regards the faith at this time, he said to cheers from the audience that there was a strange state of affairs between Ireland and England. It was the masses that kept the faith in Ireland while in England 'it was the better class that stood by the faith'.[53]

This lecture, warmly received on the night, met with strong objections from at least one Protestant minister. Rev. T.B. Robertson wrote to the

Cork Constitution requiring to be told the purpose of the talk: 'Was it to influence the religious bigotry of Roman Catholics, or to mislead his Roman Catholic audience in regard to historical truth?'[54] The minister found that the lecture had given a false impression to the audience that 'Roman Catholics – Roman Catholics alone – suffered from the Penal Laws, and other persecutions, because of their religion'. Windle was challenged because he had said that dissenters were also the subject of persecution. The minister wrote that if Windle were an impartial historian he would have told his audience that 'Protestants were largely to be excused if they persecuted, as they inherited the practice from the Church of Rome, which had bitterly persecuted Protestants, long centuries before the period known as the Reformation'. No Protestant Church, he said, would countenance persecution of any man because of his religion.[55] If Windle made a reply there is no record of it in the scrapbook.

The short-lived success of St Anthony's Hall attracted the wrath of at least one Protestant minister who had criticisms to make at the lack of hostel facilities for Protestants at UCC. Canon J.W. Tristram complained at the Church of Ireland Synod in 1913 that the academic year at UCC had been 'opened with the Solemn Mass of the Holy Ghost, the president, professors and students attending in academic state'. Windle, in a letter to *The Irish Times* on 21 April 1913, took exception to the fact that the canon had neglected to point out the following: 'that at or about the same time of year a religious Service, also held in a city church (I understand in the Cathedral in 1912), is conducted for the benefit of those who do not profess the faith of the majority in this district, and that it is also, as I am informed, well attended by the professors and students for whom it is designed'.[56]

Windle failed to understand why Tristram described the one ceremony as the 'opening' of the college and denied that title to the other ceremony in which his own co-religionists took part. Windle was driven to the conclusion that the canon was not aware of the Church of Ireland ceremony. Tristram replied on 22 April. He asked Windle a series of questions. The location of the 'city church' was, he stated, 'practically attached to the University College'. Tristram mistakenly believed that the Red Mass was said in St Anthony's Hall, formerly the Church of Ireland Berkeley Hall. He made reference to the wall being knocked between the college and the hall. Tristram admitted he was not aware that there had been a Church of Ireland ceremony. He did recall that there had been a service at St Mary's, Shandon. He concluded that in the mind of the impartial reader 'University College Cork and the National University itself are associated with the Roman Catholic Church in a manner much more close and intimate than they are with any other communion'.[57]

On 23 April, Windle replied, pointing out that the ceremony of 1912 was held in the city parish church of SS Peter and Paul. On two previous occasions, the president added, the ceremony was held in St Anthony's Hall (1910 and 1911). Concerning the Church of Ireland services for those years, two had been held – in St Mary's, Shandon, and in St Finbarr's Cathedral. Windle had never heard the late and much loved Bishop Meade of Cork, who was a governor of UCC, 'express publicly or privately any criticism or objection to anything that has been done by his fellow-governors'.[58] Tristram replied to Windle on the 24th. Beaten on the major argument, he concluded vigorously: 'I have no "objection" whatever to a religious Service on such an occasion – quite the contrary; but what I did, and do, complain of is the association with any one religious denomination of a College or University whose very title and *raison d'etre* should make it entirely undenominational, especially when Protestant winners of County Council scholarships are told that they must go there or do without.'[59]

On 25 April, Windle responded to Tristram, rejecting the canon's allegations and challenging the view that St Anthony's Hall was dominating the college and that the college was 'cowed and cowering under its octopus-like tentacles'. Windle set out the situation as he saw it. The hall had once been a Protestant-owned residence. It had failed and lay derelict for a number of years. The Franciscans had purchased the hall and ran it as a residence. The college authorities had given the students an entrance from the hall which allowed them to go in and out at a minimum of inconvenience to themselves. 'Of course,' he argued, 'it plays an important part in college life.' Windle had prevailed upon the late Bishop Meade and the late Archdeacon Powell to provide a hall of residence for their students. It was the only way to avoid having to send Church of Ireland students to reside in St Anthony's Hall. Windle gave an assurance that the governing body would give students in a Church of Ireland hall 'every privilege and convenience which they have extended to the existing institution'. Windle made reference to Trinity College Dublin, where accommodation is provided for its students. Cork had no such privileged status: 'Finally, if I may be permitted the remark, that is why it seems to me to be a little hard, not to say ungracious, that those who enjoy freely all these privileges of which we are deprived should carp and cavil at the efforts which we make to adjust ourselves to circumstances for which we are not responsible.'[60] Tristram, allowing bravado to triumph over prudence, delivered a final broadside on 26 April 1913, but it did not add materially to the debate.[61] Windle, at that point, ended his involvement in the correspondence. The correspondence, however, points to Windle's determination to protect the religious freedom and rights of the followers of all Churches among the staff and in the student body in the college. That was made very clear in the exchange of letters quoted above. Windle did not wish to confront any growth in hostility among members of the Church of Ireland towards the college. Tristram did not find support for his criticisms. Nevertheless, Windle used the exchanges in *The Irish Times* to clarify college policy and provide reassurances to members of the Church of Ireland that he did not wish to force any student to have to reside in St Anthony's Hall. The provision of a hall of residence for Church of Ireland students was the solution, a solution for which he had actively canvassed since coming to Cork.

Sr Monica did not interpret as triumphalist the initiation of the annual Red Mass, the Lenten triduum, the appointment of two chaplains for male and female students and the establishment of confraternities for men and women; the Red Mass was nothing more than the restoration of an essential feature of Christian university life which had been in existence since the Middle Ages, 'namely, a corporate act of supplication at the commencement of the year for the light and guidance of the Holy Spirit during the weeks to follow'.[62]

John O'Connell and Isabella Honan

The Dublin solicitor, John O'Connell, strongly supported Windle in his efforts to restore a form of religious equilibrium in the college. Born in the capital on 12 February 1868, he was the only son of Thomas Francis O'Connell, 10 Mountjoy Square.[63] Educated by the Jesuits at Belvedere College, he entered Trinity College where he graduated with a BA in 1889 and took the degrees there of MA and LLD in 1894.[64] He had already taken up employment in his father's law firm and qualified as a solicitor in 1889,[65] and eventually became head of Messrs Thomas F. O'Connell and Son. The firm had 'a very extensive practice, including among its clients the Dublin and South Eastern Railway Co.'[66] In 1901 he married Mary, the eldest daughter of Thomas Scally, Deepwell, Blackrock, County Dublin.[67] They lived at Árd Éinín, Killiney, County Dublin. His wife played a very active part in his public life.[68] Mary O'Connell was also very influential in the development of her husband's artistic sensibility. The couple acquired a large art collection and were prominent members of Dublin cultural circles. Following the sudden death of his wife in 1925, Sir John O'Connell decided to study for the priesthood. He was ordained in 1929 by Cardinal Bourne.

Despite a busy professional life, O'Connell found time to be an active member of all the principal Catholic and philanthropic societies where he did 'an appreciable amount of work'. His obituary in *The Irish*

Times in 1943 stated that O'Connell was 'a man of many accomplishments and interests. His charity, while generous, was unostentatious, and the cheerfulness which accompanied his gifts endeared him to all who benefited by his largesse.'[69] O'Connell was knighted in 1914 and Pius XI in 1924 created him Knight Commander of the Order of St Gregory the Great.[70] Windle and O'Connell had quickly become close and steadfast friends. Both were devout Catholics, and shared a common interest in developing a strong Catholic presence in third-level education. O'Connell was a member of the Senate of the University of Dublin and a member of the governing body of University College Cork. He was a Fellow of the Royal Society of Antiquaries of Ireland, of the Royal Irish Academy, a vice-president of the Statistical and Social Inquiry Society of Ireland, and a member of the Board of Superintendence of the Dublin Hospitals.[71] He was also a director of the National Bank Ltd.[72]

O'Connell was a justice of the peace in Cork and was a solicitor to the prominent Honan merchant family as his father had been before him. His links with that Cork family brought him into very close contact with Windle and with UCC. Having had much success in Birmingham attracting philanthropic donations to the university, Windle was on the lookout for similar sources of funding in Cork, but Cork was not Birmingham. But it did have a number of prominent, wealthy families. Isabella [Belle] Honan was the last surviving member of that distinguished merchant family. Originally from Limerick, the Honans had been prominent in the business life of that city in the late eighteenth century. It is not very clear when they came to Cork. But there is a listing in Lucas' *Commercial Directory*, according to Richard I. Henchion, that Robert Honan married Catherine Moylan, the second daughter of Richard Moylan (then deceased), at Douglas Farm. The latter had been in partnership with his brother in an emporium at Kyrle's Quay. He was a nephew of Francis Moylan (b. 1735) who became a Catholic Bishop of Cork. Henchion speculates: 'It is probably not unkind to the Honans to declare that much of their subsequent liberality to church institutions had its origin in the Moylan connection.' Robert Honan founded a corn and butter exporting firm that was to trade under his name for a century. The business was situated at 19/21 St Patrick's Quay for the processing of butter and at 10/11 King St (now MacCurtain St) for the sale of grain. The Metropole Hotel occupies the latter site. Robert Honan was a frugal and parsimonious character who used to bring his lunch to work daily like any school child. He died at his residence in Sydney Place on 6 June 1865, leaving the sum of £60,000 to be divided among his family. The business history of the Honan family in pre and post famine Ireland has yet to be written.[73]

Isabella Honan first made provision in 1910 for the allocation of a scholarship fund of £10,000 to UCC. Most UCC professors at the time earned £500 a year. Servants would have received no more than £30 a year. In 2004, according to the Secretary of UCC, Mr Michael Kelleher, the original Honan bequest of £10,000 was worth over £1 million on the books of the college. In 2010, the bequest is worth only a fraction of that sum, the banking crisis of 2009 having dissipated most of the share value of the fund. However, that first act of generosity by Isabella Honan had a great personal impact on the lives of many students who would other-wise never have had the means to enter the university.

Isabella, who died suddenly while on holiday in a hotel in Crosshaven on 18 August 1913, left her fortune to be used for altruistic causes. An obit-uary described her as belonging to 'an old Cork family which had long been associated with charitable enterprise in the city'. The short news item also referred to her own charitable work, including the donation of £10,000 for scholarships to UCC.[74] The *Cork Examiner* gave more extensive coverage to her funeral, which took place on 19 August 1913. The reporter reflected on the 'munificence of the deceased lady' as the Mass was being chanted in St Patrick's – where 'much of the furnishings of the church must be a monument to the kindly disposition of the late Miss Honan'. The report added: 'Shrines and statues, monstrances, ciboriums and chal-ices perpetuate her memory in the parish of which she was such a faithful member. Full of the spirit of Christian charity her vast worldly wealth only spoke to her the opportunity of doing good and lavishing favours on her less fortunate fellow-creatures; and in a no lesser degree the means of propagating the Faith she held so dear, and of alleviating the financial troubles which often times beset the rugged path of religious Orders who select the ministering of comfort and solace to the poor and lowly as their special mission.'[75]

O'Connell, among the mourners at her funeral, had been called upon to advise Isabella Honan. She had made her will in Dublin on 27 July 1901. A codicil was added on 13 August 1904 in Bray, County Wicklow. A second codicil was added on 16 April 1908 in Cork City. (This was after the death of her only surviving brother, Robert.) A third and final codicil was made on 13 August 1908 in Crosshaven, County Cork.[76] O'Connell was made executor of the will. According to the second codicil, O'Connell was to use Honan's money 'amongst such charitable purposes in Cork as he should in his unfettered discretion select'. He wrote to Windle, who was on summer holidays in London, of the windfall for the college – a sum of between £30,000 and £40,000. The only condition was that Windle would remain at UCC as president. If he went, the money was to be devoted to other charitable works. Windle wrote immediately to Birrell in confidence, as the news of the gift was to remain secret for some months.[77] This was a large fortune.[78]

Windle returned to UCC for the autumn term buoyed up by the news of the bequest. Despite the controversy caused earlier with Tristram over the manner in which the new academic year should be opened, Windle changed nothing. The Red Mass for 1913/14 was held, as previously, in SS Peter and Paul's church. The rector of the Irish College in Rome, Mgr Michael O'Riordan, delivered the sermon. The press reported that about 600 students and fifteen professors were present together with a large number of clergy and city officials. O'Riordan challenged his listeners to explore the mysteries of their faith. He made reference to the early Christians and to those who followed. There was nothing esoteric in Catholicism. The early Christians did not philosophise about it. O'Riordan told the congregation that the higher one went in the sciences the more faith would be confirmed: 'The man who drives a tram-car knows the practical results of the sciences of electricity as well as the professor who investigates its principles in his laboratory; the dyer and the farmer know the practical results of chemical science as well as the professor who makes the analysis of bodies, and probably can use these results better. Thus the poor and the illiterate knew how to grasp the Christian Mysteries, can take in practical teachings of Christianity as well as the philosopher, who often succeeds only in thinking foolish things and in saying and writing them.' After speaking for nearly an hour, he concluded by telling the students present that they were reaping the harvest of what their fathers had sown in the winter and spring with much labour and sacrifice; that they had opportunities which were denied to their fathers, but which their fathers had won for them. Those are great gifts, he said, and they entail great responsibilities – of using their cultivated intelligence to leaven and to lift up by the lives they lead, by what they say and do in public and in after life in the midst of those with whom their lot is cast.[79]

The *Cork Examiner* gave extensive coverage to the occasion:

> While in other countries this spirit of bigotry seeks to divorce religious teaching and education, and even men of the highest intellectual attainments have followed mistaken pathways, there is in Ireland ever-increasing evidence that here still remains one of the great founts of Christianity, and that while religious teachings may be vanished from the schools of other countries the youth of Ireland will still receive a training which will fit them to withstand the great temptations which to-day are to be met with in all walks of life. An example of the fidelity of the Irish people to the faith was the scene in SS. Peter and Paul's Church yesterday when at the opening of the academic

year Professors and students as well as many members of the Governing Body joined together and besought the blessings of God on their labours.[80]

In February 1914, Windle received a note from O'Connell offering the Honan bequest. The solicitor felt that 'it would entirely fall in with her wishes, to which I was most anxious to give effect, if I were to apply a substantial part of the residue left in my direction for charitable purposes in Cork, for the benefit of an institution in which she had exhibited so much interest'.[81] O'Connell had made inquiries with the Franciscans to discover that it was the definite and final direction of the minister general of the Order of Friars Minor to sever connections with St Anthony's. O'Connell conferred with Windle about the purchase of St Anthony's Hall. He sought out the Irish Franciscan, Dillon, and made an offer to buy the building. He wrote to Bishop O'Callaghan on 5 February 1914 that he had reason to feel that the offer would be accepted. O'Connell also wrote to tell the Bishop of Cloyne of the developments. On 4 April 1914, O'Connell completed the sale, costing the Honan bequest £6,000. He also purchased 'the grounds thereto adjoining being all that situate in the Parish of St Finbarre of Gill Abbey Barony of Cork . . . Held in fee simple to the intent that the said premises with the appurtenances and the chapel and such other buildings as may be erected thereon'. In order to avoid any accusations of secrecy, the most important letters relating to the purchase of the hall were published in the *Cork Examiner* a few weeks afterwards.

O'Connell developed the idea for the reconstitution of the hostel under a permanent Catholic governing body. That would prove of immense benefit to the Church and to the entire Catholic population of Munster, 'and one which would have been peculiarly pleasing to Miss Honan herself'.[82] O'Connell felt that the hostel should be run by a warden 'who, for obvious reasons, should be a married man'. He wrote that that part of the 'matter was simple enough.' But, he continued: 'it was an important part of my scheme that there should be a proper Chapel, suitable to the dignity of a University, with a chaplain resident in the Hostel, responsible for the spiritual welfare of its inmates, and provided for by endowment.'[83] O'Connell added: 'As I have already hinted, the existing Chapel seems to me to be inadequate to the needs of the residents in the Hostel, and of the Roman Catholic members of University College, and I intend at once to proceed with the building of a Chapel on a scale and design which, it is hoped, will not be unworthy of its sacred purpose.'[84] He was allocating from the bequest a sum of £3,000 for the erection of a biological sciences institute. O'Connell felt that all the projects should bear the name of the donor, Isabella Honan. In a letter of 5 April 1914, Windle acknowledged that he owed it to O'Connell's 'forbearance for which I now express my thanks – that the house was not closed to students some time ago'. He said that he was 'beginning to fear that this would be the result, when you came to the rescue and by your generous assistance, the institution will now be placed on a permanent footing and will be an abiding source of advantage to the Catholic parents of Munster'.[85] The *Cork Examiner*, in a leading article, welcomed the generosity of the Honan family and the wisdom of Sir John O'Connell in the manner that the bequest was being spent. The government was criticised for not providing 'ready means of residence for students coming from a distance to attend the courses in the College. However, nothing of this kind was done.' The editorial said parents would expect that the Honan grant would feed the residents and that their temporal welfare would be looked after: 'What they could not get elsewhere is the Catholic atmosphere, the spiritual guardianship which under the scheme outlined by Dr O'Connell, and warmly approved of by the Bishop, they will be able to enjoy in what is now to be known as the Honan Hostel.'

A short news report, together with an advertisement, appeared in the *Cork Examiner*. It announced the newly named Honan Hostel would re-open on 20 April 1914. Professor T. Smiddy was appointed acting warden. The chaplain was Rev. D. Cohalan PhD. The paper welcomed the news and anticipated a very successful career for the institution under its new arrangements.[86]

The Honan Hostel, the culmination of nine years of work by Windle, was duly opened on 20 April 1914 and named after the benefactor, Isabella Honan.[87] The Honan Trust was established on 5 January 1915 under Royal Charter of His Majesty King George V. The first meeting of the governors was held at the Honan Hostel on Tuesday 26 January 1915.[88] The first action of the first meeting was to express gratitude to Sir John O'Connell for 'having presented the Hostel to the Governors'. The royal charter was taken as read. 'The grant of Arms to the Honan Hostel, Cork by the Ulster King-at-Arms was read and accepted.' A local Corkman had prepared the common seal. This was examined and adopted as the seal of the governors. The by-laws, which had been circu-lated to the governors, were approved subject to small amendments.[89] The deed of conveyance in trust, from Sir John O'Connell to the trustees of the Honan Hostel, was examined and approved. The common seal was attached to the said deed. The title deeds were handed over by O'Connell to the governors and entrusted to the warden. They fixed a seal to the transfer of assets representing the endowment of £8,000 to the hostel.[90]

On the motion of O'Connell, it was agreed that Windle, Bishop O'Callaghan, Professor Molohan, Professor Patrick Thomas O'Sullivan and Professor W.J. Dunlea be appointed as a sub-committee to oversee the affairs of the hostel until the meeting of the governors. Three of the above should form a quorum. It was further directed that the warden should procure a suitable deed box with two sets of keys – one to be retained by the chairman and the other by the warden. The box was to be placed in the strongroom of the college if the president so permitted. The seal also had to be kept under lock and key, one key kept by the warden and another by the chairman. A.J. Magennis, South Mall, was appointed auditor of the accounts to be presented on Founder's Day. The annual fee was to be five guineas.[91]

The Archbishop of Cashel, John Harty, proposed a motion, seconded by Bishop O'Callaghan of Cork, to give thanks to O'Connell for his generosity in endowing the Honan Hostel out of the Honan funds 'and for his personal labours in connection with the endowment and foundation of the institution'. Professor T. Smiddy, warden, was secretary to the meeting.[92] The capacity of the hostel was about forty and it was usually full during term time. The hostel was closed in 1991.

The Collegiate Chapel

Having secured the Honan Hostel as a hall of residence for male Catholic students, Windle also harboured an even more ambitious plan – to build the collegiate chapel which would serve the Catholic staff and student body of the college. In that connection, he bravely stepped into a world of controversy and artistic debate. Windle and O'Connell were determined to break with copycat architecture, imported second-rate artwork and the building of shabby, drab churches. While discussing the plans for the Honan Hostel, O'Connell had, in a letter to Windle in early 1914, raised the building of a chapel. He concluded his letter to Windle: 'I am sure that it will be your wish as much as it is mine, that all the works referred to in this letter shall be carried out in Ireland, and so far as possible in Cork, by Cork labour, and with materials obtained from the city or county of Cork. It is an additional gratification to me, and will I am sure, also be to you that the expenditure of the necessary monies will lead to a considerable amount of employment for Cork workmen.'[93]

In his reply on 5 April 1914, Windle pledged that he would undertake to 'make every effort to see that no penny which can be expended in the country goes out of it, and that as far as possible the pennies expended in the country shall be expended in Cork'.[94] An editorial in the *Cork Examiner* on 6 April – the day that the O'Connell–Windle correspondence was published in that paper – also welcomed the building of a new chapel in the Celtic Romanesque style, 'and which we are glad to learn will be made of Irish materials, and will afford much needed work for Cork workmen'.[95]

James F. McMullen MRIAI, who had been the architect employed on the renovation of St Anthony's Hall/Honan Hostel, was chosen for the challenging task of bringing the ideas of O'Connell into bricks and mortar. The plans were drawn up. The building contract was given to John Sisk. The first meeting of the governors was held on 26 January 1915.[96] On 18 May 1915, the second meeting of the governors records: 'at the conclusion of the business on the agenda, the governors adjourned to the site of the Hostel Chapel where the laying of the foundation stone was performed by the Most Rev. Thomas A. O'Callaghan D.D., Bishop of Cork.'[97] The *Cork Examiner* reported extensively on the ceremony and carried photographs of the occasion.[98]

McMullen, on the basis of his earlier work and style, was very sympathetic to the artistic views of O'Connell, or more accurately stated, the O'Connells. On the instructions of his client, he visited 'many of the twelfth century ruins which abound in the historic County of Tipperary and, in the words of His Grace the Archbishop of Cashel "received inspiration which he has put to the best advantage". Cormac's Chapel in Cashel, County Tipperary, was a major influence on the architect. O'Connell gave McMullen no choice. He instructed the architect to erect the chapel in the Hiberno-Romanesque style.[99]

The architect gave O'Connell credit for providing the inspiration for the building of the chapel. However, it is important to stress at this stage that O'Connell himself gave full credit to his wife, Mary Scally, for her central role in the artistic creation and execution of the chapel.[100] Living in Dublin in the 1890s and the early twentieth century, the O'Connells had both witnessed and participated in the revitalisation of the arts and crafts movement.

O'Connell's sister-in-law, Ethel Josephine Scally, was a prominent figure in that movement. She worked, up to the time of her death in Cork in July 1915, on a commission for the Honan Chapel – designing the 'cloth of gold' set of vestments for High Mass consisting of a cope, chasuble and dalmatic. Although she did not live to see her designs executed, the finished embroidery consists of medallions of the four evangelists, taken from the Book of Kells, set in bands of intertwining serpentine ornament. The work was carried out in the workshops of William Egan and Sons (founded in 1823) which was then under the manager, Barry Michael Egan. About thirty women were employed to make the vestments over an eighteen-month period.[101]

The innovative Honan Chapel architecture was enhanced by the choice of stained glass. Originally, the commission for most of the windows was to go to the Sarah Purser studio, 'An Túr Gloine' (Tower of Glass) and to the artist, A.E. Child. But a brave decision by Windle and

O'Connell enhanced the artistic value of the church. A past pupil of Belvedere College, Harry Clarke, was beginning to make a name for himself in the early pre-war period as a coming force in the international world of design and stained glass making. Born in 1889, he was the son of Joshua and Bridgid Clarke. His father had set up a business as a church decorator and manufacturer of objects of art.[102] Harry Clarke first came under the notice of another Belvedere College old boy, Ambrose Laurence (Larky) Waldron;[103] the latter introduced the artist to Joseph Maunsell Hone for whose publishing firm he began to illustrate Coleridge's *Rime of the Ancient Mariner*.[104] O'Connell, who had gone to the same school, lived close to Waldron. They shared an interest in culture, literature and in the contemporary arts and crafts revival. Waldron's household was a centre of lavish gatherings. Windle, when visiting the city, regularly stayed with Waldron.[105] All three men – Waldron, O'Connell and Windle – were involved in the decision to employ the young Harry Clarke.[106] In October 1914, Waldron approached Harry Clarke on behalf of Sir John O'Connell concerning the design of stained glass windows for the Honan Chapel. Clarke recorded in his diary that he had met O'Connell on 19 October and had agreed to submit, within five weeks, designs for a number of Chapel windows.

In January 1915, Windle gave him the commission for three windows on the basis of his drawings. Those windows were put on display in the studio of Clarke's father in Dublin in summer 1915. They were of Saints Brigid, Patrick and Columcille. So impressed was Windle by the richness of the production, he ended by giving Clarke a commission for another eight windows. Windle travelled to Dublin in February 1916 'to see Harry Clarke's windows, which are quite wonderful beyond all'.[107] In the end, Windle had taken absolutely no risk by giving the young artist the new commission. Clarke had come to the notice of Thomas Bodkin, appointed director of the National Gallery of Ireland in 1927. He admired the artist's work greatly and, in particular, the four newly completed Honan windows which were exhibited in the family studios in North Frederick Street in June 1916; they were of Saints Ita, Finbarr, Columcille and Brigid. Miraculously, they had survived the British bombardments which helped crush the 1916 rising in central Dublin. Clarke lost drawings and blocks for his illustration of *The Ancient Mariner* in the offices of the publisher Maunsel – a casualty of the rising.[108] Bodkin described Clarke's work as 'a very notable achievement. Nothing like them has been produced before in Ireland.' Bodkin added: 'The sustained magnificence of colour, the beautiful and most intricate drawing, the lavish and mysterious symbolism, combine to produce an effect of splendour which is overpowering.'[109] Bodkin felt that the Honan Chapel would become a place of pilgrimage for lovers of great art if the other windows lived up to the accomplishment of those already completed.[110] The judgment of successive generations attests to the genius of Harry Clarke. Looking at the altar, five of the windows on the right hand side of the church were all executed by him: Our Lady, St Joseph, St Ita, St Brendan and St Gobnet. St Bridget, St Patrick and St Columcille are above the main entrance. On the left hand side, again facing the altar, there are three Clarke windows out of seven: St Finn Barr, St Albert and St Declan. The remaining five windows were from the Purser studio. The completion of the chapel, which had employed in its building and furnishing the best artists and artisans, was a matter of celebration – not least in UCC and in Cork.

Solemn Opening of Honan Chapel

Windle took great pains to organise a dignified and memorable opening for a chapel which symbolised the end of Catholic 'inferiority' in the country. The building blended the traditional and the modern. It represented the historical presence of Christianity in Ireland through the centuries. There was nothing second rate about the artisanship and the artistry which had gone into the completion of the project. It was a building of which Catholics could be proud.

The solemn opening of the collegiate chapel took place on Sunday 5 November 1916. The *Cork Examiner* took pains to report almost every detail of the colourful event: at 11.30 Solemn High Mass was sung by the Archbishop of Cashel, John Harty. The Bishop of Cork, Daniel Cohalan, presided. The Bishop of Ross, Denis Kelly, the Bishop of Cloyne, Robert Browne and other senior diocesan clergymen also occupied seats in the sanctuary. Various religious orders were also represented. The Lord Mayor of Cork, T.C. Butterfield, and the Mayor of Waterford, J.J. O'Sullivan, were in attendance together with other senior politicians of the region, the president, Sir Bertram Windle, and a large body of the professorial staff (nearly twenty) and students of the college. The architect, James F. McMullen and Sir John O'Connell, the inspiration behind the project, were also present.[111]

Led by Archbishop Harty of Cashel, the prelates and clergy processed into the chapel as the (North) Cathedral choir sang 'Ecce Sacerdos'. 'Ave Maria' was sung at the offertory. The Bishop of Ross, Dr Kelly, preached the opening sermon after the end of Solemn High Mass which was characterised by its eloquence and erudition. It was also very progressive in tone and far-sighted in its appeal to practical cooperation in politics, commerce and the development of the nation between Catholics and Protestants, between nationalists and unionists. He took as his text

Apocalypse XXI.2: 'I saw the Holy City, the new Jerusalem, coming down out of heaven prepared as a bride adorned for her husband.' The early part of the sermon dwelt upon the history of St Finbarr and the establishment of a great seat of learning in Cork where he became the first bishop and his church became the first cathedral. In early Christian Ireland, the cells of those monks and scholars were, he said, the nucleus of the city of Cork.[112] Kelly recalled that St Finbarr and the men of his time associated the school with the church. They could not conceive the one without the other, but modern progress, which had given birth to the brilliant idea of divorcing man and wife, also divorced the school and the chapel. Hence at the start, their college (in 1848) had to ignore the existence of St Finbarr's Cathedral, and should have no connection with any other church or chapel: 'To-day, by opening this chapel we have restored once again St Finn Barr's ideal: we have linked together the Church and the College.' The Catholic clients of St Finn Barr could now fulfil the duties of their religion in the beautiful chapel, erected in the site sanctified by him; his Protestant student clients have St Finbarr's Cathedral on the same site, for their religious exercises; thus, they, all of them, Catholics and Protestants, could rejoice together in the common joy that they had re-established the sanctity and the indissolubility of the marriage of religion and education. [113]

Bishop Kelly continued with a perceptive comment that appeared on the surface to be a statement in tune with the Counter-Reformation. But when the statement was unbundled, it had a progressive meaning: 'In the practice of religion Catholics cannot join with Protestants. It is notorious that Protestants, non-conformist as well as Episcopalian, whatever may be their professions, are, in matters of religion and education, at least as exclusive as us. We rejoice that they act up to our principles. But in all other matters – national, municipal, industrial, social – we are not only free, but eager to join with them for mutual benefit, and for the promotion of the welfare of our common country.' He said that that was the law of Christian charity by which all men should love one another in the Fatherhood of God and the Brotherhood of the Saviour of all mankind. Referring to a recent statement, released by the Protestant bishop, clergy and members of the synod of the diocese of Cork, Cloyne and Ross, Bishop Kelly acknowledged its importance. The statement, which followed a meeting in St Finbarr's Cathedral, expressed the desire for unity and cooperation with all their fellow-countrymen in the promotion of the good and prosperity of 'our common country'. They longed for a settlement of the national question on national lines. Kelly added: 'From St Finn Barr's new chapel today, on behalf of the Catholic Diocese of Ross – and I believe the same is the opinion of the Catholics of Cork and Cloyne, all Ireland – I hail with satisfaction those sentiments of that representative body of Corkmen. Catholics are not only ready to co-operate with them, but we want to bring those sentiments into immediate operation.'[114] Bishop Kelly then turned to trends in the wider world. He felt that they were living in revolutionary times. After the war effort in the countries involved, he said, a tremendous host of problems would be treading on one another's heels clamouring for attention and solution. The disbanding of the men of the various services – finding new occupations for them and for the millions of persons now engaged in war work, the provision for the disabled and for their dependants, and the dependants of the killed, the reconstruction of the huge industrial system, the picking up again of the broken and scattered lines of trade and commerce – such were specimens of those angry and explosive problems.[115] It would be an inestimable boon to Ireland, Bishop Kelly argued, to have a settlement put in operation during the war; and thus to escape being dragged into a post-war maelstrom of confusion. That would be more to the advantage of unionists than nationalists. It would be an immense relief to Great Britain to have the Irish question off her hands before grappling with her own difficult and dangerous problems.[116]

Kelly linked the present and ancient past. In the days of St Finbarr, strife and turmoil reigned in Great Britain and on the continent of Europe. The Roman Empire was dismembered and modern nations were struggling into life. Roman civilisation, learning, laws, arts and institutions were shattered into fragments. Wreck, ruin and chaos were widespread. Ireland stood apart, surrounded by the Western Ocean. She advanced rapidly in learning and art. From all Europe scholars flocked to her schools; she sent out teachers and missionaries to many countries, and played a most important part in establishing in Europe Christian learning and civilisation. If she had been a party actually concerned in the re-parcelling of Europe she could not have become the apostle and civiliser of many peoples.[117]

Having dwelt so long on the history of this site, Kelly turned to the new chapel itself. He quoted again the text of the sermon and added: 'Your chapel is so fair, so beautiful, so perfect, that it seems to have dropped down from Heaven, not made by hands. It is, indeed, like a bride, fresh, fair and charming, adorned for the bridegroom.' Kelly continued: 'In innumerable passages of sacred Scripture God reveals His desire that His House should be rich and beautiful. The Psalmist sings – "I have loved the beauty of God's house and the place where his glory dwelleth," and those words were repeated by the priest in every Mass that was celebrated.'[118] The bishop told the congregation that there was in man an inborn love and admiration of the beautiful in nature, literature, art and music. But he felt that the public taste in modern times had been 'perverted and debased as the natural consequence of modern utilitarianism and materialism.' He continued: 'A steam-engine is not a thing of beauty; a motor car is not a thing of beauty; nor is an aeroplane, nor a submarine. Hence we have grown tired of beauty, we have grown sick of Grecian prettiness, and we worship the ugly. We now prefer the glare of the city to sylvan scenes; in literature we seek after what is revolting, shocking and dreadful. Art, music, dress, all showed a depraved taste.'[119] It was, therefore, a happy idea of Sir John O'Connell, with the support of the Isabella Honan bequest, to place before the students of UCC a 'work of true art, correct taste, and genuine beauty'. Bishop Kelly praised the architect and the artists who drew designs and gave helpful suggestions. The artificers, he added, also deserved a meed of praise for the care, cunning and skill with which they carved out the various designs. Kelly added: 'We thank them all for the masterpiece which they have raised for the honour of God, St Finn Barr, and for the sanctification and artistic education of the community of Cork University College.'[120] The ceremonies concluded with the architect, James F. McMullen, presenting Bishop Cohalan with a wrought gold key of beautiful design in Celtic ornamentation, surmounted by the Cork Arms, and bearing suitable inscriptions on both sides.[121] Windle gave a lunch in the Honan Hostel for fifty-five people. Bishop Cohalan officiated, at four o'clock, at Solemn Benediction of the Blessed Sacrament at which there was a large attendance. The (North) Cathedral choir sang in plain chant the 'Te Deum', 'O Salutaris' and 'Tantum Ergo' unaccompanied.[122]

Windle provided a more intimate account of the events in his diary entry for 5 November 1916:

> Blowy and some showers but on the whole decently fine. Deo Gratias. After breakfast and seeing things all in order. Opening of chapel. Procession (1) mayors and councillors (2) staff and Governing Body to mace and self (3) clergy. Mass sung by Archbishop of Cashel – Sermon (the best I ever heard from any man) by Kelly of Ross – with a cry for unity to professors. Bishop of Cork (who didn't seem to like sermon) presided – also Bishop (Cloyne) – chapel full and many students. A splendid ceremony with choir of 65 and everything done in dignity and order – an object-lesson to the staff-students. Lunch of 55 people at the Hostel and speeches – toasts [?] to Government – King and Pope O'Connell – Bishops and church, Munster O'C – Cashel Cork – Honan Hostel. Lord Mayor – Smiddy. Chairman – self – Then Benediction (Bishop Cork) and a full chapel. A tiring day.

Thus ended one of the most important and successful days in Windle's fifteen years at UCC.

The Honan Chapel in Historical Context

Sir John O'Connell published a book on the Honan Chapel in 1916. A reviewer, J.J.H. (almost certainly John J. Horgan), wrote in *Studies*: 'The history of the project is in itself significant. It is in reality a successful attempt to accomplish that feat so dear to every Irish heart, of driving a coach and four through an Act of Parliament. The University Act of 1908 solemnly enacted that whatever sums of money might be provided for the new University or any of its constituent colleges, no part of it should be applied for "the provision or maintenance of any church, chapel, or other place of religious worship or observance." It was to evade this absurd and scandalous provision that the Honan Hostel Chapel has been built, in order that some sort of building which would answer to the first need of Christian university life, a chapel.'

Horgan continued:

> But something far more than this was attempted, and something far more has been done. . . . We strongly advise anyone interested in Irish ecclesiastical art – and surely this category ought to include all educated Catholic Irishmen – to procure this interesting book which describes and fully illustrates the chapel and its contents, and also to seize the first possible opportunity of visiting the building for themselves. The young Catholics of Munster, who will be educated by its art and inspired by its beauty, will have good cause to remember the munificent generosity of the Honan family and the providential destiny which placed its disposal and direction in the hands of such men as Sir John R. O'Connell, Sir B.C.A. Windle, the President of University College, Cork, and Mr J.F. MacMullen [sic], the Architect. They have brought to their task not only enlightened taste and feeling, but a sincere desire to revive the great religious and artistic traditions of their native land.[123]

An unsigned review in *The Dublin Review* pointed out that the building of the Honan Chapel 'should call into new life the spirit and the work of the age when Irishmen built noble churches under the impulse of native genius. There was a happy confidence that such a building would win its way to the hearts of the ardent youth of to-day.'[124]

In the historical context of 1916, the building of the collegiate chapel at UCC was not in any sense an act of Catholic triumphalism. The opening was overlaid with meaning and symbolism for Windle, the culmination of his policy to normalise relations between the university and the Catholic community in the Munster region. By charter, the Honan Chapel was Catholic. Between 1914 and 1916, Windle managed to secure both his major presidential ambitions – and in the process to normalise college relations with the Catholic Church. He had provided a hall of residence and a chapel for the students of his faith. UCC was no longer a 'godless' college. It was a university where all faiths and Churches were to be treated with dignity and respect.

CHAPTER 5

Radical Politics, the First World War and the 1916 Rising

In late 1913, the successes resulting from the Honan bequest were largely in the future. Windle was recovering from the humiliation of having to defend his actions in public over the removal to UCC of the Knock-shan-a-wee ogham stones. That controversy was much more than a dispute over the best practice in handling priceless cultural artefacts; it also reflected a new radicalism in Cork politics where the actions of a UCC president were not above criticism or reproach. The local Gaelic League was divided and politicised. The radical faction of that body had led the recent criticism of Windle. He was also a figure of suspicion in Irish Republican Brotherhood (IRB), trade union and Gaelic Athletic Association (GAA) circles. The UCC president was not that popular among the members of the Ancient Order of Hibernians (AOH).

Windle would constantly criticise in his diaries the activities of James Joseph (J.J.) Walsh, who began life as a post office clerk, devoting much of his free time to extending the GAA throughout the county. In politics, Walsh supported William O'Brien's All-for-Ireland League. He was elected in 1911 to the corporation for the centre ward. In 1912, he formed a rifle club in Cork City. In response to the rise of paramilitary force in the north-east corner of the country, Eoin MacNeill, the Professor of Early and Medieval Irish History in UCD, wrote on 1 November 1913 'The North Began', in Patrick Pearse's *An Claidheamh Soluis.* On 11 November 1913, MacNeill and Pearse, supported by Roger Casement, set up the Irish Volunteers. The new organisation was launched on 25 November at a public meeting in the Rotunda Rooms in Dublin. About 3,000 enlisted on that first night. The secretary of Cork Industrial Development Authority, Diarmuid L. Fawsitt, was one of those who signed up.[1] He also became a member of the IRB. Returning to Cork, Walsh played a leading role in the foundation of the Irish

Volunteers there. And enlisting the support of Liam de Róiste, he also
helped to organise the Volunteers in the city. Fawsitt, Walsh and de
Róiste wanted to hold a public meeting in the city to recruit volunteers.
Walsh contacted MacNeill, who agreed to speak in the city hall on
Sunday 14 December 1913. J.J. Walsh, chairman of the Cork County
Board of the GAA, took the chair. His fellow organisers were de Róiste
(Gaelic League) and Fawsitt (IDA). MacNeill and Roger Casement travelled to Cork for the meeting. They discussed their plans for the meeting
with J.J. Horgan in the Imperial Hotel. While willing to speak, Horgan
declined to do so on the grounds that, as a member of the national
directorate of the United Irish League, he might compromise the new
volunteer body and also the IPP. Redmond had not given the green light
for the party to identify publicly with the new movement. There had
been rumours of tension between the different nationalist groups in the
city. The first six rows of the meeting were occupied by members of the
AOH. A very large crowd attended, among them Tomás MacCurtain and
Terence MacSwiney, a founder of the Celtic Literary Society. Fawsitt
opened the meeting by reading the manifesto of the Irish Volunteers.
Walsh told the audience that Cork was prepared to follow Dublin,
Galway, Kilkenny and Kerry in forming a local volunteer movement.
MacNeill then addressed the meeting and, to boos and hisses, called for
three cheers for Edward Carson and his volunteers. Members of the
AOH, positioned near the front, roared themselves hoarse, 'hissing,
groaning, and uttering threats at the speaker, who blandly smiled and
awaited a subsidence of the tempest'.[2] The stage was stormed and Walsh
was injured in the mêlée.[3] 'Stormy meeting in Cork – violent assaults on
speakers', headlined *The Irish Times*.[4] Roger Casement claimed later in a
letter that the meeting had only been disturbed but not broken up. He
had not been jostled or touched by anyone, nor were his notes torn from
his hand. He had received a very courteous and kindly hearing from a
very large gathering. He said that some 700 names had been given in by
men wishing to enrol in the Volunteers. MacNeill, in another letter to the
press, supported Casement and rejected *The Irish Times*' statement that
he was a supporter of Sinn Féin. He said he had been a supporter of
John Redmond.[5] Windle was not impressed, writing the night of the
meeting: 'J McNeill's [*sic*] ridiculous meeting broken up in wild disorder.'
Unsettled by the drift of events, he noted in his diary on 5 December:
'Telegram from *Irish Independent* – asking if true that I had accepted a
post of importance in England – alas I haven't nor the chance.'[6] He was
stuck in Cork for the time being. He witnessed the rise of the Irish
Volunteers in the city and in the county. A number of those named on
the provisional committee were those Windle liked least in the public life

of the city: J.J. Walsh, Seán O'Hegarty, Terence MacSwiney and Tomás MacCurtain and two UCC students, Liam Owen and Daniel Enright. P.S. O'Hegarty was also active in the organisation.[7] A military council, which maintained control over drilling and training, was formed in July 1914; MacCurtain and Seán O'Hegarty were among its members. There was real tension, however, in Cork and elsewhere between the followers of Redmond and the more radical elements.

Windle was not a party to any of those developments. The early months of 1914 were taken up with negotiations regarding the Honan project. There were numerous meetings and discussions which moved towards a positive conclusion. In spring 1914, he was invited to give an address to the Catholic Institute. He worked hard on the text in parallel with an effort to complete his manuscript on 'The Church and Science'. He came to Glasgow on 23 March as the guest of Professor Phillimore. Windle had been an external examiner in the Department of Anatomy at the University of Glasgow before taking up his duties at UCC. He went to Dowanhill convent where Sr Monica was teaching. He also met Anne Hardman, the daughter of his close friend, John B. Hardman. (Her name in religion was Sr Anne.) He met the superior of the convent and principal of the Training College, Sr Mary of St Wilfrid (Mary Adela Lescher). His diary also makes reference to meeting 'other nuns including the biologists'. That may have been the first occasion on which he met Sr Monica.[8] He dined that evening with Judge Lord Skerrington and Professor Phillimore. He gave his address on 'The Argument from Design', and noted in his diary: 'It went very well.' Out of the meeting between Sr Monica Taylor and Windle flowered a prolonged intellectual relationship. The exchange of letters, which lasted until his death in 1929, began in 1914. In May, Windle received the good news that Gasquet had received the 'red hat'.[9]

Windle's diary records his continued preoccupation with the drift of Irish politics. Between 21 and 24 July 1914, an unsuccessful attempt was made at the Buckingham Palace Conference to reach agreement between the different parties on the Ulster question. Windle's growing anger towards Carson was recorded on 14 July: 'No trouble in Ireland after all but [why] does [somebody] not geld that ass Carson.' On 26 July, rifles were landed at Howth, County Dublin, and distributed to waiting columns of Volunteers. The Dublin Metropolitan Police (DMP) and troops of the King's Own Scottish Borderers unsuccessfully attempted to stop the distribution. Returning to barracks, the troops opened fire on a crowd on Bachelor's Walk, which was six miles away, killing four civilians and leaving thirty wounded. Windle wrote on 27 July: 'News of abominable outrage in Dublin by soldiers and police.

What a government and what a scandalous differentiation between the forces of Ulster and the genuine Irishman.'

Windle spent his summer holiday as usual in Harrogate in July and August 1914.[10] On 2 August, he met Neville Chamberlain: 'War specials all day. England so far out of it but God knows how long it may be.' On 3 August, he noted: 'Great anxiety about war.' Windle, who was still in England when war broke out on the 4th, made immediate preparations to get back to his university: 'got berths and space for car [on 7th] and saw it on at 1 a.m. – boat sailed late with many soldiers and cackling idiots of women to 2 of whom I gave going-over not likely soon to be forgotten. Very rough passage. Boat going like an arrow to get across.' Upon returning, he put the college on a war footing, writing in his diary on 10 August: 'Deputation from students wanting to form Volunteer Corps. Highly approved.' Windle felt a sense of exaltation at what he perceived was a great spirit of determination to fight and win the war. He believed that the country (Ireland) was united as never before, as he told Humphreys in a letter on 10 August: 'I felt it my duty to place the college at the disposal of the military and naval authorities as a Base Hospital, with myself as its administrator and my medical Professors as its surgeons. (I am now in communication with all sorts of people on the subject.) It is a disastrous business altogether, but the Government have behaved splendidly, particularly Grey. Redmond's speech was magnificent, and except for a few sore-hearted dissentients, Ireland is a united country and what a Godsend that is! And it is boiling with patriotic fervour and a desire to fight for the Empire! What a miracle!'[11] Redmond's stirring words in the House of Commons were, in part: 'I say to the Government that they may tomorrow withdraw every one of their troops from Ireland. I say that the coast of Ireland will be defended from foreign invasion by her armed sons and for this purpose armed Nationalist Catholics in the South will be only too glad to join arms with the armed Protestant Ulstermen in the North.'[12] Windle wrote to Redmond: 'Your manifesto this morning is not merely, as I think, the finest thing you have ever done, but one of the most perfect and stirring pieces of English prose which I have ever read.'[13] On 12 August, his plans for a field hospital had progressed. He had two nurses holding themselves in readiness and he had sourced stretchers, beds and other necessary materials. On 13 August, he visited the neighbouring Bon Secours hospital and got a commitment that they would provide nurses, later arranging the delivery of beds and bedding. He spoke at a fundraising meeting for wives and families of soldiers and gave a donation of £10. On the 14th, he continued his work preparing the hospital on campus and on 15 August, he wrote: 'Beds being got into Examination Hall.'[14] UCC was ready to play its part in the war effort.[15] On 20 August, the president wrote: 'Walked to Penrose Quay in [city] and melancholy to see the soldiers going off in thousands to this diabolical war. Back at the university.' On 22 August, he wrote of the death of Pius X: 'Evidently this awful war killed him.' Most of his diary entries for the following weeks are filled with gloom and despondency. On 4 September, he wrote: 'A lovely day but news as gloomy as it can be – God help us – How is this to end.' The war had disrupted the running of UCC, as he explained to Humphreys on 16 September: 'There has been a whole chapter of misfortunes here. Registrar ill in bed. Three professors hung up by war. A fourth detained away by serious illness of his wife. All meaning more work for me. Finally, our Vice-Chancellor died in the summer and has no successor as yet. The Senior Pro-Vice-Chancellor is hung up in Copenhagen, and I am next, and have had to arrange all sorts of things with Dublin, over the telephone, as so many External Examiners are prevented from acting.'[16] Professor Stockley, who was married to a German, was one of the stranded professors referred to above. He had been on holiday in Germany at the outbreak and Windle, with great difficulty, succeeded in securing him passage home to Cork. The Professor of German, Wally Swertz was not so fortunate. She remained stranded in Germany, dying there in 1917.

Meanwhile, the war had immediate consequences for the implementation of home rule, Asquith bringing in a Suspensory Act on 15 September. The Home Rule Bill and the Suspensory Bill received royal assent simultaneously on 18 September.[17] That meant the postponement of its implementation until some time in the undetermined future. Windle wrote to Humphreys on 16 September: 'For one thing I am profoundly thankful, namely, that Home Rule is now settled . . . However, enough of politics – when Asquith comes to this country he will get the reception of his life. I have never known a time when feeling in favour of England ran so high in this country amongst all classes, and I fully believe that the miracle of South Africa is going to be repeated here – God grant it may be! Amen.'[18] Asquith visited Dublin on 25 September, and, speaking in the Rotunda, he talked optimistically about the end of the war and the emergence of an international organisation to keep the peace.[19] He was very warmly received.

Five days before, John Redmond, in a speech at Woodenbridge, County Wicklow, had committed his party to support the war effort and urged nationalists to enlistment.[20] The following day, the provisional committee of the Volunteers repudiated that pro-war interpretation. Within a fortnight, the Volunteers had split. Redmond had formed the National Volunteers and had taken 170,000 with him. About 12,000 remained as Irish Volunteers under Eoin MacNeill. Windle's son-in-law,

J.J. Horgan, took up a commission in Redmond's organisation confident that home rule would be implemented after the war had been won.[21] The Irish Volunteers had been infiltrated by the Irish Republican Brotherhood. Not content to wait for home rule, the war offered a different possibility for those revolutionaries – the opportunity to stage a revolution against British rule.

Meanwhile, in UCC, there had been a generous response from staff and students to the call to the colours. Professor Edgar H. Harper, who had been appointed to the chair of Mathematical Physics in 1913, joined up in 1914 and died in action in France on 10 July 1916. He had obtained a commission in the Royal Munster Fusiliers in May 1915, transferring to the South Staffordshire Regiment where he was promoted to lieutenant. He is listed on the Dungannon War Memorial and is commemorated on the memorial in the 1937 reading room, Trinity College. His younger brother, Ernest, Royal Munster Fusiliers, was killed at the Dardanelles on 9 August 1916. By the end of the war, UCC staff, students and ex-students had lost 29 dead out of 354 who had served. Fifty-four had been deco-rated.[22] Three had been awarded KCDGMs, eleven got Order of the Bath 'Companion's (CBs), five were given CMGs, six got Distinguished Service Orders (DSOs), twenty-two were given Military Crosses (MCs) and eighteen got the Legion of Honour. One was awarded the Royal Flying Cross, one got a Distinguished Service Cross and eighteen were men-tioned in dispatches. UCC medics were strongly represented among those who had served: Royal Army Medical Corps (RAMC), 162; Indian Medical Service (IMS), 29, Royal Navy (RN) (Medical); 37, distinctions gained, 25; killed or died on active service, 14.[23] The heroism and the full horror of a prolonged war became part of the history of UCC, although a plaque or monument has yet to be erected to the memory of those staff and students who died in the First World War. Two UCC war casualties merit special notice. Vincent McNamara was a 2nd Lieutenant in the 136th Fortress Company, Royal Engineers.[24] A student of civil engi-neering, McNamara played on a highly successful rugby team with Harry Jack, J.F. Linehan, George Murphy-O'Connor and T.F. Sheehan. He was part of a golden age of UCC rugby between 1911 and 1915, winning three international caps for Ireland in 1914.[25] Vincent (Macky) McNamara died, aged twenty-four, on 29 November 1915, at Gallipoli. He was buried there in the Lancashire landing cemetery and is commemorated on panel 9 of the Lancashire Landing Memorial, Turkey.

Another student engineer and athlete, Patrick J. Roche, was also a casualty of the war. Born in 1886 at 10 Spring Lane, he was a Catholic, entering Queen's College in 1906. He was already an established athlete, having won the 220 yards Gaelic AA Championships the same year as he began his engineering studies. He was Irish champion at the 100 yards from 1907 to 1910, and the 220 champion in 1907. He was one of 154 athletes selected to compete in the 1908 Olympic Games for Great Britain and Ireland. Roche competed in the 100 and 200 yards, reaching the semi-finals of both competitions. He shared the Hibernian record for the 100 yards at 10.15 seconds. He graduated in 1910. He enlisted in the Royal Engineers in 1914. By 1917, he was a lieutenant and awarded an MC. He died that year of enteric fever in Baghdad.[26]

For Windle, like so many others of his generation who were not at the front, the war had a deep and scarring impact on his life. A regular flow of visitors serving – including his brother – brought him details of the horrors of modern warfare. He never wavered in his support for the war effort, but any optimism about it being over 'early' was quickly dissipated as he watched one year roll into another.

On 5 November, Windle wrote in his diary: 'Nothing but intrigues here . . . What with the climate which is bad and the people who are ten times worse this place is certainly not a bed of roses – All the same if you fly from one Cross you get a worse says T[homas]. à K[empis] and I'm inclined to think he was right – Anyway if I live, I must stick it out three and a half years here and then . . .' On 6 November, he wrote: 'Well I must stick it 3 and a half – 4 years more if I live or then good-bye to this place.' On 4 December, he wrote gloomily: 'But of all the mean-minded races [commend] me to the ordinary Irish – One is up to ones neck in shine in this place and cant even have a clean bath elsewhere because of the war.' On 5 December, he mused that if the war had ended 'and my time here up, things would become cheerful. However I do not doubt that God put me here and keeps me here and beastly as the place and people are I must try and do my duty.' On 31 December, he wrote: 'So ends a year of unparalleled anxiety and trouble all brought about by autocratic militarism.' On 3 February 1915, Windle again had an opportunity to welcome the lord lieutenant and Lady Aberdeen to the college. They were met at the entrance door of the Great Hall where the daughter and the son of two of the professors presented Lady Aberdeen with a 'handsome bouquet'. The lord mayor and the city high sheriff accompanied the party together with a large number of the members of the governing body. The photographs of the visit reveal a great sense of celebration and ceremony.[27]

Those photographs, however, did not tell the full story of the struggle Windle faced to keep the college functioning normally in wartime. He wrote to Sr Monica on 7 May: 'Several of my staff have gone to the war and I have had a good deal of trouble in supplying their places and in keeping back others who wanted to go but are, in my opinion, much more needed in training medical men for the services than in looking after the wounded. I wish one could see the end of the war looming in the distance; some think it is nearer than was supposed likely.'[28]

But the war, continuing until the end of 1918, saw the evaporation of the great euphoria and unity in Ireland at the beginning of fighting in August 1914. Windle's respect for Asquith deteriorated and he noted in late April: 'The Parliamentary intrigues still in full blast. Can it be supposed that there is any person outside parliament who still retains any vestige of respect for that most contemptible body?' The prime minister, on 25 May 1915, capitulated and established a coalition government with Labour and the Conservative Unionists. Carson accepted an invitation to join the cabinet. Windle, a long-time home ruler, was dejected at the idea of having 'that scoundrel Carson' in the cabinet, as he recorded in his diary on 16 April.[29] Redmond, seeking to maintain the traditional policy of independence, declined the invitation and also refused to nominate a leading member of his party to the cabinet.[30] John Dillon feared that the coalition experience would result in the 'hopeless discrediting of Asquith and others of the Liberal ministers'.[31] On 28 June, Windle wrote disconsolately: 'Can anything in this world cancel the misery of last year?' 'No,' he replied to his own question and then reflected on the loss of the *Lusitania* which had been torpedoed on 7 May 1915 off the Old Head of Kinsale at a cost of 1,198 lives. Only 800 survived. Windle could not believe that the Germans thought that the ship was armed or carrying munitions. He heard about the sinking while at a governing body meeting on 7 May: 'a dastardly job by which 1,000-1,500 innocent . . . were drowned.' The following day, he wrote: 'My 57th birthday and the worst owing to bad news about Lusitania and Russians. God grant this hell-hole war may be over before my next and I a better man.' Horgan, Windle's son-in-law, had been appointed coroner in 1914. He presided over an inquest in Kinsale on 8 and 10 May on the bodies of five passengers who had been drowned in the tragedy. Two days later, the jury, as directed by Horgan, returned a verdict of 'wilful and wholesale murder' against the emperor and government of Germany. The verdict had reverberations beyond Kinsale, the words becoming a rallying cry in Britain on posters, in newspaper headlines and cartoons.[32] What impact his son-in-law's meteoric international fame had on Windle is not recorded in the diaries.

Windle blamed the government for the breakdown of the nationalist consensus in Ireland during the early months of the war. He witnessed the radicalisation of Irish politics with battle lines being drawn between nationalists and unionists. He also saw the growth of real tensions within the Irish Parliamentary Party as Redmond failed to deliver home rule. Windle also saw the growth of cultural radicalism. The Gaelic League he had joined at its foundation had been transformed and – much against the wishes of its founder, Douglas Hyde – it had become an instrument of radical politics. Patrick Pearse, the progressive educationalist he had worked with on St Enda's in 1910, had become a member of the Irish Republican Brotherhood and a supporter of physical force. That radicalism was also to be found within the gates of UCC both among members of the staff and within the student body. Senia Pašeta's revealing study, *Before the Revolution: Nationalism, Social Change and Ireland's Catholic Élite, 1879–1922*, concentrates her study on Dublin in the main.[33] But a much more politically diverse picture might emerge of the political allegiance of students if a similar study were undertaken for either UCC or UCG and the feeder schools from which both colleges recruited. Radical nationalist politics held its attractions for the younger generation, and that was certainly the case in UCC.

Fergus Campbell's work on *The Irish Establishment, 1879–1914* helps illuminate the complexities and frustrations of upward mobility of middle class Catholic Ireland in business, the professions, the administration, the police and the army. Part of the problem the British administration faced in Ireland between 1914 and 1918 was that it was not sufficiently 'green' to understand the contradictory and conflicting impulses in Irish society and to mount successful policies to counteract the rise of radical nationalism.[34] Windle was an agent of change for Catholics. He had hoped that British society would change sufficiently swiftly to counter the rise of radical nationalism within the UCC student body.[35]

The greening of Dublin Castle may have progressed under Birrell. Lawrence McBride argues: 'The appointment of Augustine Birrell as Chief Secretary in January 1907 was one of the most important events in the transformation of the Irish administration . . . The period of Birrell's administration largely marked the greening of Dublin Castle. Irish civil servants were becoming more broadly representative of the people they served. The rank and file shared the popular enthusiasm for home rule.'[36] But the opening up of Catholic recruitment into the Irish administration in the pre-1916 rising period was not sufficient to absorb even a fraction of those looking for posts, and the glass ceiling continued to apply. The war may have further reduced the opportunities for Catholic professionals in the colonial civil service. Irish history might have had a different outcome had the British government introduced home rule in 1913 and thus provided greater opportunities for Catholics to enter and gain higher promotion in the police, army, civil service and the professions.

Windle repeatedly revealed his fears in his diaries about what he thought the delay in implementing home rule meant to a new generation. As the war progressed, he became more and more despondent. His mood was not improved by being unable to leave the country in summer 1915 to holiday in England; the Windles rented a cottage, 'Listarkin', in Union Hall, west Cork. It became Windle's retreat from UCC and 'the world', until he left Ireland at the end of 1919. The couple used their wartime summer holiday time to collect large quantities of bog moss, sphagnum, to be used for the dressing of wounds.[37] Windle had a large shed erected in the college grounds for drying the harvest. Edith founded a women's guild, which sent books to the soldiers of Munster, cared for the prisoners, and also collected and cleaned the sphagnum.[38] The War Work Guild and Sphagnum Department at UCC collected £483-10-2; the number of articles collected and dispatched was 3,894; the number of sphagnum dressings prepared was 2,790; the number of prisoners regularly supplied with food parcels was twenty-two. Finally, the amount collected for spending on Munster soldiers was £231-0-5.[39] Meanwhile, Windle's brother Reginald, who was an officer in the medical corps, was sent to France to command a hospital of 1,040 beds.[40] Windle himself never considered enlisting as a doctor.

Windle had been buoyed by the initial response in Ireland to the outbreak of war. He admired and idealised the level of unity and loyalty the call to the colours had evoked. This was in contrast to the reaction of the United States to the war, with Windle hoping on 7 September that the 'lily-livered yanks' would be stirred to action. On 12 September, Gasquet echoed Windle's feelings about Ireland, home rule and British policy: 'I am glad to hear what you say about Ireland. The Irish in Rome are not too loyal I fear but it doesn't much matter now. I quite agree about Home Rule. It should come without any doubt directly we are in peace. One of the lessons the war should teach is that no people can or should be governed against their will.'[41]

After a difficult term, the Windles spent the Christmas holidays at 'Listarkin'. On 31 December, he wrote: 'Thus ends 1915 – a blasted year. Constant alternations of hope and despair – or not quite that – chiefly due to the bickerings and squabblings of as mean a gang of politicians as ever intrigued. They run the brothel-keeper very close for the lowest rung in humanity. It is pitiable that decent people should have to suffer for their follies.' He listed eight of his friends who had died during the year. He was thankful, however, that he and his wife were in reasonable health: 'no grave illness (tho' both of us had pretty sharp influenza) thank God and Edith still spared to me - Please God 1916 will be a better year and may I be a better man at the end of it.'[42]

Academic, Author and Public Intellectual

Amid the storms of war, public life and the running of an expanding university, Windle never wavered in his commitment to his personal academic life. He produced an enviable scholarly output, as the following brief section will illustrate. In 1907, he published *What is Life: A Study of Vitalism and Neo-Vitalism*. This book project started out as a lecture delivered in the hall of Westminster Cathedral in March 1906, entitled 'The Secret of the Cell'.In the final text, he brought forward such biological evidence 'as had come under his notice in favour of a vitalistic or a neo-vitalistic explanation of living matter'. He had not intended to deal with the question of the human soul and its relation to the activities of the human body, 'since that is a matter for theologians rather than for biologists to deal with'.[43] He expressed his gratitude in the preface to Fr M. Maher SJ, 'to whom I owe more than I can express for his kindness in reading my manuscript and supplying me with many most useful suggestions'. He also thanked his wife, Edith, who had redrawn the figures for the book.

As a Catholic and an academic, Windle had – and would – spend a great deal of his life in the public arena defending the Catholic Church's approach to science and debating the question of evolution.[44] He combined those interests with publications on literature, archaeology, local history and education. Windle published nearly twenty-five books and articles between 1904 and 1919 while president of UCC.

In 1912, he edited *Twelve Catholic Men of Science* to demonstrate that there were 'numerous stars of science' who were also 'devout Catholics and found no difficulty in maintaining both positions simultaneously. It ought to be superfluous to maintain such a thesis, and it would be so if persons who propagate such accusations as are made against the Catholic Church would, first of all, investigate the facts of the case. But, as the statement has been made, it may be well to give some definite examples of the co-existence in the same individual of scientific enthusiasm and reputation with a steadfast attachment to the doctrines of the Catholic Church.'[45]

Windle thought it desirable that such a selection should embrace a collection of subjects as varied as possible. The people whose lives were sketched in the book were from different countries, different ages and from different branches of science – biological and physical. Some were churchmen and some were lay. Others spent their lives among Catholic surroundings, while others lived 'largely in a non-Catholic environment'. Most of them were born in the Church, but some entered in later years. Some lived 'in times when profession of their religion was at least no disadvantage, others . . . when it was either a positive disadvantage or, at least, in no way in their favour'. In one thing only all were alike, he wrote, 'and that is in their attachment to their religion'.[46]

Windle, having chosen a distinguished panel of authors, oversaw the individual publication of their essays, in most cases, as Catholic Truth Society (CTS) pamphlets. He then brought the essays together in a single volume, writing himself about Thomas Dwight, Professor of Anatomy at Harvard University. The latter was the great-grandson of John Warren, the founder of the Medical School at Harvard, and grandson of John Collins Warren, the founder of the chair of Anatomy at Harvard.[47]

In 1915, Windle published one of his most important works: *A Century of Scientific Thought and other Essays*.[48] He dedicated the book to his friend Fr M. Maher SJ, 'in grateful remembrance of much kind help on many occasions'. A number of chapters in the book had appeared in *The Dublin Review, Catholic World* and *Studies*.[49] He reviewed the *Argument from Design* before, during and after the Darwinian controversy, examining where such an argument stood in his day. He made a reference to 'the one serious conflict with science in which a mistake was made by the then rulers of the Church'. That was 'on the physical side, for the dispute with Galileo raged around the geocentric and heliocentric theories of astronomy'. He noted that Cardinal Newman had remarked that the Galileo case was the 'one and only definite case which can be brought up, and is invariably brought up, as an example when the Church is accused of being the enemy of science'. He defended the Church against such a charge. Reviewing the arguments about Darwinism, he wrote: 'But there is one thing which she [science] cannot tell us now or ever, nor can pretend to tell us. She presents to our knowledge a universe composed of matter, and that matter everywhere in motion. But she cannot tell us how that matter came into being, or how it came to be in motion. This limita-tion of science is of course recognized by everybody. We Catholics, in common with all Christians, say that God Almighty, existing from all eter-nity, created matter, and endowed it with the wonderful properties which it possesses. It is at least a simple and a sufficient theory.'[50] Windle argued further: 'What I want to emphasize is this, that science has its own corner – a large one – but that there are other corners; that science cannot tell us anything about the other corners, any more than the other corners can tell us about science. Finally, that science admittedly cannot give us any convincing answer as to how there come to be any corners at all. All this has been long and well known, and fully recognized by writers of the first importance.'[51]

Windle posed the question of what shattered the *Argument from Design*. The formulation of the theory of natural selection was its apparent

nemesis. But Windle argued that natural selection could not cause variations. But what causes the variations? That was, for Windle, the kernel of
the whole matter and it was one on which science at present could shed
but little light: 'It is no good saying that there is an inherent tendency in
all living things to vary: that explanation is purely verbal. To say that a
thing inheres in, or sticks in, something else, does not explain why it
inheres or how it got stuck there.' Windle concluded: 'What I have been
anxious to show is, that the argument which held the field before the
storm, when the lake was comparatively calm, now that the tempest has
raged over it, still remains, restates as we may suppose the waters of the
lake to have rearranged themselves during the commotion to which they
were subjected, but essentially the same, and the same because founded
upon what we cannot but regard as being the Eternal Verities'.[52]

Windle concluded that the 'Lawgiver whose existence has to be postulated in order so that the whole may work is, whatever paraphrase may
be used, the God whom we reverence as the Creator of all things'.[53] He
further refuted the theory of natural selection in another essay:

> It is quite clear that the plant must have within itself a tendency to
> vary and to vary in certain directions, a force which enables it to make
> those sudden and complete mutations which have been described in
> this paper. It is not the environment which provides them or even
> calls them forth, so far as we can at present see. It is an inherent func-
> tion of living matter, a function which we can appreciate without in
> any way understanding it, a function whose laws we can only guess
> at. That natural selection may come into operation after this function
> has been exercised is possible; that it has anything in the world to say
> to the causation of the function, as some have seemed to imagine, is
> obviously and entirely absurd.[54]

In an essay on the human skull, Windle concluded: 'so far as the cran-
iological evidence goes, those who desire to prove the evolution of man's
body from that of a lower form have completely failed to make out their
case.'[55] Entering the debate on the 'earliest man', Windle concluded: 'It is
when geologists – and still worse anthropologists – try to set these
periods down in terms of years, that we enter the domain of chaos. But
with all this it may be said quite definitely, that the point of appearance of
man upon this earth must be put back to a very much greater distance of
time than was dreamed of by writers up to a comparatively recent date.'[56]

Windle published his most important work, *The Church and Science*, in
1917. Dedicated to Gasquet, it went into a second edition the same year
and was reprinted in 1918, in 1920 and again in 1924.[57] This volume was
a *summa* of a lifetime of Windle's scientific thought and a stout defence of
Church teaching in the area. He criticised those who considered the

Catholic Church 'as a fossilised organisation incapable of any intellectual life and, on the other hand, as torn by fierce and internecine quarrels as to questions of doctrine'. But he was quickly at pains to point out that his book was not 'a compendium of Apologetics'. His position was briefly as follows: 'assuming that the Church is what she claims to be, what are the exact relations which she bears to the science of the day and those which the science of the day bears towards her? Having thus defined the exact scope of this book, it may be well to define the terms which we have just been employing, on the excellent principle that we should be quite clear as to what we are talking about before we begin to talk about it.'[58] Following a detailed discussion, he concluded 'that Science, in the opinion of the world, is justified in regarding the objects with which she deals as realities. But we also learn that the whole range of knowledge and experience does not come within the scope of Science.'[59] His concluding chapter warned readers from being carried away by 'the hot-gospellers of the daily and weekly press, or by the enthusiasms of ardent and sometimes ignorant disciples'.[60]

Windle concluded his book as follows: 'Let us learn humility and patience from Science if we learn nothing else: but we shall miss its greatest lesson if it fails to teach us the greatness of the Creator, from whose Idea all these wonders took their origin.'[61] It is worth stressing that Windle completed his academic research and writing amid a very busy teaching and administrative career. His powers of concentration and self-discipline were great, but there were occasions when the flow of national politics disturbed his equilibrium – and no event more so than the 1916 rising.

Windle and the 1916 Rising

Radical nationalist and separatist ideas grew rapidly throughout 1915 in Ireland. Wartime measures exacerbated feelings of grievance and alienation. The Defence of the Realm Act, introduced on 8 August 1914, had, by December 1914, suspended the publication of *Sinn Féin*, *Irish Freedom* and the *Irish Worker*. Windle, ever conscious of the danger of revolution, viewed the march of events with growing concern. Surprisingly, he made no comment in his diary on the funeral on 1 August 1915 of the Fenian, O'Donovan Rossa, with the graveside oration by Patrick Pearse: 'but the fools, the fools! – they have left us our Fenian dead, and while Ireland holds these graves, Ireland unfree shall never be at peace.' By the summer of that year, plans were being advanced by the IRB for revolutionary action.

Windle commented on the Conscription Bill on 7 January 1916:

'Introduction of Conscription majority 300 in house of 400 – but to the devil with all politicians. If we had a real man for King he would half [?] the lot and carry on for a time to everyone's satisfaction.' On 8 January, Windle was angry about the outcome of the bill in the House of Commons: 'Ireland's exemption from the Bill an insult! "I'm not going to make you fight because you are doing it already!" is an insult. What a people and what an opportunity they have lost!' Redmond, in contrast, told the House of Commons on 18 January that he considered the application of conscription to Ireland as being 'impracticable, unworkable, and impossible . . . It would play right into the hands of those who are a contemptible minority amongst the Nationalists of Ireland, and who are trying, and unsuccessfully trying, to prevent recruiting and to undermine the position and power of the Irish Party because of the attitude which we have taken up . . .'[62] On Saturday 29 January 1916, Windle went to town to see Canon Roche. He wrote: 'When one thinks over it, it is wonderful how the country had come through this conscription crisis and what a good spirit has been shown.'

In parenthesis, Redmond was correct to be concerned about the intentions and actions of the 'contemptible minority'. The Irish Republican Brotherhood, very much a minority, had reformed and regrouped in the previous few years. In May 1915, the Supreme Council of the IRB had set up a Military Council comprised of Pearse, Joseph Mary Plunkett and Éamon Ceannt. By the end of the year, there were definite plans to stage an uprising, and with German support. Between 19 and 22 January, James Connolly – the leader of the Irish Citizen Army – was brought into the plans to stage a revolt. The planning was very much in the hands of Patrick Pearse, Tom Clarke, Joseph Mary Plunkett and Seán MacDermott.

Meanwhile, in UCC, there was a meeting of the new governing body on 9 February 1916. The president congratulated a former student of the college, Cllr Butterfield, upon his election 'to the important office of Lord Mayor of Cork'. A vote of congratulation was sent to the outgoing lord mayor (1911–16), Sir Henry O'Shea, 'on the signal honour conferred on him by His Majesty'.[63] Throughout the early part of February, Windle wrote sparingly in his diary. On the 14th the closing line read: 'Black stories of Sinn Féiners – a scurvy crew.' There is a long entry for Sunday 27th. He went to town for the paper and was cheered by the news from France: 'After lunch Lucas White-King and wife (a sister of the scoundrel Northcliffe, but apparently decent herself) to see College . . . and stayed to tea.' He also met an officer returning wounded from Suvla Bay who was very critical of, what Windle termed, weak generals: 'This confirms my view of the older class of officer – those now coming in may have more sense.' This is a reference to the military disaster at Gallipoli. (On 6 August 1915, a major attempt was made to break the deadlock at the Battle of Gallipoli with a landing intended to support the Anzac sector, eight kilometres to the south. The British commanding officer, Lieutenant General Sir Frederick Stopford, was dismissed for gross incompetence.) On Monday 28 February 1916, Windle went to Dublin where he encountered news of the slaughter in Turkey; a Fr Stafford who was just back from Salonika, having been through 'whole Suvla Bay . . . an awful business in which he says he prayed that he might die. Exactly same thing about older officers whom B. said were like clowns trying to play Hamlet.' On Tuesday, 7 March, he ended his entry: 'Verdun stationary but how long can such slaughter go on?'

On the home front, Windle encountered problems with some of his older professors. On 15 March, he had a meeting with 'pre-1908 people – Alexander and Stockley. And such a gang of asses surely never came together in one room – After trying to get ideas into their impenetrable heads (some of them especially ineffable [George] Stokes [Professor of Philosophy and Jurisprudence] the dark caverns of whose mind no bit of sense ever penetrates) I sent them away and told them to think it over – determining to find another way. By the way [David] Barry [Professor of Physiology] at once burst out that he must have another Demonstrator and I wiped the ground with him to the delight of the others.' The entry for 17 March 1916 revealed a warmer side of Windle in his attitude towards professorial staff. During lunch he received a telegram with news of the death of the Professor of Irish, Fr R.H. Henebry: 'God bless his soul. I had a deep affection for him poor, wild, erratic, kindly, lovable holy creature.'

Windle despaired about the handling of the war. He regarded Asquith as being weak and under the control of the military and press barons, Northcliffe being a pet hate. The latter had begun life as Alfred Charles William Harmsworth near Dublin in 1865. He became a press baron, championing the tabloid format. He had begun publishing the *Daily Mail* in 1896 and had great success with *The Sunday Dispatch*. He also owned *The Times*. Harmsworth became Lord Northcliffe in 1905. His press empire helped bring down the Asquith government in 1915. For that reason, and his championing of Ulster unionism, Windle held him and his publications in great contempt. On 6 April 1916, Windle returned to Anglo-Irish politics: 'Why they don't hang that traitorous piece of vanity Carson and his brother Jackass Harmsworth [Lord Northcliffe] is a constant source of amazement to me.' On 18 April, he wrote: 'The Parliamentary intrigues still in full blast. Can it be supposed that there is any person outside Parliament who still retains any vestige of respect for that most contemptible body? Here too we seem to have the ill-effects of the arch-prig

Jarett in forcing a swine of the Curzon and Milner type.' On 19 April 1916, he wrote: 'Meanwhile our dirty intriguing scoundrels in Parliament – surely rungs in the ladder below night-soil-men go on bickering and intriguing and earning the loathing of every honest man. Northcliffe – that beggar on horseback – the arch pimp' and on 20 April, he wrote: 'Intrigue still flourishing and Northcliffe still unhung, his carrion carcass fouling the air.' On 21 April 'Crisis over but alas Lloyd George still in Government. Northcliffe thought he was going to win and be made Prime Minister. But is on his scaly [?] bum down in the mud, so it appears.'

While Windle was, as his diary entries show, fully absorbed in the political crisis in London, he revealed no awareness of the cataclysm which was about to befall the British Empire in Dublin. On Easter Sunday, 23 April, Windle attended Mass in the local church at Union Hall, and went out for a walk with Edith: 'O'Connells to lunch and then walk . . . Great shipping activity and something evidently up, though impossible to see what. O'Connells back to Glandore after tea.' On Easter Monday, he noted: 'Poured all night and practically all day – misting when not raining – and in afternoon and evening being heavy. Took cook into Skibbereen and packed her off to Cork. Then back. Edith in evening developed aches . . . and went early to bed.' Windle's diary does not contain any warning about a rising, though he feared constantly the rise of radical nationalism. Both he and O'Connell were members of an inner circle of Catholics trusted by the British administration. But they did not suspect or expect trouble.

Revolutions were not supposed to take place on a bank holiday Easter weekend. A biographer of William O'Brien, Michael MacDonagh, wrote: 'So the Commander-in-Chief of the Forces was on holiday; the Chief Secretary was in London; the Lord Lieutenant had arranged to go on a state visit to Belfast that very day. Most of the officers of the Dublin garrison were at Fairy House races.'[64] The under-secretary, Sir Matthew Nathan, had wired Birrell in London for instructions to arrest the most important Sinn Féin leaders on Easter Monday. But the order did not come. The leader of the Irish Volunteers, Eoin MacNeill, had, with great difficulty and with the help of the clergy in Dublin, successfully counter-manded a general mobilisation of the Volunteers for Sunday 23 April. Dublin Castle authorities, therefore, took their leave with a certain peace of mind. But Patrick Pearse and other members of the IRB were, despite that setback, intent on going ahead with an uprising. Action was merely postponed for a day. On Monday 24 April, an attack on the GPO and other targeted buildings in Dublin took the British authorities completely by surprise.

Windle's diary entry for Tuesday the 25th, the day martial law was declared, reads as follows: 'Raining all day – Edith better and with some hesitation back to Cork two and a half hours in bad weather. Stopped by policeman in Bandon and on reaching home hear them say [there had] been a somewhat serious Sinn Féin rising in Dublin (nothing in papers) and all trains to Dublin stopped – what a foolish mischievous curse for it can do nothing real. Others say it was Connolly (late Larkin's) Citizen army. Whoever it was, if the Government had, as they should have done, shot Carson when he first began these games there would have been none of this nonsense. The first news to-day however is that a ship under Norwegian colours but German carrying arms for landing was sunk. All on board, including that black scoundrel Sir Roger Casement, taken prisoners to Spike.'

On the day of the rising, John Horgan and his family were on holiday in Macroom. They, too, returned to Cork on Easter Tuesday. When he heard the news from Dublin, he immediately opposed the actions of the revolutionaries, agreeing with Tim Healy MP that it was a revolt of 'a minority of the minority'. Horgan quoted his own father (MJ), an old and loyal Parnellite who was seriously ill at the time: 'May God save Ireland from such devils.'[65] The latter died on 14 July 1916 despondent about the future of the country. His son, although a member of the Irish Parliamentary Party, had a good insight into the psychology of those who took part. Writing with the benefit of hindsight in the 1940s, for him, the immediate causes of the rising were as follows: 'Recruiting blunders, the formation of the first coalition Government in England with its implications of a postponement of Home Rule; the possible imposition of conscription in Ireland; and above all the pressure of Irish American and German intrigue on extreme opinion were no doubt immediate causes of the Rebellion.'[66] But Horgan also provided a contemporary explanation when writing on 31 May 1916 to Colonel Maurice Moore: 'The reasons for the wretched rebellion are as clear as daylight. They are (1) the way which Carson and Co. were permitted to break the law with immunity. (2) The distrust of Ireland and the tinkering with Home Rule. On both these counts the English misgovernment of this country stands indicted before the world and the sooner they make up their minds to settle the Irish question in the only way it can be settled – namely full and immediate self-government – the better for England and Ireland.'[67] Windle and Horgan were not so far away from each other in their respective diagnoses of the causes of the rising.

For both Horgan and Windle, the rising was an aberration of little historical consequence. However, for those who took part the revolution in Dublin was merely a beginning on the road to national independence. P.S. O'Hegarty, Windle's critic during the ogham stone crisis, read the events in a very different way: 'But when Tom Clarke faced the firing squad in Kilmainham, he knew that he had won, and that the soul of Ireland would go back to the old heroic thoughts and heroic ways. Those May morning volleys blotted out the old Ireland.'[68] Windle, part of that 'old Ireland', was myopic about political change and the future of radical Irish nationalism.

Windle, with *sang froid*, decided to continue college business as if nothing had happened.[69] But, quite naturally, the events in Dublin had consequences. On Wednesday 26 April, he described the disruption caused by the rising as being a 'great bother'. It had '[Isaac] Swain [Professor of Geology and Geography] hung up in Dublin – also Miss [Mary] Ryan [Professor of Romance Languages]'. Nevertheless, he conferred degrees and chaired a meeting of the Medical Faculty. That evening, he wrote: 'Papers now break suddenly into Dublin affair saying – Liberty Hall is shelled from river – 10,000 troops with artillery brought into city – matters satisfactory. Martial law proclaimed.' Liberty Hall and the GPO were severely damaged by gunfire from Trinity College and from a fishery protection ship, the *Helga*.

Unknown to Windle, on the 26th, the pacifist, socialist and supporter of women's suffrage, Francis Sheehy Skeffington, and two others, Thomas McIntyre and Patrick Dickson, were summarily 'executed' at Portobello barracks on the orders of a Capt. J.C. Bowen-Colthurst from Dripsey, County Cork.[70] On Thursday 27th, Windle chaired three meetings and gave an address to national teachers on university and elementary education which 'was well received'. He wrote: 'O'Connell and Lucy to tea and yarn after yarn as to Dublin to which still no access. Trouble there very serious but getting under [control] though all sorts of wild rumours about, no doubt most of them untrue.' On the 28th Windle received a Mr Byrne from Listowel, County Kerry, who told him that he had been in Tralee where there had been 'no disturbances of any kinds' – thus killing off rumours about the rising having spread to other parts of the country: 'So much for the 70–700 killed there. What lies!' He added: 'However, Dublin is clearly bad enough – nowhere else – May all these ruffians be put underground!'[71]

Windle walked up to Farranferris with Edith to inquire after the Bishop of Cork who was dying. He had the O'Connells to tea: 'O'Connell as pessimistic as ever – nevertheless it is clear apparently that the Bosches are foiled at Verdun'.

On Saturday 29 April, General Sir John Maxwell, newly arrived in Dublin as commander-in-chief, extended martial law to cover the entire country. Windle wrote: 'Very fine warm day – Town and Canon Patrick Roche – long talk on all sorts of things. Bishop Cohalan has evidently acted a man's part in keeping back these foolish Shinners here in Cork. Dublin rumour of end [of rising] confirmed by official representative. That poor mad Pearse – the Commander – Good God that anyone should accept such a thing – a pure visionary – a scholar – has chucked up the sponge D.G. This will end the thing so we all think.'

On Sunday 30 April, Windle recorded the surrender in Dublin: 'complete collapse of Irish rebels – Pearse – *President* – of Irish Republic – wounded and will I hope be hung with Connolly before I write again in this. Also the megalomaniac – for that is what he is – Casement.' Windle wrote on Monday 1 May: 'All Dublin commanders gave up and many others in country – Reasonable British success at Flanders part owing to German gas having blown back on them.' Birrell had returned to Dublin on 27 April. He resigned on 1 May and Sir Matthew Nathan followed. Both men felt that they had not provided due warning of the rising to the British government and did the honourable thing.

On 1 May, Windle did not know that over 400 insurgents, rounded up after the rising, had arrived at internment camps in Britain. Hundreds more arrests and deportations followed. On 2 May, Windle went to work in his office in the college, noted that Bishop O'Callaghan was dying and that Bishop Cohalan 'really doing a fine work calming down rebels. A number of the local Sinn Féiners gave up their arms, the rest were taken from shops etc. and lodged in gaol. It appears that besides mad Pearse and Connolly the Provisional Government (!) had unclean[?] Joseph Plunkett – (who will not be crushed) among its numbers. That strumpet Markievicz in the thick of it, and Mr Sheehy Skeffington, her in bright green uniform and high boots with tassels! Commander of the South Dublin Union. And for these apes and lunatics £2,000,000 of damage has been done and hundreds of lives lost.' Reports also reached him indicating that the rebels were 'thoroughly cowered down'.

On 3 May, the governing body met at UCC. Beforehand, Windle was given details by the lord mayor, Thomas C. Butterfield, about the rising in Cork City: 'military agreed to wipe slate for Sinn Féiners in Cork, unless mixed up with foreign enemies, if arms given up. If not would shell each house in Cork where arms were. Arms given up. Then by some stupid mistake they arrested 13 leaders – He [lord mayor] got them out at 7 pm and saved a riot. Last night a considerable tumult – mostly boys singing outside gaol.'

The situation in the city had remained tense for a number of days. Negotiations took place between the Irish Volunteers and Bishop Cohalan, the lord mayor and the British military. Credit must go to Cohalan, who was Auxiliary Bishop of Cork at the time. He mediated between the British authorities and the Volunteers. The arms, it was agreed, were not to be confiscated but handed over to the bishop and the lord mayor before midnight on 30 April. The transfer took place on 1 May. The lord mayor, unable to guarantee that he could keep the arms securely, handed them over to the military.[72]

The events in Dublin were not mentioned at the meeting of the governing body. However, indirectly, they discussed a technical question regarding the reappointment of professors.[73] Windle wrote revealingly the same day that the meeting was 'quite short to settle appointment but one and all declared no Sinn Féiners. Glad to say none on staff for Stockley is only an ass.' A vote of condolence was passed, marking the death of the Professor of Irish, Fr R. Henebry.[74] On 3 May – the day the governing body was meeting in UCC – three of the leaders of the rising – Patrick Pearse, Thomas Clarke and Thomas MacDonagh – were executed. On 4 May, Windle wrote cold-bloodedly: 'Pearse shot and the others shot and a good thing. 3 others 3 years P. S. [penal servitude] too little. Recorder, who dined with us, says military officer who searched Pearse's house told him that he found a quantity of German correspondence there. Letters now beginning to come in. Miss Ryan and Porter both back [from Dublin] and interesting experiences. Miss [?] R[yan] wandered all through Dublin including O'Connell St on Tuesday. Quite quiet but sniping in Leeson St.'

On 4 May, Joseph Mary Plunkett, Edward Daly, Michael O'Hanrahan and William Pearse were executed. Windle commented on 5 May: '4 more Shinners shot and a lot sent to penal servitude. Poor Plunkett (Count) Son (married day before shot) – The arch scoundrel J.J. Walsh[75] [Cork politician, 1880–1948] 10 years P. S. [penal servitude]. But things quietening down and here the people seem quite quiet.' Windle turned his thoughts to unionist and Conservative politicians: 'The arch-traitor Carson impudently blocking aided by his fellow villain Milner. Why don't they get ten years?'

On his way down to the city on 5 May, he 'saw 6 Shinners marched to gaol by soldiers. No excitement. Sir H. Blake, [retired colonial governor living in Youghal], really one of the most offensive beasts I ever met.' Windle has a terse entry on 6 May: 'Major McBride – spared after Boer war where he led a Boer Regiment – shot. Had married Maud Gonne and I think separated from her – In employ of Dublin Corporation . . . Prisoners keep coming in from outlying districts but place seems quiet.'

On 7 May, Windle wrote: 'Another violent and unsuccessful attack on Verdun. Markievicz strumpet [sentenced to] death, but commuted to penal servitude for life. Better if they keep her there, but they won't – Two Plunketts (said to be sons of George Noble) 10 years each.' On 8 May – his fifty-eighth birthday – Windle went to town with Edith: 'Things quieting down.' Con Colbert, Éamonn Ceannt, Michael Mallin and Seán

Heuston had been executed that day. In the House of Commons, Redmond warned that the executions were alienating many who had not the slightest sympathy with the insurrection. Windle had no such scruples about the draconian policy pursued by Maxwell.

On 9 May, he wrote: 'Not a great deal of news though "Cyrino" White Star lost by torpedo. No passengers but what will the lily-livered [President Woodrow] Wilson say to this. Presumably nothing. The sentimentalists in England beginning to hector[?] at executions. However the worst blackguards (except Connolly) are under the sod.' It is worthy of note that on 9 May, Asquith had reassured Redmond that he had, the previous day, sent Maxwell a strong telegram and that he hoped – unless in an exceptional case – the executions would cease.[76] That was· not to be the case. That very day, Thomas Kent, a farmer from Coole, near Fermoy, was executed in the barracks in Cork. He, his brothers and his mother, had resisted arrest and during the subsequent fight a head constable had been killed. His brother, William, had been acquitted.[77]

On 9 May, the day of the Kent execution, the *Cork Examiner* carried a joint letter signed by Bishop Daniel Cohalan, the lord mayor, T.C. Butterfield, the high sheriff, W. Harte, William Murphy, George Crosbie, James McCabe *and* Windle's son-in-law, John J. Horgan which read in part: 'Voicing we believe the opinion of the great majority of the citizens of Cork we desire to protest most strongly against any further shootings as the result of court-martial trials and against indiscriminate arrests throughout the country. We are strongly of opinion that such shootings and arrests are having a most injurious effect on the feelings of the Irish people, and if persisted in may be extremely prejudicial to the peace and future harmony of Ireland and England.'[78]

Windle wrote on 10 May: 'The politicians are on the rampage after their polemics returning like the dogs they are to their own nauseous vomit and asking if men are to be shot down in cold blood – i.e. the rebels who never did it themselves! Amongst the pack Mary's delightful husband. It's enough to sicken anyone of humanity.' The reference to 'Mary's delightful husband' was overlaid with sarcasm and disapproval.

John Dillon – a politician Windle disliked intensely – had been trapped by the fighting during Easter week in his house in North Great George's Street. He travelled to London on the 10th. The Irish Parliamentary Party met and passed a resolution calling for a public inquiry into the causes of the rising. In the House of Commons on 11 May, Dillon pleaded for an end to the policy of executions: 'You are letting loose a river of blood and make no mistake about it, between two races who, after three hundred years of hatred and strife, we had nearly succeeded in bringing it together.' The repression of the rising was 'washing out our whole lives in a sea of blood'. He then shocked many members in the House who shouted 'Shame' when he said: 'That may horrify you, but I declare most solemnly, and I am not ashamed to say it in the House of Commons, that I am proud of these men. They were foolish. They were misled.' He was not defending murderers, he said. They should be brought to trial, open trial: 'But it is not murderers who are being exe-cuted; it is insurgents who have fought a clean fight, a brave fight, however misguided, and it would have been a damned good thing for you if your soldiers were able to put up as good a fight as did these men in Dublin – three thousand men against twenty thousand with machine-guns and artillery.' His speech was fiery, indignant and radical and no less so when he gave the House details of the death of Sheehy Skeffington.[79] Despite Dillon's eloquence and common sense, the following day, 12 May, James Connolly and Seán MacDermott were executed – the last of the rising leaders to die by firing squad. Meanwhile, Windle referred on 11 May to the politicians 'carrying on *à faire vomir* – how the night-soil man shines by the politician than when the brothel-keeper (possibly) is one stage lower only and at the bottom of the ladder'. On 12 May, he gave his verdict on the Dillon speech: 'Dillon's speech in House of Commons a characteristic example of his incredible habit of doing the right thing in the wrongest possible way. He has been scourge of this country for years and of course now lets loose the oratory of Paddy Meade [?], Jerry Kelleher and all the other unwashed and un-regener-ated ruffians of the Cork Corporation – God knows what is to become of this country under such scoundrels.' On Saturday 13 May, Windle motored to west Cork with Edith: 'Stopped twice going and twice returning for permit which has to be got from police'. A man called Hayes 'half-drunk and meandering about the brave men who died in Dublin, and he would be proud to be in the grave with them. I suppose a type of the ill-balanced mind – a sort of village Dillon.' He drove back to the college to find that Professor Alexander had put up the Bishop of Ross's pastoral 'underlined in places on his notice-board and getting back of students up. He and Stockley at opposite poles are enough to drive anybody mad.'

Asquith arrived in Dublin on 12 May and remained until the 15th when he went to Belfast, returning to the capital on the same day. He visited Sinn Féin prisoners at Richmond barracks and entered into con-versation with them. On 17 May, he attended a meeting of the Privy Council in Dublin Castle. He travelled to Cork on 18 May and returned to London that evening. Windle wrote on the 14th: 'Much rumours about Asquith's visit to Ireland and its results which every one hopes may be good. At least he has shown courage and done the right thing in seeing the rebels – It is a sad business badly influenced by the wicked *Morning Post* and *Irish Times* on the one hand and by injudicious persons – often I fear priests – on the other.' On 15 May, he made a reference to 'injudicious (but perhaps less than might have been expected) letter from Bishop Cohalan in [*Cork*] *Examiner*'. He then made a very curious reference to Sheehy Skeffington: 'As G.C. [George Crosbie] says it is tragic to think that none can mention Sheehy Skeffington's death without laughing. He was bound to be shot.'

Windle had lunch on 16 May with John O'Connell who had come down from Dublin for a Honan Hostel meeting. He stayed the night and both men had an opportunity to discuss the events in Dublin in detail. O'Connell 'confirms my idea that the Sinn Féiners thought Germany would come to their aid by story of soldier friend taken prisoner by rebels and to 4 courts. There met Plunkett with whom he had been at school. They said Germany will relieve us on Wednesday or Thursday at latest. By Friday spirit quite taken out of them. Of course Germans never intended coming – afraid poor silly old Plunkett really has run his foolish head into trouble. O'Connell acts for Pearse's landlords and had many interesting stories about him – an honest creature with a distorted mind.' Later on 16 May, Windle worked in his office and then chaired a two-hour meeting of the Honan Hostel. His diary (16 May) reveals that he learned at that meeting that the Bishop of Cloyne (Robert Browne) 'thinks Cohalan's letter a mistake. So it was and another this morning (17th) foolish creature'. (Cohalan had written two letters in the *Cork Examiner* setting out his views on British policy.) Windle agreed with Bishop Browne: 'This it is to take a man from Maynooth with no experience of the world and make a bishop of him.' Windle's view of Cohalan became more and more critical after the latter became Bishop of Cork on 29 August 1916. However, it was not entirely accurate to suggest that he was devoid of all pastoral experience in his younger years. Born at Kilmichael, County Cork, in 1858, he was ordained in 1883, and served for three years as a teacher, a chaplain in the city's military prison, and as a curate in the parish of Tracton. Cohalan held the post of Professor of Moral and Dogmatic Theology in Maynooth between 1886 and 1914. He had been appointed Auxiliary Bishop of Cork on 25 May 1914.

On 17 May, Windle went to Dublin by afternoon train where he stayed in the Shelbourne: 'Up *before* time. Scenes of ruins in Sackville Street can hardly be imagined. All panes of glass in lower rooms of Shelbourne broken.' He had a long talk with a staff officer who was 'rounding up suspects'. The 18th was 'a long hot summer day'. After attending an unpleasant NUI Senate meeting, Windle visited O'Connell Street: 'went to see ruins an awful spectacle – Post Office and most of

Sackville St. gone – why didn't they wipe the whole dirty place and its dirty people out while they were about it?' On 19 May, he met a friend: 'Waldron tells me that that strumpet Countess Markievicz is now in a lunatic asylum as a sexual maniac. Her letters were simply horrible. Count Plunkett's house was stuffed with ammunition of every kind.'

On 20 May, he was back in Cork where he met a number of people including his close friend, Canon Patrick Roche: 'Everybody talking about Birrell's evidence on Irish outbreak which quite splendid in its perception and truth. C. Roche fears many of the clergy were involved though he had not thought so previously – impudent fledgling priests I expect for the most part.' Windle went back to Dublin on 22 May for another NUI meeting where [Sir Joseph] McGrath [registrar] told him that he had heard the following: '(1) that Ireland was surrounded by German subs and British could do nothing. (2) that Dublin was the last place to rise and all the rest of P.[?] was theirs. (3) That the Pope on Easter Sunday sent them his special blessing through Archbishop Walsh – This is what they all believed.' The latter point confirms – in a not entirely accurate way – the general belief that Count Plunkett had secured a papal blessing for all those about to go out in the rising.[80]

The British government continued its policy of coercion. Throughout the country, hundreds of Sinn Féin 'sympathisers' were rounded up, the number being over 100 from the Cork area. All were interned in England and Wales. In an effort to find a way out of the Irish political impasse, Asquith entrusted Lloyd George on 23 January to negotiate a settlement. His solution was to exclude the six northern counties. Windle and other nationalists were not surprised. They saw him pandering yet again to Carson and his hardline unionist associates. On 26 May, Windle noted: 'Lloyd George to try and pacify Ireland to settle thing. God grant he may.'[81] On 31 May, Windle gave vent to his frustration with Irish politicians: 'Unutterable guff being talked by every vote-hunter in this den of lies – Ireland – I wish I could be out of it, but alas there is no chance.' Another entry spoke of 'more hot-air from the rotten politicians especially local and so we go on with these hellhounds of politicians'. Windle reserved some of his most choice prose for members of the hierarchy he did not like, particularly Bishop Thomas O'Dwyer of Limerick, a formidable prelate who had played a prominent part in national politics since the 1870s.[82] Windle may have disliked his 1916 pastoral. According to his biographer, Fr Morrissey, 'the religious spirit, the felicity of language, and the hard realism [of the pastoral] could not fail to make an impact'. It earned high praise from Pope Benedict XV: 'he has written a fine pastoral'. Translated into Italian and into other languages, it had a wide impact.

In the aftermath of the rising, O'Dwyer received an ultimatum from General Maxwell, dated 6 May, demanding his cooperation with regard to two priests 'whose presence in the neighbourhood' he considered to be a 'dangerous menace to the peace and safety of the realm'.[83] O'Dwyer replied defiantly to the general, transforming him into an unlikely episcopal champion of radical Irish nationalism.[84] Because of censorship, there had been a delay in publication. His letter first appeared on 27 May in the *Cork Examiner* and was carried by the Dublin-based media a few days later. O'Dwyer's letter had all the greater impact because the Irish bishops as a body had issued no joint statement on the rising. Windle, a devout Catholic but no admirer of the leadership of the rising, took strong exception to what the Bishop of Limerick had written. Feeling that the bishops had disgraced themselves by their collective silence, he regarded O'Dwyer as a major threat to the future well-being of the Catholic Church in Ireland.[85] On 3 June, he wrote: 'Bishop Limerick – that cake of devil's faeces at it again. This country is enough to make an atheist of any but the strongest or the most careless . . . My god what a country and what a people. Town and Canon Roche and spoke my mind about the bishops and Coffey who are enough to make any weak-minded Catholic abandon his faith – would God I could get away from these surroundings and leave this gang of liars and backbiters.' Every day, the papers carried stories about the rising and its aftermath. Capt. J.C. Bowen-Colthurst was tried on 6 and 7 June by court martial for the murder of Francis Sheehy Skeffington and two other civilians. He was found guilty, but was deemed insane and was lodged in Broadmoor asylum until his release on 26 January 1918. He made a new life for himself in Canada.

The Irish Parliamentary Party, regrouping after the rising debacle, met in the Mansion House in Dublin on 10 June to discuss proposals being brought forward by Lloyd George on the future of Ireland. The proposal was to bring forward home rule immediately. That would be accompanied by an amending bill as a strictly War Emergency Act. It would cover only the period of the war and a short specified time afterwards. During that period, the Irish members would remain at Westminster. The six north-eastern counties would be left under the British imperial government for the duration of the war. After the war, the final settlement would be determined by Imperial Conference. On 10 June – the same day as the parliamentary party met – Windle wrote: 'As to this country it is now again delivered over to the vile band of cowardly blatherers temporarily held down by J. Redmond – an honest man – and the loudest of them is that misbegotten crank and hysteric J[ohn] Dillon.' On 12 June, he wrote: 'things here unsatisfactory – a degraded and ignorant priesthood, narrow-minded from never leaving the country and a bum-sucking gang of local "not to say national" politicians and no decent people mingling in the mess – What can one expect? The country is I fear almost hopeless.'

On 12 June, the Ulster Unionist Council accepted Lloyd George's proposal for the immediate implementation of home rule. Six counties in Ulster were to be temporarily excluded: 'we feel, as loyal citizens, that in this crisis in the Empire's history it is our duty to make sacrifices, and we consequently authorise Sir Edward Carson to continue the negotiations'.[86] On 13 June, Windle wrote optimistically: 'chance of settlement of Home Rule matter if these impudent, ill-bred, half educated priests, whom we laymen keep alive will hold their arrogant tongues. Wait till we get Home Rule and we will sort them.' On 14 June, he wrote: 'Northerner [Carson] agreed to Lloyd George scheme and others here will do it. But oh! the impudent curates'.

Windle presided over a series of college meetings on 14 June. The governing body passed a vote of sympathy on the deaths of Royal Navy surgeons Capps and Sydney Punch, and Lieut. T.K. O'Brien, Connaught Rangers, all of whom had been students of the college and it was directed 'that this expression of their sympathy be sent to the relatives of the deceased officers'.[87] Windle referred on 15 June to the death of the Bishop of Cork: 'Making arrangements about bishop's funeral which will be a dreadfully long business.'

On 17 June, Windle attended the funeral of Bishop O'Callaghan at the North Cathedral. He noted: 'four seats reserved – for the first time quite properly – privilege.' He gave a long description of the funeral, ending: 'These things always much too long.'

A conference of nationalists from the six Ulster counties, meeting in Belfast on 23 June, proposed to be excluded from inclusion in the Government of Ireland Act which they had accepted in view of all the circumstances of the present situation in Ireland. Windle commented on the same day: 'The Ulster Nationalists agree to separation – a *most* patriotic and noble action – majority 210 in 700 so quite clear – William O'Brien and his gang hold a disorderly meeting.' On 27 June, Windle wrote contemptuously of the unionists and their entourage: 'Same old gang going on with the aristocratic wretches [might alternatively be *bitches*] who are always poking their saddled noses into politics but it looks as if it would be defeated and Carson and Bonar Law seem to be playing fair. Is it possible to trust Lansdowne.' On 28 June, Windle was of the view that the 'Unionist intrigue seems breaking up.'

The report of the Royal Commission on the rising was published on 3 July. On 11 July, Windle commented: 'Asquith's speech regarding Ireland reveals nothing new.' On 13 July, he noted cryptically: 'Irish matter again

in chaos owing to Lansdowne's speech.' The following day, he referred
to 'rotten Irish intrigues'. On 17 July, he wrote: 'Irish matters going from
bad to worse. Can the Shinners be right? It is impossible to imagine anything more inept than that English handling of Ireland. Ape of Norfolk
and Hunt, the imbecile, as usual amongst our worst enemies.' On 18 July,
he added: 'The Salisburys and Norfolks and other spawn of Belial doing
their best to upset things in Ireland.' On 19 July, he wrote of 'fools of
Englishmen and dastards of Irish unionists'.

Lloyd George had assured Redmond that, once an agreement with
Carson had been reached, the cabinet would carry it out. If not, he would
resign. But when the unionists in the cabinet sabotaged the agreement
Lloyd George did not step down. Redmond's relationship with him was
never the same again. A fundamental bond of trust had been breached.
John Horgan quoted the following lines about Lloyd George:

> Count not his broken pledges as a crime
> He meant them, how he meant them – at the time

Horgan felt that no Irishman of that period could forget Lloyd George's
act of *Punica fides*. On 25 July, Windle concluded: 'Asquith, as Dillon said,
prefers Lansdowne to Ireland and gave the whole thing away – a weak
fool. Let him carry his stinking carrion burden on his shoulders –
Redmond's and Carson's speeches excellent and a rapprochement ought
to be possible. But Asquith and Lloyd George just faecal vomit. Never
trust an Englishman still less a Welshman.'

Windle returned from England to Cork, driving on the 26th to
Skibbereen, where he was caught up in the crowds at an agricultural
show: 'Place full of people busy and drinking themselves into the gutter.
What a country.' Windle, disappointed by O'Dwyer of Limerick, had little
time for Archbishop William Walsh's nationalist sympathies and added to
his distaste for the leadership of the Irish Catholic Church – a disaffection
which grew during his last years in the country.[88] He wrote on 27 July:
'Archbishop of Dublin writes a vile letter – one of these days we will
perhaps be able to better these conditions. Impudent fool.' He had a
declining respect for the archbishop whose stance in the wake of the rising
had angered him. Walsh had, due to illness, not met Asquith on his visit to
the city.[89] But he had agreed to act as chairman of Cardinal Farley's Irish
Distress Fund, later known as the National Aid Fund.[90] Windle could not
accept such a contradiction in the actions of the Archbishop of Dublin.

On 1 August, Windle returned to his denunciation of the Asquith government: 'the government and Asquith in particular have covered
themselves with infamy by knuckling under to Lansdowne and Co. Irish
members speak well and the general feeling of England is against

government.' Asquith compounded his mistakes, in the eyes of Windle, by appointing a unionist, Henry Edward Duke KC, as successor to Birrell. On 1 August 1916, he described him as being a man who had never been in Ireland and 'most undoubtedly will leave it ruined as politician for every man's hand will be against him. One must now hope that the war will be won by the Russians and French not the English.' Windle wrote on 12 August of 'picture in the paper of [new chief secretary] Duke arriving in Kingstown with a fine smile on his face which may soon be on the other side of his mouth when he leaves – a tragic history for an apparently promising man.' His term as chief secretary between 1916 and 1918 was far from distinguished.

Seeking refuge from the disappointments of his professional and public life, Windle came to rely more and more on his visits to Listarkin – a very special place of refuge. There, he was close to his relatives at Castletownshend, visiting the Somervilles on 28 July: 'Went over to see Miss Somerville – just past her 90th birthday and full of life and in possession of all her faculties.' But even the Listarkin idyll was blighted in August 1916 when his favourite dog, Sally, was accidentally poisoned by 'some scoundrel' who wanted to stop dogs barking at night.[91] On 5 August, Windle wrote that it was 'a hard thing for me having so few things to care for or to care for me. Buried her with many [lamentations]. A bad night. It is ridiculous to think of leaving . . . because one has lost a dog but my interest in Listarkin is killed and can never revive. If I live two years I will clear out of this accursed country where every prospect pleases but oh how vile is man.' After attending Mass on Sunday, 6 August, he noted: 'Fretted all day about Sally. Hard to lose a creature which really loved one when there are so few that do. This holiday quite ruined by this event.' On 9 August, he remembered the death of his only son who died after only a few months: 'Twenty years ago Lawrence was born and might have now been fighting had he lived. Yet he too might have been a disappointment like the other two [his daughters] and like so many other things in this world.'[92]

Windle had been in England for part of the trial of Roger Casement which was held from 26 to 29 June. On the 29th, Windle recorded: 'Casement condemned to death – made the usual bumptious speech – a one-idea'd vain man who will not be put to death and ought to be in a criminal lunatic asylum.' The prosecution was led by the attorney general, Sir Frederick Edwin (FE) Smith. The tactics were particularly robust, with a strong emphasis upon his active homosexuality. This trial was conducted before a generation with a strong memory of the trial of Oscar Wilde in 1895. The tactic of demonising Casement did not work in Ireland but held sway in court. He was found guilty of high treason and sentenced to death. A strong campaign was mounted to commute the sentence. But all public pressure failed and he was hanged on 3 August in Pentonville, London. Windle wrote in his diary on the 4th: 'Government hanged Casement. Fools to make a martyr where they might have made every one think him a spy.' Casement's trial and execution gave a major propaganda victory to Sinn Féin.

Windle returned to UCC for the new term. On 11 October, a meeting of the governing body recorded a letter from Dean Shinkwin acknowledging the governing body's letter of sympathy on the death of the Bishop of Cork, Dr O'Callaghan.[93] The meeting also recorded a resolution of sympathy on the death of Professor Harper: 'The Governing Body desire to convey to the relatives of the late Professor Harper the deep regret with which they have learnt of his gallant death in France as an officer in the 10th South Staffordshire Regiment and to place on record their sense of the loss to the College caused by his untimely end.'[94] At the same meeting, the Professor of Physiology, D. Barry, had written that he wished to take up a temporary commission in the RAMC due to 'a great dearth of doctors in the army'. The governing body sanctioned Professor Barry for leave of absence to give 'evening lectures on Alcohol and Venereal Diseases'.[95]

Windle's dislike of Bishop Cohalan grew in intensity. The bishop, according to him, had insulted the memory of UCC's great benefactor, Isabella Honan: 'Dr Cohalan refused to say Mass for Honan family unless paid for same and in one of the most vulgar and impudent letters I have ever read – what a clergy this unhappy country has! Any Catholic of education who keeps his Faith in it, is proof against anything.' He wrote again: 'What a gang the bishops and priests of this country are? . . . one has to remember that the church's treasure is in earthen (very earthen) pots.'

On Saturday 4 November, Lieutenant General Bryan Mahon, a Catholic, replaced Sir John Maxwell as commander-in-chief in Ireland. That appointment, while it paved the way for a possible thaw in hardline British policy towards Ireland, was an opportunity for Sinn Féin to intensify its propaganda war. The British government came under increasing pressure from Australia and the United States to release all internees and the chief secretary, Henry Duke, succumbed – a great coup for Sinn Féin, using the occasion of the return of so many internees to press for even wider support for their programme.[96]

On Sunday 5 November 1916, Windle enjoyed one of the best days of his entire years in UCC – the occasion of the opening of the Honan Chapel. Bishop Kelly gave a very strong sermon to a packed congregation. On 8 November 1916, he wrote of an inspection [of the Honan Hostel] by Bishop Cohalan which he could not avoid 'though disliking him greatly'.[97] On Sunday 12 November, Windle went reluctantly to Cohalan's installation in the North Cathedral. But he did so 'much against the grain for I think little of him and the praise which is poured out on him by those who think as little as I do makes one sick.' Cohalan, however, surprised him: 'Bishop has made quite a straight speech about politics declaring himself – Redmondite – though he will take no part in elections.'

As 1916 came towards an end, Windle was despondent about the future of the Irish Catholic Church. He had no respect for the overwhelming majority of bishops. He observed with alarm the rise of radical nationalism in the country and Windle watched helplessly as the British government and Dublin Castle made a complete mess of running the country. On 4 December, he wrote in his diary: 'How the whore shines by the side of the politician and how we want a Cromwell or some one like that to purge this vile House of Commons.' He was watching the final days of the Asquith government. He commented on 5 December about the manoeuvrings by Lloyd George to oust the prime minister: 'Government intrigues still on . . . I cannot trust a Welsh nonconformist attorney – the combination must bear a liar and a knave – Asquith no doubt is a ruffian of the worst kind but what of Bonar Law? May or may not be honest. Probably not as he is a politician.' Bonar Law, at that point, was rumoured to be the next prime minister. Windle certainly did not relish the prospect of unionists, together with their press baron supporters, coming to power; writing on 6 December, he asked: 'Why that foetid gutter-snipe Northcliffe has not been hanged long ago beats me. However the thing may be politics is a vile game and played as low down in England as it can be. But for the fact that this country (and incidentally) all my family are tied up with it, I could wish England no good.' Windle wrote on 7 December that 'this Northcliffe–Lloyd George combination thinks and rightly that it can do down Asquith'. He did not have to wait long to see his prediction come true. On 8 December, he wrote: 'Lloyd George Premier. Asquith refuses Garter and an Earldom – Carson – First Lord of the Admiralty – God in Heaven what a gang – gutter-snipes *in excelsis!*'

The new government was made up of fifteen unionists/conservatives, and by members of the Liberal and Labour parties none of whom had served in cabinet before. Lawrence McBride described the change in the composition of the British government in Ireland in the post-rising period in dramatic terms. Birrell had been replaced by a military regime. That in turn was given over to a unionist-led administration breaking the Irish Parliamentary Party's *de facto* influence over Dublin Castle.[98] The British had transformed the Irish administration from a regime of government into a force of occupation, justifying such a shift on the basis that all nationalists were potentially disloyal. According to McBride, the big losers in the new system were John Redmond and his party. Perhaps both Redmond and Lloyd George underestimated the political danger posed by Sinn Féin 'to the hegemony of the Irish Parliamentary Party'.[99]

Windle, wishing to get away from all the depressing news, drove to Listarkin in mid-December in three hours.[100] He went to see Miss Somerville on the 20th. She was past ninety and 'mind as clear as a bell'. On the same day, Cardinal Gasquet wrote: 'Ireland has been making history and I only wish I could have a long talk with you about many things, which are not at all clear. When I was in London in the summer I saw several of the Irish Nationalist party and gathered that they are not at all in the Good Graces of the Bishops and clergy. But what is the use of discussing anything at the present moment. Let us hope that this coming year may see the end of this awful war and the only end that can secure civilization from this attack of German Kultur.'[101] Windle was not full of the season of goodwill when, on 22 December, he wrote about President Woodrow Wilson: 'Wilson's note published. His lily-liver pines for peace at any price or else he is trying to pull the chestnuts out of the fire for the unspeakable Hun. I hope we shall have nothing of it but with the gang of lawyer politicians we have anything is possible.' On Christmas Day, he went to Mass in Union Hall and, in the afternoon, 'Edith down village distributing toys with great delight.' Windle wrote in his final 1916 entry: 'So ends this dolorous year in which I at least have had many things to be thankful for – but a depressing year on account of the perpetual political intrigues. Surely politics is now a card-sharpers game fit for bauds and brothel-bullies not for gentlemen. When jackeens like Northcliffe and Carson hold the reins, it is time that a thorough purge was given to the country and but that we are tied to it why should England be cherished?' Windle saw out the old year on that forlorn note.

CHAPTER 6

The Rise of Sinn Féin and
the Irish Convention

Windle began 1917 more in hope than in the expectation of the British government returning to a sane and sensible Irish policy. He had a low opinion of Lloyd George and an even more disparaging view of many members of his cabinet and their press baron entourage.[1] Windle was witnessing – whether he was fully aware of it or not – the passing of the old Irish Parliamentary Party order. Windle believed that the pro-unionist policies of the British government, which were undercutting Redmond's popular roots and that of his party, were liable to end in disaster and that, for him, meant the victory of Sinn Féin – a radical nationalist coalition forged out of the rising and out of its brutal repression. Éamon de Valera, turned down for a professorial post in UCC in 1913, was one of the main rising stars of a new Irish politics. Windle, who had disliked him in 1913, did not have cause to change his mind during his remaining two years in Ireland. The old order was indeed passing and Windle, now so much a part of the British establishment in Ireland, was very late in seeing Sinn Féin's potential for ultimate victory.

Besides his loss of faith in the Irish policies of the government – and even at times in British democracy itself – Windle had also become alienated from the overwhelming majority of the Irish episcopate and their nationalistic brand of Catholicism. By the end of 1917 he held the Irish Catholic Church and its leadership in even less esteem. For example, two unfortunate episodes in early 1917 destroyed his tentative friendship with Bishop Cohalan of Cork. He wrote on 6 January: 'Mass – letters. Accompanying one from Bishop Cohalan respecting recognition of technical school as to which he knows nothing yet objects. Why is it that when a man becomes a Bishop he at once ceases to use all sense of decency. A weak man afraid to have it thought that he is being led by others. How these fools are throwing away their inheritance and how anti-clericalism is swamping this country.' Windle also had a personal reason for disliking the local bishop. His close friend, Canon Patrick Roche, had – against his will – been moved from the centre-city parish of SS Peter and Paul to Ballincollig in the countryside. Roche found the unnecessary move 'very distressing', according to Windle, and 'I think a rotten stroke. Probably doesn't want strong man near the throne.' On 9 January, Windle met Cohalan outside the college, and noted: 'a curious, mean obstinate man of a very narrow type.' He called on Roche who was 'seething with annoyance'. 'What a gang our clerics are', Windle wrote on 20 January.

Windle's dislike for Cohalan was surpassed only by his detestation of Bishop O'Dwyer of Limerick. On 24 January he recorded the victory of the Unionist Sir Stephen Quinn in the contest for the Lord Mayor of Limerick by twenty-three to ten – 'I hope a slap for the lousy Limerick bishop.' Noting on 18 February that he had issued a pastoral, Windle commented that it was 'so base, so lying, so dishonest as to outdo anything ever done even by those dregs of humanity – the Irish bishops'. He added: 'why a miserable pimped up little peasant should be allowed to do these things is a mystery. For me it determines me not to go near Catholic things (outside personal religion).' Windle's opinion of Bishop O'Dwyer did not mellow before his death on 19 August 1917. He remained quite unforgiving. On 29 January, he noted that it was the Kaiser's birthday: 'May he spend his next in that part of the other world where alone he could be happy viz in Hell or the most inflamed part of Purgatory.'[2]

Sinn Féin enjoyed its first major political breakthrough on 5 February 1917 when, in a by-election, the voters of North Roscommon returned George Noble Count Plunkett to Westminster. The father of one of the executed leaders of the rising, he declined to take the seat in accordance with Sinn Féin policy. Meanwhile, Windle noted the same day about the British 'yellow press', with particular emphasis on 'the lies' of the *Daily Mail*: 'What a land England is to be swayed by such lying garbage as is spat out by Northcliffe.' Meanwhile, the Irish Parliamentary Party fought in the Commons to advance the forlorn cause of home rule. William Redmond, who had enlisted in 1915, had returned to the House in December 1916 and spoke passionately about the unity of Orange and Green in the trenches and of how nationalist and unionist officers and men had forged bonds of comradeship and friendship: 'no one, I say, can see these men passing with this [green] badge on the roads in France and Belgium, in comradeship and friendship with the men who have on their shoulder the Orange badge, without being struck by the newness of the situation, if you like, but with the great hope which is in it, and with the lesson that it teaches.'[3] Before returning to the front, he left the following letter with his solicitor: 'If I should die abroad I will give my wife my last thought and love, and ask her to pray that we may meet hereafter. I shall die a true Catholic, humbly hoping for mercy from God, through the intercession of his Blessed Mother, whose help I have ever invoked all through my life. I should like all my friends to know that in joining the Irish Brigade and in going to France I sincerely believed, as all Irish soldiers do, that I was doing my best for the welfare of Ireland in every way.'[4]

In the absence of his brother, John Redmond and his fellow MPs continued the parliamentary fight to press the British government to move on the question of home rule. Windle, on 6 March, wrote of 'base English intrigues against this country and its prosperity constantly going on'. He recorded on 8 March: 'Debate in House of Commons the most disgraceful episode even in English history. Lloyd George's behaviour what might have been expected from a leprous Welsh Calvinist meth[odist?] attorney. Healy covers himself with his own faeces as with a cloak. How can anyone expect Ireland to be loyal and why should Irish men fight for such a country?' On 9 March, he wrote: 'Evidently Healy has sold what is left of his lecherous little soul to the scurrilous gang of Tory intriguers.' On 14 March: 'Lloyd George I hope sinking in public estimation as an obvious and branded liar,' and on 15 March: 'further rumours about Home Rule – How much longer are the stupid English going to allow that ex corner boy Carson to sit on their hands? What a fatuous race!'[5]

On 17 March, Willie Redmond returned to the House of Commons to deliver his most famous speech. He spoke on a motion calling on the House 'without further delay to confer upon Ireland the free institutions long promised her'. He said:

> Mistakes – dark, black, and bitter mistakes – have been made. A people denied justice, a people with many admitted grievances, the redress of which has been long delayed, on our side, perhaps, in the conflict and in the bitterness of contest, there may have been things said and done, offensive if will, irritating if will, to the people of this country; but what I want to ask, in all simplicity, is this, whether in face of the tremendous conflict which is now raging, whether, in view of the fact that, apart from every other consideration, the Irish people, South as well as North, are upon the side of the allies and against the German pretension today, it is not possible from this war to make a new start; whether it is not possible on your side, and on ours as well, to let the dead past bury its dead, and to commence a brighter and a newer and a friendlier era between the two countries?

He asked what stood in the way of a settlement: 'Canada everybody is proud of. Australia has done her part splendidly in this struggle. Why cannot you listen to them? Canada five times in her parliament has begged you to deal with the Irish question on broad and free lines, and Australia has done the same. In God's name, why cannot you do it? I do not believe there is an Englishman in Europe who would not this very night agree to a full and free measure of home rule if the Irish people themselves would demand it.' Redmond then appealed to Sir Edward Carson: 'If there ought to be an oblivion of the past between Great Britain and Ireland generally, may I ask in God's name the first lord of the admiralty [Carson] why there cannot be a similar oblivion on the past between the warring sections in Ireland?' What was it that stood in the way of Ireland taking her place as a self-governing part of the empire, he asked the House. Ireland was the only part of the empire fighting which was not self-governing, he answered.[6]

Windle, a friend of Willie Redmond, was not impressed by the immediate response of Lloyd George. He described the English as 'a wooden-hard crowd' on 23 March when making reference to the recent debate in the House of Commons. Two days later, he wrote: 'First signs of Carson's utter incompetence as First Lord in papers. May that impostor and traitor soon be hounded out of Public life. Poor [Eoin] MacNeill at Parkhurst and Carson in cabinet and that is justice as she is taught in England.' Gasquet wrote to him on 28 March about the state of Irish politics: 'We are all hoping and praying that the Irish question may be nearing an end. I have heard once or twice from T.P. [O'Connor]. As far as I can see the Bishops in Ireland are not working with the Irish Party and they would seem to me to be playing a very dangerous game from the church's point of view . . .'[7] The cardinal thanked Windle for a copy of his recently published book on religion and science, and noted that he was arranging for a presentation copy to be given to Pope Benedict XV.

Woodrow Wilson – much maligned by Windle – made a dramatic appeal to the US Congress on 2 April to declare war on Germany. That development brightened Windle's spirits. He wrote on 4 April: 'Wilson at last calls for war – great enthusiasm in U.S.A.' On 6 April, he wrote: 'American Senate by overwhelming majority declare for war. I feel I must apologize to Wilson for derogatory remarks. He really may be the great man of the war . . . Moreover, his address a Masterpiece.'[8] With the United States in, the future looked immediately brighter for victory. But it also meant that there was a new imperative for British politicians to solve the Irish question. Dr Bernadette Whelan has written a comprehensive overview of Irish-American relations during this troubled period.[9] Failure to bring about a political resolution in Ireland would mean an added complication at the post-war peace conference. The Imperial War Cabinet had been formed in March 1917. Headed by Lloyd George, it included the prime minister of Canada, Sir Robert Borden; the prime minister of South Africa, Louis Botha; the prime minister of Australia, Billy Hughes; the prime minister of New Zealand, William Massey; Jan Smuts of South Africa and the British secretary of state for India and other senior ministers from Britain and the dominions. The Dominion prime ministers, now members of the Imperial Cabinet, put pressure on to find a solution for Ireland. Lloyd George angled to implement home rule in twenty-six counties, leaving the northern six counties under unionist control. That had been his consistent line in the latter part of 1916.

On 9 April, Windle returned to a theme which preoccupied him during the latter years of the war – the need to do away with despotic monarchs: 'Kings and Head nobles are an abomination – and with private property in land (and mines!) should disappear' in the post-war settlement. On 12 April, Windle wrote: 'I hope I may live to see the day when these islands get rid of their junkers and live in peace with one another.' He looked forward to an end to the old hegemonic world order. Windle wrote on 22 April: 'A perfectly transcendent day – nothing can be more beautiful than the sea and sky and shores – but for vile man and his vile rats [?] – i.e. vile autocratic men – Let us hope the end of the war may mean the end of all monarchies and hereditary titles. Such things are the dung-heaps on which the fungi of oppression and iniquity grow. Yet democracy is the dunghill on which Lloyd George and suchlike poisonous [bullies?] flourish and anyway George V is a gentleman which heaven knows Lloyd George is not.'

The Irish Parliamentary Party suffered yet another setback on 9 May, losing the South Longford by-election: 'Longford election – Shinners in by 30 votes . . . But this Government deserves anything and everything it gets if it allows itself to be bossed by the [. . .] unspeakable Carson,' he wrote on 10 May. As the very future of the Irish Parliamentary Party was now in doubt, Lloyd George had come forward with a set of new proposals to settle the Irish impasse. By May 1917, Lloyd George proposed to introduce a bill to apply immediately the Home Rule Act, with the exclusion for five to six years of six Ulster counties. His Plan B was to hold an Irish Convention of all the parties in order to find agreement on a scheme for self-government. On 21 May, the prime minister announced the setting up of just such a body. The idea got a mixed reception in Ireland. On 5 June, Windle wrote: 'Great doubts about Irish Convention.' The following day, he recorded: 'Dillon the difficulty. *And* no wonder. Also lice-like Bishop of Limerick and Co. and no wonder. Still things move.' The death in action of William Redmond on 7 June at the Battle of Messines helped introduce a more sober note into Irish politics. He was buried in the grounds of the Locre Hospice, Flanders, and on 12 June a requiem Mass was held for him at Westminster Cathedral.[10] Reflecting the views of many Irishmen, Windle had written on 9 June: 'News of Wm. Redmond's death – a very great loss.' Life went on.

William Redmond's death may have helped pave the way for a greater receptivity to the idea of political compromise and moderation. The convention idea offered such a course of action and it was actively taken up by constitutional nationalists in Cork. On 8 June, Windle wrote that Sherman Crawford planned to hold a meeting in the city in support of the convention idea: 'All want me to be chair and had to agree.' But the Irish Parliamentary Party was divided on the proposal. Windle wrote: 'Dillon – that misbegotten ass who is the real difficulty in Ireland today.' However, John Redmond gave his support to the idea. On 11 June, Windle hosted a convention planning meeting in Cork: 'long and interesting and arranged all about Thursday's meeting. Saw bishop and got him to promise to speak.' In introducing his plan to the House of Commons on 11 June, Lloyd George made a direct reference to William Redmond: 'there were political tasks at home which his genial presence, his great personal popularity, and his moving powers of speech would have been useful to aid. He elected instead to face death on the battlefield.' Asquith said that the success of the convention would be 'the best and most enduring tribute and monument we can raise to his memory'. Carson, too, linked the calling of the convention to the death of Redmond. The *Cork Examiner*, on 11 June, wrote: 'If those taking part in it exhibit the fraternal feeling that was the keynote to the success of the Irish troops at the storming of the ridge of Messines then it cannot fail . . . The death of Major Redmond should help to draw together the men who have in the past been estranged . . . It must not be said of Irishmen that they can agree everywhere but at home.'[11]

On Thursday 14 June, Windle presided over a large meeting in the city hall which was, according to his entry for that day, attended by 600 business and professional people representing all the major interests in the city and region 'wishing success to Convention'. Horgan, who was also at the meeting, claimed that 'an organised attempt' had been made to break up the meeting by 'a small body of young men representing the Sinn Féin party'. Windle wrote that there had been 'much disturbance by 40–50 youths and boys who sang, whistled and carried on, making my position in the chair not very pleasant'. Horgan, writing in the late 1940s, believed that the 'young hooligans' of 1917 were 'the precursors of the Black Shirts and the Storm Troopers'.[12] A resolution of God-speed to the convention was passed, despite the organised Sinn Féin disruption.[13]

Windle continued with his daily duties, commenting at night in his diary on the state of the country. He wrote on 15 June: 'Amnesty to Irish prisoners – If the strumpet Markievicz can break her neck or become heavily pregnant she may keep quiet – not otherwise – Should (?) be chaste is out anyway.'[14] He wrote on 26 June: 'Sinn Féiners seem to desire no more rows [and] further "order"their members to keep off the streets so as to avoid trouble. Pity a few more of them couldn't have had a whacking of some sort to teach them sense.' Meanwhile, Windle placed his hopes on the convention being a way out of the impasse. Gasquet wrote to Windle on 30 June: 'We are all praying that this Convention may effect some settlement of the Irish question. I looked down the names of those who attended your meeting. I see many Protestant clergymen on the list but not a Catholic – I fear that religion will suffer from this stand-off policy.'[15]

The outcome of yet another by-election underlined – if that were necessary – the need for a bold initiative in Irish politics if the Irish Parliamentary Party were to be rescued from the danger of going into oblivion. A vacancy had occurred in East Clare due to the death of William Redmond who had represented the constituency at Westminster for twenty-five years. Éamon de Valera, recently released from jail, was selected to stand for Sinn Féin. Windle wrote on 5 July: 'but Oh God the asininity of the Shinner and sins [are] certainly reincarnated in that bloody ass de Valera. Old Spright says Clare farmers will have nothing to do with him or S.F.'[16] But Windle's informant proved unreliable. De Valera had arrived in the constituency on 23 June. He canvassed with Professor Eoin MacNeill supported by election posters which said: 'A vote for Ireland a Nation, a vote against Conscription, a vote against partition, a vote for Ireland's language, and for Ireland's ideals and civilisation.'The IPP candidate, Patrick Lynch, a Crown prosecutor, had strong support. He, too, canvassed on the record of his party in preventing the extension of conscription to Ireland. But the IPP were in disarray and very few of the party leaders turned out to support what headquarters thought was a safe seat. Éamon de Valera swept to victory on 10 July with a majority of 2,975 votes (5,010 to 2,035), appearing on the courthouse steps in Ennis in the uniform of the Irish Volunteers, flanked by Countess Markievicz, Count Plunkett MP and Arthur Griffith.[17] Commenting on 12 July, Windle revealed his quandary: he was unable to accept 'that the Sinn Féin evidently are anxious to avoid disturbance and seem to want a constitutional movement for a Republic – an impossible dream. May I get speedily out of this country! Yes: but where? Should I take the wings of the morning.'

The Irish Convention

While Sinn Féin celebrated a great political victory in East Clare, Windle was 'overwhelmed' to receive a letter on 13 July from the prime minister 'asking me to be a member of the Irish Convention. How this came I can't think. Very averse to it as it will smash my holiday and certainly give rise to much work and worry, but could not possibly refuse so wired and wrote acceptance.' Speculating about why he was asked to serve, one source said 'why isn't Sir Bertram Windle put in to match Mahaffy and represent NUI?' Windle wrote to Horgan on 15 July: 'What I heard in England leads me to think that the attempt, if any, to burke the Convention, will be much resented and personally I think better of its chances than you and others seem to do.'[18] Windle immediately started to prepare for his new role. He read George Russell (Æ)'s pamphlet on the convention which 'really is an admirable piece of work – also J.J.H's [his son-in-law] draft of an Ulster settlement which I also think admirable and workable'.[19] He also read Erskine Childers' *Framework of Home Rule*, which impressed him greatly.[20] The latter was appointed an assistant secretary to the convention. Windle wrote to Humphreys on 18 July that he had been assailed by a sense of duty and that, once offered the position, he could not refuse 'though it knocks the bottom out of my holiday, which I shall spend gassing and being gassed'. However, he had the satisfaction of feeling that 'I shall be engaged in important and useful work. I have never refused to do anything that I could in connexion with the War, but have always felt that I was doing but little in comparison, for example, with what you have been doing, not to speak of thousands of others.' If he could help bring about a settlement 'in this distracted country I shall have done as useful work as if I were in the trenches at the hinder end of a gun'. Windle was convinced that 'we have a great and unexampled chance if we have sense enough to make use of it'. He believed, in fact he knew, that there was a 'great body of sensible, moderate opinion in this country which has never become articulate, but may yet do so, now it has its chance'. Windle noted that a great deal of non-sense had been written about the convention, but 'no man can truthfully say that it is not a wonderfully representative body'.[21]

Windle wrote to Sr Monica on 22 July from Listarkin, telling her of his acceptance of the invitation to the convention: '. . . I am off to Dublin to-morrow to the destruction of my holiday but it is a clear piece of duty. This is far too long a letter but it is a great pleasure to write to you and indeed I find it impossible to realize that we have only met once and may never meet again in this world. However I hope this may not be so. Do not forget me in your prayers and remember that I rely greatly upon them. I am your affectionate friend.'[22]

The membership of the convention quickly became clear. Sinn Féin simply refused to participate. John Redmond committed the Irish Parliamentary Party to the new initiative and led its delegation. However,

John Dillon did not support the convention and William O'Brien, too, refused to become involved. Tim Healy was another conscientious objector. However, William Martin Murphy, the entrepreneur and owner of the *Irish Independent*, played a very active role on the nationalist side. The chairmen of the thirty-three county councils, the lords mayor or mayors of the six county boroughs, and the chairmen of the urban councils throughout Ireland were requested to appoint eight representatives, two from each province. The Ulster Parliamentary Party and the Irish Unionist Alliance were each invited to nominate five representatives. The northern unionists were led by Hugh T. Barrie, Londonderry and Abercorn. The southern unionists were led by Lord Midleton. The Church of Ireland was represented by the archbishops of Armagh and Dublin. The moderator of the General Assembly represented the Presbyterian Church of Ireland. The chairmen of the Chambers of Commerce of Dublin, Belfast and Cork were invited, together with Labour organisations. The representative peers of Ireland were asked to select two of their number. In addition to one member selected to represent the Trades and Labour Council of Belfast, six persons were appointed to represent various labour organisations, and fifteen other people were nominated by the government, making the total membership of the convention ninety-five. During the lifetime of the convention, three members died and two resigned.

The Catholic hierarchy had difficulty selecting episcopal representatives. Cardinal Logue saw the convention as a way of both deflecting the onward march of Sinn Féin and of providing a possible solution to the dilemma of constitutional nationalists. Archbishop Walsh was not a supporter. He had moved a significant direction towards embracing Sinn Féin as represented by de Valera – a man Logue never really liked or trusted. Neither of the two archbishops favoured sending the Bishop of Raphoe, Patrick O'Donnell, as a delegate. He had been weak in his opposition to partition in 1916, but he was selected by his fellow bishops as were also the Archbishop of Cashel, John Harty, and the Bishop of Down and Connor, Joseph MacRory.[23] The Bishop of Ross, Denis Kelly, was prevented from attending frequently due to bad health.

Professor R.B. McDowell, in his study of the Irish Convention, helpfully describes its composition as follows: 'From what has been said it is clear that taking the convention as a whole it undoubtedly contained a remarkable number of men of ability and personality. Politically speaking the 95 members who accepted invitations were divided as follows: 52 were nationalists (two of whom, [Edward] MacLysaght and [George William (Æ)] Russell, were in advance of the others), two were liberals ([Earl of] Granard and [Lord Antony Patrick] MacDonnell), six were labour, nine were southern unionists, twenty-four were Ulster unionists, [John Pentland] Mahaffy is hard to label, and [Horace] Plunkett, as will be seen, strove to be detached. Grouping the members theologically – which many Irishmen at this time would almost automatically attempt to do – there seem to have been 53 catholics and 42 protestants.'[24]

As finally constituted, according to Horgan, there were ninety-five members, of whom fifteen were nominated by the government, forty-six elected public representatives, while the remainder were delegates of the Churches, Irish peers, political parties, trade unions and chambers of commerce. 'It was in fact a very representative body,' wrote Horgan,[25] who, in preparation for the convention, published a series of articles in *The Leader* during June and July entitled 'An Irish Constitution'. His friend, Edward Martyn, wrote to him on 13 July just after de Valera had won the Clare by-election: 'I put off writing to you until after the Clare election which shows that Sinn Féin is going through the country like an epidemic. I must say I do not pity the Parliamentary Party, they are responsible practically for everything. If ten years ago they had tackled the British Government vigorously we would never have had Carsonism out of which everything else has grown . . . However, I have now come to the conclusion that as long as England is a great power she will never relax her grip on Ireland if she can possibly avoid it. They may talk of Home Rule and get up bogus conventions to gain time, and tide them over their difficulties, but nothing short of irresistible pressure will make them give it. That is why I see the only hope in the Sinn Féin idea of going before the Peace Conference.' When men like Martyn thought along such lines, it was very clear just how far Sinn Féin had advanced on the road to political victory.

The convention proved to be a hopelessly divided body. Windle, writing an overall assessment of the parties involved at the end of his 1918 diary, will serve as a guide to the following analysis:

CONVENTION,

As for my own views on the people I came across and, so to speak, lived with for eight months:

(1) Ulster. If to make money and the best of this world is all, Ulster is right, but if not, *not*. They have no 'vision' beyond money, so it seems to me, and are not really Irish. Can they ever amalgamate with the rest of the country? It is difficult to imagine it. Look at [John Stoupe Finlay McCance, Unionist Antrim County Council] – educated at Oxford, pleasant privately I'm told – an absolutely revolting bounder in the Convention.

(2) Southern Unionists. These are the men who really appeal to me and of course by birth and associations I belong to them and

understand them. They are gentlemen, and you know that their word is their bond. I liked all of them, though I began with the greatest prejudice against [Viscount] Midleton, [Andrew] Jameson and several others, e.g., [George Francis] Stewart. Yet I was wrong. These men acted in a most patriotic spirit, and if all the rest had been like them the Convention would have been a great success.

(3) The Protestant Bishops.[26] [Archbishop of Dublin, John Henry] Bernard excellent and goes with Southern Unionists. [Archbishop of Armagh, John Baptist] Crozier had a hard task and got bogged at the end. Everybody liked him, but he has not the brains of Bernard.

(4) The Catholic Bishops. Proved to me that Ireland can do no good till the priest (and parson) is eliminated from politics. Save [Denis] Kelly who was early eliminated by illness, they neither sought peace nor ensured it but went for the utmost limit. Raphoe's ill temper when beaten was anything but edifying – altogether they did no good to religion amongst their own who were disedified nor amongst the others who said 'What did we always tell you?' As to the Southern Unionists nothing could change view that the bishops meant strangling Home Rule by excessive demands.

(5) County Council Chairmen. In the lump an excellent sensible body of men who would make good M.P.s. Some asses, but very few.

(6) For the rest – the assembly was at least as good as any House of Commons in England, and would have made a thoroughly sensible parliament.[27]

However, such judgments were formulated after the event and were based on Windle's bitter experience of attending virtually every session of a convention that ended in failure.

Delegates had begun with high expectations. On 22 July, Windle had lunch with Horgan at Listarkin and they discussed the convention: 'Wild yarn as to riot in Cork and two priests killed.' The rumour came from Skibbereen. But on returning to Cork the following day, he learned that the reports about violence were 'an absolute lie about any trouble in Cork – not a vestige of ground for this lie. Who starts such things?' Windle travelled to Dublin for the first meeting of the convention on 25 July. It met in the Regent House, Trinity College. Windle was one of those proposed for the chair: 'Convention began at 11.00 to speech from Duke – Very good.' That afternoon, 'John Redmond announced names of chair H. Plunkett and F[rancis John Stephens] Hopwood (secretary).' After some discussion the meeting broke up. Windle, who was seated behind Redmond and Joe Devlin, wrote: 'John Redmond, Devlin and I walked away together.' Plunkett 'was the only man all would agree on. I understand my name was considered.' Windle commented: 'John Redmond seems well but harassed – could he be otherwise.'

On 26 July, Windle wrote that he had been elected to the Procedure Committee: 'general view is satisfactory – nobody particularly wanted Horace Plunkett as chairman but himself and I suppose Æ [George Russell] who I suppose is an able person but lord is a complete *poseur* . . . Hopwood obviously A1. To Cork by 3.00'. Gasquet wrote to Windle on 28 July:

> I am very glad that you have been appointed a member of the Great Convention. I sincerely hope that it may succeed in coming to some conclusion. I believe that England would be ready to give Ireland anything it wanted to secure a permanent peace. Even a Colonial Constitution though I cannot see how it [Ireland] could live and flourish on those lines. What I do fear is for the future of the Church and its interests under new conditions. As you say – the Bishops do not appear to realise whither they are drifting. However matters have gone too far now to draw back and there does not seem to be any strong man to take the lead. Two things I deeply regret – one that the Irish nationalist party is treated as it apparently is and that after all his real work for his country John Redmond finds his position attacked by the clerical party and by the revolutionary element. And (2) that the B. Government have insulted Irish sentiment by the way they have played up to Carson. I have always maintained that however able a man, after his declared intentions to resist the will of Parliament by rebellion, he should have for ever been retired into private life. I shall be glad to hear anything you are able to say of the convention. I look upon it as the most important matter now pending and it has all my wishes and prayers for success.[28]

The convention, guided by Plunkett, had begun on 25 July with a series of debates on Irish problems in general. The chairman wished to steer clear of controversy during those early days. In August, a grand committee of twenty was set up to draft proposals for discussion that addressed the problems which had cropped up during those early weeks of debate. Windle had a number of interesting observations on leading scholarly and political figures in his diaries during the early weeks of August. On 3 August, he wrote: 'Can a man be a greater ass than Eoin McNeill is? He has carefully and completely killed the Irish language question by his silly manoeuvres as I told him a year ago he would and one may never hope that he will sicken people of this silly, futile Irish Republic idea.' On 7 August, Windle returned to UCC from west Cork. He made this note in his diary: 'Sir F. Hopwood there and a great help. King very interested in convention and has letter from Hopwood after each meeting . . . Carson no good at administration?' On 8 August he was back in Dublin where he attended a reception given by the Lord Mayor of Dublin. He was on the train back to Cork the following morning and then drove to Skibbereen.

While the convention members believed that they were charting the future of the country, the political reality in the countryside was somewhat different. Pat O'Brien, a nationalist MP and chief whip of the IPP, had held a seat in the constituency of Kilkenny City from 1895 to 1917. He was a close friend of John Redmond and spent the days of his final illness at the party leader's home in Aghavannagh, County Wicklow. He died in July 1917. His death came within a month of William Redmond's. It was recorded that at O'Brien's funeral, 'then, and then only in his [Redmond's] lifetime people saw him publicly break down; he had to be led away from the grave'. Sinn Féin put forward as its candidate in the by-election on 10 August William T. Cosgrave, a member of the GPO garrison in 1916 who had initially been condemned to death and was in jail at the time. This future president of the Executive Council of the Irish Free State won by 772 votes to John Magennis's (nationalist) 392. Windle commented on 12 August: 'Shinners said to have won by 100 in Kilkenny. If so, this was what was expected. The contemptible unionist curs did not vote at all – anxious, I suppose, further to embarrass Redmond who is trying to save them. My God – what a crew.' He wrote the next day: 'Shinner – the usual enthusiast – in at Kilkenny by 2–1 majority . . . The strumpet Markievicz talking of "our allies" Germany and Austria! What is to be done with a mad bitch like this?'

Windle, unconscious that Irish politics had moved decisively in a new direction, was unable to fathom the depth of the change in the country. He was invited to dinner in Bantry by William Martin Murphy, the owner of the *Irish Independent*. J. Campbell, Erskine Childers and Tim Healy were also present. Windle commented on Healy's contribution to the evening – 'a pessimistic train all through and a bitter one – A man I neither like nor trust.' On Saturday 18 August, he motored to Skibbereen where he called for a few minutes on Bishop Kelly: 'Horace Plunkett (and he) averse to cantonal settlement but I think it may come – in his Ulster Minister.' On Monday 20 August, he called again on Bishop Kelly *en route* to Cork. The latter 'would rather to have no Home Rule than Home Rule to Ulster sub-parliament. I wouldn't.'[29] On 21 August, he was back in Dublin for a meeting of the convention. William Martin Murphy, entrepreneur and former nationalist MP, made a presentation. In the afternoon, he listened to a speech by Lord Londonderry and then went out in the evening to Kingstown and dined with John O'Connell. On 22 August, he prepared a speech 'which I didn't get off. Saw Plunkett and much talk.' He complimented the 'splendid speeches' by George Russell (Æ) and by Joe Devlin – and Mahaffy 'who proclaimed himself for a Home Ruler'. He spent Saturday 25 August preparing his speech for the convention before returning to Listarkin. Windle went back to Dublin on 28 August and stayed with Plunkett. He went in the evening to the Vice Regal Lodge to a party – 'saw all sorts of people hadn't met for long time'. On 29 August, he wrote to John Humphreys: 'There is a desperate lot to read up about all sorts of points, and we are in the midst of a long general debate of great interest and importance on the whole question.' He said his speech of that day, lasting forty-five minutes, had been well received. On Thursday 30th, he returned to the convention and listened to a series of speeches. That night he returned to Kilteragh. The following day he wrote of a conversation he had with Horace Plunkett: 'He thinks thing may go to Government commission in October . . . I think he is sanguine.' In conversation later that evening, one of the guests said that there was 'no man in the convention more anxious for a settlement than Midleton – If so he has a queer way of showing it.' Windle wrote to Horgan the same evening that 'the convention barometer is steadily rising and we may even make the Country a welcome Christmas box'. He was pleased that the articles that they had both written for the *Cork Examiner* had had a good impact on the convention secretary, Sir Francis Hopwood. He would tell Horgan more if he would come to tea with Mary on Sunday. On 2 September, he wrote to Horgan that an attempt was being made to impose the Swiss federal system on them. He felt it would fail but, as a last resort, it might be necessary to accept it.[30]

On Monday 3 September, he took the train to Belfast for a meeting of the convention. He attended all day on the 4th when he heard Redmond speak. There was, he declared, no length 'consistent with reason, sense and justice' to which he would not go to meet the views of Ulstermen. The speech was 'one of the finest', according to Windle. Lord Midleton shook Redmond's hand warmly after he had finished. It appeared as if the basis was being laid for a workable compromise. Windle was back in Cork on Friday 7 September where he worked most of the day: 'rumours of Sinn Féin and Labour trouble', he wrote. He noted on 8 September: 'Sinn Féiners announce meeting for 23rd – a deliberate attempt to break up the Convention. The whore, the fool and the maniac are to be here – my god – what a country? No wonder England is sick of it. I very nearly am myself, yet it contains a multitude of delightful people.' His diary entry also read: 'Met [Stanley] Harrington – thinks as I do – that suppression of Sinn Féin meeting would be fatal. Let them blow off. John J. Horgan to tea – agrees with S

Harrington and self.' He referred to his erstwhile friend and patron William O'Brien: 'simply malignant – always was.'

On 9 September, writing to Sr Monica, he spoke of the stress under which he was working:

> The convention is a terrible tax and a very heavy responsibility. We meet for three days every week and for five to six hours on each of those days. When I got home at midnight on Thursday I had been away for ten days continuously and I go up to Dublin again tomorrow. It is a most curious thing that I took up scientific work first of all because I thought that it would provide me with a quiet studious life with the result that for five and thirty years nearly I have never been out of action; re-organising educational institutions; sitting on Boards innumerable; never have I known what it was to have peace and all my researching and writing has had to be done in the intervals. And now I am landed with share in the gigantic task of constructing a Constitution for a Nation. 'Oh cursed spite! I quote to myself from Hamlet and have only one consolation; Lots of people intrigued to get on this Convention: at least earnestly desired to be members and many are hopelessly disgruntled because they are not there – why Heaven only knows. I can say this that I not only did not raise a little finger to be made a member but I neither expected nor desired it. Hence I am bound to look upon it as the wish of God that I should be there for some purpose unknown to me but doubtless quite clear to Him; consequently I think I am entitled to ask for prayers for the success of the undertaking and also have some reason to hope that I shall not want assistance in it.

On 10 September 1917, Gasquet wrote to Windle, acknowledging receipt of his 'very interesting letter', and expressing that 'we are deeply concerned for the results of the convention. If some real success will attend it it will be worth all the trouble you are having and the prayers which are being offered up. What has been the bane of Ireland up to this, has been the way in which people with different views have been kept apart and differences rather than points of agreement have been insisted upon – So "more power to your elbow."'. He added that he had reread Windle's book (*The Church and Science*) 'and esteem it even more highly than I did when I first went through it'. It should, he thought, have many editions. He would, when he got back to Rome, take the pope's copy to him and 'personally explain its importance'.

The convention moved to Cork. On 22 September, Redmond wrote to Windle: 'Very many thanks but you must forgive me if I don't accept your kind invitation. I am really not up to parties at present. I have already refused John Horgan. I know you won't misunderstand.'[31] Still grieving the death in action in June of his brother Willie, Redmond was also battling poor health. On 24 September, Windle put up Plunkett and Hopwood in his home. Horgan gave lodgings to Erskine Childers and to Stephen Gwynn MP. Windle wrote on the 25th about the convention meeting: 'W.M. Murphy a bit troublesome and venomous as usual underlies suave exterior.' The meeting was adjourned while the government brought forward a scheme. Windle wrote: 'this means a month at least [off] "Hallelujah!"' There were many formal occasions surrounding the convention visit to Cork. Plunkett and Hopwood went to the ceremony at the mouth of the harbour where the lord mayor, asserting his authority as admiral of the port, threw a dart into the sea. Windle noted in his diary: 'lunch given by Harbour Board – the usual dull – tedious – overlong–speeches of Lucy and Plunkett excellent'. The latter had sounded a note of 'justifiable optimism'.

Before assessing the outcome of the convention session in Cork, delegates received news of a major and tragic development. Thomas Ashe, a prominent Sinn Féin leader, died in Mountjoy jail on 25 September under, as Dorothy Macardle writes, 'the ordeal of forcible feeding'. A school teacher from Kerry, a native speaker and a member of the executive of the Gaelic League, he had been sentenced to death and then to life imprisonment for his part in the 1916 rising. He served hard labour at Dartmoor and then at Lewes. Transferred to Portland and released under general amnesty in June 1917, he was accompanied by Austin Stack back to Tralee on 20 June where they were welcomed by 4,000 people. Ashe was rearrested and jailed on 18 August, and went on a hunger strike together with forty other prisoners, to achieve political status. The prisoners destroyed the furniture in their cells; Ashe was left to lie on the floor. The Lord Mayor of Dublin, Laurence O'Neill, visited him twice and found him in a deplorable condition. The second time, he noted that strenuous efforts had been made to force-feed him. The circumstances of his death led to public outrage. Ashe was given a hero's funeral, as, dressed in the uniform of a Volunteer, his remains were laid out in the city hall, Dublin, accompanied by a guard of honour. Thousands filed past the remains and dense crowds lined the streets as 200 priests followed the cortège to the cemetery. On 30 September, some 30,000 joined in the funeral procession, described by Macardle as 'a pageant of the nation'. Ashe's death won concessions for the Sinn Féin prisoners.[32] Tim Healy MP acted for Ashe's family at the inquest; his death, he said, was 'another blood stain on the Irish Calvary'. He held a letter from the governor of Mountjoy which he described as 'Ashe's death warrant'. Counsel for the government withdrew, describing Healy's behaviour as 'a disgrace to the bar'.[33] Windle wrote in his diary on 10 October: 'the conduct of T. Healy at the Ashe inquest is so gross that no barrister has ever prostituted his profession to the same extent. No decent person should ever sit at the table with him and I never will again if I can help it.' But Ashe, IRB man, Gaelic Leaguer and revolutionary nationalist, was more dangerous dead than alive. The chief secretary, Ian Macpherson, said that his death did more 'to stimulate Sinn Féinism and disorder in Ireland than anything I know'.[34]

Shocked when he heard the news of Ashe's death, Plunkett told his friend in the British embassy in Washington, Shane Leslie, that it was 'a bolt from the blue'. Constrained by censorship from writing openly about what was happening, he had to content himself 'with saying that the mere fact that, in my belief (though not in that, I think, of many other people) the occurrence will not shake the Convention, above that, if I am right, its roots have gone down'. He was leaving that night – 3 October – to meet a number of important people. A grand committee had been charged to prepare a proposal and they had a fortnight to complete the work: 'On the whole though I am bound to tell you that my optimism is not general. I think you may share it. I see a great deal of John Redmond now. His health, I am afraid, is not at all good and his spirit seems broken. The convention delegates are very fond of him, and Devlin has also made an excellent impression; but the Party is in a very bad way. It ought to be reconstructed completely and, if his health is restored, Redmond should be the first Premier.'[35] However, Redmond's ill-health meant that he had not taken the chair, as was the general will, of an important subcommittee to set down a plan of action. Instead, the Bishop of Raphoe, Patrick O'Donnell, was given that responsibility. The latter lacked Redmond's ability to craft an agreed compromise.

During the latter months of 1917, Redmond – despite his rapidly declining health – worked energetically behind the scenes to lay down the basis for a settlement. He believed that the southern unionists could be won over to home rule. With the support of Lord Midleton and his group, the Ulster unionists would be left isolated. Redmond had moved to a position, ruling out the possibility that all nationalist demands could be met, that an agreement with southern unionists would be the only viable way to break the logjam. The British cabinet now included the Dominion prime ministers, all of whom were eager for a settlement of the Irish question. Lloyd George had given a public pledge on a settlement. But Ulster unionists acted as if they had a veto over the progress of the convention. Carson had explained to the Ulster Unionist Council that participation in the convention did not commit them to anything. Lord Cushendun wrote about Ulster unionist participation: 'It was a bone thrown to a snarling dog, and the longer there was anything to gnaw the longer would the dog keep quiet.'[36] However, Redmond had accepted at face value Lloyd George's public commitment.

Windle's diary references to the Ulster unionists and to Carson during the latter months of 1917 illustrate the depth of his antagonism towards what he considered to be an intransigent and implacable block. On 13 October, he wrote: 'Conduct of Irish Government viler and viler and seriously prejudicing convention. What a gang of hogs the Castle herds!' On 18 October: 'Government still playing the ruffian under that vile knave Carson's instigation.' Gasquet wrote to Windle on 31 October: 'How goes the Convention? I hope that good may come out of all this chaos, but really there seems in Ireland an evil spirit, which always turns things topsy turvy at the worst possible moment. Here we are all very anxious about Italy. Will it be able to resist the German pressure? *Chi lo sa*. Of course, we don't know yet the true story of the attack – possibly never shall.'[37]

Windle wrote to Sr Monica on 4 November, wishing for a quiet life: 'You will be amused to know that in the past three months – two of them supposed to be vacation! I attended 52 meetings – presiding at more than half of them and spent 29 days or parts of them in Dublin. That is what I have slipped into and I can only suppose that it is God's pleasure as I never looked for that kind of life for myself and do not like it.'[38] Meanwhile, Plunkett, ever the optimist, told Leslie on 2 November that the 'convention was working hard and well'. He had 'four earnest committees exploring various subjects. The problem of Irish government – at all times inherently complex – has been further complicated by the war.' He assured Leslie: 'Of course we are only considering a solution within the Empire and, even if we were to be a republic, any man of sense knows he should have to have business relations of some kind with Britain. What the political structure of either or the commercial policy of the latter will be five or even one year hence, no one can tell and yet, in framing a constitution for Ireland, these things must be taken into account.'[39]

Redmond, sensing the seriousness of the crisis in November 1917, wrote to Lloyd George stating that the situation had become 'exceedingly grave' and predicting that the convention would be 'abortive' unless efforts were made to persuade Ulster unionists of the need for compromise. The securing of fiscal autonomy was of paramount importance. Assurances had been given to the Ulstermen in the form of concessions regarding an upper and lower chamber. There was also a provision for both chambers to vote together in all disputed matters. Redmond told Lloyd George in a letter on 13 November that it was up to the prime minister and Carson to act. They had it 'in their power to do so'. Redmond told Lloyd George 'the plain truth'. There was not a moment to lose. Otherwise, he said, the convention would break down and 'before Christmas you will probably have violence and bloodshed all over the country'.[40]

Windle found by the end of 1917 that Sinn Féin ideas were held by a small minority of UCC professors. On 11 December, he wrote: 'That ass of asses Stockley could speak at de Valera's meeting tonight but could not come to the academic council.' The following day, he met with a man 'who says Cork City Shinners the most malignant in Ireland'.[41] The Jesuit Fr Michael Maher wrote on 19 December: 'I was particularly pleased to know that you are still hopeful about the Convention. I feared much that the enemy would have been successful in sowing his cockle during the recess . . . But the great point will be to get the Convention solution, on whatever it may be, as soon as possible as a war measure. The marvellous way in which the Lords have swallowed this big Reform Bill is hopeful. The Government – even Tory – cannot shut their eyes to the awkward-ness of an Irish problem when they go into a European Conference, depending on America . . . I hope the Convention work will soon end for your sake also, and that you will then get at least partial quiet – man is not born to live in a railway carriage.'[42]

On 18 December, the convention was plunged into crisis. Lord Midleton put forward, on behalf of the southern unionists, a proposal 'to establish Home Rule on a broader basis than the Act of 1914, while retaining to the Imperial Parliament full control over customs and excise, as well as national defence'.[43] Windle thought that Midleton's offer was 'a fair one and in a very conciliatory speech'. He reserved his anger for the northern delegates: 'But the Ulsters are a vile crew. You have to only look at their vile, unspiritual countenances to see the swine they are at heart. Barrie better but then Scotch – The real Belfaster is the vilest thing living.' Windle considered the afternoon meeting 'a sheer waste of time', returning to Cork frustrated and disillusioned. The political crisis deep-ened as Bishop O'Donnell, splitting the nationalists, stood out for fiscal autonomy. He wrote to Redmond on 22 December stating that it would be a disastrous blunder to agree to the Midleton proposal without first receiving guarantees regarding Ulster: 'but any compromise that is not with the North is no good, for an agreed settlement at least . . . I have never been sanguine about a settlement. But my hopes at present are as high as they were at any time, or higher.'[44]

Joe Devlin also warned Redmond on the 22nd of the gravity of the sit-uation. He supported the position of Bishop O'Donnell. Plunkett, concerned about outright failure, told Redmond: 'In any case, if the Bishop persists a settlement in the Convention becomes impossible, and the Irish question, so far as Ireland is concerned, is where it was, unless external circumstances and Sinn Féin come in to solve it. Personally I think that among your followers there may be some who will not approve of any such policy. But of this you are a better judge than I am.'[45] Redmond corresponded with O'Donnell over Christmas in an effort to find room for compromise. On 26 December, Windle wrote asking Sr Monica to say 'special prayers and get them said next week for the Irish Convention which will be at its most critical point that God may guide it to a right decision and especially for me, if as seems likely, I have to speak, that I may be helped to say something useful. But it would be well worth doing if it brought peace to this distracted country.' His diary for the same day read: 'Edith had Christmas tree for children of village under 12. Great excitement. No post. No letters. As arranged this the most wearisome season of the year.' Windle wrote to Humphreys on 27 December: 'My holiday has been badly cut down by the Convention. No sooner was I down here than I was summoned to Dublin for a meeting. It took me from 9.45 a.m. on a bitterly cold day until 8.45 in the evening. I spent all next day at meetings – left Dublin 7.35 a.m. on the following day and got here at 4.0 p.m. Now I must leave on Monday for further very important meetings and do not know whether I can get much more holiday. It is very tiring, and there seems to be no end to it. However, if we can bring about a settlement, it will be a great task accomplished.'[46] Windle made the last entry into his diary on 31 December: 'So ends a dreadful year. The last part a nightmare of travel and meetings. I suppose I have done from 10–15,000 miles in trains and car. Weariness insufferable at meetings and much unpleasantries. I hope God will accept it for part of my most just Purgatory. On the other hand health wonderful on the whole. Edith well and Nora [his daughter who was in London] kept safe in air raids – for all such things D.G.'

Windle was ready to go back in the new year to the convention refreshed and determined to press for a solution. Due to illness, Plunkett was not in the chair when business resumed on 3 January. He wrote: 'vile speech by [northern unionist leader, Hugh Thom] Barrie – Good by [Capt. Stephen] Gwynn.' In the afternoon, Windle spoke for an hour. The following day – the 4th – Redmond delivered what was generally regarded as one of the great speeches of his political career:

> If we break down in despair and helplessness God only knows how terrible and far-reaching may be the consequences. Far better, for us and the Empire, never to have met . . . I would be ashamed to speak of surrender of such things as sacrifices when I remember the kind of sacrifices our brave boys have made and are making this very hour, while we are safe at home talking. I cannot trust myself to speak

upon this matter. Personal loss I set aside. My position – our position
– before the War was that we possessed the confidence of nearly the
entire country. I took a risk – we took a risk – with eyes open. I have –
we have – not merely taken the risk, but made the sacrifice. If the
choice were to be made tomorrow I would do it all over again. I have
had my surfeit of public life. My modest ambition would be to serve
in some quite humble capacity under the first Unionist Prime
Minister of Ireland . . . No, we must come to a settlement. We must
rise to the occasion, if only to save ourselves from a life-long remorse
for wrecking, for what the historian of the future would describe as a
crime against the Empire in her hour of deadliest peril, and a crime
against the peace and happiness of our own beloved and long-
suffering country.[47]

Windle wrote that day: 'Splendid speeches by Redmond – the finest I
ever heard.' In contrast, he had to listen to 'the most awful antiquated
tosh from Londonderry'.

At that point, Windle started counting heads. He felt that there was a
strong block favouring the Redmond proposal. He counted 95 per cent of
the nationalists and all the southern unionists as being in support, feeling
also that six out of seven of the Labour representatives would be in favour
together with an unknown number of the remaining delegates. Windle
made a brief visit to Cork, returning on 14 January to hear Redmond's final
appeal to the convention. He wrote that Redmond's position was 'very
statesmanlike'. Later, Plunkett explained to a friend what happened next,
fiscal autonomy being the roadblock on the road to consensus: 'On this
rock the convention stuck on January 15th when Redmond introduced an
amendment to a resolution of Lord Midleton's proposing a compromise
upon which the Southern Unionists and the Nationalists could unite. It
gives to Ireland far wider powers than were contained in the Act of 1914,
the only reservation of powers being the levying and collecting of customs.
Even excise was to be transferred to the Irish parliament.'

Plunkett explained further: 'My policy all through has been to try and
change the Irish political situation from being one in which three-
quarters of the population – all Roman Catholic – were for Home rule,
and one quarter – all Protestant – against, to one in which the proportion
would be over four fifths one way and less than a fifth the other – the religious cleavage ceasing to exist. Then I was convinced that the opinion of
the world and the circumstances of the time would have overborne the
governmental pledges to Ulster and the whole question would be rapidly
solved. Redmond, I think, took this view and he therefore offered to
accept the southern unionist compromise on condition that the government would give legislative effect to it forthwith.'

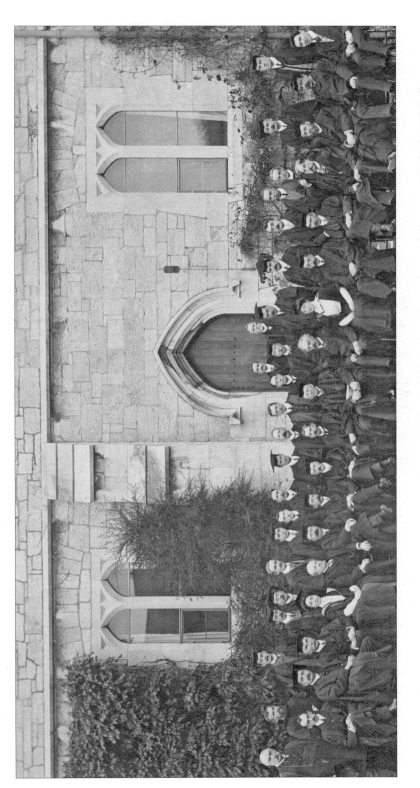

Academic staff of UCC in 1910. Mary Ryan is in the front row left and on the right is the Professor of Education, Elizabeth M. O'Sullivan.

Above and right:
Professor of Romance Languages,
Mary Ryan, 1909–38. She was the
first woman professor in the
British Isles and was appointed
under Windle.

Windle in UCC
presidential robes.

Left: Chief Secretary of Ireland,
Augustine Birrell, who was
responsible for the passage of
the Irish Universities Act 1908.

Sir John O'Connell, driving force with Windle behind the building of the
Honan Hostel and Chapel.

Honan Chapel.

UCC coat of arms on main gate of the Honan Chapel with college motto:
'Where Finbarr taught let Munster learn.'

Main door of
Honan Chapel.

Below: Interior of Cormac's chapel, Cashel, and north doorway were a source of
inspiration for the architect of the Honan Chapel.

Above: One of the stations of the cross.
Below: Round tower detail on interior pillar.

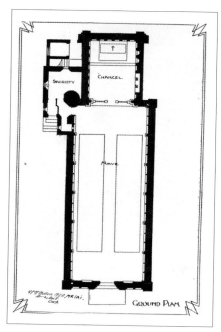

Ground plan of the chapel.

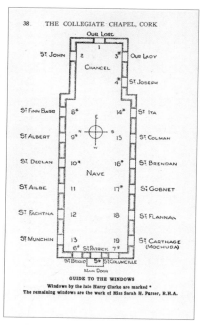

38. THE COLLEGIATE·CHAPEL, CORK

GUIDE TO THE WINDOWS

Windows by the late Harry Clarke are marked *
The remaining windows are the work of Miss Sarah H. Purser, R.H.A.

Plan of stained glass windows
in Honan Chapel.

Interior of Honan Chapel, 2010.

Plunkett explained to Leslie that Redmond knew that a few faithful followers would back him, namely Stephen Gwynn, [John Joseph] Clancy, John Fitzgibbon: 'But he had been ill and had seen little of his rank and file. So it came to pass that on January 15th, a few hours before he was to move his amendment, he discovered that Devlin and the bishops had deserted him and taken most of the minor Nationalists in the Convention with them. They insisted on full fiscal autonomy, which they knew none of the Unionists would accept.' Windle captured in his diary the drama of 15 January: 'Redmond finds he can't carry his party and withdraws his motion. Consternation! Bishop MacRory holds for customs, and what he says is quite true but doesn't help – Devlin bolts the ticket – stampeded by William Martin Murphy and afraid of Shinners, but attacks the Ulsters. [Northern unionist Sir Robert Newton] Anderson replies not very effectively. Pathetic letter from Bishop Kelly, from "his sick, almost his death bed" asking for settlement. Things looking very bad . . .'[48] Windle concluded his entry in *red ink*: 'This was the real end of the convention.'[49]

It was certainly the end for Redmond. Leaving the meeting, he told a parliamentary colleague that everything was wrecked, and he saw nothing ahead for his country but ruin and chaos. Redmond was convinced that Sinn Féin would be the architects of that ruin. For a man who had given distinguished service to his country since before his election to the House of Commons in 1881, some members of the younger Irish generation had little regard for the sixty-two-year-old veteran MP. He had begun to encounter an atmosphere of confrontation and intimidation on the streets around Trinity College as he walked to and from the convention. Todd Andrews, later a Fianna Fáil minister, spoke of his chance encounter as a seventeen-year-old with Redmond outside the main gate of Trinity College where the 'Lloyd George Convention' was sitting: 'One of the first to emerge was John Redmond, the Irish Party leader, always referred to by us, derisively, as Johnny Redmond. He was easily recognisable and someone in the crowd began to boo. The booing was taken up by the rest of us and as the crowd grew larger and larger the boos grew louder and louder while Redmond walked along Westmoreland Street. By the time he reached *The Irish Times* office, the crowd was transformed into a threatening mob. Some passers-by with a sense of responsibility threw a cocoon round Redmond taking him into the office of *The Irish Times*, the crowd then dispersed . . . I am quite sure that if any of the mob had offered physical violence to Redmond I would have joined in.'[50]

Midleton, who had risked his political credibility by supporting Redmond, was very bitter in his attitude towards the Irish bishops, and, in particular, towards Bishop O'Donnell of Raphoe who, he felt, had torpedoed the compromise. Writing to Sir Edmund Talbot (Lord Fitzalan) in December 1920, he explained: 'In 1917 the last chance of a united government of Ireland passed away, when the Bishop of Raphoe decided to break down the agreement between North–South on which alone it was possible to avoid a split. The North said: We must have 40 pc of the Lower House or a thoroughly sound Senate to vote with the Lower House on disputes. Redmond agreed. The Financial question had then to be faced. The Southern Unionists proposed to give Ireland *excise* – and Ulster with many heart-searchings were willing to concede this if customs remained Imperial. Redmond said, "I will settle if Lord Midleton can obtain the undertaking of Lloyd George that this will be put through at once." I went to London and got a paper signed by Lloyd George and Curzon to this effect.' Midleton explained that Raphoe persuaded Devlin to oppose. He also went to the Archbishop of Armagh, Michael Logue, and got a 'fiat' 'to resist on customs'. Raphoe opposed and Midleton 'denounced him'. Dillon pressed him to withdraw his threat of withdrawing 'all protection to minority' on the question of the Senate. Midleton explained that Raphoe then fell back on customs as a reason to vote against the settlement. The collapse was due 'from first to last' to the Bishop of Raphoe. In contrast, Midleton praised the role of Bishop Kelly of Ross who despite being 'at death's door' in Dublin was not visited by O'Donnell.[51]

Meanwhile Plunkett, despite the collapse in mid-January, sought to preserve an air of normality at the convention: 'January 15th was the first day of the week's three days session and we had to try and keep the debate going through the week so that I could run over to London and put the situation before the government,' he told Shane Leslie. On 20 January 1918, a dejected Windle wrote to Sr Monica: 'Please remember me specially in your prayers on 23rd . . . as it is the 35th anniversary of my reception into the Church one occasion in my life one may note on which I did not make a mistake.' He noted that 'Bishop of Cork very kindly said Mass for me at College Chapel'. His diary entry for 24 January reveals his disagreement with the hierarchy over their strong stance in the convention – a most troubling spiritual development for the president. Windle wrote on 1 February to Sr Monica: 'I must devote a short time to thanking you, as I do trust sincerely for your very kind letter. I very greatly appreciated it for – though you might not think it – I live in great isolation here, having hardly anyone but my wife to talk to – I had a great friend a priest but he has been moved into the country – a great loss to me . . . Ireland is the worst place in which an intellectually minded Catholic could live – the most trying for his Faith. If I come through that test nothing will wreck it. Of course one has to keep before ones mind the difference between the treasure and the vessel in which it is kept.' Windle wrote frankly about his attitude to the local Irish clergy: 'no wonder there is so much anti-clericalism in this country, and, though it has not led to loss of Faith as yet, it is a step and, as France has shown, is a dangerous one in that direction. I am very much troubled about this as I fear a religious debacle some day in what is ironically called Holy Ireland. Perhaps I ought not to bother you with such things but I have no one here to talk them over with and there is a relief in speaking or writing of [it].' Windle concluded with the hope that the prime minister, in whom he had no great confidence, might be able to do something to improve the situation in Ireland when he returned from France.

Plunkett strove very hard in the last two weeks in January to save the convention, pressing for an initiative from Lloyd George. A fifteen-man delegation did not find the cabinet responsive. It took a long time to interview the leaders of the several groups separately and to confer with the delegation as a whole. On 20 January, Carson resigned from the war cabinet, giving as one of his reasons that he felt it might be to the advantage of the cabinet to discuss the matter of an Irish settlement without his presence.[52] On 8 February Windle's diary stated: 'Carson to breakfast enough to produce emesis for the day.' Windle got news on 17 February about new proposals being made by Lloyd George.[53] He recorded that police and customs would be retained by London until after the war, matters then to be decided by a committee with an impartial chairman. Horgan heard from his friend Erskine Childers that although failure was not inevitable, if it occurred, the British government would be wholly to blame. The British government found it very hard to engineer a way out of the convention dilemma. Plunkett wrote to Leslie: 'And when all this had been done, the Cabinet found themselves in as big a difficulty as the Convention and had to stay on in London waiting to get a decision out of home until the midnight of the 25th February.' Out of the political crisis, Plunkett felt had emerged a serious proposal which came in a long letter from Lloyd George: it was, in Plunkett's view, 'the most generous offer which has ever been made by England to Ireland'. He said the government 'was for the immediate transfer of full powers over all direct taxation and, of course, of all other powers in the Act'. Certain powers were reserved until after the war – customs and excise, police, and the post office: 'Unfortunately, Redmond is ill and so is the Bishop of Ross, who is far the wisest economist and financier in the Convention. The Bishop of Raphoe therefore leads the nationalists and he takes the extreme line on the fiscal issues – sincerely, I believe, but fanatically and without any real economic knowledge or, of course, acquaintance with commercial and industrial affairs. Not unnaturally, the rather over-bishoping of the Convention is making comment and I am not sure that it is altogether wiser from the clerical point of view. It gets known outside and I have heard it whispered that Maynooth is at its old game – Customs being a mere stick with which to beat democracy when it might, if not kept in order, set its profane hands to education. My personal belief is that the Church is genuinely apprehensive of the growing revolutionary forces and is anxious to be in with a constitutional Irish government which may possibly hold them in restraint.'Plunkett felt that the Ulster members of the convention were anxious to settle: 'Therefore, if I can only get agreement in the rest of the Convention, I expect negotiations to be opened up between the North-east corner and the rest of Ireland,'he wrote.

On the morning of 26 February, Plunkett called the convention together to hear the decision, 'so you may imagine the circumstances under which I had to convey it to the Convention and give them my advice as to how they should act'. But the chairman had underestimated the depth of unionist and Catholic episcopal opposition. Cardinal Logue, one of the most conciliatory of the Irish bishops, wrote on 1 March 1918 to the administration in Dublin: 'I have carefully read over the proposals of Mr Lloyd George; and I am sorry to say, in my opinion they will settle nothing. I believe that, if published at present, they would be promptly rejected with contempt, and would strengthen the hands and complete the influence of the promoters of disorder.'Having dismantled the settlement proposals, Logue wrote: 'It may be uncharitable, but I find it hard to resist the conviction that this whole business, Convention, and all, is a piece of clever play – it would be disrespectful to call jockeying – to keep the Irish question floating till the war is over, and then leave Sinn Féin, Carsonism and Socialism to fight each other over the fate of unfortunate Ireland. This is the view which the public will certainly take of futile proposals of settlement. Hence I believe it is the duty of the Nationalist members of the convention to insist on the earliest possible report, or reports, as the case may be, and leave to the Government the responsibility of acting or refusing to act on the report of the majority.'[54]

On 3 March, Windle wrote to Sr Monica about his deep concerns over the failure to reach consensus: 'I got home late on Friday night from Dublin; I return there to-morrow until Fri; I expect to report the process next week and probably there the week after; then I hope the convention will be over. This is a desperately critical time and one of very great and harassing anxiety for me. So please have me frequently in your prayers . . . I greatly appreciate your letters and still more your prayers – particularly now, for, apart from the Convention and its work, so strenuous and so engrossing and worrying, and my work here which has to be compressed into such short periods, I have looming in front of me as possibilities other pieces of work – unsought by me . . . What I would love more than anything (and my wife too) is to retire to our little house in West Cork with a modest income and live a life of writing and country. Apparently I shall never have it, and if that is God's will, it must be so. All the same it's a hard thing to give it up.'[55]

Windle wrote that evening – 3 March – that Horgan had visited him in the afternoon, reporting that the 'Bishops want to settle but must have formula to save their faces'. Windle felt that the large majority of nationalists would oblige the bishops and go with them. He noted that Midleton was 'down here yesterday holding a meeting – What done is not known.' On 5 March he wrote: 'Things clearer a bit but Bishop Raphoe (who is I think disgusting a good many) and Murphy – (in a vile temper as no one will back him) made fierce speeches.'

Redmond, ill for some time, went to London in early March to be operated upon to remove an intestinal obstruction. The intervention helped relieve his pain, but he died of heart failure on 6 March. Windle learned 'sad news of John Redmond's death. On Tuesday Devlin was with him; he was sitting up in bed reading the paper and told Devlin to go back to the convention. Then he [had] heart failure.' Fr Bernard Vaughan, a close friend, said that one of the last utterances to fall from his lips was: 'I am a broken-hearted man.' Tributes came from all the leading politicians, including Carson: 'Indeed, we were not very far apart in our attempts at a settlement of the Irish question.'[56] John Dillon, refusing to write an obituary of Redmond, wrote emotionally to the journalist C.P. Scott on 6 March: 'I feel so bitterly and deeply the tragedy of Redmond's fate that if I were to attempt to write about him just now I would be irresistibly dragged into a bitter attack on George, Asquith and British ministers in general, and into drawing the moral from his fate of the madness and folly of any Irish leader putting any trust in the promises of English ministers.'[57]

After a funeral service in Westminster Cathedral, his remains, escorted by John Dillon, were taken on 9 March for burial, not to Glasnevin cemetery, Dublin, but to the family vault in Wexford town. People gathered at each station along the way to pay their last respects. A huge crowd attended his funeral, his coffin draped in a flag used at Parnell's funeral. Redmond's old party opponent, Dillon, gave the graveside oration, extolling Redmond's lifetime of work to advance the cause of reconciliation: 'Is it too much to hope that the grave we have closed to-day may cry out with an irresistible voice to his countrymen to take and put into effect the lesson of his life, and to bury for ever the discords and dissension which have been the curse of Ireland throughout the centuries, and consummate the work of John Redmond's life by uniting all Irishmen to work for the good of Ireland.'[58]

Despite the honours paid to Redmond at his funeral, Horgan wrote that the deceased leader of the IPP had suffered in the months before his death 'not only the perfidy of British politicians but, what was far worse, the base ingratitude of his own people', manifesting itself on the streets of Dublin while on his way to the convention. So often accosted as he approached the gates of Trinity College, Redmond had been forced in the end to use another gate. Horgan described him as a character of 'exceptional charm' who utterly lacked 'vanity or pride'. 'Jealousy, that devouring canker of small minds,' Horgan wrote, 'was utterly foreign to his nature.'[59] Dillon, on 6 April, told T.P. O'Connor that the last two years had added 'one more great tragedy to the tragic story of Ireland and his [Redmond's] fate is a terrible warning to all Irish leaders who have to deal with British statesmen'.[60]

Windle's friend, Fr Maher, wrote on 7 March: 'The news of John Redmond's death arrived to-day. How are all passing over! RIP . . . I was naturally very sorry to hear there was danger ahead of a split on the Catholic side. Anyway, I have been praying my best both for the cause of the country and for you.' Maher felt that, if Windle was drifting into a position of opposition to the Irish bishops at the convention, it would be 'wiser for you to return over here – I mean, of course, religious, not merely political questions, though it is often not easy to separate them in Ireland'. He concluded in the following surprising way: 'Meanwhile I do most sincerely hope and pray that you will not drift into anything approaching an anti-clerical position – both for the sake of your spiritual welfare and your solid happiness, especially now in the evening of life. May our good Lord take care of you and preserve you from such a misfortune after your years of good work for His interest.'[61]

Windle was deeply wounded by the attitude of Archbishop William Walsh towards the late John Redmond. His diary entry on 11 March states: 'Great criticism of Archbishop [of] Dublin's action in neither having a requiem for John Redmond nor uttering one word of sympathy as to his death. Can a man who thus carries a vendetta beyond the grave really be a Christian? He certainly alienates many from the Church which has the misfortune to have him for an archbishop.'

Windle wrote again on Easter Sunday, speaking about going to Dublin for the last two meetings of the convention: 'I can't say how thankful I am that it is over, or nearly so, for it has not only been a very anxious job, but a more than wearisome one. Can any good thing come out of it? Well, not as much as might have come but for the dreadful prejudices of the Protestant North, and its ingrained hatred of, and contempt for, our religion – still a great deal has been done and will, I think, last – Please God we may get a settlement out of it.' He hoped that the prime minister was in earnest and would keep the solemn promises made to the delegates. On the day the final report of the Irish Convention was published – 12 March – Windle wrote: 'Began by usual waste of time. Badgering Horace Plunkett as to an "ill"-judged but well-meant letter. Got up in my wrath and hotly denounced this waste of time and actually stopped it. . . . Then vote and what a vote – we won 38–34. Our 38 = most of the Nationalist Party and all of the Southern Unionists and 5 Labour. Theirs the rest of the Nationalists and *all Ulster* who voted for Customs and Excise which they would never give up on the plea that they are against constitution of finality – The most cynical piece of dishonesty I ever came up against. Pure wrecking . . . Raphoe furious and vulgarly indignant – Scrape under and you find the peasant.'

The following day, 13 March, Windle returned to vent his anger on the Bishop of Raphoe: 'The peasant arrogance and bad temper of Raphoe – impudence of Down and Connor, the unblushing lies of Barrie and the dour enmity of W.M. Murphy – I can't think [?] has he and of course Barrie and Co don't want any settlement. Do the bishops? Many people doubt it and think they [the bishops] would rather go on as they are having more power than they would have under Home Rule. I cannot make up my mind on this point.' On Thursday 14 March 1918, Windle wrote: 'Convention 10.30–5. After change owing in part to storm of yesterday and no point to Conference organised by Granard at his house. Anyway Bishop hands in his gun and will help to settlement . . . We unite and beat Ulster 51–18.' On Friday 15th, Windle recorded that 'Ulster votes against everything – Barrie seems to me to be the type of the Parliamentary hypocrite. Plunkett [was] doing a bit better. Spoke several times on various points.'

John Dillon, for whom Windle had but little respect, was elected the new leader of the Irish Parliamentary Party. Windle wrote to Sr Monica on 18 March that the convention was in its final stages and needed progress more than ever: 'I got back from Dublin at midnight on Friday and return to-day. Please be very insistent about the Convention this week as we are at its final stages and need prayers more than ever. So does this distracted country where so many of the Bishops and clergy are doing all that they can to drive anyone with any education out of the church. Nothing more shocking nor unchristian than their behaviour with regard to John Redmond – not only a great man but a fervent and edifying Catholic was ever known. For me, all that I can say is "Lord to whom shall we go?" and stick to the church as I hope I should have done in Rome under the Borgias – But it is not pleasant and not encouraging least of all edifying.'

On 20 March, Windle went to a Requiem Mass for John Redmond at Gardiner Street in Dublin which had been organised by the Clongowes Wood Union. He wrote: 'poor Mrs Redmond's grief – sat just behind her. Feeling about Archbishop very hurt. Feeling much better all round but Plunkett awful. No other word – botches everything.' On 21 March 1918, Windle wrote that the convention 'went very well. Raphoe [for] once really statesmanlike. The children of Sodom and Gomorrah will do anything. Vile herd. Horace Plunkett got a good ragging about his proposed report which he wants to begin by Council of Trent and its effects on Ireland. Oh what asses men can be – even the best – when eaten up with vanity.' On 22 March, he wrote: 'Fierce day at Convention, and for a time seemed as if all were up. Horace Plunkett more daft than ever. Got a good going over about his report (as he calls it) from all of us, including self, in a speech much cheered. Then attempt to put report as a whole, which could only have been carried by a very small majority. No one really wanted this, and we ended up by having no such motion, nor was it wanted.'

There was some excitement at the hustings in Waterford in the latter part of March. Captain Archer Redmond DSO had been MP for Tyrone East since 1910. Upon the death of his father, he resigned his seat and set out to hold his father's seat in Waterford. He campaigned in his army uniform, wearing a black armband to signify that he was in mourning for his father and his uncle, Willie Redmond. On 23 March, Windle travelled to Listarkin. He wrote: 'Tar barrels and people rejoicing in village over Capt. William John Redmond's return for Waterford.' That was a small crumb of comfort to people like Windle who now had to contend with a pro-Sinn Féin administrator in the Union Hall parish. The priest had, according to Windle, 'preached two S.F. sermons and set this quiet place in sections. What asses our clergy are many of them – or worse than asses and how they are throwing their heritage away.'[62]

Plunkett had invited John Dillon to take Redmond's seat in the convention. Writing on 25 March, he refused politely but firmly. On 30 March, Plunkett circulated the draft report of the convention and it was discussed by delegates on 4 and 5 April amid rumours that the British government was about to introduce conscription in Ireland.[63] It was all over. The Irish Convention report was a statement of incompatible positions. Consensus had not been reached. Windle felt that the Irish episcopal delegation had thrown away that chance in January when Redmond was prepared to go so far to achieve agreement.[64]

Windle, having put so much physical and intellectual effort into the proceedings, was bitterly disappointed by the outcome. Writing on 4 April as discussion on the report continued, he stated: 'An Acrid morning

– probably well meant but asinine efforts of Crozier. Raphoe offensive beyond words! In the end got the report by 44–29 . . . Thus ends the Convention, the most wearisome thing I ever was in and one which has lowered my opinion of human nature and made me a convinced anti-clerical to the extent that I would have all the clergy and especially bishops kept rigidly out of public life.' He exempted Bishop Kelly from criticism but called Bishop O'Donnell 'a vile peasant type set on horse-back'. As the convention was engaged in a face-saving exercise during those days, Windle made an assessment of the two figures who had dom-inated the proceedings, Plunkett and Redmond. Plunkett, he felt, had 'made a bad chairman yet may have got things through better than another. Weak, verbose especially in rulings and utterly failing to see the [??] when he could get a vote. But an honest, kindly gentleman whom everyone respects.' John Redmond, who had died on 6 March, was 'the great figure while he lived – one of the greatest I have met and the finest speaker I have heard'. He mentioned Antony McDonnell as 'being a broad-minded man who *might* have brought in Ulster'. On 8 April, he noted: '*J Redmond* incomparably the greatest man in the Convention. [?] of his great speeches especially the last in which his followers say he exceeded anything he had ever done, simply the finest I ever heard. His last short speech withdrawing his resolution – beaten down by beastly bishops, the most pathetic – Redmond outed by that vile Raphoe!'

During the weeks of meetings in Dublin, Windle had changed in his political thinking. He had grown quite close to the southern unionists. With the emergence of Dillon as leader of the IPP, he had no other home in Irish politics but to seek refuge with Lord Midleton. However, he did not so much make a conscious choice to join the southern unionists as stand back from all politics. He was profoundly disillusioned with parlia-mentary democracy itself, and the British variety in particular. The war had made him even more pessimistic about 'vile man'. Exhausted after the months of travel to Dublin and long meetings, he wrote in his diary on 6 May that he found the outcome of the convention 'but a sorry busi-ness of 51 meetings'.[65] Published on 13 April, Windle gave his damning verdict: 'Irish convention report out today but might almost be waste-paper. It would be a tragedy if all that time and energy had been wasted.' While the convention had not been a waste of time, it is unsurprising that dejection was the dominant emotion felt by people like Windle, Midleton and others. As Irish politics entered a new and uncharted phase, it was 'end game' for any hope of a home rule settlement for Ireland.

CHAPTER 7

The Conscription Crisis and the 'German Plot'

A new crisis enveloped Ireland on virtually the same day as the ill-fated Irish Convention report was published. On 9 April, Lloyd George introduced the Military Service Bill with a provision to extend conscription to all men over seventeen residing in the Channel Islands, the Isle of Man and Ireland. Catholic and Protestant clergy were also included in the provisions of the bill. The negative reaction was so overwhelming in Ireland and elsewhere that Lloyd George reversed his decision to enlist Catholic clergy. On 13 April, Windle noted that the decision not to conscript clergy 'eases the situation a bit'. Windle wrote on the day of the announcement: 'As to conscription I note (a) the government ought to have collared the hordes of shirkers (very largely Jews) who fill Dublin, Cork and other places and who have fled from England to escape fighting (b) There is an unseen undercurrent here of people whose sons and children are fighting and who don't see why others shouldn't – A man said to me: "I've four at the war and why wouldn't the farmers who have been living on the fat of the land have theirs go too?"' That was not an entirely unsympathetic response. But Windle was not representative of those who supported radical nationalism. His was the view of a man committed to the war effort who saw shirking going on around him.

Horace Plunkett, writing on 6 May – a month after the conscription crisis erupted in Ireland, explained: 'My own firm belief is that the simplest explanation of the government's blunder of April 9th is the true one. The Cabinet was being bombarded with threats that their draft of the older men would be wrecked in parliament, unless the younger men in Ireland were taken.'[1] From the perspective of the cabinet and its supporters, the measure was both reasonable and inevitable. In a letter to the *Freeman's Journal*, Sir Arthur Conan Doyle said: 'The world is a strange picture at present. Belgium in slavery; France bleeding from a hundred

202

wounds, but still keeping her brave pale face to enemy; Britain sending her last man and her last pound to hold the murderer off from his victim; America straining every nerve, with real cause for fear lest she be too late; and Ireland, as fat as butter, wrangling over her parish pump.' He urged Irishmen, for God's sake, to be awakened to their duty, 'or an Irishman will be ashamed of the blood which runs in his veins. If peace were to come now, where in the wide world would Ireland find a friend.'[2]

While the reaction was swingeing in the nationalist press, an editorial in *The Irish Times* felt that the government had been 'extraordinarily timid and foolish in its treatment of this question'. How could, noted the paper, quoting a journalist, the British government 'dare to conscript middle-aged men in England, Scotland, and Wales, so long as there are still 200,000 young men in Ireland'? The paper warned the government that the justification for conscription was enrolment of at least 200,000 recruits into the British forces.[3]

Horace Plunkett, who might have been expected to support conscription, refused to do so, writing on 6 May:

> Every man who works for Ireland must make up his mind whether he will or will not die of a broken heart. I long ago decided that as I shall inevitably be tempted to do so, I would resist the temptation. Otherwise I think Lloyd George's speech on April 9th would have sent me down the *via dolorosa* of Irish servants. Next to the Phoenix Park murders, I do not think the deity who presides over Irish destinies ever did us a worse turn than making England hurl conscription to Ireland just when the report of the convention was going to open up a real prospect of a peaceful settlement. For such was much more definitely in sight than the public generally believe, or in the light of this untoward event, will ever believe. The Convention, by uniting the Redmondite Nationalists and the Southern Unionists, had made a fundamental change in the Irish question and a parliament for all Ireland would have been set up with execrations from Ulster, which I think might have been a healthy offset to the execrations of the Nationalists who had gone over to Sinn Féin, including, unfortunately, the R.C. hierarchy.[4]

Caught between despair and optimism, Plunkett wrote:

> The convention is not such a washout as the eclipse of its report by the conscription issue would lead one to suppose. Some ninety, more or less influential persons, have had for the first time in their lives, a training in the elements of government and also have got to know each other's own points of view as never before. Things are formed more quickly and the situation may be brighter than it is now by the time you get this. You and I have been sorely afflicted by

the government's mad folly in torpedoing the convention with Conscription. I think, however, the chaos they have caused is bound to produce a reaction. The convention really did good work in Ireland, and you have done splendid work in America. Against stupidity the gods strive in vain and we are both temporarily knocked out: but if we are right our opportunity will come again and I do not regret any of the work either of us have done or regard it as wasted.[5]

Éamon de Valera was as critical as Plunkett about the conscription initiative but from a very different political perspective. He called on nationalists to unite to a man in order to prevent the enforcement of conscription in Ireland. He said that the English always wanted revenge on the Irish people because they were not ready to go as slaves and fight her battle and allow her to have business as usual.[6] The leader of the Irish Parliamentary Party, John Dillon, pledged his opposition to the bill.

On 9 April, the standing committee of the Irish bishops issued a statement opposing conscription and began to mobilise clergy and religious to lead a campaign against the bill's implementation. The bishops regarded the bill as 'an oppressive and inhuman law which the Irish people have a right to resist by every means that are consonant with the law of God'.[7] Horace Plunkett, surprisingly, praised the actions of the hierarchy but felt that they had gone too far: 'The R.C. Church in Ireland have been in an extremely difficult position. Personally, I think the action they took saved us from a wild outbreak which would have deluged the country in blood.' He did not think it wise, however, to question the sovereign power of the imperial parliament in military matters. 'If the bishops had contented themselves with the strongest possible protest against the action of the government and taken up a definite stand upon a constitutional issue which is not really in the domain of faith and morals, I believe they would have produced the same effect in Ireland and a far greater effect outside.'[8]

In spite of the overwhelmingly negative reaction in Ireland, the British government carried on regardless. On 10 April, by a three-to-one majority, the bill had passed all stages in the House of Commons. However, there was an immediate rethink in British circles. *The Irish Times* reported on 12 April that there was a strong possibility, if not certainty, that the conscription of priests, clergymen and ministers of religion would be dropped from the bill.

On 15 April, Windle, postponing a visit to Dublin, wrote of the mood in Cork: 'seething indignation about conscription. Crowds to match a circus go through Cork! No one knows what may happen at any moment. Great mass meeting to be held to-night in Grand Parade. Bishop and Lord Mayor – unless Tories have pushed Lloyd George with this in return for Home Rule it is impossible to understand this madness. Nothing has ever stirred the country so deeply and indeed it is slavery and nothing else to coerce a country without its consent into conscription.'[9]

But it was too late to prevent mass mobilisation of all nationalists. On 18 April, a conference was held at the Mansion House, Dublin, with representatives of Sinn Féin, the Irish Parliamentary Party, the All-for-Ireland League, the Irish Labour Party and the Irish bishops attending. This was the climax to the anti-conscription campaign. It was a historic meeting. All shades of nationalist opinion were represented on the podium – John Dillon, Éamon de Valera, Arthur Griffith, Joseph Devlin, William O'Brien, T.M. Healy and various labour leaders all shared a common platform. A statement of Ireland's case was drafted by Tim Healy MP and Éamon de Valera of Sinn Féin. This was to be presented to the president of the United States, Woodrow Wilson.

After the meeting, a delegation went to Maynooth to see the Irish bishops who were meeting there at the time. The delegation was made up of de Valera, John Dillon, T.M. Healy, Larry O'Neill (Lord Mayor of Dublin) and William O'Brien (Labour Party). The outcome was the unification of the Church with all shades of nationalism against conscription. The momentum grew as a national campaign was mounted. Irishmen were asked to take a pledge 'to resist conscription by the most effective means at their disposal'. A 'committee of defence' was established in every parish to organise resistance.[10]

In contrast, the Protestant archbishops of Armagh and Dublin, according to *The Irish Times*, spoke out in favour of conscription. Both hoped that, when conscription was introduced in the country, 'their fellow-countrymen will accept it cheerfully as a sacred duty to themselves and to the Empire. It is certain that in the case of Irish Unionists of all the churches that hope will be fulfilled.'[11]

The day the Conscription Bill received royal assent, 18 April, Windle wrote to Sr Monica covering a wide range of issues: 'I am back at the mill and never in my life under less pleasant circumstances. It is not only that the war news is not by any means as good as it might be but things in this country could scarcely be worse. I don't suppose you bother your head about politics but nothing could be more foolish than the way in which the government have handled this island. In 1914 it was more friendly than I have ever known it to England. At the moment nothing could be worse than the feeling – How foolish to have thrown this asset away to please a number of highly placed people – highly placed socially! We may be on the verge of a revolution here – no one can say and only the most careful treatment of the country can abate it. I am sure you will pray for us and for me and my wife that we may be brought safely through this troublous time. And if – for nothing is impossible – I were to be killed I am sure you would not forget me in your prayers either. I don't anticipate this but one must be prepared for anything and anyway it is what is happening to thousands daily.'

On 19 April 1918, Windle wrote of his meetings in the college with the secretary of the students about their conscription meeting, which he allowed, but had refused to preside at: 'I refused to close the college which some of them wanted, said I could not keep students there but must provide teaching for those who wished to have it.' He said that a general in the Cork garrison told him that he was sending for Stockley to interview him: 'Told him Stockley was an ass and wanted to be a martyr and should so be treated.' He added: 'The attitude of our Bishops makes me furious. What right have they to be dictating to the country what it should do about conscription? How badly we want Home Rule to clip the crumbs of these people!'

Windle wrote to Sr Monica on 20 April giving her details of another honour being bestowed upon him: 'To my intense astonishment and dismay (I don't conceal that fact) I got two days ago a letter saying that Mr Balfour was sending a mission to America to bring about a closer relationship between the universities there and ours and asking me to be a member. The number is 4 only – so that the compliment is a high one and of course it is a good thing for the Church that of so small a number one shall be Catholic . . . All the same I am greatly upset by the whole thing and by the state of affairs here which is as bad as it can be. God help us all and God help those who have no religion for how they can get on at all simply baffles me. I needn't say every plan that I had ever dreamed up for the immediate future is now knocked on the head.'

The Irish Parliamentary Party met in Dublin on Saturday 20 April, and passed a resolution declaring that the act was 'one of the most brutal acts of tyranny and oppression that any Government can be guilty of'. It was also agreed that it was the highest and most immediate duty of everyone of the party to remain in Ireland, and actively cooperate with their constituents in opposing the enforcement of compulsory military service in Ireland.[12]

On 21 April, Windle wrote in his diary about the situation in Cork: 'Town quiet enough. Great taking of pledge against conscription I read. This means that Episcopal shame bless me being riveted still firmer round the people's necks. Can I or can I not get out of a country which is bossed by bishops into one where Catholicity is a pleasanter religion to live in?'

Archbishop Harty, preaching at Mass on that Sunday, denounced conscription and said that the Irish nation had the right to decide freely about its own taxation system: 'I proclaim here that the Act of Conscription is unjust, hypocritical, and I shall now proceed to the

Confraternity Hall to sign the protest against it. Every man with a drop of Irish blood in his veins should do so. We shall march to victory and shall plant the flag of Ireland in an impregnable position, proudly floating over this free nation.'[13] That message was echoed that Sunday at Masses all over the country. Tens of thousands of people signed in parishes the pledge: 'Denying the rights of the British Government to enforce compulsory service in this country, we pledge ourselves solemnly to one another to resist conscription by the most effective means at our disposal.'[14] After Mass at the Pro-Cathedral in Dublin, people signed in Banba Hall, Rutland Street. At other churches, the pledge was signed outside the church. Where it was not possible for a person to be present at Mass, the names were sent to the parish house on a slip of paper.[15] Some 150,000 people signed in Dublin alone. The Cork and City Parochial committee, of which Horgan was secretary, collected funds and hundreds of signatures. Windle's son-in-law, who had been in favour of the Redmond policy of enlistment in 1914, had, in the changed circumstances, taken up a strongly anti-conscription stance.

On Monday 22 April, Windle was approached by students requesting a day off from studies to participate in the national stoppage due to take place the following day. He did not approve. The demonstration organised by the trade union movement was a success, however, and as Horgan noted, it 'paralysed the normal life of three-fourths of the country'.[16] Windle was confused by the course of events, and on 27 April he wrote of his willingness to accept the new challenges posed by the political changes and their impact on the university. But he was ill at ease: 'Still I don't like it but if it is God's will what does one do? No question one ought to follow it and I must and will.' On 28 April, he noted: 'Meanwhile every kind of asininity being perpetrated in this country. I see (Monday) that Home Rule bill is to be brought in on Thursday. Irish MPs to stay away until they see what it is. J. Dillon is capable of any possible folly – that I believe. If this be thrown up – this Bill – I will clear out the moment I can get something in England and if I go to U.S.A. they must give me something when I return.'

The British administration was again in crisis. The chief secretary, Henry Duke, resigned and the lord lieutenant, Lord Wimborne, followed. Both men had left their posts in protest over the failure of the British prime minister to take into account the report of the Irish Convention. They were replaced by Edward Shortt and Lord French respectively.[17] On 29 April, Windle wrote: 'Addison! A 3rd rate ass who has never set foot in Ireland is one of the 3 men in charge of Home Rule Bill. Shortt (never in country either) another! What a gang politicians are!' Windle was so unsettled, he thought of leaving the country as soon as possible. On 5

May, he wrote: 'Long talk with Edith as to returning [to England] of which I am seriously thinking.'

Sir Horace Plunkett, who had seen the Irish Convention report shelved, was also very disillusioned by the political tack of the British government. He wrote in *The Irish Times* on 6 May 1918: 'At the gravest crisis with which the British Empire has ever been faced the Government have staked their existence upon a two-fold Irish policy – conscription and Home Rule. They cannot achieve both: at the cost of much present bloodshed and lasting hate they might achieve the first, thereby making the second impossible; in my opinion, for what it is worth, they would fail in the attempt and have to go, leaving both undone. Their successors would then have to find a way out of the worst Irish situation in my memory, which goes back to the Fenian days of fifty years ago and has had burned into it every agrarian and political agitation since.' Plunkett felt that the way out of the cabinet's disastrous policy was to set up government in Ireland. He believed that the Irish people, given their own government, would quickly show the world their real attitude to the war: 'It may then dawn upon Englishmen that we have in Ireland no pro-Germans except . . .'[18]

Contrary to Plunkett's advice, British policy hardened. The attorney general, Arthur W. Samuels, sought information from the inspector general of the RIC, Brigadier-General Byrne, as to whether the 'constabulary could be fully relied on if called upon to arrest the Priests who in the anti-Conscription Campaign are preaching from the Altar and at Chapel and other meetings to their Congregations, and telling them to assassinate the soldiers and police if they come to conscript them, and are endeavouring to suborn the police to betray their allegiance'.[19] Byrne told him that the 'agitation led by the Hierarchy and pushed actively by the Priests was telling on his men, and so serious on the R.C. Members of the Force was the effect of the Bishops and Priests urging resistance as a "moral"and "religious duty"that the Constabulary could not be trusted to carry out such arrests and that if they were put to it the results might even be so disastrous as to break up the Force.'

Later that day – 10 May – Samuels had a meeting with the county inspector of Kilkenny, Power, in the presence of the inspector general. Power, who was a Catholic like Byrne, told him that, 'having regard to the Bishops and Priests urging resistance to Conscription as a "moral duty", the R.C. police could not be safely ordered to carry out such arrests or to enforce Conscription.'The conclusion was the following: 'Ireland is in a most seditious and dangerous condition. The Sinn Féin organisation is a treasonable conspiracy preparing for another rebellion – is looking for German Assistance. Rebellions would occur at any favourable moment were it not for the large number of troops in the country. There is well-grounded apprehension of outrage and sabotage – threats of it are frequent and the number of claims for malicious injuries before the courts has been very great. Large subscriptions – amounting now to about £60,000 – are being given or exacted at the Chapels for the "national Defence Fund" to resist conscription . . . Isolated Protestants in the South are being intimidated to subscribe and to sign anti-conscription pledges.'[20]

Samuels was of the strong opinion that the Criminal Law and Procedure (Ireland) Act, 1885 should be brought into operation by proclamation. That legislation had, he believed, been most effective in restoring order at the time of the Land League: 'The people knew what it means, and if the country were Proclaimed under it the peasantry would at once believe that the Government was in earnest and meant to Govern, and the effect would, I believe, be a welcome relief to all well-disposed persons.' He wanted the Sinn Féin organisation proclaimed under the act by special proclamation as a 'dangerous association'. Samuels felt it imperative that 'the leaders of the Sinn Féin organisation should be at once deported and interned'.[21]

Samuels felt that it was impossible to hope that any home rule measure would at present be accepted by nationalist Ireland. He argued that the Sinn Féin body had completely captured the IPP and any proposal for federal home rule would be rejected. The southern unionists, he said, had hardened their positions, owing to the anti-conscription revolt of the nationalists and the attitude of the hierarchy and the priests. They were 'now unanimously of opinion that no scheme of Home Rule such as their delegates supported at the Convention could be safely introduced'. The Ulster unionists were more determined than ever against home rule. Samuels, therefore, felt the government was fully justified in postponing the introduction of a home rule measure: 'The temper of Ireland is too bad to hope for any reconciliation at present, and it would be a much safer and practical course to postpone the general enforcement of conscription for the present – postponing also the introduction of any Home Rule Bill during the present parliament, and to take in hand the restoration of order and public confidence.' Samuels believed that the 'universal opinion' was 'that at the moment it [the introduction of home rule] would make things far more unsettled and be accompanied by greater antagonism and sectarian animosities than unhappily now predominate'.[22] As hardline thinking crystallised in Dublin and London, Windle continued to write a commentary in his diary on Irish affairs. On 11 May, he was visited by Professor Hartog and Thompson of the *Daily Mail*. According to the visitor, Thompson, the government was going to drop both home rule and conscription. Windle commented: 'What a worm Lloyd George is and what a Godforsaken lot are British politicians.'

At the Colonial Office, Walter Long had been sufficiently concerned with the Irish situation to write to Cardinal Bourne for 'advice, counsel, and if happily it be possible, for active assistance'. His letter of 11 May referred to the 'perilous condition of affairs which has arisen in Ireland. I fear that it cannot, must not be, beyond the power of statesmanship to avert the awful disasters with which we appear to be threatened.'[23] The cardinal met Long and mentioned Windle as being a central person to consult on the Irish situation. Windle was quickly summoned to meet Long at the Colonial Office. His diary recorded on 15 May that he expected it to be 'a job of some sort no doubt'. The visit was to be kept 'absolutely secret'. On 17 May, he wrote: 'Colonial Office and with Walter Long 11–1.15 and very interesting talk as to what is to be done in Ireland and found myself in general accord with him.' Long then told him that he had gone to Cardinal Bourne to get the name of a reliable person in Ireland: 'Bourne says above all men – one – B.C.A.W.' Precisely what Long had in mind for him is not made clear in the diary or in related correspondence. But the British government was in a terrible quandary over Ireland and sought advice outside official channels. The dilemma may have been whether or not it was prudent to take decisive action against nationalist conspirators. Windle was convinced that it was necessary to 'draw the sword'.

On 17 May – the day Windle met Long – Sinn Féin leaders, including de Valera (president of Sinn Féin), Arthur Griffith (vice-president, Sinn Féin), Countess Markievicz (member of Sinn Féin executive), W.T. Cosgrave (MP for Kilkenny), Darrel Figgis (honorary secretary of Sinn Féin) and Count Plunkett were arrested simultaneously with the publication of a vice regal proclamation which alleged Irish collaboration with Germany. The arrests were made on Friday night and early Saturday morning by Superintendent Brien of 'G' Division. *The Irish Times* reported that the arrests were carried out quietly and the prisoners were conveyed to detention in covered military motor wagons and motor cars. The streets of Dublin were practically deserted during the night, and no disturbance took place.[24]

The RIC carried out raids and arrests outside Dublin – in Cork, Skibbereen, Clonmel, Cashel, Carrigaholt in Clare, Tralee, Killarney, Dingle, Drogheda, Dundalk, Kilkenny, Athlone, Tullamore, Gorey, Sligo, Galway, Loughrea, Westport, Roscommon, Gort, Strabane, Belfast, Carrickmacross and Mayo. Two raids were carried out on Sinn Féin headquarters in Harcourt Street and on the National Aid Association in Bachelor's Walk. The latter was an organisation set up to help the relatives of those who had died in the 1916 rising. When the raiding party of troops and policemen came out of the premises, a large crowd had gathered there, uttering what *The Irish Times* described as 'disloyal cries, such as "Up the Rebels" and booing took place'.[25] Some seventy-three detainees were deported to Britain.

Lord French had counselled Lloyd George that a tough military stance would secure the country. He needed 37,000 soldiers based in Ireland. With the help of the Royal Air Force, he would 'play about with either bombs or machine guns . . . and ought to put the fear of God into these playful young Sinn Féiners'.[26] Fortunately, he did not get the forces for which he had petitioned. His militaristic solution might have resulted in an Amritsar-style massacre.[27] On 18 May, Lord French issued a proclamation calling on all loyal subjects of his majesty 'to assist in every way His Majesty's government in Ireland to suppress this treasonable conspiracy, and to defeat the treacherous attempt of the Germans to defame the honour of Irishmen for their own ends'. There was a further call on loyal citizens to crush 'the said conspiracy, and, so far as in them lies, to assist in securing the effective prosecution of the War and the welfare and safety of the Empire'. There was a call to facilitate and encourage voluntary enlistment in Ireland in the British forces. Conscription, it was announced, had been temporarily abandoned.[28]

Windle returned to Dublin on the night mail boat, recording on 18 May: 'Hot-foot on this follow French's Proclamation of the German plot and the arrest of a number of people. Saw 2 or 3 in handcuffs on Limerick Junction platform with file of soldiers with fixed bayonets – said to be from Clonmel. There are a number of people who would be the better for being mopped up. Crossed in boat with Sanderson. The noted Colonel – a H.R.! says, and truly, that times are changed. NB. As I came through Kingstown Harbour I saw a cruiser and 2 submarines. On the cruiser I suppose were de Valera, Markievicz and the other people who were arrested in the night for the plot.' Back in Cork on 19 May, Windle wrote: 'City quite quiet – aeroplane out and about several times first to "look-see" I suppose. I do not know what to say of our people. They have of course been abominably treated but their credulous representatives is [sic] amazing. Ignorance and insularity [are] an awful combination!'

Windle wrote on 19 May to Cardinal Bourne about his meeting in London: 'The friend in office, of whom you spoke concerning me (and I understand in very kind terms) sent me a message on Sunday last and as a result of which I crossed to Holyhead that night . . . However one must put one's own convenience aside in times like this and as I had two and a half hours with our friend I came over to some purpose.' Having supported the rounding up of Sinn Féin leaders, Windle's diary reveals an alienated figure in a political world with which he has ever diminishing sympathy. He wrote on 20 May: 'Ireland *per* John Dillon and company making a complete, hysterical ass of itself.' The following day, he recorded: 'As to this country it is . . . suffering from a violent fit of shameless, indecent hysteria. Dillon that ass joining with Shinners to protest against deportations of conspirators.' The IPP leader was strong in condemnation of the arrests, claiming on 26 May in a speech in Bailieborough, County Cavan, that over 100 men and women had been arrested within the previous ten days. The authorities had not published any evidence against the detainees, he said. He felt that there was a campaign to convince the American people that the Irish were in league with the German government: 'A more abominable libel than that was never levelled against the Irish people since the days of Richard Pigott (hear, hear), he said.'[29]

Windle went to Dublin on 24 May where he attended a meeting of the NUI: 'Thence to vice regal lodge on invitation of His Excellency and one hour's talk with him and W. Long. Heard *all* about Sinn Féin plot which as bad as it can be. Strongly urged proceeding against plotters so as to make matters clear, since the publication of details, unproved might be called a mere invention. The whole story is marvellous and discreditable.' He travelled on to London where he had a meeting with a priest: 'long talk – told him everything – Thinks I should stick it – a great responsibility to refuse unsought of offices pressed on me.' The latter reference may allude to an offer made to him during his meeting with the lord lieutenant in Dublin. On 29 May, he met his friend Cardinal Bourne and 'told him everything he wanted to know'. He recorded that the cardinal 'says Fr Stafford told him that he stopped hunger strike at Frongoch – where he was chaplain – by telling men no absolution for those who were committing sin by abstaining from food. This cardinal says is quite right – yet when Ashe committed suicide in this way Archbishop Walsh sent his carriage to his funeral. Either he thought Ashe irresponsible or he has no religion.'

Meanwhile the chief secretary, Shortt, was asked in the House of Commons on 30 May 1918 whether the prisoners brought to England had the same rights and liberties of persons awaiting trial and whether they would be tried in Ireland or in Great Britain. Shortt, in reply, gave the number of those arrested as sixty-nine. The condition of their detention was under consideration, he said. Sir George Cave, the home secretary, was asked whether the legal representative who acted for the detainees had applied for leave to see his clients. That application had been refused for the present, he said.[30] Four of the detained were MPs – de Valera (East Clare), Cosgrave (Kilkenny), Plunkett (North Roscommon) and J.

McGuinness (South Longford). That matter was raised again in the Commons on 3 June 1918. However, the detainees were left to languish in a legal twilight zone. The security of the realm took precedence over respect for individual rights.

On 31 May, Windle returned to Ireland, remaining on deck most of the night: He wrote: 'Perfectly lovely – flat calm. Sea-birds peaceful – exquisite colours of dawn and fears of a torpedo all the way. Only man is vile and he *is* vile. – NB. An odd thing – third consecutive Friday night on which I have crossed channel. First time for using Passport which has certainly cut down numbers.' Confined to his room in Cork suffering from hay fever, he wrote on 4 June: 'Curse this hysterical strumpet of a country carrying on as per usual.' The following day, he noted: 'Government must be quite satisfied. Home Rule scheme breaks down according to papers. *Que faire*? [What to do?] and personally *que faire*? [What am I to do myself?] Is there any good toiling at the oar when the tide is over-masteringly against one?' On 6 June, he wrote: 'What the Government is up to with this country I can't imagine and as to the country itself its attitude is enough to turn the strongest stomach. General belief that Home Rule is given up. Carson I suppose again.' He commented on 8 June that the government was 'filling all Castle posts with Tories and Protestants. What they are up to no man can say.' On 10 June, he commented: 'Irish affairs no better – given over to every kind of hysterical rubbish.' And 12 June: 'Irish news as bad as ever – this country exactly like a hysterical girl – I wish I could get out of it being thoroughly ashamed for the first time in my life of being an Irishman.' The next day, he entered: 'Ireland as foolishly hysterical as ever – Truly a land of *opera-bouffe*. Why couldn't one be born a French man and belong to a land of which one could be proud as one can't of this?' On 17 June, Windle noted: 'Shinner (Kent! brother of a murderer and that the reason) elected Chairman of Cork County Council – My God what a country but what can be expected of a country in which you have wigged asses like Hallinan talking of the bogus Irish-German Plot (as if they knew which they don't) and declaring Sinn Féin to be the people's path to Liberty. The impudence of these half-educated peasants beats everything.'

On 20 June, a by-election was held in East Cavan. Arthur Griffith (Sinn Féin) was elected by 3,795 votes to the nationalist, J.F. O'Hanlon's, 2,581. The defeat of the Irish Parliamentary Party's candidate was a crushing psychological and political blow for John Dillon. On 21 June, Windle wrote: 'News that Conscription and Home Rule are both dropped which is what Sinn Féin has done for us and they get their man in (Griffith!) for E. Cavan by 1,200 majority. My Heavens what a country!'

On 20 June in the House of Commons, the chief secretary for Ireland, Edward Shortt, sought to justify the action of the British government over the 'German plot'. Asked whether he now had sufficient evidence to enable a prosecution for treason to be brought against the Irish men and women who had been deported and interned, he replied: 'There is sufficient evidence but no prosecutions for treason are considered either necessary or advisable.' He was asked why he would not proceed against the detainees, particularly in light of the fact that there was a commonly held view in Ireland that the action had been taken to suppress a political movement and that the whole charge had been 'faked up'. Shortt replied: 'I should think the reasons were obvious and certainly no such views are held widely.' He was then asked: 'Is the reason that the evidence is mostly collected by *agent provocateurs*?' 'No, certainly not,' replied Shortt.[31]

John Dillon argued that the British government had acted against the advice of every single man who had had any serious acquaintance with Ireland, and against the advice of his party, turning its back on the constitutional movement and arresting Sinn Féiners 'for doing that which they permitted the Ulster Orangemen to do'.[32] On 3 July, Windle wrote: 'Not much news of any kind. Dillon and Co now going back to the House of Commons which has been too thankful to have been without them and their absence from which has done nothing but made them laughing-stocks to everybody. What a state the Irish Parliamentary Party has fallen into for want of Redmond and on account of the subservience to the bishops. If they had faced them at the Convention what a difference.'

The British government resorted to another tactic with which Windle only partially agreed. On 4 July, he wrote: 'Government make a move and proclaims Sinn Féin – Cumann na nGael . . . Gaelic League (!) as dangerous organisations. As to the last that seems strong meat however something had to be done to stop raiding and lawlessness and the pendulum now going from Do-nothing Duke to the opposite extreme.' On 5 July, Windle received a letter from the colonial secretary, Walter Long. We have not found that letter. On 8 July, he wrote: 'Certainly this is a bad country for a Catholic to live in . . . though in every way, it would be good to have priests who weren't almost all peasants and if peasants born then peasants always. Maynooth doing nothing [in] the way of breeding others . . . to live as a Catholic in England is a pride and a joy, here it is a mortification and a misery. The treasure is there and one cannot do without it, but would that it were not hidden in such a very very dirty pot.' On 9 July, Windle wrote: 'What is happening to this country? You take a group of clever – even brilliant peasants – you educate them in Maynooth – the narrowest groove in the world. You give them Professorship there.

They work 15–20–25 years at Theology or what not. Then they are made Bishops and *at once* with no breeding for it or preparation, in most cases capacity; they pose (and worst of all are accepted) as political leaders – until their power is broken down – political of course – nothing can be done in this country. They know that and hence not a bit of Home Rule do they want in my opinion.'

On 10 July, Windle's entry read: 'Nothing much in the way of news . . . The lying Irish (and some of the English) papers who go on printing that there never was a "plot" . . . Meantime a man is arrested (yesterday) in Skibbereen – with hidden arms, ammunition, money and German literature – The populace resent this "because he is being taken away from his poor old mother who has no one else." We are a vile and a hysterical people and I don't wonder the English farmers are sick at lusty Irish harvesters going over there, exempt while their own sons are conscripted.'

While at Listarkin on 18 July, he wrote to Sr Monica:

> 'Every prospect pleases and only man is vile', in other words, there is a fly in the apothecaries' ointment, since last summer. We then had two excellent priests. The administrator was a rough kind of man but well read and learned and an excellent preacher. The curate was an admirable young man who had spent several years on the mission at Goran which had done him a lot of good. One cannot expect very superior priests in a little place like this where for miles and miles there isn't an educated Catholic except a few doctors, and ourselves. However we got on very nicely these two have been shifted and we have as administrator a man whom I have not called on nor shall nor would admit to my house if I could help it – a vulgar, political Sinn Féin priest of the worst type – Fortunately he lives 2 miles away – the curate is a decent, quiet little thing who was ordained last November. And doesn't count. I am having a rather trying time for the past 12 months from the clerical point of view. There was one admirable priest in Cork who was my confessor for more than 12 years. He has been shifted into the country alas! And I have no friend now amongst the local clergy. Of course I go to confession but it's just a business and don't get the help I did from my former confessor. I suppose there is some good reason for all this but never in all my Catholic life have I been so ecclesiastically stranded as now. Since there is not a single priest in the city of Cork to whom I could or would go if I were in any trouble.[33]

Windle continued his analysis of the Irish Catholic Church for the edification of Sr Monica:

> Conditions are so different here that it is hard for anyone to understand them who does not know the country – most Catholics being

poor or being lower middle class the average priest more or less matches them and you don't meet him in the better homes where I suspect he could feel like a fish out of water. As a general rule too he is much more 'professional' – He will give you absolution or many of the sacraments in a perfectly business-like manner but you won't get much spirituality out of him. That is the rule though of course there are exceptions and amongst the orders there are here and there men of quite different calibre. This it is which makes it difficult to think of settling down here when one retires: things are very different in England. Yet of course I prefer my own country – but it is hard to live without what one may call the pleasure of Catholicity and those, except the internal one, one never gets.[34]

In his diary for the 18th, Windle returned to the theme of criticising the Irish clergy: 'Asses of priests bringing gifts to Mr de Valera and talking absolute hog-drivel. How is it possible to settle down in a country where a Catholic is tied up with such swine and has to endure their gruntings and be tarred with their brush.' 'Ireland no better,' he wrote on 20 July. On 21 July, he commented: 'Vile sermon by our local yokel.'

The Windles returned to Cork on 24 July. The following day, he wrote: 'I suppose so large a band of asses could not be got outside the lands of Kerry where they grow from the ground. Strikes in England due to pure damned foolishness of Government and officials. I want the Hun smashed but not by England though indeed any stick will do to beat a dog.' On 26 July, Windle received a pamphlet in the post from Horace Plunkett: 'fine but what good suggesting anything to the lying Bush-Baptist who now bosses things.'[35] On 7 August, Windle's low opinion of the chief secretary, Shortt, was expressed as follows: 'Instead of a genuine attempt to settle education in Ireland as I had urged, Shortt sets up two parliamentary commissions . . . neither of which can or will do anything but waste time and money.'

Gasquet wrote to Windle from the Holy See on 10 August: 'How many things have happened since you last wrote to me from a sitting of the Convention! To us out here it is very difficult to follow this situation in Ireland. Probably it is almost as difficult for you in that "distressful country" itself. I wish it were possible to have a long talk with you about the situation. The policy of the new Nationalist leaders is nearly as hard to follow, as that of the Government is. The playing of the latter with King Carson is enough to make honest Irishmen savage. Is there no one at all who has the gift of vision? Or are they all timid?'

On Sunday 18 August, he noted with relief while at Listarkin: 'C. Roche said Mass 8.30 so we escaped the terror who came on the rest at 10.00.' Windle continued his commentary on the inadequacies of the

Irish clergy in his diaries on 21 and 22 August. He said that Canon Roche's views on Maynooth College 'exactly agree with mine viz: that it is the curse of this country and that decentralisation in ecclesiastical [area] is badly wanted'. On 22 August, Windle motored to Skibbereen to have lunch with Bishop Kelly: 'Very pessimistic as to Ireland – hasn't a friend left which is fine. Thinks the counsel of despair is success of Sinn Féiners at election. A whole body of MPs not going to Parliament would shock world? Would world care a damn? *je m'en doute*.' Referring to the Irish Convention, he noted that Kelly 'had implored that abominable Raphoe and his ruffians to fall in with Midleton. Told them nothing would induce him to accept the responsibility of rejecting such an offer. Raphoe (impudent, sullen – head drunk of conceit) said government couldn't give less than Midleton and might be forced into more – Hence our position.'[36] On 26 August, Windle noted that the Bishop of Ross said 'real obstacle to Home Rule are the Presbyterians (a vile, vile gang *je l'admets*) who think if they had the Six Counties they would have a purely Presbyterian enclave in which they could do as they like. They have all the low vileness of that triple scoundrel John Knox.'

On 23 August, Windle received a letter from Horace Plunkett asking him to be a member of the Irish War Aims Committee. Windle wrote that he did not much like the idea. He would not go public and engage in speaking commitments: 'I want the Hun beaten – no one does more but I don't want England to be top-dog,' he wrote. Membership would have involved him in the production of propaganda of one kind or another. He would also have been employed as lecturer to help raise support for the war. (On 31 August 1918, Windle suggested to Horace Plunkett the names of two additions to the War Aims Committee.)

Alienated from Church and state, Windle unburdened himself to Cardinal Bourne on 29 August. He apologised for the 'inordinate length' of his letter and stressed that his personal views 'are of a highly confidential character'. Windle wrote very frankly as follows: 'Until something is done to reverse this policy I must confess that I see no hope for us.' He explained that he had had lunch on Saturday with Bishop Kelly, 'who is not only my Diocesan but my P.P. this being a mensal parish'. Windle was sure that the cardinal knew the bishop 'and will be glad to hear that he is looking very well though he says he is not going to live long and is glad of it. He is about the only Bishop in this country who has my real confidence; if we had two or three more like him we should be in a more hopeful condition.' Kelly's views very much 'coincide with mine and he thinks that it will take fourteen years of more or less bitter struggle to bring us back to where we were a year ago when the Convention was called together not to speak of where we were in 1914'.[37]

Windle recalled for the cardinal the view of the late John Redmond:

> Time after time at the Convention, Redmond said that its failure
> would make things ten times as bad as they were. Yet in the face of
> that the other Bishops there – of course Raphoe was the only one that
> counted – pressed an impossible solution; split the National party
> and kill Redmond. God may forgive him; I never will. Bp. Kelly told
> me that he called the other Bishops to what he thought was his dying
> bed, for he then was given twenty-four hours to live, and adjured
> them to accept the Midleton compromise telling them that if he was
> offered to be cleared of all the evil he had done in his life (I'm sure not
> much) to stand with them, he would not accept the responsibility. Yet,
> thinking in their own self-conceited way that, by asking for more
> than they knew they could get, they would get as much as they were
> prepared to accept, they split the party, voted with the Ulster gang
> against the report and killed the Convention. Had all the convention
> save Ulster agreed on a scheme even an impostor like the present
> premier could not have avoided a settlement. Anyone but a man of
> the boundless self-conceit of Raphoe could have seen this but he
> wouldn't and we are where we are.[38]

Windle then gave the cardinal his views on the anti-home rule stance
of Raphoe: 'Politically this is bad enough but religiously it is far worse,
there are in this country heaps of quiet people who want a settlement.
Outside Ulster there are few of the old die-hards. Amongst the protestants the belief is universal, and it is held by not a few of our own, that
our Bishops (i.e. Raphoe and Co.) are really averse from Home Rule,
knowing that it would mean an end of their political domination as it
would and should; and that they dare not oppose it openly but, pretending to support it, make it wholly impossible by their demands.'
Windle could not believe that such duplicity was possible, 'but thousands
do, and, as you may imagine the opinion does no good to our religion. It
confirms the Protestant in his objections to it and it makes anti-clericals
of the Catholics; indeed I do not know any educated lay catholic who is
not anti-clerical though in no way anti-Catholic. It is not a satisfactory
position in any way.'[39]

On 4 September 1918, Windle received word of the death of his close
friend and spiritual director, Fr Maher, 'the most intimate of friends on
the spiritual side I possessed'. It would be wrong to underestimate the
deep impact of Maher's death on the morale of Windle. He was a figure
of immense importance in Windle's life and one of the people who
understood him best. The news filled him 'with a great loneliness. He was
a thoroughly spiritual man – learned – kind, affectionate – sympathetic
. . . RIP but *what* a loss to me.' (On 17 September, he wrote an obituary

notice 'of my dear Fr Maher SJ for Clongownian. His loss is quite vile …
but I hope that he is helping me in heaven.')

Back in the university for a meeting on 5 September, a letter was
waiting for him from Long which 'shows that he understands the position here in no wise. Just that ordinary Tory thick headedness. I thought
he had been better.' On 7 September he noted: 'No decent news about
this unfortunate country and its rulers appear determined to make it ten
thousand times worse than it was. I suppose Carson at the bottom of all
this mischief and his group of titled ladies. What we want is a mitigated
"Terror" to rid us of our junkers and much more our junkeresses.' About
to return to UCC on 10 September, Windle wrote: 'I can't think why I am
going back to the college – a thing I loathe when I could return and settle
down here [Listarkin] and live quietly.'

Gasquet wrote to Windle on 9 September saying that he had 'obtained from Rome the permission you asked to read books on the
Index'. The actual document had not been sent on yet but he should have
it later. 'Meanwhile you have the "faculty" – I don't think you would care
for [?] as a place to retire to, but as you say, when you do retire, the great
point is to take plenty of time to see the kind of thing that would suit.
Before that you will have to come to Rome and perhaps you will find that
after all the "Eternal City" would be the best resting place.' It was now an
open secret that Windle was hoping to retire from his position as president of UCC.

Windle was so disabused with the antics of the British government
that he hoped that they would not get the credit for winning the war. On
11 September, he wrote: 'We must of course thoroughly beat the Hun I
feel that but if it could be so managed that in doing so it should be France
and U.SA. which did it and England was an "also ran". That is what I
should like – But clearly England is a shade better than Prussia.' On 12
September, he asked: 'Irish news no better and that bitch Borthwick in
her bawdy *Morning Post* for vengeance on this country.[40] If she and
Carson could be tied back to back and cast into Gehenna there might be
some gleams of possibility of peace.'

Breaking from Windle and the world of national politics, there were
two unrelated events in September 1918 which cast his personality in a
negative light. Windle went to see three new stained glass windows by
Harry Clarke in St Barrahane's Protestant church (built in 1826) in
Castletownshend. The Somervilles, finding the original windows too
gloomy, had commissioned the artist to create a three-light east window
depicting the nativity in memory of Dr Thomas Somerville of Drishane
House and his wife Henrietta.[41] Windle wrote: 'To see Clarke's new
window – far too good for such a church and such a sect but may do

them good.' The second episode in September 1918 highlighted Windle's self-centredness and ambivalent attitude towards his grandchildren. On 9 September, he met his grandson, accompanied by a maid, off the train in Skibbereen. They were to stay a week. Windle wrote that the visit was 'a treat for Edith who badly wanted it and a scourge for me who badly didn't, but didn't say so.' On 14 September, he noted that having the boy 'in our house an intolerable nuisance to me, but adored by Edith'. It was unlikely to have been the presence of his grandchild which prompted him to copy out a prayer on 15 September from Boswell's *Johnson*: 'Grant me, O Lord, to design only what is lawful and right; and afford me calmness of mind, and steadiness of purpose, that I am to do thy will in this short life, as to obtain happiness in the world to come, for the sake of Jesus Christ our Lord, Amen.' On 16 September, he 'deposited the little boy (D.G.) and Annie [maid] in train for Cork'.

Windle returned to UCC ready to face another year. He gave much of his attention to mounting a campaign for the establishment of a University of Munster. His diary entries about the country continued to be gloomy and despondent. On 30 September, he noted: 'Ireland goes on playing the maudlin ass.' On 3 October, he wrote: 'Oh this asinine fool of a country and what is to become of it no one can say.' Referring to Londonderry and the unionists, he wrote: 'Let us hope they may be exterminated after the war.' His respect for Woodrow Wilson had grown, describing his stance as 'splendid', but 'what a contrast to England's beastly Bush Baptist!' Nothing had changed during the summer to lift his opinion of Lloyd George.

The war continued and its horrors were never very far away. The mail steamer, *Leinster*, with 687 passengers and a crew of 60, was torpedoed on 10 October *en route* from Dun Laoghaire to Holyhead. There were 180 civilians on board. The majority were military personnel from Ireland, Britain, Canada, Australia, New Zealand and the United States. The ship was sixteen miles off the Irish coast when the attack occurred. Some 529 lost their lives of whom 115 were civilians.[42] Windle wrote on 11 October: 'Diabolical Huns torpedo "Leinster" and murder over 400 helpless people. May God deal with them as they deserve.'

The British government had long since lost the loyalty and allegiance of nationalist Ireland. Walking in Cork City on 20 October, he witnessed a 'recruiting meeting in afternoon broken up by Sinn Féiners and a baton charge followed'. He believed that the country was in a state of incipient revolution. On 21 October, he wrote that there were 'rumours of a Sinn Féin rising and that things were very bad in Dublin'. Gasquet wrote from Rome on 23 October, sending on the document granting Windle permission to read books on the Index. The cardinal inquired: 'How about

Ireland? Are the government officials going to blunder again? If one is to believe the papers the Nationalist Party will be much reduced when the election comes. This is a pity as it appears to me.'[43]

In UCC, Windle had to deal with the Spanish flu epidemic. On 28 October, he noted: '9 cases of flu in Honan Hostel shows epidemic has come.' Following a meeting with his deans, it was agreed unanimously to close the college. He wrote: 'a great nuisance but I am sure the right thing. Very busy making all arrangements. By afternoon place deserted.' On 29 October, he busied himself over the 'influenza vaccine business'. (On 14 November, he noted that the flu in the college was going down.)

The excerpts from his diaries, quoted below, chronicle the depths of his despair about the country and his desire to leave – torn as he was between his God-given duty, his personal well-being and the dangers – as he saw it – to his faith. Windle began to use an even more intemperate vocabulary in his diaries directed at both Church and state between late October 1918 and January 1919. He wrote on 23 October: 'our imbecile, fat-headed bishop [Cohalan] makes an ass of himself over Sinn Féin. Why is it that a prig and pedant who has spent 25 years in doing nothing but doling out dollops of theology to our peasants should imagine himself competent to talk about politics. This country is quite hopeless and the sooner I can get out of it the better.'

A three-day convention of the Sinn Féin organisation had begun in the Mansion House, Dublin on 28 October. De Valera was elected president unopposed following the withdrawal of Arthur Griffith and Count Plunkett. On 31 October, Windle made another despairing comment about the country: 'Ireland as rotten as ever but curious Sinn Féin developments – former firebrands like the strumpet Markievicz left off Executive and poor old sheep Plunkett formerly the leader.' Michael Collins and Eoin MacNeill also won seats on the SF executive. Such contradiction puzzled Windle who had no real idea how to judge the nuances within radical nationalism.

But war, at least, was drawing swiftly to an end. On 9 November, Windle wrote about the end of an era: 'Ructions all over continent – kings and dukes abdicating right and left'. On 10 November, he noted: 'English papers this morning full of guff about the soul of great Britain and suchlike ráiméis [ráiméis=drivel].' He attributed the victory to the entry of the United States of America, noting on 11 November: 'PEACE [written in red] abroad and I wish to God there were at home for things go from bad to worse . . . Bells rung (Protestant of course – we haven't any) and flags hoisted and general good humour except for a few black-guard boys.' Cork celebrated the end of hostilities. The war had ended on 'the eleventh hour of the eleventh day of the eleventh month'. The total number of casualties, military and civilian, was 16 million dead and 21 million wounded.

The war over in Europe, Windle faced the possibility of a social and political revolution in Ireland. That was Windle's recurring nightmare. Amidst such uncertainty, he wrote: 'Lloyd George precipitates a general election which no one wants in the hope of [gaining] a way "out" which will keep him amongst the "flesh-pots"for four more years.'[44] The entry concluded: 'Many an honester man is doing Penal Servitude and yet doing it deservedly.' How did Windle view the prospects of the Irish Parliamentary Party? He had a visit on 4 December from two prospective IPP candidates, Major T. Crosbie and O'Sullivan, and commented that 'the latter [was] a splendid sample – the former dull. But what hope is there for a country which is given over to madness and folly and filled with the vilest priests on earth?' As election day – 14 December – approached, Windle gave his opinion of the Cork candidates: 'Of the 2 Sinn Féiners one mad (Roche) one a regular bad one (J.J. Walsh) a scoundrel unfit for anything. Of the 2 Unionists 1 (Farrington) the most impossible crank in Cork . . . the other a shifty hound (Williams). Of the Nationalist candidates Crosbie decent but not much brains. Neither [was] O'Sullivan a really first class man.'

The writing was on the wall for the Irish Parliamentary Party. John Horgan, a stauncher supporter one could not find in Cork, had been alienated by the attempt to impose conscription on the country. In 1918, he published a pamphlet, *The Complete Grammar of Anarchy*, addressed to the British government. It was seized by the authorities in a raid on the publishers and bookshops and later described by the Irish attorney general, Samuels, as sedition and intended to instigate rebellion and create anarchy. Horgan called, in the run up to the general election, for Sinn Féin and the Irish Parliamentary Party to hold a convention to work out a common approach. He succeeded in getting a resolution to that effect passed at a meeting of Cork nationalists and the text was sent to John Dillon. The latter was well disposed to the idea but said he would not compromise on representation at Westminster. There was no ground for compromise. Eoin MacNeill told Horgan that the parliamentary party 'cannot and does not count on being able to secure more than five seats in Ireland at a general election'. He was right and there was no need for Sinn Féin to concede or compromise.[45]

On polling day, Windle noted: 'Closed college at 2.00. Everything, however, perfectly quiet.' When the votes were counted, Walsh (SF) had topped the poll with 20,801 votes, closely followed by Liam de Róiste [Roche], with 20,506. They took the two seats. Maurice Talbot Crosbie (IPP) got 7,480 votes and his running mate Richard L. O'Sullivan 7,162.

David Williams (unionist) got 2,519 votes and Thomas Farrington (unionist) received 2,254.[46]

Dejected by the local results, he wrote on the day after polling day: 'It is a misery for an educated Catholic to live in this country where most of the priests are unfit to come into a decent house.' On 16 December, he reflected: 'I am afraid it is clear that I must stay here though two things weigh against it. (1) the impossibility of enjoying one's religion in a country where most of the bishops and priests make one vomit. Hard – as I gave up much for it. (2) The country itself which is at present in a state beneath even sympathy or contempt. Imagine priests supporting a man who said if England was fighting the devil Ireland would be pro-devil and pro-hell. *That* is what Catholicity is in Ireland. It certainly is not Christianity.'

The disaster for the Irish Parliamentary Party in Cork was repeated throughout the country. The IPP leader, John Dillon, lost a seat he had held in East Mayo for thirty years to the jailed leader of Sinn Féin, Éamon de Valera, by 8,843 to 4,451. The 'strumpet Markievicz', as Windle repeatedly called her, was returned for St Patrick's Ward, Dublin, and became the first woman to win a seat in the House of Commons.

Windle was a lost soul in the emerging Ireland. He retreated to Listarkin and went to Mass on Christmas Day in the local church: 'A lovely crisp day. Mass – and the most disedifying Mass ever as [Priest] 25 minutes late though it had been impressed on us on Sunday 10 sharp and people were there by 10. Priest cross. Boys stupid and careless. Singing more awful than ever. These are the things [that] make settling here impossible.' On 27 December, he wrote: 'Edith's Christmas tree held in Court-House – a filthy hall – overcrowded with excited children and as a result Edith home with sore throat.' 'Oh! that I could get away from this wretched country,' he wrote. And on 30 December: 'Results of elections: 75 Shinners decorate our lists. 6 Home Rulers, the rest unionists. Dillon out – (Asquith in by the bye) – only one woman elected the whore and murderess Markievicz by a respectable Christian Catholic constituency. We are now in for a bad time in this country. England can't give the Republic which by the way most of the people don't really want. She can't give Home Rule, nor for in the present temper of the people, that would mean another reason for separation. What is she to do. Doles and slaps as per ancient recipe.' After the final count, Sinn Féin had won seventy-three seats, twenty-five of which had been uncontested. Four SF candidates, including de Valera and Arthur Griffith, had been elected for two constituencies. The IPP or Nationalists took six, the Unionists twenty-five and Independent Unionist one. The majority party had won about 47 per cent of the votes cast. The old order had changed, or so it appeared, virtually overnight.[47]

Dillon told T.P. O'Connor, one of his closest collaborators, that 'the treachery and weakness of the government' were a major reason for the collapse of the IPP vote at the general election. He blamed the 'poisoning of the minds of the Irish people' for *many* years by the *Irish Independent*, the mosquito press and Sinn Féin propaganda without any effective response from the IPP. He felt that the younger generation were ignorant of that record, having grown up in 'the mephitic atmosphere of the Parnellite split, and Healyism'. Dillon accused a large section of the priests of venting their fury to destroy an 'independent lay party', in order to recover their power over Irish politics which the Parnellite movement had to a very large extent destroyed. The priests, according to Dillon, were 'most dishonestly' using Sinn Féin to carry out the purpose that they had long nursed. He also held that defeat was due to 'the outbreak in all its old savagery of the hatred of England, due to the executions and vile and idiotic policy of the government for the past five years'.[48] Had he known of the contents of the Dillon letter, Windle would have agreed with his analysis of the stance taken by the majority of the bishops and clergy.

Windle had great cause for despair. Among the seventy-three 'Shinners' returned, Sinn Féin swept the board in Cork with David Rice Kent (Cork East), Terence Joseph MacSwiney (Cork Mid), Patrick O'Keeffe (Cork North), Thomas Hunger (Cork North-East), Diarmuid Christopher Lynch (Cork South-East) and Seán Hales (Cork West).[49] On 2 January 1919, Gasquet wrote: 'I can quite understand your feeling about the present state of Ireland. It is indeed chaos and what the clergy expect to gain by supporting the Sinn Féiners I can't understand – probably they don't either. The destruction of the Constitutional party is complete I see. I think that the mistake the Nationalists made all along was not to have tried to work with the Bishops more. Now their Lordships will have to deal with a party pledged to revolutionary methods and force without any idea of obedience to law civil or religious.'[50] The cardinal sympathised with Windle for the unenviable position in which he found himself: 'It is all very terrible and I feel very much for you in the difficult position you are in as a Catholic *first* and foremost. It is a great trial and there is nothing that I can see that is likely to change the ecclesiastical outlook. The younger clergy are quite out of hand and even if the Bishops wished I do not suppose they could stay the whirlwind now they have let it ahead. It is still quite impossible for the authorities to understand the situation, especially as it is so obvious that the English government is really the cause of all the mess, through their insane backing of Carson and Co.'[51] Gasquet felt that there was one thing that could be done by them in the circumstances: 'The only recourse we can have is "prayer" that God may still the storm. Humanly speaking it looks that we are in for a new period of coercion, with all this means for bitterness and soreness.'[52]

Despite the uncertainty over the future of Ireland, Windle was – by January 1919 – in the midst of a major campaign to win autonomy and university status for University College Cork. He had reactivated the idea, first launched by him soon after his arrival in Ireland, of trying to establish a University of Munster. It was a brave if foolhardy undertaking not least because he was facing within the college a challenge from staff with Sinn Féin sympathies. His diary identified two professors – Stockley and Rahilly – as being the leaders of the new faction. For example, on 24 June 1918, he described both men as 'two pious mad fools – giving lots of trouble. How much easier and better to have to do with the really wicked than the Godly idiot. With the first one can cope and he is at times open to argument – the other swollen headed goat isn't.'[53] Windle, staking all his prestige on winning autonomy for UCC, had to contend with the Sinn Féin enemy within the campus.

CHAPTER 8

The University of Munster – Windle's Last Hurrah

Windle, in his early years in Ireland, had sought to establish a University of Munster free from the 'shackles' of the NUI. His experiences over the intervening years only reinforced his wish to achieve autonomous university status for UCC. In mid-1917, there is evidence that the time was ripe to make a major effort to secure his long-cherished goal. Sir John O'Connell, one of Windle's closest friends, wrote to him on 12 July: 'Candidly I am very glad indeed to learn that you have decided to go for a University for Cork, and I believe that you will have no difficulty in carrying the Cork people with you, as I believe there is a good deal of feeling in Cork at the present time in favour of having a University for the Province of Munster, with its seat in Cork. Moreover, such is the pride of the Cork people that I think if you succeed in having it established on the right lines, that a good deal of money will flow in to you from one source or another, and that many of the richest people in Cork will be found to follow the example of the late Miss Honan.'[1] O'Connell was also his legal adviser and, in that capacity, he wrote: 'It will of course, as you say, be necessary to set out in the Petition for the Charter the various grounds upon which the Charter for the University is asked for, and amongst these not the least important will be to show the large amount of money which has either been given to the College since the University Act was passed, or applied indirectly for the benefit of the College, such as the purchase endowment and equipment of the Honan Hostel.'[2]

Windle had agreed in mid-1917 to serve as a member of the Irish Convention and that was a full-time job in itself. While the NUI system was for Windle a form of bondage in Egypt, he was obliged to abandon mounting a campaign for autonomy at that time. But timing was of critical importance. The rise of Sinn Féin created problems for Windle – problems which would contribute substantially to the failure of his push for autonomy. While Windle felt confident that he could carry the overwhelming majority of the professorial staff of UCC with him on the matter of autonomy, Sinn Féin ideas had found their way inside the portals of the college. Windle had two strong, vocal opponents in the Professor of English, William F.P. Stockley and the Professor of Mathematical Physics, Alfred O'Rahilly.[3] (The latter was to become registrar [1920–43] and president [1943–54].) Ironically, O'Rahilly[4] had been Windle's protégé, and his role in the subsequent events must have filled the UCC president with a profound sense of disappointment, if not betrayal. But protégés in academic life have a history of turning on their patrons.

In the spring of 1918, the threat from Sinn Féin – while growing in the country – did not pose a fundamental obstacle to the plan to embark on a campaign for autonomy. At a meeting on 8 February, the UCC governing body set up a committee to draw up a report on the establishment of a University of Munster. The first meeting was held on 22 February and those present were the president, the registrar, P.J. Merriman, Downey and Sir Stanley Harrington. Both Catholic and Church of Ireland bishops sent their apologies. It was decided to petition for a charter 'but to recommend to the Governing Body to pass a Resolution pointing out the desirability and necessity for a separate university for Munster'. That was to be passed on to the prime minister, the chief secretary and the members of parliament for Munster. The governing body were to be recommended to adopt a statement prepared by the president and approved by the university committee. The resolution was also to be sent to the following to secure their support for the initiative: lords lieutenant and vice lieutenants of the counties, bishops of Cork and heads of religious bodies in Munster, MPs for Munster, the lord mayor and mayors of Munster, chairmen and vice chairmen of the county councils of Munster, chairmen of harbour boards, chairmen of chambers of commerce, chairmen of trade and labour associations, head masters and mistresses of the schools of Munster and the members of the former Cork Higher Education Committee. The committee also agreed that a petition in support of a governing body resolution should be signed by the above and forwarded to the prime minister, the chief secretary and MPs for Munster. Windle reported that he had received £61-12-1 from the Cork Higher Education Committee to be used to help fund the campaign.[5]

Conscious of the relevance of his Birmingham experience, he wrote to George H. Morley on 11 February explaining his plans. It was 'a job which I do not relish but which recalls many pleasant days which you and I spent together over a similar task'. He explained that he had most of the papers connected with the Birmingham campaign for autonomy 'but

I seem to have mislaid my copy of the Petition by the Council of Mason University College for a Charter'.[6] On 18 April, Windle thanked Morley for sending on the papers which he had requested: 'At the present moment everything in this country is thrown into confusion by the extraordinary procedure of the Government, the most stupid that I can remember in 60 years experience of English rule in Ireland. [*sic*] There may be some method in Lloyd George's madness, but if there is, I am unable to discover it.'[7]

Windle, seeking to keep the press on his side and to pre-empt any leaks of his plans, wrote on 13 February to the owner of the *Cork Examiner*, George Crosbie: 'I wanted to tell you in confidence that the Governing Body has decided to inaugurate a serious and active campaign for the obtaining of a separate University for Cork. I do not want anything to appear about this in the papers until everything is quite ready, but I can promise you that you will have the earliest and fullest information when the time arrives.'[8]

On 9 March, a special meeting of the governing body was held. Apologies were received from the Lord Mayor of Cork, T.C. Butterfield, and the Archbishop of Cashel, J.M. Harty. The former sought to be excused on the grounds that he wished to attend the funeral of John Redmond. Both expressed support for the motion in favour of a University of Munster. Bishop Cohalan, proposing the motion, told the meeting that UCC was seriously hampered by its position as a member of a Dublin-based federal university. Those disadvantages were outlined as being time and money lost in travel to attend numerous meetings and the dissimilarity in the local conditions, thus hampering UCC from being able to respond to the specific needs of the region. Cohalan proposed a motion, seconded by A.F. Sharman-Crawford, reading:[9] 'The Governing Body of University College, Cork, many of the Members of which have been associated with it since the Irish Universities Act of 1908 came into operation, desires to state that in its opinion the success of the College as an institution of Higher Education is seriously hampered by its position as a member of a Federal University. This entails not only great inconvenience owing to the distance between Cork and Dublin, the journeys for the same; but also owing to the dissimilarity of local conditions, limits the development of the College in directions which the Governing Body believe would be to the advantage and prosperity of Munster. [It emphasised] the great industrial developments which are now taking place in Cork; the further expansion which may be hoped for after the War; and the urgent necessity which exists that the College should be in a position to take the fullest advantage of these developments, and to give them the maximum assistance'.[10] Sir Stanley Harrington then proposed, seconded by Professor P.T. O'Sullivan, that the governing body support the Windle statement and circulate it to all the individuals and bodies outlined in the report of the university committee. A further resolution, proposed by the recorder of Cork and seconded by Br. E.J. Connolly, proposed that a delegation be sent to the chief secretary. A committee to draft a charter and statutes was also set up.[11] The first resolution, quoted above, was sent to hundreds of likely supporters of the University of Munster idea. A perforated form was added at the end of the page, stating: 'You may add my name to the petition which the Governing Body is promoting for the creation of a University in Cork for Munster.' Windle also circulated his pamphlet – under the name of the governing body – restating the argument for the establishment of an autonomous Munster university.[12]

A meeting of an executive committee established to deal with the University of Munster question was held in Windle's office on 16 March. Those present were Sir Stanley Harrington, Merriman, Sharman-Crawford and Downey. The president told them that he did not think it advisable to seek a meeting with the chief secretary immediately; they should wait for the opportune moment. On 26 March, the elderly and infirm Chancellor of the NUI, Archbishop William Walsh, wrote in a shakey hand: 'I have read the Pamphlet with interest. As you know, I have always advocated the Cork University idea in the most public way. I shall be delighted to sign the petition except that the grant of its prayer would place the Dublin University College in a horrible position of inferiority, – still hampered by all the admitted drawbacks of the federal system, whilst a set of new Charters would be issued on the ground that Cork should be set free from those drawbacks. It should have been easy to frame the proposal so as not to leave it open to this manifest objection.' Downey wrote to Windle on 29 March: 'It is certainly annoying about the archbishop's letter. I thought he only got your statement with "compliments" – at least that is what I understood.' Tongue-in-cheek, Downey added: '. . . why not suggest to the archbishop to join the University of Dublin with Trinity and his own as the two Colleges! Maynooth could complete the Trinity and after some time your friend Dr Mahaffy could retire.'[13]

In a letter from St Patrick's Training College, Dublin, a man named Byrne wrote on 30 March: 'The answer is that what is good enough for Belfast and Scotland and the North of England ought to be good enough for us . . . To be candid, I must say I should not be satisfied with Liverpool or Sheffield or even Manchester as a mark [?] for Cork. Excuse my candour.'[14] Even with vigorous support of that kind – together with a comprehensive campaign in Munster – Windle had little confidence in the will of the British government to deliver the necessary legislation. Nevertheless, he was determined and provided proof of the advanced state of the campaign in a letter on 10 June to Walter Long at the Colonial Office. He sent a copy of the *University College Cork Official Gazette*, July 1918,[15] and a copy of the final list of subscribers to the petition: 'It is of real importance to the South of Ireland,' Windle wrote, 'and its settlement would give great satisfaction to a large number of people.'[16] The list of signatories broke down as follows: peers and other titled persons (14), Catholic clergy (130), clergymen of other denominations (51), head masters and head mistresses of schools (48), medical men (166), lawyers (113) and engineers (25). Among those who had signed were the earls of Bandon, Kenmare and Dunraven, seventeen MPs, the Archbishop of Cashel, Catholic and Church of Ireland bishops of the region, the Lord Mayor of Cork, the mayors of Waterford, Limerick and Clonmel and the chairmen of the county councils for Cork Tipperary North and South, and Waterford. The following public bodies had passed resolutions: Cork County Council, Cork City Council, Cork Harbour Board, Cork Incorporated Chamber of Commerce and Shipping, Kerry County Council, Limerick County Council, Waterford City Council, Waterford County Council, Cork branch of the Irish National Teachers' Association and the Munster Provincial Council of the Association of Secondary Teachers.[17]

Windle sent a similar set of documents to the lord lieutenant. Receipt was acknowledged on 14 June 1918. In autumn 1918, he pressed for a meeting with Lord French to discuss the University of Munster. On 30 October, Bishop Cohalan, seconded by the lord mayor, proposed 'That the Governing Body desire once again with great respect to urge upon His Excellency, the Lord Lieutenant, the great importance to their College and to the South of Ireland of the establishment of an independent University for the Province as indicated on their previous communications and further venture again to express the hope that His Excellency will do them the honour of receiving a Deputation in connection with this matter.'[18] Slow progress was made. But in late December, Windle was invited to Dublin Castle. On 1 January 1919, he stayed at the Shelbourne where he had dinner with Sir T. Esmonde who he found 'more than pessimistic' about the future of the country. The following day, he went to UCD and met President Coffey, spending two hours with him. He went to the 'Castle' to meet with Shortt and the attorney general, A.W. Samuels. With the country in a state of incipient revolution, Windle found it hard to concentrate on his campaign. On 7 January, he referred to receiving a letter from Gasquet saying 'bishops have let loose the whirlwind and can't control it. Devil mend the beasts; they deserve anything they can get.'[19] On 8 January 1919, he again recorded: 'Sinn Féiners held their assembly;

make a protest; decide to convene assembly inviting other MPs who of course will not attend.' On 9 January, he wrote: 'Office and much work on scheme for development of university for Shortt who now made Home Secretary! Just after mastering Irish job. What is to be done under this crisis?' The following day, he noted that F.E. Smith had been made lord chancellor. His comment: 'I think that the brothel-bully is on a higher rung of the ladder than the politician.' On 13 January, James Ian Macpherson was appointed chief secretary. Windle had no objection to him *per se*; but, yet again, he had, at a critical juncture in their campaign, to build a relationship with a new man and his new team. Sir John O'Connell wrote to Windle on 11 January to report on his meeting (the 10th) with Under-Secretary James MacMahon:[20] 'I think McMahon is favourable, though perhaps not very much interested not being an educationalist or a Munster man, but I know him well and he assured me he would do everything he could to help and so far as he was concerned he was not in any way antagonistic.' O'Connell relayed that MacMahon saw two difficulties in the way, the opposition of the Treasury to giving any money and the fact that the government would not take up any bill likely to be opposed. O'Connell also reported:

> As regards the first difficulty he said he understood that the creation of a Munster University would involve your asking the Treasury for further financial assistance, and he thinks that they will not be willing to give any financial aid. As regards the second, McMahon said that the measure will certainly be opposed by any influence in Parliament which the Dublin College can command, it will also be opposed by the Representatives of Trinity college because they will naturally feel that if there was a Munster University it might conceivably detach some of the Protestant students, who would otherwise go to Trinity. That Devlin and Captain Redmond would probably be persuaded by the Nationalists to oppose the Bill and that as all the MPs of Cork City and county are Sinn Féiners pledged to abstain from going to Parliament, there will be no person to advocate the measure on behalf of Munster.

O'Connell did not think that Windle ought to be discouraged, concluding: 'I think the key to the situation of the moment is that French is the dominant factor in Ireland, that Shortt who was at cross purposes with him has gone and that the new Chief Secretary will work more in harmony with French, so that if you get French keen on a Munster University, he will carry the Chief Secretary with him.' Finally, MacMahon told O'Connell that another ground of opposition would be that there were already too many universities and that there was a feeling that there should only have been the one 'Trinity College' and 'that the Government may look unfavourably on the multiplication of Universities as tending to increase the local differences and set up, instead of breaking down, barriers between the different parts of the Country'. O'Connell offered to meet the delegation in advance of their meeting.[21]

Windle secured an appointment for a 'Munster university' delegation with Lord French on 16 January at 12 o'clock in the Privy Council Chamber, Dublin Castle. He was invited to send on his proposal by return of post, which he did. However, Dublin Castle was on a state of high alert and a University of Munster was not one of its immediate priorities. Windle was informed by 'B' on 12 January that the Irish War Council 'have a perfect scheme in case of rebellion even down to position of [machine guns] at [?] Won't last more than 3 days and would mean dreadful slaughter. Let us hope these poor deluded fools will not be led into it.' Anything was likely to happen.[22] He had a long talk on the 14th with Harrington and Sharman-Crawford: 'The latter says even [Arthur] Griffith would accept Federation within the Empire. Damn his impudence.'

Preparing for the meeting with French, he completed the requested documentation for the chief secretary and his speech for the lord lieutenant. He circulated the documents to the members of the deputation. Windle and Harrington stayed at the Vice Regal Lodge the night before their appointment: 'Lord Haldane there. Lord Lieutenant called me to him after dinner and we had half an hour talk. Said Shortt impossible. Did things without consulting him ... Macpherson excellent. Very anxious as to whether prisoners should be released. Shortt let out Plunkett without consulting him – also a bad thing.' French then told Windle regarding the university proposal: 'Not to think he was cold-watering our scheme if his official reply was not too encouraging.'

The following morning, 16 January, Windle went to the Privy Council Chamber where the delegation had assembled. It was made up of the Lord Mayor of Cork, Professors Hartog, Merriman, Pearson, Sir John O'Connell and the recorder. Neither of the two bishops of Cork was able to attend. Sharman-Crawford pulled out at the last minute. Harrington introduced each member to the lord lieutenant. Windle outlined the case for an autonomous university, speaking, according to himself, 'well I thought' for half an hour 'and others said'. The lord lieutenant stated that the arguments in favour of the proposal were 'strong' but 'there were difficulties'. He then gave 'his personal view which [was] more favourable', according to Windle. Afterwards, he spoke to the under-secretary 'who said French quite firm and advised as to next steps'. Windle was asked to 'prepare a short Bill'. The following morning, Windle had 'much talk ... to Lord Haldane who thinks he knows everything but doesn't about Ireland – a pompous thing who looks like a butler'.

Upon his return to Cork, Windle instructed the UCC legal adviser, Michael Murphy (41 South Mall) to work on a draft bill, replying on 18 January that he did not 'think it would be very difficult making the draft quite short as the method adopted in the Act of 1908 forms an excellent precedent'.[23] Leaving matters in Murphy's hands, Windle went to England. On 20 January 1919, he wrote: 'Humphreys came over – long talk. Very full of idea I should be Provost of Birmingham University. Said I would if offered but *most* unlikely.' On 21 January – the day of the first meeting of Dáil Éireann – Murphy reported that he had a text roughly worked out 'and I find that by incorporating the applicable provisions of the Act of 1908 I can keep it within small compass'. Assuming that Windle did not wish to 'antagonize the National University more than is inevitable', he was leaving the £20,000 which had been divided by the 1908 act between Dublin and Belfast out of the bill 'as an attempt to make thirds of it, or to get any share would bring both in against us'. Murphy said that he was 'quite at a loss to know what to do about the transfer of existing graduates to our new University. I do not suppose very many would elect in favour of a change, and if that be so it might avert opposition if no provision at all were put in.'[24]

Windle, still in England when Murphy sent the above letter, had been quite wrong to assume that Sinn Féin deputies to Dáil Éireann would take their seats in Westminster for the £400. In Oxford on 22 January, he met a number of academics, one of whom had never been to Ireland but was a 'bigoted ass'. Returning to Cork on 25 January, he continued to misread very badly the direction of Irish politics. He wrote on 28 January: 'general opinion that Sinn Féin is on the wane – stopping hunting is a nail in their coffin. Yet I wonder.'

Windle knew that the key to getting a bill safely through parliament depended upon securing maximum support from nationalist politicians. But all the Sinn Féin deputies were opposed. Dublin Castle was nervous, given the rise of Sinn Féin, and the political will was not there to steer legislation through the House of Commons. The attorney general, A.W. Samuels, told Windle in a letter on 3 February that he had been staying at the home in Cambridge of William Ridgeway who had been Professor of Greek at Cork from 1883 to 1894. Samuels wrote that 'it would be of great importance' if the Munster university idea had the support of the northern MP, Joe Devlin. Samuels asked Windle to get Devlin to speak to him 'if you are sure he would help', adding: 'Time is of great importance as we have a great amount of work [to do].' He said he would speak to the chief secretary the following day provided he was back at work. But the chief secretary was in bed and their draftsman, who was out with influenza, would not be back to work for at least a month. 'So you can imagine my pressure,' he wrote.[25]

Given what Samuels had said, it was all the more important to produce the text of the draft bill as swiftly as possible. Murphy told Windle on 4 February that he had a draft, adding: 'I have some misgiving as to the extreme brevity of the bill but I see the force of your desire to make it as simple as possible and if the government are willing to help there will be no difficulty in adding matters that might well be in it.' Windle, once he had received the draft, made some preliminary notes for a draft charter, envisaging a visitor, a chancellor, a vice-chancellor and a Senate to replace the existing governing body, an academic council, faculties, convocation, students' representative council, etc.

Windle reported to the governing body on 6 February. He had worked hard to get a full attendance, writing on 31 January to Bishop Browne of Cloyne stating that he was seeking a meeting of the governing body to prepare a draft charter for the proposed Cork university: 'The time is now approaching when we shall be asked to declare our hand. I am exceedingly anxious that you should be present at this meeting.' He did not make the meeting but Bishop Cohalan was present. On 6 February Windle reported that 'The Deputation was most favourably received by His Excellency and the President was subsequently asked to prepare a brief draft Bill for the consideration of the Irish Government.' That work, he said, was in train under his direction working with the solicitor to the college. The draft contained no details 'but was a small permissive Bill to enable the king, if so pleased, to constitute by Charter a University for Munster in Cork. All the details would be contained in the Charter which would be necessary to consider at an early date.' Windle, having outlined financial matters, requested that members of the governing body 'regard this report as absolutely private and confidential'.[26] The governors endorsed the report.

Meanwhile, Gasquet, at the Holy See, was kept informed by Windle of the most recent university and national political developments. From Rome, he observed the deteriorating situation in Ireland with apprehension, reading a recent letter from Windle with 'painful interest', and wrote on 9 February: 'Where are we all going. The whole world at present seems "topsy turvy" and the spirit of revolt is found everywhere – even in the Church.' He added: 'It is an epidemic and very catching and I fear we are going to have trouble in all countries in one form or other. I have followed the events in Ireland as far as the papers reveal them and I confess that I cannot see *what* the people want. For it would seem that it would be impossible for Ireland to exist by itself. I have always thought that the only remedy for the actual state of things was the most generous Home

Rule, within the Empire. I think that this is just and possible, but the present proposals go beyond this and people must know that they are asking for the impossible. What you say about the rising anticlerical feeling makes the idea very dangerous to religion.' Gasquet quite understood 'how painful' Windle must have found 'the present chaos and particularly the attitude of the clergy – especially that of the younger clergy'. The cardinal felt that it was a

> very serious state of things but it is almost impossible for the authorities to act, except as taking part in politics of some kind. The Pope's position is very difficult. When it suits people they say 'they object to Rome having any part in the politics of a country'– When *they* are touched they say 'Why doesn't Rome come down on the people and especially the priests, who are engaged in upsetting my applecart.' I know that the affairs of the 'most distressful country' are giving grave [?] causes of anxiety to the authorities, but what should be done it is difficult to say . . . It is easy to say 'have patience', but not so easy to have it and I am sure at least of this, that by sticking to your post, you will have a reward, as in doing this you are keeping things together at least in [your] sphere. If you were to give up the chaos would enter into the precincts of university college.[27]

On 6 February, Windle had written to the under-secretary, MacMahon, seeking some feedback on the draft bill and wondered whether it should be sent directly to the chief secretary or to the lord lieutenant.[28] By 10 February, he was in a position to send a copy of the draft bill to the chief secretary: 'You will understand that this was in no sense done with the idea of dictating the form which Government action should take, but solely to show that it was possible to produce such a Bill with practically no contentious matter contained in it. Once the principle of founding such a University is conceded, that is to say the first clause carried, the rest of the Bill is quite uncontentious and is mostly taken, as you will see, from the Irish Universities Act.'[29] Windle also said that he had a committee to draw up a charter but 'again a model exists in the shape of the Charter drawn up by the Queen's College, Belfast' when it was being given university status. Windle stressed that UCC was asking for additional funds for the University of Munster: 'We are, of course, applying to the Chancellor of the Exchequer for additional funds for this college – funds which are needed whether it is converted into a University or not.'[30]

On 15 February, Windle convened a meeting of a Charter Committee composed of Merriman, Bishop Cohalan, Bishop Dowse, Professor Pearson, Professor E.M. O'Sullivan and Downey. Windle argued that the general fabric of the proposed university would be similar to that of the National University and the college. The architecture of governance would remain much the same. However, a Senate would replace the governing body, made up in the first instance of the existing governing body. Windle gave further details of the composition of the new Senate. He suggested that there would be a chancellor, the first being named in the charter. He noted that the provost of Trinity College Dublin was appointed by the Crown while the vice-chancellor of Queen's was appointed by the Senate. When Windle came to discuss the appointment of professors, he said that they 'should be governed by all guarantees against political and religious preferences contained in the existing documents'. The 'final power of appointment must lie in the hands of the Senate' but he attached considerable importance to the role of the academic council in that regard. The report, as outlined above, was sent to the governing body which accepted it at a meeting on 15 February with some minor amendments.[31]

On 22 February, Attorney General Samuels sent a 'private and confidential' letter to Windle, relaying depressing news. He told him that 'the question of setting up an independent university in Cork has not come before me officially in any way'. He had not been 'brought in touch with the results of the deputation to His Excellency'. At a personal level, however, he was as supportive as ever: 'I may perhaps mention that I have been long of opinion that it would be of the greatest advantage that Cork should have an absolutely independent university and I am now more than ever convinced of it.' His attraction to the project was rooted in 'the distinctive artistic, literary and intellectual aptitudes of the Munster people and particularly of the people of Cork itself'. He was convinced that 'the sound development of Cork intellectualism and its educational progress will be seriously hampered unless the College is emancipated and left free to work out on its own responsibility a career of its own as a university'. He told Windle that he had discussed the matter with the Cambridge don, W. Ridgeway, who was 'intimately acquainted with the possibilities of Cork as a university centre, and who is of course a very distinguished expert on English Educational matters both in Ireland and England'.[32] Ridgeway had been Professor of Greek in Cork between 1883 and 1894. Samuels, while 'very strongly in favour of your having a separate university', pointed to a defect in the UCC documentation; there was no treatment of the financial aspects of the case and he advised Windle that he would have to make the financial case in the event of legislation coming forward. He promised Windle his 'heartiest support', and had already told Shortt that he was strongly in favour of a Munster university. He also promised that he would speak to the chief secretary, Ian Macpherson, 'at the first possible opportunity'.[33] Windle drafted a memorandum – dated 26 February – on the financial question, making the strongest possible argument in favour of independence. He listed all the savings the establishment of the Munster university proposal would provide to the NUI. It was a detailed and – Windle hoped – a persuasive document.[34]

While Windle anticipated obstacles at the government level, he was alarmed at the growth in organised opposition to his proposal within the NUI. In order to counteract the influence of Coffey of UCD, he wrote to Laurence Waldron on 22 February: 'I take it for granted that you never read the Agenda of the Senate, but if you have not already thrown it into the waste paper basket please turn to that abominable document and observe Item No. 5, in which Coffey proposes to raise the question of the Independent Cork University. I assume that he means to move a resolution against it and think that he might have stated that in his Notice of Motion.' Windle appealed to Waldron to attend and support the Cork scheme: 'I know how you hate going to the meetings of that body; so do I. But on this occasion I do earnestly press you to attend . . . I am of course taking it for granted that you are still alive: for all I know you may be lucky enough to be on the other side of the Styx.' Waldron must have been still in the land of the living as Windle invited him to dinner on the 26th.

Windle had also written to Fr William Delany SJ requesting that he attend the meeting of the Senate. The elderly Jesuit wrote on 24 February, sending his pledge of support: 'I am and *have been for many years clearly convinced* that Cork should have a University of its own. I fear that on account of my somewhat shaky health I may not be able to be present at the meeting of Senate. But I cordially hope that the senate may approve of it.' Windle wrote on the 26th urging him, were he not in a position to attend, to send a letter of support to the registrar which could be read out at the meeting. He thought that the Cork proposal would meet with 'selfish opposition' from representatives of other colleges. On 10 April, Delany confirmed to Windle that he could not attend the Senate. He mentioned that the very 'thorny subject I had to deal with 34 years ago in St Stephen's Green was the question of *centralisation* or independence'.[35]

The NUI Senate met on 28 February. It was noted that a letter had been received from Windle, dated the 27th. A letter was also received from the under-secretary, Dublin Castle, enclosing a copy of a draft bill to give effect to the proposal recently laid before the Irish government for establishing a University of Munster. The University of Munster appeared under item 6 on the agenda with the rider: 'Such a change would, of course, completely alter the present organisation of the National University.' On the motion of the Professor of Experimental Physics at UCD, John Alexander McClelland, the Senate decided that the matter should be referred to a committee consisting of the standing committee, with Professors McClelland, Mary T. Hayden and Sir Plunket Barton.[36]

They were empowered to get the opinions of convocation and of the colleges. If necessary, a special meeting of the Senate would be held to discuss the outcome of convocation. The registrar was instructed to write to the government 'expressing the hope that nothing further would be done until the senate had time to consider the matter'.[37] That evening, Windle wrote: 'Meeting Senate (1) Government had sent draft Bill for consideration! Looks like going on. Very pleased. But senate hummed like hive of bees and a lot of work. Finally to go to Special Convocation with others added, and to Senate before end of April. Doesn't of course matter much.' Windle appeared to be very pleased with the outcome. His entry also referred to Trinity and that Mahaffy would 'do his best to get a permissible resolution of his Board. Saw D.F. Dixon and E. Gwynn on same and got warm promises of support from them. 3.50 train . . . home. 10.45 – train 20 minutes late.'

Windle was very single-minded. He worked tirelessly on winning support for his proposal. While the Munster Sinn Féin MPs were opposed, he singled out others who might be helpful. Having written to T.P. O'Connor on 27 February, he received the following encouraging reply: 'Of course I will do everything I can to help the University to become independent, but I do not think I can do very much at the moment. My communications with Ian Macpherson must be very careful and infrequent, as he has no policy for Ireland I am sure, but that of his chief, who will not touch Ireland until he is forced to do so and until he thinks he can do it with full safety to his own continuance as Prime Minister.'[38] Windle replied on 1 March: 'Of course I am aware that you cannot do much, if anything at present, but I may tell you confidentially that I have very good reason to hope that the scheme may be brought before the House at perhaps no distant date, in which case your acquiescence and support would be of great importance, and I shall look to you at that time for the assistance which you so kindly promise.'[39]

Windle wrote to Samuels at the end of February 1919, explaining that a bill had been prepared at the suggestion of Dublin Castle: 'It was of course in no way intended to dictate to the Government how they should proceed, though the suggestion for the preparation of the draft came from the Castle. It was merely to show that the legislation was of the simplest and most non-contentious character, once the establishment of a University was conceded.'[40] He also enclosed other material, including the completed petition. He wanted his advice on a point which was of 'great *personal* interest' to him: 'If there is a chance of a University being set up here I would be prepared to remain, if I were alive and if my health permitted, for some years in order to get it well rooted in the ground. If there is no chance of a University being set up the probability is that I shall retire and take the modest pension which I can now claim. You will understand that I am well aware that my going or staying is a matter of absolute indifference to the Government which will not have to fill up my position. It is, however, as you will readily understand a matter of considerable importance to me, and one about which I want to make preparations in advance.'[41]

Besides the strain of having to run the campaign for a University of Munster, Windle's detestation of what was happening in Ireland was being recorded almost daily in his diary. On 3 March, he wrote: 'I do not think words can describe the asininities of the Shinners. They make one ashamed of being an Irishman for they have made my country ridiculous.' Two days later, he noted: 'Lord Mayor of Dublin appears on platform with one of the escaped from Lincoln in I.R.A uniform. How can such things be allowed.' On 7 March, he wrote: 'Gaol-birds to be let out.'

Meanwhile, the Professor of Anatomy at Trinity, Andrew Francis Dixon, wrote in confidence to Windle on 5 March saying that the registrar had written or was to write, saying that the board had passed a resolution 'that while the Board of Trinity does not desire to interfere with the internal affairs of other universities, it recognises that . . . Federal universities can only be regarded as temporary expedient and in so far as the Board is in favour of a University for Munster. I am not sure of the exact words but this is certainly the sense of the resolution. This [is] merely for your private ears.'[42] In fact, the provost of Trinity, Rev. Sir J.P. Mahaffy, had written to Windle on 4 March saying that he had 'with some difficulty' got a resolution passed in favour of a university of the south. On 5 March, Windle replied: 'I heard yesterday from Samuels who has been staying with Ridgeway, who is an old professor of this place and is quite aware of the conditions and as much in favour of an independent University as you are yourself.' He added: 'It is impossible for me to say how grateful I am to you for what you have done for us. Without your aid we never could have obtained this resolution from the Board, and I am sure that it will be of the greatest possible service to us. Coupled with the letter which you were good enough to promise to send to Mr Macpherson I am sure that it ought to practically settle the matter.'[43]

Buoyed by that news, Windle wrote to Samuels on 5 March, sending on the draft charter: 'This is the sixth Charter in the construction of which I have had a large share so I think I may claim to have some knowledge of such documents, and as the verbiage of this is almost entirely taken from the Belfast Charter (which is a very good one) I do not think that your draftsmen will find it necessary to make many alterations.'[44] He made reference to Professor Ridgeway, who he remembered very well from their days at Trinity, 'though he was senior to me'. He had often met him since, 'the last time being at the excavations at Avebury'. Windle was saddened by the news that he was 'becoming so blind, but he thoroughly knows this place as an old Professor, and I am sure that his opinion would have great weight with you'. He reassured the attorney general that Irish MPs would support a bill, mentioning Joe Devlin and T.P. O'Connor as having written to him recently pledging their support.[45] He was reassured that 'you will not get opposition from the Irish Members if you introduce such a Bill'. Windle also mentioned the Trinity resolution: 'This ought to be a great assistance to us, as many people thought that Trinity would take up a selfish attitude or opposition. I saw Mahaffy last week and he promised me that he would write himself to the Chief Secretary. He is very warmly interested in our movement.' Windle told Samuels that the same could not be said for the NUI Senate: 'We shall of course get an adverse vote from the Senate of the National University founded on purely selfish reasons. Convocation will I assume at least manage to raise a quorum (which it very seldom does) and pass an adverse resolution. Convocation however consists of a small number of Dublin graduates, for of course Cork graduates never bother to go near it. In fact I think very few of them are members. But I do not attach much importance to these things, nor I am sure do you.'[46]

Windle, seeking to avoid confrontation at the Senate, wrote to the registrar of the NUI, Joseph McGrath, on 5 March urging that negotiations should be conducted in a friendly way. But the tone of his letter was over-confident if not foolhardy:

> I want your wise opinion as to whether it would be or would not be better for Merriman and myself to attend. I feel that we are in a somewhat delicate position and I want to explain to you privately what it is. Let me begin by saying that unless something unexpected happens we are going to get that University and get it speedily. What the other Colleges really ought to do is to offer observations as to what they would like to occur in the event of our being separated from them. I do not know whether each of them wants to be set up as a separate University or whether they prefer to keep on as they are. In either case I regard your position as absolutely safe for in the second instance you would go on as you are, and in the first the worst that could happen would be that you would be retired on compulsory retirement terms which means, I believe, practically the whole income for life with nothing to do for it – the kind of position which all of us are looking for.

Windle found a parallel in the break-up of the Victoria University in England: 'This was occasioned by the determination of Liverpool (oddly enough the second largest of the three Colleges) to obtain a separate

University. At first there were symptoms that Manchester and Leeds would resist this project. Finally they agreed to seek the same thing for themselves. Then Sheffield intervened. This college had just been refused admission into the Victoria University. It was weak but it made a great plea to the Government and four Universities were created instead of one. Of course I have no idea whatever of what Dublin and Galway may think in this matter. If they are going to content themselves with an attitude of blank negation they are doing a foolish thing for themselves and I think little harm to us.'

Windle recommended that the best course for the NUI was the following: 'We regret the decision of one of the Colleges to endeavour to obtain University powers, and should the Government decide to accede to their request we venture to claim – and then go on to claim whatever they want. I am very anxious that this change should be made in a friendly way and not as the result of a struggle. There is so much educational lee-way to be made up that it would be a great pity that our time and the time of the two other colleges should be wasted in wrangling for what is a foregone conclusion. Further I would give any influence which I possess to any reasonable scheme proposed by the N.U.I., and I am sure that they could get it.' In addition, Windle wondered in his letter whether it would be best for him to go quietly to the committee and say what he had just said in a friendly manner.

Windle told McGrath that he could not gauge the intentions of the government but he did not think that they would not have committed themselves to asking for a draft bill 'and sending it to the two Universities without intending to go through with the matter'. He told the registrar: '[I] should not commit myself to anyone but you to the statement that I think our efforts will be successful.' Windle concluded: 'I think it quite certain that we shall get this University in time and more than probable that we may get it quite soon . . . What I want you to consider is whether in the interests of peace it would be better for Merriman and myself to go up and say something of this kind, quietly and in a friendly manner, to the committee. I think perhaps it would be well and well also for them to understand that whatever their action is we are going on with this movement until it is successful.' [47]

Windle, who had a good sense of the refinements of academic politics, must quickly have realised that his letter was bombastic and provocative. Despite having the support of Mahaffy and a draft bill, Windle had no grounds for arrogance or over-confidence. Within a day, he had sent a second letter to McGrath who replied on 7 March referring to the receipt of 'both your letters'. Referring to the TCD resolution, McGrath said it was 'a decided kick on for you!' He thought that it was very important for both

Merriman and Windle to attend the meeting of the special committee as their presence might prevent 'irresponsible and inflammable talk which can do nothing but harm'. He told Windle that he knew he could rely upon him always.[48]

Throughout March, Windle wrote a large number of letters seeking support from all sectors of society and across the political divide. On 18 March, he wrote in quiet confidence to Lord Midleton, a man he had admired and befriended during the Irish Convention: 'Confidentially I may tell you that it is quite probable that the matter may come before Parliament before very long. I have seen the Lord Lieutenant, the Chief Secretary and the Attorney General concerning it. The first and the last are warmly in favour of the project and the second gave me an exceedingly sympathetic hearing last week.' Windle hoped that if the bill were to come before parliament 'it will have the support of yourself and those with whom you are associated because I think that it really is an important piece of reconstruction'. He explained further: 'At the present time we are tied by two Colleges in the national University with which we have very little sympathy and are rather unfairly tarred more or less with the same brush. For my own part I do not think I can stand very much longer the connection with those places which I dislike exceedingly, and which allows us no freedom of action whatsoever.' Windle pointed out that Midleton would appreciate as a southerner 'the fact that it has been signed by all the Catholic and two out of the three Church of Ireland Bishops in Munster – which I consider very significant – and by not less than 51 non-Catholic clergymen. When I tell you that it was not sent to curates, either Catholic or Protestant, but only to Rectors, Parish Priests, and the like, this 51 must form a very large percentage of the whole number in Munster. This University has been clamoured for steadily for eighty years by the people of Cork and Munster generally; it could afford the greatest satisfaction to all sorts of people if it were granted; it is not a political question.'[49]

Midleton replied to Windle on 21 March that he felt on safe ground following any suggestion made by him on education 'but I confess the extraordinary course taken by the Catholic Bishops in the Convention seemed to me to indicate a desire on their part to crush all progress in Ireland and to indicate no desire to cooperate in any movement on undenominational lines. This, writing to you privately, has discouraged me in Irish matters more than anything else, and I have felt that the only possible hope for the Southern Provinces is that while we should proceed in a broad spirit of tolerance, Catholics of all descriptions should unite in making it clear that our co-operation would be welcomed in all movements. I gather that you hope that you have achieved something like this in regard to the University, and I will certainly talk to my Southern friends about it.'[50] Midleton wrote again to Windle on 26 March pledging his support for the project: 'Be sure, I will give the university scheme the best consideration I can, and help you if it is possible.'[51]

Bishop Cohalan had written encouragingly to Windle on 20 March that it was thanks to the president that the movement for an independent university of Cork was going so satisfactorily: 'I dare say the Senate of the National University will oppose. The representatives of U C Dublin should not oppose. There would not be much difficulty in solving the Dublin question if it stood alone. The Dublin College, with its fine staff, its big roll of students and its established character, could become a university, or it could be united with Trinity under the one University of Dublin.' The bishop felt that the trouble would be with Galway and Maynooth, or even with Galway alone. He thought that if Cork was successful, Maynooth could become a recognised college of a Dublin university. The National University could remain with Cork dropped out, and Dublin and Galway the constituent colleges, and Maynooth a recognised college. However, he sounded a note of warning: 'But with Cork out I am afraid that Dublin would not be content with a federal university in which it would be federated with Galway only. The Dublin men, I suppose, have no fault to find with the existing arrangements; Galway and Maynooth do not expect a better system; and hence I am afraid there is not much hope of their assistance in securing an independent university in Cork, which would imply throwing the whole National University question into the melting pot again.'[52]

Cohalan was correct to be concerned about developments within the NUI. On 21 March, McGrath set out the meeting schedule for the NUI Standing Committee and Senate. There was a proposal to meet on 20 May with the special committee on the University of Munster to meet prior to the full Senate meeting. In his sick-bed on 22 March, Windle wrote in his diary: 'I suspect Coffey to put Munster U. question on long finger.' Infuriated by what he saw as procrastination, he sought an explanation from McGrath in a letter that same day.

He also contacted his friend, Professor McClelland, pointing out by letter that the Senate originally was to have made a decision by the end of April: 'These dilatory tactics strike me as being of an underhand character and I am sure you are not privy to them. May I ask you to help me to have the very distinct pledge given at the last meeting of the Senate adhered to?' (McClelland had told Windle in a letter on 17 March that he had proposed the sub-committee 'but that does not mean that I am opposed'.) Waldron, mentioned earlier, went on 26 March to a meeting of the governing body of UCD, writing to Windle the following day: 'The question of the Munster University came up. The Cork University – Coffey said it was called in the title – I can see that he is bitterly – savagely – opposed to it and that his policy is procrastination . . . After much discussion – I was to some extent supported by McClelland – Coffey moved to refer the question to the general purposes [committee] of University College. He said power should be given to them to have full legal advice to the effect regarding the proposed severance . . . Now you know all I can tell you. It must be treated by you as strictly confidential, it would not be cricket for me to tell you what took place . . . The surpliced ruffian Corcoran S.J. told me he favoured the Cork proposal.'[53]

On 30 March, Windle wrote to McClelland that whatever happened in Dublin and whatever attitude the NUI might take up 'we shall continue to struggle for this measure until we have obtained it. I am convinced that we shall obtain it, and I think before very long. What I am seriously anxious about is that it should be obtained, if at all possible, peacefully, and not as the result of a struggle in which friction and unpleasantness are bound to occur. There is so much educational lee-way to be made up in this country that I personally should deeply regret having to deflect my attention from that to the struggle for a local University . . . As it is, a great deal of my time is and has been occupied over this matter . . . I am well aware that it is utterly useless to appeal to the persons of the mentality of [Joseph] Pye, but I had thought that it might be possible to carry with us the more sensible and sober-minded members of the Senate.'[54] Windle contrasted the workings of the NUI to the decision-making capability of a centralised Trinity College which got its opinion in within a week and 'the sprawling concern like ours'. He felt that the Trinity 'entirely favourable' decision, which had been sent within a week, revealed 'the difference between the workings of a real University and a sham' one.[55]

In frustration, Windle wrote to Samuels on 28 March that he had heard that UCD, 'which of course absolutely controls the University, is to procrastinate as far as possible'. As UCD had no valid reply to the UCC statement, according to Windle, they fell back on the selfish argument that 'they prefer things as they are'. 'I think you will agree with me,' he wrote, 'that this is hardly playing the game, but this is the kind of thing that I have had to put up with for ten years and of which, as you will readily understand, I am heartily sick. A number of the Senate do not seem to be capable of understanding how negotiations are customarily carried on by gentlemen.'[56] Windle wanted Samuels' advice on courses of action open to him: 'Would it be better for me to go on pressing for a meeting? e.g. I can write a formal protest to the Chancellor, which I have not done, or I can threaten publication of the correspondence. Neither of these things, and especially the latter, appears to me to be very desirable, and what I want to know is whether it would better suit your book to let things slide and for you to be in a position to say: "We asked for observations, but we waited, say, two months. We received none and under the circumstances do not feel disposed to wait any longer."'[57] Having done everything he could to get a meeting called, the only further step he could take was to approach the chancellor on the matter and make 'to him a respectful but strong protest'.[58] Samuels responded on 1 April saying that he would have a word about the matter with the chief secretary who was expected 'over here tomorrow . . . I had a conversation with Devlin and also with Whitla, Q.U.B., who are quite agreeable.'[59]

Although he did not know it, Windle was facing a humiliating defeat. His confidence in Dublin Castle was sorely misplaced. His diary entries show that he was also unplugged from the realities of Irish politics. On 24 March, he wrote: 'Lord Mayor of Dublin proposes to meet President (!) de Valera at the gates of the city and conduct him to the Mansion House to deliver a message to Ireland! My God what a country!' On 27 March, he wrote: 'Shinners and impudent de Valera carrying on like asses.' On 31 March, he noted: 'A policeman shot in Western Road and an R.M. in Westport. What this country is coming to under the British rule and the coward Bishops God only knows.' No matter how withering his analysis of the overall performance of the British government and its capacity to function, paradoxically Windle had a misplaced faith in the capacity of Dublin Castle to deliver a University of Munster.

While Windle was organising his campaign to win parliamentary support for the scheme, opposition was beginning to manifest itself within UCC. The president was attacked in the March edition of the student magazine, *An Mac Léighinn/The Student*, which argued that UCC should no longer be considered a place for 'shoneens and drunkards, swanks and idlers . . . We are on the high road towards a wee Irish speaking Republic in University College Cork. The Professors had better look up or we shall soon not understand lectures delivered in a foreign tongue.' Windle was attacked for being a member of the Irish Convention. Stockley and O'Rahilly were praised for their Sinn Féin sentiments.[60] The April issue used even more intemperate language, referring to the president 'and the four other degenerates who run and ruin our university'.[61] Michael Murphy, the college lawyer, advised that, although the president had been libelled, 'I implore you as a friend to take no notice of this thing.'[62]

On 4 April, Windle wrote: 'Letter from McM[ahon] saying Irish Government are seeking a reply from N.U.I. before May. Letter from Rahilly expressing regret at scurrilous article in 'Student' on me – It appears they described me and others as 'degenerates!' Mr Murphy advises doing nothing – I quite agree.' There was a meeting of the Students' Representative Council and the University Graduates' Sinn Féin Club. On 15 April, O'Rahilly, who attended, wrote anonymously in *The New Ireland* that the governing body had no authority to recommend the establishment of an autonomous university. He said that a 'handful of intriguers' were trying to turn UCC into a 'crown university'. The same day, Windle wrote about a Senate meeting: 'Coffey acid – McGrath as usual facing both ways. Pye more inane than usual! [John A.] McClelland – swollen as wheat also as usual. [Rev. John A.] McCaffrey [president of Maynooth] and [Sir Plunket] Barton never opened their lips. Inches dilatory – nothing really to say. Bitter and vicious hatred of us obvious.'

Windle returned from Dublin and was in UCC on the 17th. He noted the following day: 'very disconcerting news as to Student Representative Council passing resolution against university.' He believed that to be 'Sinn Féin work', and added: 'With this on one side and the idiocy of [the Professor of Botany, H. Ashley] Cummins and [the Professor of Engineering, Connell W. O'D] Alexander on the other how is anything to succeed. Very upset and feeling very much played out by overwork and worry.'

As the Irish Universities Bill was to be sent to the NUI Senate on 20 April, Windle received a letter from the Professor of Physiology, David T. Barry, commenting on the agenda: 'About No. 11 on the Senate Agenda, there is an aroma of Coffey about it; it seems to me preposterous. I shall certainly oppose it.' On 19 April 1919, the *Southern Star* published a resolution, signed by all the Sinn Féin TDs of Munster, including Michael Collins, Liam de Róiste, Terence MacSwiney and Austin Stack, protesting against the 'hasty and secret attempt to secure an Act of the Westminster Parliament in order to empower the English Crown to erect a University in Cork'. The signatories were of the opinion that 'these secret steps are in no sense authorised by our constituencies' and demanded its deferral until 'the paramount national issue now before the country is settled'.

The sister of Terence MacSwiney, Mary, the honorary secretary of the Graduates' Sinn Féin Club, wrote to the secretary of UCC on 22 April. She enclosed a statement from her own organisation, which she said was also supported by the Students' Representative Council: 'No decision can be reached without impartial investigation and full opportunity for free discussion, especially by those educational associations and public bodies which are directly concerned.'[63] The statement considered it 'most inopportune for effecting such an upheaval'. It argued that the governing body, having deferred its re-election until January 1920, was not in any sense representative of the people of Munster and had no mandate to carry such a project into effect: 'Moreover, it is simply ridiculous to assert that the people of Munster, who, with overwhelming unanimity, have repudiated representation in the English Parliament, have authorised any individual or individuals to petition on their behalf at Dublin Castle and Westminster for a University Act and Charter.'[64] The statement, calling on all public bodies to join in passing a protest, was read at a meeting of the governing body on 24 April along with a letter and resolution from the Sinn Féin TD, Liam de Róiste.[65] The motion desired to enter 'an emphatic protest against the hasty and secret attempt to secure an Act of the Westminster parliament in order to empower the English Crown to erect a University in Cork, for whose efficient administration in the national and educational interests of Ireland the people of Munster have no guarantee. We are of opinion that these secret steps are in no sense authorised by our constituencies, and that any movement to erect an independent university in Munster should be deferred until the paramount national issue now before the Country is settled, and until the public bodies of Munster can adequately safeguard the people's interests in such an educational scheme.'[66] The Gaelic League also opposed the bill.

Windle, by way of response to the above motions, argued that the governing body resolution, circulated to all public representatives and public bodies, be sent out as a rejoinder. Proposed by Bishop Cohalan, and seconded by Harrington, the motion was carried and acted upon.[67] However, the governing body statement simply provoked another round of protests. The University Graduates Sinn Féin Club, Cork, and the Students' Representative Council issued a reply to the governing body's statement which appeared in the press on 21 April: 'If the Bill is passed, Viscount French will be perfectly free to set up any kind of university he pleases; he can increase the number of Crown nominees and curtail the elected representatives. Dublin Castle can set up a second Trinity College in Cork.'[68] On 26 April, Windle responded in the privacy of his diary: 'a characteristic Rahilly – calling himself S.F. Graduates Club . . . Decided to take no notice of it.' Liam de Róiste replied on 2 May rejecting the initiative on the grounds that there was no guarantee that the national and educational interests of the people would be safeguarded: 'All those things are the secret of some small coterie, which is not representative of the people, nor responsible to the people in any way.' Much more formidable opposition, in the form of a long letter from Professor Eoin MacNeill, appeared on 3 May in the *Irish Independent*. He said that the UCC governing body statement 'hardly exceeds in candour a Phoenix Park affidavit'. He questioned whether the petition, signed nearly twelve months before, accurately reflected the current position of the signatories. He contrasted the openness of the process surrounding the drafting of the 1908 act and the secrecy cloaking the new bill. MacNeill argued that it handed a 'blank cheque' to Macpherson. Where there would be no great harm in putting a new university bill on the statute books, together with home rule, MacNeill said the new charter as drafted should be sent to the British Museum. It would require national and democratic authority to establish a new University of Munster, he said. The people of Munster and the rest of Ireland, he added, would 'not be convinced by the statement that they have read that any reputable body of Irishmen has assigned absolute power in a matter of Irish university education to a British Ministry which is acting as the present Ministry is acting in Ireland and holding us up to their own people and to the world as a nation of miscreants and assassins.'[69] In Sinn Féin and nationalist circles, MacNeill's arguments carried weight. The provost of Trinity College, Mahaffy, who was 'a curious man of great prowess and much wit' according to Windle, died on 2 May and in his passing an ally had been lost in the fight for a University of Munster.

Although Windle had his critics among the professorial body at UCC, he was not without significant support. The Professor of Archaeology, Rev. Patrick Power, wrote on 29 April to Windle to express his opposition to the scurrilous attacks to which the president had been subjected in the previous weeks: 'For several reasons, and on various grounds, I feel much pained at, and not a little ashamed of, the recent public correspondence etc in opposition to the proposed University Bill. The spirit manifest – whatever its origin – is deplorable, and the opposition – such as it is – seems to me ill-reasoning, ill-mannered, unjust and foolish. You are free to make any, and whatever, use you think well of this paragraph.' On 3 May, Windle thanked him very much for the latter part of his letter: 'Vulgar abuse and ignorant criticism in the long run defeat themselves, and I am inclined to think that these persons are really doing our cause a great service. Still it is disappointing to think that some members of the staff should lend themselves to such things, but I suppose one cannot expect among so many that all would be honourable, well-balanced, and polite. None the less, I am very grateful to you for what you have been kind enough to say.'

Such had been the furore in UCC over the criticism of Windle, the May edition of *An Mac Léighinn/The Student* carried an apology to the president: 'We keenly regret the tone of one short article in our last issue. It was written by a youthful contributor in an excess of indignation, and unfortunately, owing to inability to secure proofs, it appeared as it was written. We therefore tend to Sir Bertram Windle an apology for any unpleasant and unnecessary personalities which appeared in our last issue.' Professor Stockley published his own three-line admonition: ' I beg to be allowed to recall Goethe's words, that if one makes oneself *grob* [German for coarse/uncouth] in a controversy, one proves nothing about the adversary; one only proves oneself a *grob*.'[70] A final reaction, from A.J.R. [probably O'Rahilly], sought to condemn the tirade but hold firm to the opposition to the University of Munster plan: It 'would be unfortunate and disastrous of University men, instead of rising and ennobling the conduct of public controversy, [if they] were to descend to mere vulgar abuse and undignified tirades'. He felt that 'the remarks in the previous issue were the thoughtless and hurried outcome of well-meaning emotion'. He enjoined the editorial board 'aim at a higher ethical and literary standard and to cultivate a proper sense of responsibility in journalism'.[71] But it was further stated that the apology 'must not be construed into an acknowledgement that we withdraw any of the severe strictures which we passed on the University Plot. Let us get a sense of proportion. The few epithets – three, we think – complained of are quite irrelevant to our case . . . Those against whom our contributor used over colloquial language have, after all, been guilty of a very underhand attempt to hand our College over to the tender mercies of Dublin Castle. Personally, we prefer the blunt language of a cornerboy to the secret plottings of a politician. Still two wrongs do not make a right ... And when a Castle-made, secretly-planned University was being foisted on us, who first called for publicity, who first denounced the plot? – *The Student*.'[72]

Windle was not drawn into making a public comment, continuing to conduct his own campaign. On 3 May, he summarised for H.R. Chillingworth, Baily, County Dublin, how he assessed popular opposition to the bill: 'It is matter of public notoriety that the Sinn Féin people – acting on the principle that as they are impotent then no one else must be allowed to do anything – have got up an opposition to this University matter.' Windle explained that the current campaign against him was being 'engineered by a gentleman of the name of Roche who calls himself De Róiste and who was one of a small number of persons who in 1908 did their best to upset the then University proposals, on the ground that nothing should be taken from England through English legislature – one of the most fatal pieces of policy that can well be imagined. He and his little gang were unsuccessful then, and I think that they are at present a good deal more helpful than hurtful. You are at liberty to mention that Roche who is an opponent at present was an opponent in 1908 since this is matter of public notoriety.'[73] Windle explained that, in his view, the National University was 'pursuing the characteristic policy of dragging out the matter in the hopes that the Irish Government may change their mind, or the skies fall, or something else happen which will put an end to the scheme. They cannot offer any but a selfish opposition to it, and they do not like to do that.'[74]

Windle's mood had changed from one of optimism in March and early April to despondency and gloom by May. He confessed to his friend, Humphreys, on the 7th that he could hardly write as the future was 'so black and uncertain'. He said there had been 'a desperate Sinn Féin opposition against the Munster university scheme on the grounds perfectly ridiculous – that nothing should be asked for from a British parliament – which really means that Sinn Féin, not being able to do anything themselves, don't want anybody else to do anything. If I do not get the University this year I think I must resign; at present I see nothing else for it. I can't go on for ever standing the strain of low intrigue and the constant stream of abuse directed at me as at anyone in this country who tried to do anything for it.'[75]

In anticipation of the upcoming meeting of the Senate, Windle had sent a letter to the NUI on 5 May: 'as the only business appears to be the Report of the Special Committee, which can only be accepted, rejected, or amended,' he did not consider it necessary to be present at the meeting. But he was deeply concerned about the possible negative outcome and did what he possibly could to influence members to support his position. He wrote to Plunket Barton, one of the members of the NUI sub-committee, on 9 May: 'We have quite made up our minds here about this matter and are not going under any circumstances whatsoever to settle down quietly under the yoke of the Dublin college in the National University . . . What I really would wish is a peaceful settlement of the matter so that we might go our own way and the other Colleges theirs, and I cannot see any reason why such mutual agreement should not be arrived at. With Coffey where he is and what he is, it is I fear impossible.'[76]

Correspondence was read at the Senate meeting on 9 May from the registrar, dated 1 March, 6 March and 8 April, and from the under-secretary, dated 7 March and 4 April 1919. Magennis proposed, and McClelland seconded, a motion, which was passed unanimously – what amounted to yet another move to procrastinate: 'that the report of the Committee to the Meeting of May 7th be referred to the Senate Meeting of the 21st, so as to secure proper opportunity for a discussion by the Senate regarding the proposed University for Cork, as the Government have in their letter of April 4th again pressed the Senate for its observations on the Draft Bill.'[77] Windle wrote a long entry on the meeting that evening, though he did not attend. Merriman reported that President Coffey was 'for delay – others for going ahead'. McGrath said: 'ah Castle is not going to do anything, but admitted he had had 3 letters' asking for 'clarification'. 'Let them go on,' commented Windle sharply. Sensing the inevitability of defeat, Windle also wrote on 9 May to Laurence Waldron, another Senate member, explaining that the recent debate in the NUI Senate had been 'long and wearisome, for Merriman, who went to the last meeting, informs me that they spent two and a half hours wrangling over the apparently small Resolution'. He asked Waldron, as a great favour, to remain at the meeting until the vote was taken. Windle said he would make a brief statement of his position and 'otherwise we shall not take up the time of the meeting, though I am sure that there will be plenty others to do so'. He further asked Waldron to rise 'at the proper moment' and propose that a vote be taken: 'The opposition which is being got up in Cork to the proposal is purely of a Sinn Féin character and is based on the kind of motive that as they cannot get anything themselves no one else must be allowed to get anything either,' he wrote.[78]

Sinn Féin opposition to the bill intensified in the first two weeks of May. Writing in *The New Ireland* on the 10th under the pseudonym 'Graduate', O'Rahilly represented the president and the delegation that had visited the Privy Council Chamber in January as being members of a 'private and secret . . . plot', representing nobody but themselves in a 'private mission to the conscriptionist viceroy'.[79] O'Rahilly was not below character assassination: Windle was an Englishman who had already been described in *The New Ireland*. Sir Stanley Harrington, he claimed, was 'a notoriously bad employer in Cork'. Merriman, in his view, had 'consistently opposed the national ideal in the university election and elsewhere'. Sir John O'Connell was, he wrote, 'a Trinity College graduate, lives in Killiney, and has no right to interfere with the matter at all'. Professor Charles Pearson was 'the head of the Freemasons in Cork'. Professor Hartog was described as 'an elderly naturalised gentleman who cannot claim to represent even the Hebrew community in Cork'. O'Rahilly urged the people of Munster 'to say whether they have placed their national educational affairs in the power of such men who wished to hand them over to the English Lord Lieutenant in the privy council chamber of Dublin Castle'.[80]

Under attack from within his own university, Windle soon had tangible evidence of the invertebrate nature of the British government. On 10 May, Professor Ridgeway wrote to him from Cambridge a 'most confidential' letter, conveying unwelcome news: 'The Irish Attorney-General is here for the week-end. He asks me to say that the Government are naturally much crowded by the Irish legislation already in the House of Commons, but if you could arrange to have your Bill introduced into the House of Lords, and set agoing there as soon as possible the Government would probably give it all help in the House of Commons. This would save much time, and do a great deal towards getting it through this Session. He has been naturally so busy with other very important matters that he has not had time to write to you to suggest this.'[81] On 12 May, Windle received a confirmatory letter from Dublin Castle saying Samuels 'wants bill introduced in House of Lords. All right but he must get someone to do it.' Whether Windle realised it or not, that news spelled the end of any hope of getting the legislation for a University of Munster put on the statute books. Windle knew that the attainment of autonomous university status was drifting away from him. He wrote again to the chief secretary in mid-May. In a reply on the 16th, he received news that the chief secretary was 'on the sick list at present and I have not been able to consult him about your letter'. Law, who wrote on his behalf, agreed to have inquiries made 'and if there is anything that can be stated about the position of the Munster University question I shall let you know'. He was invited to drop into the Irish Office 'on chance' when next in Dublin.[82]

Windle had cause for further alarm when he received a worrying letter, dated 19 May, from James C. Meredith KC, who was appointed in 1919 president of the Dáil Éireann Supreme Court.[83] He had just received a notice of the convocation on 6 June 1919. As matters stood, it did not appear to Meredith that 'it will be possible to get the question discussed at the meeting on the merits'. He was struck by the fact that the bill gave too much power to the king by charter. He told Windle that the bill 'allows the King to make all the statutes and cuts the jurisdiction of Parliament'. Regarding the financial aspects of the bill, Meredith felt that the act would require amendment 'if the University of Cork is not to suffer loss'. He did not wish to trouble Windle with his observations, but he thought that he should let him know how the draft bill had struck him. Windle alerted Michael Murphy, and, on 24 May, the latter sent two pages of amendments to the bill prompted by the letter from Meredith.[84]

The NUI Senate met on 21 May and discussed the University of Munster question. A motion to accept the original report of the committee, the text of which was in the minutes of the Senate for 7 May, was lost by nine votes to eleven. Agnes O'Farrelly of UCD proposed, and Joseph P. Pye of Galway seconded: 'That the Senate of the National University of Ireland deprecates the hasty introduction that will destroy the constitution of a university the foundation of which was accepted a few years ago as a settlement of the university question, and it claims that sufficient time be given to set forth its reasoned opinion on the subject.'[85] It was also decided that 'the Senate, if not prepared to go into full details with regard to the various questions involved in the establishment of a University in Cork, give an indication both to the Government and to the country as to their attitude towards the proposal'. This was carried by seven to six.[86] Windle's diary entry for that day was laconic but revealing: 'Most unpleasant and difficult meeting. Perfectly hateful.'

On 22 May, Windle noted: '*Samuels* says all Irish Government want it and mean business – But begin in House of Lords. No need to talk any more to them.' He believed that it was necessary for him to travel to London to muster support in official circles for the bill. (He had received a letter dated 16 May stating that 'Mr Chamberlain would be happy to see you here at 10.30 am on Friday, May 23rd – subject of course to any unforeseen contingency when he would make another appointment.'[87]) He also sought an opportunity to see Midleton while in London. On 23 May, Windle met Chamberlain: 'kind but bothered and would have no voice in matter.' He then went to the Admiralty and made an appointment to see Long. He later met Cardinal Bourne who 'thinks Toronto would be a good thing.' (This is a reference to a possible job offer from St Michael's College, University of Toronto.) The cardinal was 'shocked at Irish condition'. He advised him to see Lord E. Talbot and 'did so after some trouble'. He was very kind and said he would help. Windle was also advised to see the Irish draftsman. He did so, 'but found him most unsympathetic and stalled with work'. At one point in their conversation, Samuels came into the room. He said he wanted the bill first brought into the House of Lords 'by private member then government would probably take it up'. Windle 'said this would never do and left – fairly hopeless of him at any rate'. Believing against the odds that he might succeed, Windle continued to conduct a spirited campaign in London. He wrote on 24 May to Macpherson, Whitla, Carson ('! Such my despair') and S. Harrington.' The second name on the list was Sir William Whitla, Professor of Medicine, Queen's University, Belfast.

Despite his sense of hopelessness about the bill, he continued to lobby. On the 28th, he went to see Long. His diary recorded that the latter was 'very friendly and said "why on earth not go on with this thing?" I replied: "Why indeed". Long then said: "I'll write to L.L. [Lord Lieutenant] p.s. [private secretary] to-day and say it should be introduced after Whit tide." So there you are – now what will happen?' Windle saw Lord Midleton on 31 May and found him 'very pessimistic about all Irish things but would do what he could [for Munster University].' His deliberations in London ended inconclusively. Windle sailed for Ireland on 1 June enjoying a 'perfectly flat passage'. On arrival, he went to Mass and took the train to Killiney where he had a meeting with Sir Arthur Chance. On 9 June, the NUI Convocation met in UCD, Earlsfort Terrace. Dr Michael Francis Cox presided. He was a physician, a senator and the first chairman of the Convocation, a position he held from 1910 until 1925. Cox was a friend of John Redmond and other leading members of the IPP. But in such changed times there was little he could do from the chair to influence the outcome of the vote on the University of Munster. A resolution, signed by the nineteen Sinn Féin TDs, was read out. It had already been said to the UCC governing body. The Cork Sinn Féin Graduates' Club also sent in a statement against the proposal to establish an independent university.

The chairman, in submitting the message regarding the proposed Munster university, said that he was present at the Senate and took the liberty of asking what government of Ireland had submitted the bill to the Senate and by what authority had it done so. The lord chief justices, who had subscribed their names to the submission, could hardly be said to represent the people of Ireland, he said. It would be a loss to the National University to lose 'the genius of the people of Cork'.[88]

Professor O'Rahilly proposed a motion which opposed the proposal of independence for UCC as it 'provides no solution of the alleged difficulties of the existing federal system of the National University of Ireland; and, secondly, would hand over to persons not responsible to the Irish people and their elected representatives the most absolute powers to regulate the whole constitution and administration of the proposed new university.' The motion also stated that the proposal had been brought forward at a most inopportune time and apart from the principle involved, on which it offered no opinion at that time, 'the preparation of this arbitrary, vague, and incomplete measure has been attended by many objectionable circumstances, which are a menace to the national character and academic freedom of Irish education'. Concluding, O'Rahilly said there was no proof that Cork wanted the bill, stating that nineteen out of twenty Munster TDs had opposed it. The UCC governing body was out of touch with the people. The motion, he said, opposed Lord French and Macpherson being given a free hand under the bill to set up anything that they liked in Cork and call it a university. The motion was adopted by 115 votes to 4, with 27 members not voting.[89]

After Convocation – 6 June – Windle wrote: 'The Irish Government refuses to give us a University because of opposition of N.U.I. – Of course, a mere excuse. £6,000 additional only for college – not enough.' The following day, he noted: 'Rahilly – who asked for leave for rest! (liar) [?] rejection of Cork scheme in Convocation. Of course armed by large majority – matters little now.' His mood was dark and he had determined to quit the college.[90] Windle chaired a meeting of the university executive on 11 June: 'much talk over Government and their giving this away to Sinn Féin. Said I was adamant as to going. S Harrington said no one could blame me.'

The governing body met on 13 June. The mood was sombre and deflated. The minutes include the text of a letter from the Chief

Secretary's Office, stating that, in view of the attitude of the NUI Senate the bill would 'certainly not be unopposed'. Owing to the congested condition of parliamentary business, 'His Excellency regrets that he cannot hold out any hope at present of the promotion or support by the Government of the proposed establishment of a University of Cork.' A bill, dealing with the matter, might be introduced in the House of Lords, the letter concluded.[91] The minutes also recorded the text of opposition to the University of Munster.[92] By way of response, Windle put before the governors a memorandum setting out the alternatives before them. Firstly, it noted that the Irish government had refused to undertake to bring in a bill for the establishment of a Munster university during that year: 'The excuse made for this is that the Bill would be opposed by all the influence of the National University. That it would be opposed by that University is unquestionably true though I cannot bring myself to believe that such opposition would have been in any way serious had the Government been in earnest about the matter.' Windle laid out the following alternative courses of action open to the governors:

> 1 – The Govern Body can accept the situation and say and do nothing further; 2 – It can make a strong protest. Should it decide to do this it might pass a resolution at the present meeting; 3 – it might appeal to the Visitor for a Visitation to consider the position of the College; 4 – it might apply for alterations in the Charters of the college and the university which would remove some of the grosser inequalities complained of in the statement of the case. The probability is that a concession of this kind would be given by the government as it would not entail legislation. But the GB must bear in mind that, should it obtain this concession, the Munster University movement must be regarded as shelved for at least the next ten years. It is very urgent that the GB should know its own mind about this matter, and I hope that the members will be prepared to discuss the question fully and come to a decision as to their policy for the immediate future.[93]

After a discussion, Bishop Cohalan proposed: 'That the Governing Body desire with great respect to express the deep regret with which they have received the communication from the Irish Government stating that it was impossible to introduce legislation at present for the foundation of a Munster University. The Governing Body desire to reiterate their opinion that real progress is impossible under the present system. Further they desire respectfully to point out that the reason alleged by the Government for their inaction in this matter is in itself an argument in favour of the project. The Governing Body have shown that the Senate of the University, not to speak of Convocation, are and must be dominated by a permanent majority from University College Dublin. This they consider a most serious obstacle to the development of this College. They regret exceedingly that the project of a Munster University has been dropped even temporarily.'[94]

The UCD governing body met on 26 June 1919 and passed the following motion, unanimously opposing 'the break up of the National University of Ireland as involved in the proposals contained in the Draft Bill submitted to the Senate, and if necessary, will forward a reasoned statement for the opposition'.[95]

Windle, exhausted and dejected, saw no point in continuing as president of a college now foredoomed to stagnate: 'Mind now made up to clear out at Christmas,' he wrote disconsolately on 6 June 1919.

CHAPTER 9

'Years of Harvesting':
Canada, 1920–1929

Windle was both exhausted and humiliated by the manner in which his campaign failed to free UCC from the bondage of the NUI. He had been abandoned by the British government and he had faced subversion of his plans from within the gates of UCC. However, the collapse of the campaign helped finally to lift the burden from his shoulders of feeling that he had to remain as president of UCC in order to fulfil a divine plan. On 17 June, he wrote: 'very worried about whether to go or not – so much both ways – must leave it to God but would that He could make it clear to me what He desires.' Windle had not entirely left the matter in God's hands. His dissatisfaction with UCC, the NUI and Ireland had been known to his friends and to the authorities in Dublin Castle for quite some time. News of his unsettled state had even reached the wider Catholic world where his academic reputation was highly esteemed in many centres of learning. Therefore, it was not surprising for him to receive an offer to teach for an extended period from one such institution. On 21 June, Windle received a letter from St Michael's College, University of Toronto, 'offering £500 and passages for Edith and self for three months' lectures. Cabled acceptance. *alea jacta est* [the die has been cast].' What began as a commitment to a short lecture series would turn into a permanent move to Toronto where – but for one short return trip to England in 1921 – he remained until his death in 1929, occupying the twin positions of Professor of Anthropology in the Philosophy Department of St Michael's College and Special Lecturer in Ethnology at the University of Toronto.

The prime mover behind the offer was Fr Henry Carr CSB (1880–1963), a leader of Catholic education in Canada, the founder of St Michael's College and co-founder of the Pontifical Institute of Medieval Studies, University of Toronto. Later, both Windle and Carr became the firmest of friends. On 24 June, Windle wrote to a close friend, Mgr Parkinson: 'Do not mention it to anyone except (if you wish) the two archbishops – but I am leaving here at the end of the year and am going to deliver an annual three months course of lectures on science and Christian philosophy in St Michael's College, Toronto. The rest of the year I shall live near or in London – The state of religion – under the surface – is lamentable in this country and [it is a] real severe trial to Faith, for one gets tired of saying that the Church's treasure is sometimes in earthen vessels.'[1]

Windle could hardly contain his anger when, the previous day, he had written in his diary about the growth of lawlessness in the province and in the country. That day, the IRA had shot dead in Thurles, County Tipperary, an RIC district inspector, Michael Hunt, who was returning from a local race meeting. 'Bishops protest against English rule,' he wrote on 25 June, 'but say not a word about murders especially the poor D.I. shot at Thurles. What a gang and how can this country have any blessing.' In the circum-stances, he was relieved to receive on 18 July a further letter from a group in Toronto asking him to give an after lunch talk on 7 January 1920. Windle received a letter on 29 July from Gasquet who was very conscious of the fact that his friend was having a very unpleasant time in Ireland: 'What an extraordinary state of affairs! The Government seem to be letting every-thing drift and how is it going to end?' The cardinal told him that he was 'very glad' to hear that he had accepted the offer to go to Toronto: 'To secure a man of your importance and ability is a great move and I wish you every success.'[2] Windle received further good news from Canada on 4 August: 'Then most satisfactory letter from Toronto – the clearest possible to which replied. It certainly seems a *most* clear door opened by God and how thankful I shall be to go through it.' He received another incentive to leave when, in Listarkin on 8 August, he wrote: 'Outrages on police and constabulary [?] and not ONE word from our bishops or clergy – what a gang!' The shortcomings of Irish Catholicism, as he perceived them, were again manifest on 10 August: 'Mass three quarters of an hour late and then stinking [?] yokel priest read Acts and Collect in Irish which I suppose one person in 100 could understand – yet these are the prayers for the people to join in – what a clergy and how they are throwing away their chances! What other people would wait three quarters of an hour and then have no apology or explanation?' Seeking consolation from such behaviour, he visited Bishop Kelly on 15 August: 'Very kindly and said I should do great good where I was going and would be following in the work of my life.' Windle received on 4 September 'two splendid letters from the Dean of Toronto – right to stop all worrying'.

The Windles had spent their last summer in Listarkin and in Ireland. By early September, the house was emptied of personal effects. 'State of country so bad that it does not bear mentioning,' he noted as they prepared to leave on 9 September. Two days later, he wrote that 'Heavy goods off at 9.15 . . . Good-bye to Listarkin and thank God for many pleasant days there.' Upon his return to UCC on 13 September, he told close friends that he was leaving the presidency. If Windle thought that the news of his departure would be greeted with regret, he remained somewhat naïve about the nature of academic politics. News of his departure immediately sparked off intense speculation about who would be likely to succeed him. 'No one cares a thraneen about my going but all agog as to who is to succeed me,' he wrote on 1 October as the smart money was being placed on the registrar, Merriman, to take his place.

Whatever about reaction in the college, Windle's announcement of his departure was a shock to the local community. The *Cork Examiner* did not let the occasion go unmarked. The editor employed the services of 'an esteemed correspondent', probably Horgan, to write an appreciation: 'The occasion is one worthy of some consideration and reflection by the public. The President is not in ill-health, nor is he old, nor are his intellectual faculties failing. He is in the prime of life, on the contrary, with twenty years of full activity before him in the natural order of probability; his great reputation as a scientist and scholar is growing every year in every civilized country in the world; a great Canadian University has snapped him up already to teach a great subject on which, by consent of the learned, there is no greater authority living.'[3] Windle was also remembered as being a fine administrator and a kind and helpful mentor to graduates: 'His administrative ability is unimpaired, and any one who wants to know its quality will compare the Queen's College Calendars of 1904 and 1919 or the report just issued now. His readiness and capacity to help his graduates in careers in life have grown as the years went on, and the young men and women that he has placed by his good will and wide-spread influence in responsible quarters are to be found in nearly every walk of life at home and abroad, well on the road to success.'[4]

The writer spoke about his courageous decisions to champion the cause of Irish nationalism and to convert to Catholicism: 'His patriotism is not in question either, nor could it be. In 1882, when Sir Bertram Windle, beginning life young in Birmingham, declared himself an Irish nationalist he cut away half the ground from under his feet. In English eyes then it was equivalent to professing cattle-houghing and dynamite as legitimate political weapons. It was before Sir Edward Carson made treason safe and fashionable. In the following year when he became a Catholic, leaving his near relations all in the established church, on the Episcopal bench, in the peerage, and high in the great public service, he cut away the rest of his ground, and left himself only his personal merits to support himself in his struggle for success. Handicapped with two unpopular and self-assumed badges, that struggle passed from triumph to triumph for over twenty years.'[5]

Ending on a critical note about UCC, the city and the region, he wrote: 'Very long ago a good man left his home in Rome to work out his life in his own way in a foreign land. After many years he returned unrecognised to his own people. He accepted the hard knocks of his position and did his day's work daily, but did it perfectly. As he died, his identity and his goodness were recognised together. "Ah", said his own people, "if we only had known who was our servant". He was duly honoured – afterwards.'[6] Windle received no such honour from the city of Cork.

Windle sought to disengage gracefully from the university and from Cork. He did not attend a meeting of the Academic Council on 7 October. There, his old friend, Marcus Hartog, proposed: 'That this Council expresses its deep regret at the resignation of Sir Bertram Windle from the Presidency of the College which during his tenure of office has enjoyed a prosperity and undergone a development unparalleled in its history. It desires to place on record its sense of his brilliant abilities and entire and continuous devotion to the interests of the College, which alone have made possible this prosperity and this development. And it wishes to convey to him its best for his future success and happiness in the new sphere to which he is now called.'[7] The tribute to Windle was unanimously adopted.

But, as mentioned above, the speculation about his succession had begun with indecent haste. There was now the possibility of an outside candidate for his position, an old and bitter rival from UCD: 'That filthy Dublin Dock rat [Professor William] Magennis canvassing for my job – will put a spoke in his wheel,' he wrote on 7 October. Windle noted on 9 October that his UCC pension would be £574 and that his Toronto salary would be £500. He added £200 per annum from another source and that gave a total of £1,350. 'Not too bad,' he commented. Bishop Cohalan had called to his office earlier that day before the governing body met, and asked him 'to reconsider resignation for a year – said I couldn't'. Windle was unanimously requested to reconsider at the governing body meeting that followed, but he again declined. Cohalan proposed, and the Archbishop of Cashel, John Harty, seconded, the following motion: 'That the Governing Body hereby express its intense regret on hearing of the decision of Sir Bertram Windle to resign the Presidency of the College, and desires to place on record its appreciation of his invaluable services, not merely to the College which has prospered notably under his administration, but to the whole educational world. During the 15 years of his Presidency the College has made phenomenal progress to which the increase in the number of its students and the brilliant role of their achievements testify so eloquently; while at the same time he contributed to the advancement of education outside its walls by his fruitful efforts in everything appertaining to the welfare of the nation. The Governing Body sincerely wishes that in the New World he may continue his great work and find in it the happiness and the prosperity which he eminently deserves.'[8]

As one of his final acts in the college, Windle presented the annual report for the year 1918–19. It was, in all respects, a positive, realistic appraisal of the state of college affairs. He reported that 354 UCC staff, students and graduates had taken part in the First World War. Fifty-four had gained distinctions and twenty-nine had died in action.[9] 'There were 629 students enrolled for the session,' he said, 'an increase from 566 for 1917–1918', noting that during the previous session 'the city was visited by a terrible epidemic of influenza, which for some unknown reason, attacks young adults much more than elder persons.' Five students of the college had died. On medical advice, he had closed the college for a month. A request to postpone all examinations until the autumn was sent to the NUI, but that request was quite inexplicably refused. Windle described that as 'an excellent example of the treatment which our College receives from the hands of the University and the utter state of bondage in which it lies'. He then spoke about his efforts to win autonomy for UCC and of his visit to the lord lieutenant to pursue that goal. But the campaign failed. Windle concluded: 'That decision, as I have said, leaves the College, as it has been in the past, tied hand and foot and at the mercy of a permanent majority belonging to another college.'[10] Addressing the unsatisfactory nature of the college finances, he reported that he had petitioned Dublin and made two trips to London to secure increased support, but the government had given a grant for that year which was not adequate and made the future uncertain.

Turning to personal matters, he said that it had been his intention to retire as soon as he could claim a pension. This he wished to do for more than one reason, not the least being the 'incessant, unpleasant and unnecessary work and exhausting train journeys due to our connection with the National University'. It required a constitution of iron to carry on the work of his office, he said,[11] adding that he had always wanted to find time to write and study. His pension had fallen due the previous autumn. But he could not leave while the war was still on and would not leave if the government had granted the autonomy which was so unanimously requested by the university and the region. He would have felt obliged to remain as president in order to carry out the transfer to full autonomy. Further, the work would have been lightened and the incessant struggles with outside bodies ended. But the government, he said, had relieved him of any such responsibility. He therefore intended to tender his resignation to the lord lieutenant, having the satisfaction of knowing that during his fifteen years at UCC he had seen the college nearly double in buildings, nearly treble in number of students and become the only college in Ireland to receive substantial gifts, amounting to over £100,000.[12]

Windle spent the days after the announcement of his retirement in England visiting friends. Back by 15 October, he busied himself tidying up his personal affairs. He had a visit from Shane Leslie on the 18th. That afternoon, Hartog told him that the money collected to mark his departure would leave a 'substantial balance after paying portrait which they propose to give to college for a scholarship or a medal! And a fountain pen to self and to Edith!! What a singular disposition! Portrait evidently going to become infernal nuisance.' On Sunday, 19th, he noted that graduates had presented him with a silver cigar case and a pouch. Edith was given lace: 'much touched and the *only* thing I shall take away from Cork as far as I can see after 15 years work for the vile hole.' On 28 October, Windle met Downey and Br Connolly 'on presentation to me and it appears that Hartog, the bumbling old loveable ass has been talking through his hat'.

Although very busy, Windle had to be available to the artist, Harry Scully RHA, for long sittings for his portrait which had been commissioned by the college.[13] On 2 November, he told Sr Monica of the hectic pace during his final weeks in Ireland: 'I have only another fortnight of Cork now, and then a wandering period up to December 20 when we sail. I do hope we shall have a priest on board, otherwise we shall miss Mass on two Sundays and a Christmas Day, a thing which has never happened to me before.'[14] Gasquet[15] wrote on 8 November: 'I can't say that I am pleased that you should transplant yourself over the Atlantic. But I think you are quite right and I believe and indeed am sure that you will do a vast amount of good in Canada and the U. States, where most of the learning is very superficial. Once you get known over there you will be in constant demand and they at least know how to pay for work done. Don't have any doubt you will do great service to the Church – far more than you could do by remaining in Cork.'

On 10 November, Windle had his last sitting for Scully. That day he said goodbye to his daughter Nora who left to return to London. He also gave away his dog Peg – 'a great wrench. Perhaps foolish to bind oneself to a dog but without a dog, life seems wanting in something.' On 13 November, Windle wrote: 'Office – Last time!' and had a long talk with the Church of Ireland Bishop of Cork, Charles Benjamin Dowse. Windle's equilibrium was upset by having to attend a meeting of 'colleges (GAA) association – that lying rogue there R. Sexton in chair. Rugby forbidden –

My god what a country, and this in the name of liberty. I offer my grateful thanks to Him that I am escaping from it.' That evening, his daughter Mary and her husband came to dinner. The reconciliation between Windle, his married daughter and her husband remained more correct than cordial.

On 14 November, Bertram and Lady Windle went to the Aula Maxima for a farewell ceremony. The Bishop of Cork, Daniel Cohalan, presided. The chairman of the subscription committee, Br Ignatius Connolly (Presentation order), unveiled the life-size portrait of Windle by Harry Scully. He presented it to UCC. Lady Windle received a small *replica* of the portrait and a set of furs.[16] 'Edith spoke very nicely', Windle noted. Hartog gave the encomium, during the course of which he spoke of the recent failure to gain autonomy for UCC: 'At the same time an agitation, founded on the misunderstanding and consequent misrepresentations to which we have referred above, had arisen against the scheme. The Bill had to be abandoned for the present; and our late President has told us that the heart-sickening deferment of his hopes counted for a large part in his decision to resign, and bring to a premature close his career in the guidance of the College, while still a young man as Presidents go.'[17]

The following day, the 15th, Windle went to Ballincollig to spend the evening with Canon Roche. They walked together on the 16th and saw Bishop Kelly later that day. He said his goodbyes to senior college officers, including Downey, on the morning of the 17th and later had his daughter 'Mary to lunch and good bye and cried a lot. Fonder of me than I thought,' he noted with a straight face.[18] The comment may appear strange but not to those who have read the earlier chapters of this book. That night, he wrote:

'So Ends Cork! 15 yrs hard work – spoilt by base intrigues and certainly some of the basest people I ever met. *In Exitu Israel de Egypto*

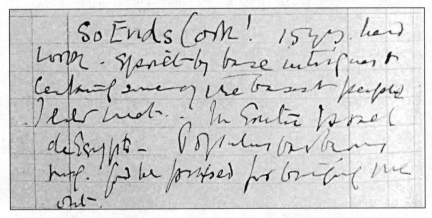

Windle's diary entry, 17 November 1919, on his final work-day at UCC.

– *Populus barbarus* [?] God be praised for bringing me out.'[19] Windle had escaped from the darkness of Ireland and out of the hands of a barbarous people.

Canon Roche wrote a warm letter of appreciation to him on 6 December: 'It costs me much to repress reminiscences. I prefer to look confidently into the future, and see there the hand of God leading you into other corners of His pastures – truly one might say "fresh woods and pastures new". Better work, even than the past, lies before you there, and its complete novelty, its noble aim and the grip it will take on you, will be at once your inspiration and your consolation. You carry with you the reverence and gratitude of everyone who, from within and without, has any knowledge of your fifteen years of wondrous successful labour here. I meet no one *now* who does not deplore your loss and lament that no strong public movement was started to keep you in your old position. I meet people of every class, and this is what I hear on all sides. Sometimes I am unchristian enough to feel that it serves us right.'[20]

Before sailing for Canada, Windle visited Glasgow on 3 and 4 December to give lectures and to meet Sr Monica and the Notre Dame community.[21] He arrived at 9.41 and went to the Training College at Dowanhill, Glasgow, 'and long talk with Monica and community'. He spoke that evening to the Catholic Students Society at Glasgow University on the topic 'Prehistoric Man'. Sir Donald MacAlister presided. He went to Dowanhill the next morning, had lunch and spent the afternoon there, presumably talking to Sr Monica. After tea at 8.00, he talked to her students on the 'Scientific Hypothesis'. His lecture, she stated, was 'the last which Sir Bertram delivered on this side of the Atlantic, and, as the reader will gather, it was given at the cost of much inconvenience to himself'.[22] Sr Monica, who would meet him only one more time, continued to correspond with him until his death in 1929.[23]

UCC selected a new president in the weeks that followed Windle's departure. The governing body met on 29 November 1919 with the acting president, Professor Charles Pearson, in the chair. A letter was read from the Chief Secretary's Office, dated 30 October, accepting the resignation. Windle's letter of resignation, effective from 30 November, was also read out.[24] There were six applications for the vacant post, four professors from UCC and one other academic: the registrar and Professor of History, Patrick J. Merriman, David T. Barry (Psychology), Patrick T. O'Sullivan (Medical Jurisprudence), Timothy A. Smiddy (Economics) and Dr Butler. The Professor of Metaphysics from UCD, William Magennis, was the only candidate from outside. In accordance with the statutes, the meeting decided to send up three names to the senate. It was decided to get the first name by holding a series of ballots on which the lowest candidate in each poll fell out. There were four polls. The result of the first poll was: Butler (0); Barry (8); Merriman (6); Magennis (5); O'Sullivan (5); and Smiddy (2). On the second poll, the results were: Butler (0); Barry (8); Merriman (6); Magennis (5); O'Sullivan (7) and Smiddy (0). The results of the third polls were: Barry (8); Merriman (9) and O'Sullivan (9). On the final polls both Merriman and O'Sullivan each got 13 votes. The meeting decided that that would be the selection of the first two candidates. Another ballot was held to vote on one of the four other names: Butler (0); Barry (15); Magennis (7) and Smiddy (4). Barry's name was added to the list.

Magennis was not a good loser. He alleged that the outgoing governing body had 'fixed' the election. A new governing body was due to take office on 1 February 1920. However, the three names went before the senate on 16 December 1919. Professor Magennis, on a point of order, argued that 'what purported to be the act of selection of three names on the part of the Governing body in Cork was illegal, and that the Senate should not complete the appointment so begun, but have a visitation to decide the matter'. It was ruled that the senate proceed with the selection of a president. Merriman got 20 votes, O'Sullivan received 5 and Barry got 4. Merriman was declared elected as President of University College Cork.[25] The decision was welcomed by the governing body at UCC on 18 December, which also accepted the new president's resignation as Professor of History. He was asked to fulfil the duties of the chair until a new professor had been appointed.[26] Merriman, a mild-mannered man, was a little shaken by the vigour of the challenge mounted by Magennis. He was also surprised by the collapse of the opposition to appointment from inside UCC. On 25 January 1920, he wrote to Windle apologising for not having written earlier to thank him for his congratulations and kind wishes. He told him that he had not attended the contentious Senate meeting at which Magennis spoke for an hour, reading extracts from huge tomes on company law and declaring that the proceedings in Cork had been invalid as two candidates had been present at the meeting. He also objected on the grounds that the statute required the acting president to be appointed only when the president had resigned or was incapacitated. Magennis had wanted a postponement of the vote, and the appointment of a visitator. Those requests were denied and the meeting lasted until 7.00 p.m. The votes, according to Merriman, were as follows: Merriman (20) (although Bishop O'Dea and Barton were unavoidably absent), P.T. O'Sullivan (5) and Barry (4). Merriman added: 'The funny thing is that the evening before in Cork, Barry boasted that he would have practically a walk over.' Another meeting had been called for 16 January but, at the time of writing, the matter of the UCC presidency was closed: 'I have been very fortunate and thank you very warmly for the help, especially for the encouragement, which you so ungrudgingly gave me.'[27]

The new president, who was succeeded as Professor of History by James Hogan, concluded with a reference to the situation in Ireland: 'You doubtless read of outrages in the American papers, but these cannot give a proper idea of the situation. When we open our newspaper at breakfast, we do not know what to expect, and we are fast getting beyond surprise or even indignation. Still, I believe things are at the worst, and, with God's help, a satisfactory settlement will soon be found. In Canada you are free from this spectre-like political obsession, and can direct yourself *sans arrière pensée* [without ulterior motive] to the great work of education.'[28]

Writing on 22 January, Windle gave his reaction to Sr Bonaventure in Cork: 'I do not envy him [Merriman] his task . . . I wanted nothing better than to serve the college but when it was obvious that I was not going to be allowed to do so without unceasing friction and underhand cabals, I felt it was time for me to get out of it, and just at the right moment, God opened this door for me.'[29] The composition of the new governing body would not have been to Windle's liking, including the Lord Mayor of Cork, Tomás MacCurtain and other Sinn Féiners. The 'greening' of UCC was taking place apace. Before the governing body, on 19 March 1920, voted to appoint a new registrar, the president referred to the attempt that had been made on the life of Professor Stockley, proposing that the secretary 'be directed to convey to Professor Stockley the condemnation of the Governors on the attempt and their congratulations on his escape'.[30] Later in the meeting, Mary MacSwiney, St Ita's School, Cork, was nominated for co-option to the governing body. She received ten votes, Rev. T. Tobin got thirteen, Br E.J.T. Connolly also got thirteen and Br J.P. Noonan got twelve. All were declared co-opted. The meeting then proceeded to consider the question of the appointment of a new registrar. Professor Smiddy was proposed for the vacant post by Merriman and seconded by Hartog. The Lord Mayor of Cork, Tomás MacCurtain, supported by Professor P.T. O'Sullivan MD, put the name of Professor Alfred O'Rahilly forward for the position. It had been a mistake to run Smiddy as a presidential candidate. He had secured only four votes on one ballot and two on another in the presidential election. The vote was taken by secret ballot, both Smiddy and O'Rahilly leaving the room and not voting. O'Rahilly won by thirteen votes to eight, a significant personal reverse for the newly-appointed president who had to live with the consequences.[31]

On 20 March about 1.15 a.m. – the night following the election of the new registrar by the governing body – the lord mayor, Tomás MacCurtain, was murdered in his bedroom by disguised members of the forces of the Crown. At the next meeting of the governing body, on 18 May 1920, President Merriman, having referred to the 'tragic death of the Lord Mayor', proposed, and the registrar seconded, that 'the sympathy of the Governing Body be conveyed to Mrs MacCurtain and family', which was adopted.[32] Political violence had come very close to UCC.

As UCC entered a new and more nationalist era, in spite of Merriman, Windle took a declining interest in his former university and in the affairs of Ireland. He was building an exciting new career in Toronto; his time there was happy, productive and fulfilled. He made very good friends, in particular with Fr Carr. He told Sr Monica: 'We often dine out with friends. Last night I dined at Victoria College to meet [Viljalmur] Stefanson, the great Esquimaux explorer, and a number of other interesting people. It is very nice to have a really intellectual society.'[33] He found the kind of academic society he craved in St Michael's, which played host to many of the most prominent Catholic intellectuals of the period.

The Windles first lived in a spacious flat at 89 St Joseph's Street.[34] He wrote on 23 January 1920 to Sr Monica: 'Since I wrote to you [28 December] we have got settled down into our flat and are very comfortable in it. It is a new scheme of life in which one has no servant but it has its compensations. I clean the boots and my wife gets the breakfast – all other meals we have in the café – but one soon gets accustomed to that mode of life and it is certainly set off a good deal by avoiding all the bothers of servants. Besides everything is arranged in this country on the principle of saving labour and it is surprising how much can be done in that direction by a little thought.'[35]

At the college, Windle was given 'two nice rooms, one in which I could sleep if I wanted to, and a good sitting-room'.[36] He told Sr Monica that he was 'now well into the work of lecturing' and his only embarrassment was that the priests in the nearby house attended those talks and the provincial 'takes most copious notes'. He hoped that meant that they were interested in what he had to say. He was due to begin a series of six lectures for the university on some aspects of the pre-history of the British Isles. They were open to the public. He would be giving four lectures to women attending the university who were in the St Joseph's and Loretto colleges. He had to go to Montreal to give a lecture at Loyola University: 'You will gather from all this that I am not being idle, but it is a great pleasure to be engaged in work which one thoroughly likes, and which is, I hope and believe, really useful.'[37]

Windle's scholarly output during the last nine years of his life was extensive. He published *On Miracles and Some Other Matters* in 1924 and

Evolution and Catholicity in 1925. He published *Who's Who of the Oxford Movement, Prefaced by a Brief Story of that Movement* in 1926. He dedicated that work to his 'dear and valued friend Monica Taylor, Sister of Notre Dame and Doctor of Science'. *The Evolutionary Problem as it is Today* appeared in 1927. This was dedicated to his friend, Fr Henry Carr, in 'a small recognition of many kindnesses'. *The Catholic Church and its Reactions with Science* was also published in 1927. He dedicated that work to Cecily Anglin, 'who was promised the dedication of a book but could not stay to see it'. Windle published a third book in 1927: *Religions Past and Present: An Elementary Account of Comparative Religion.* That was dedicated to another friend, Dr John Stenhouse.

A number of the works were based on his highly successful and popular lecture series at St Michael's College and the University of Toronto. He expended great energy in those final years travelling and giving talks to academic and to general audiences, visiting Buffalo, Rochester, New York, Boston and Washington. He also broadcast on the Paulist radio in New York. That was a very dynamic output for a man who was on the board of governors of St Michael's Hospital, vice chairman of the university's relations committee with the hospital, the Norton Memorial Lecturer of the American Anthropological Institute, a lecturer to the students of St Michael's on philosophy and to the students of the University of Toronto on ethnography.[38]

Historians are hampered by the unavailability of his diaries from 1921 to 1929. Other sources help only partially to provide a fragmented picture of his reaction to events in a country where he had toiled for fifteen years. In that first year outside UCC, 1920, Ireland intruded somewhat more frequently than in subsequent years. On 9 August, Gasquet wrote: 'Poor Ireland appears to be getting worse and worse. The Government don't seem to have any definite policy and the religious state grows worse. At present we are expecting Dr Mannix and I believe that the powers that be are determined to make a martyr of him, though he is certainly an aggravating person.'[39] Gasquet also told Windle that he had been invited by the British prime minister, Lloyd George, to lunch at 10 Downing Street during his recent visit to England. Bonar Law and Lord Curzon were also present: 'It was interesting and *inter alia* I upbraided him with letting you leave this country, saying that they should have given you some position that would have made it worth your while remaining in England. To my astonishment he agreed and regretted that you had already shaken the dust off your feet – Really the mismanagement of the Government is wonderful and the new military law for Ireland is no remedy and as I told Lloyd G. they will have to come to Dominion Home Rule and shelve the Bill which they propose. He appeared to agree. I was struck with the man

– about the most fascinating man I have ever come across. I believe, however, that he changes like the moon.'"[40] Windle may have smiled ruefully at the idea of Lloyd George regretting his departure to Canada.

Windle wrote on 11 September, having received a copy of a newspaper marked in red ink '"passed by the Censor (*sic*) I.R.A'": Impudent thieves. I hope government will stick it over these hunger-strikes and let them commit suicide and so go to their own place.' Windle wrote on 18 October: '. . . first hunger striker died in Cork. Got engaged *in prison* a week before and wanted to be married! What a picnic. Blasphemous effusions by McSweeney [*sic*] . . . But that it *is the* church, no one would ever want to be a Catholic these times with the way Bishops and priests go on in Ireland.' The reference was to the new Lord Mayor of Cork, Terence MacSwiney, whom he had known as a student, graduating from UCC in 1907. A playwright, a poet and a revolutionary nationalist, MacSwiney was elected in 1918 for mid-Cork to Dáil Éireann. MacSwiney, who succeeded the murdered MacCurtain, was arrested on 12 August and sentenced to two years. Windle, in a letter to his close friend Shane Leslie, confessed on 20 October: 'I thank God daily that I am out of Ireland and wish my married daughter and her belongings were. It is very hard at this distance to get at the real facts but personally I cannot away with the Hunger Fasting which seems suicide and silliness to me.'[41] On 25 October, MacSwiney died in Brixton jail after seventy-four days on hunger strike. His death provoked worldwide protests. Tens of thousands filed past his coffin as he lay in state at Southwark Cathedral, London. On 28 October, Windle commented: 'This making political demonstrations out of religious ceremonies must do the Church infinite harm.' He made pejorative mention of Archbishop Daniel Mannix of Melbourne and of the Bishop of Plymouth, Cotter, who he described as a 'duffer'. He could not understand why the Archbishop of Southwark, Amigo 'the rock scorpion', was involved. 'Has *he* no sense?' he asked. MacSwiney's remains were diverted to Cork by the British authorities. Arthur Griffith delivered the graveside oration at St Finbarr's cemetery. On 29 November, Windle noted: 'Constant murders in Ireland and outrages by Irish in England. How much longer will the hypocritical cry of "Holy" Ireland be kept up.' On 11 December, Cork city centre was burned by the Black and Tans, prompting Windle to write two days later: '[£] 3,000,000 of property burnt at Cork. Larkinites no doubt, but people will say soldiers, and the scoundrel [J.J.] Walsh and idiot [Liam] Roche are off on that tack. I see that mad vile bad Rahilly [Professor Alfred O'Rahilly] has an article in *Irish Theological Quarterly* proclaiming killing of soldiers and [?] in Ireland no murder.[42] On the other hand, Bishop of Cork issues edict anyone taking part in a murder or ambushing is excommunicated *ipso facto*.'

The parish priest of Dunmanway, Canon Thomas J. Magner, was shot dead by a member of the British auxiliary forces on 15 December 1920, ostensibly for refusing to toll the church bell to commemorate Armistice Day. But Fr Donal O'Donovan's study argues convincingly that he was shot in cold blood by Cadet Sergeant Vernon Hart on a country road before eyewitnesses. A few moments before the 'execution' of Magner, Hart shot dead a twenty-three-year-old local man, Tadhg O'Crowley.[43] Bishop Cohalan influenced the Cork and Bandon Railway Company to put on a special train from Cork for those wishing to attend the funerals. On 18 December, the *Cork Examiner* reported:

> Dunmanway was yesterday the scene of a most imposing and most impressive demonstration of grief and condolence. It was the occasion of the double funeral of the victims of the appalling tragedy, when the deeply-loved and revered pastor of the parish – Very Rev. Canon Magner, P.P., and a promising young parishioner, Mr Tadhg O'Crowley were brutally done to death a short distance from the town . . . a striking feature of the obsequies was the extremely large and representative gathering of the clergy of the diocese of Cork, and adjoining diocese of Ross and Cloyne. The town was in deep mourning, every place of business being closed, and the attendance of the general public from the town as well as other centres in which the deceased ministered added a further and abiding tribute to his memory. The remains of Canon Magner rested on a catafalque in front of the High Altar, and on the side of the Altar rested the coffin containing the remains of Mr Crowley . . . Solemn Requiem Mass was celebrated at 11 o'clock, his Lordship Most Rev. Dr. Cohalan, presiding. The celebrant was Very Rev Jeremiah Canon Cohalan, P.P., V.F., Bandon, a nephew of the Bishop of Cork.[44]

Fr William Sheehan preached the panegyric, in the course of which he described Canon Magner as 'one of the gentlest and most inoffensive men that ever lived. If ever there was one who would be called "a man of peace and a lover of family" it was the poor Canon that we laid to rest on Friday'. The killing was so atrocious, and so revolting in every circumstance, that 'one finds it hard to speak with moderation or to observe the law of charity', he said. In order to understand how unjustifiably cruel and shocking the killing was, he continued, 'we must remember that since the present troubles began, not a single member of any of the forces of the Crown was molested or interfered with in any way whatever within the borders of the parish'. Fr Sheehan relayed the 'extreme sympathy and regret' of the British military. On 5 January, following a court martial in Cork, Hart was found guilty of the offences with which he was charged, but was insane at the time of their commission. He was committed to an asylum. His subsequent whereabouts were not traced by Fr O'Donovan.[45]

On 30 December 1920, Windle ended his year with a reference to Edith and Ireland: 'Vile day. Edith poorly rash and pains . . . Labour in England making a pompous ass of itself about Ireland – Why can't someone put a ring in its asinine tongue – meantime *Cork Examiner* smashed because it published the bishop's pastoral and Cork Corporation passed resolution against him. Holy Ireland!' Writing to Mgr Parkinson on 22 January 1921, Windle reviewed the terrible events of the previous few weeks.

> The print [press] is very interesting – I knew Canon Magner slightly; he was a fine type of the real priest – also too few in Ireland. My personal friend was and is Canon Roche (Paris and Louvain *not* Maynooth) who D.G. is still in the land of the living. I had a letter from my daughter Nora who is in Cork looking after her late sister's children for a short time. She says (and I corroborate it from my own knowledge) that the way the priests go on is enough to drive anyone out of the church. Here is the chain of events.
>
> 1 – The Bishop preached against murder on either side and issued an edict excommunicating *ipso facto* murderers and ambushers.
> 2 – When this was read 100 men got up and walked out of Mass at the principal parish church.
> 3 – The Corporation's 95% Catholic in name passed a resolution censuring the Bishop.
> 4 – The Catholic daily paper [*Cork Examiner*] published an article supporting the Bishop.
> 5 – Men went in to the printing office of this paper and smashed the machines doing £40,000 worth of damage – because the paper supported the Bishop.
> 6 – No protest that I have heard of.
>
> How much longer can Ireland be called a Catholic country? [46]

Windle wrote to Sr Monica on 12 September 1921: 'It is a great pity but it is part of that gigantic humbug, the holiness of Ireland which deludes so many faithful souls in other lands. In my opinion the educated, thinking man or woman who can keep his or her faith in Ireland can hardly lose it elsewhere. Thank God I emerged with mine comparatively uninjured and never, if I can help it, will I ever set foot in that island.' He ended his letter: 'Other men's daughters have always been much more devoted to me than my own ever were. But that is the way of the world.'

Windle and his Daughters

Mary, Windle's married daughter, fell ill in winter 1920. On 9 November Windle received a cable from his son-in-law, J.J. Horgan: '"Mary dangerously ill. Encephalitis lethargica took her." Dreadfully upset.' Her father wrote again in his diary on 10 November: 'Cable "no change" but as we were going to bed news of her death came. God help her husband and children and Edith who loved her beyond anyone but myself and God forgive me if I was ever unfair or unkind to her at time of estrangement or any other time.' The following morning, 11 November, he wrote: 'A fine day but miserable one for us.'[47] Later that evening, he wrote to Sr Monica: 'Last night I got cablegram saying that my elder [and married] daughter was dead. I do not know how I am going to stand up under this. After my wife there is no one I shall miss so much. There's three little children and a most loving excellent husband – Oh, why is this thing when old people (pining to die) hang on and scoundrels fester in the streets? God knows and that is my only comfort – It is well with the child – but oh it is ill with me and how am I to bear the heartache? Do pray for Mary Horgan and ask the prayers of your community and do not forget her broken hearted father.'[48]

Madoline, her only daughter, was five at the time of her mother's death. When Mary first fell ill, she was sent to stay for a while with an aunt, Jennie Hogan, who lived in Douglas. Nobody in the family ever told Madoline when she was allowed to come home that her mother had died: 'In those times, such things simply weren't discussed,' she recalled over eighty years later.[49] In that regard, the world has changed for the better.

Windle wrote a letter of condolence to John J. Horgan: 'It is just a year since I left Cork and bid good-bye to Mary. Till that moment I did not really know that she was so fond of me as was the case and now I shall never see her again in this world.'[50] Windle was devastated by her death. He had reason to have many deep regrets about the way he had treated her. While it was most unusual for him to lose his composure and his reserve, he did so when he wrote to Sr Monica on 9 December: 'There had [been] a lot of trouble in my life and all sudden. My little boy – a baby but a boy can be a great loss – died after less than 24 hours illness. My first wife died half an hour after . . . My terror is lest I should lose my wife for we are everything to one another. Please make it a special subject of prayer that she may be spared to me.'[51] Windle wrote forlornly in his diary on 24 December: 'One year since we arrived Toronto knowing no one. But many good friends and much kindness and success during this year for which God be praised.' He concluded: 'Mary gone – a bad blow and dreadful for Nora, children and husband.'[52]

Some months later, Edith, a most thoughtful and resourceful person, took practical steps to try to ensure that Horgan might meet another suitable partner. Mary Brind, Windle's former secretary, worked for Paramount Film Studios in London where he had kept a fatherly eye on her progress. Before his daughter's death, he wrote to Sr Monica on 23 September 1920, describing Brind as 'a genuinely good girl and I am sure has never had a doubt [about religion] cross her mind . . . She is an artless, lovable creature who will make an ideal wife and will, I hope, get a good Catholic husband. Any way she is in excellent hands though her father, nominally Catholic, has no religion. But he has gone back to his Indian fastnesses.'[53] Horgan, probably through Edith, met Brind some time later. On 2 February 1923, Windle wrote to Sr Monica of their engagement: 'I was not greatly surprised at the news about Mary and I knew that it was a pet project of my wife's and her manoeuvres are at times successful. I was a little surprised at her accepting him but she did not like work – few girls do – and he can and will make her very comfortable [says he will send on a letter she had written] . . . I hope she will be happy and not sacrificed on the altar of the grandchildren which have been my wife's objects of solicitude and on whose behalf she has spread her nets. My interests are entirely in Mary and if she is happy alright; if not, I shall be greatly upset.'[54] Windle wrote to her again on 22 March: 'My Mary is to be married on April 26th so please say a prayer for her happiness on that day. She is a darling and loves me better than anybody but my wife and I hope, as in a sense I am the cause of this marriage – at least it would never have taken place but for me and my relations with her – that it may turn out happily. I have my fears and hope they may be baseless. It is a pang to me to think that I am never likely to see Mary again.'[55] Windle wrote again on 10 May: 'My Mary was married on the 26th of last month and I do most earnestly hope she will be happy. I had a letter from her written at 12.45 am on that day saying she was very happy and loved me more than ever so I hope she may have a happy married life and as she has been able to take the man I do not see why she would not for it is certain in that his least desirable characteristics are mostly external.' Windle then allowed himself a reflection, perhaps ironic, in which he contrasted the female and male minds: 'But the female mind is a dark, impenetrable jungle around the outskirts of which, holding his breath in awe and terror, the male may timidly walk but enter which he never can. How different to the airy, sunny, breezy even, glades, like unto a great cathedral, of the simple male mind so pervious to vision?'[56] One would like to think that the last sentence was written with a sense of irony and self-mockery. Mary continued to write to Windle, and, on 2 August, he wrote again to Sr Monica: 'As to Mary she has loathed Cork ever since she began to live there and long before she knew me or ever imagined that she would come to live there. So that no influence of mine is in that decision. I hope she will be happy but I have my fears. They are a vile people tattling and small-minded and I fear Mary will give her visitors short shrift. However there she is and there she has to live and as I have told her she should make the best of it for she has a lovely house and garden at any rate and a generous husband tho' I like him not.'[57] On 6 September, he added: 'Mary gets on all right with her husband – which is the main thing after all, but loathes Cork and its people and no wonder for ever there was a place where every prospect pleases – and it does – and where man is vile that is it and except Belfast which is viler even in its own way – you can't beat Cork. Yet it is poor Japan that gets the earthquakes.'[58]

John Horgan and Mary Brind had two children, David and Joan. They continued the tradition of running an open house with large social gatherings, great hospitality and conviviality. He founded the Cork Drama Society in 1925, was active in the local literary society, was the Irish correspondent for *The Round Table* and was chairman of the Cork Opera House. They gave hospitality to Arnold Bax and Sir John Barbirolli and to prominent Irish actors. The Horgans were patrons of the sculptor, Seamus Murphy, and the painter Patrick Hennessy stayed at Lacaduv for a long period while impecunious.[59] Mary Brind, who was much younger than her husband, was a source of great strength throughout their marriage. In the 1940s when John Horgan, having convinced himself that he had made a bad mistake in a legal case and fell into a deep depression, was persuaded by his wife to write a book to help him overcome his illness: *Parnell to Pearse*, published in 1949, was the outcome. Horgan died on 21 July 1967 aged eighty-six.

Madoline described her stepmother as a very good and loving person who helped open her young eyes to many things. She had a progressive outlook and strongly encouraged her stepdaughter to study medicine: 'I was always grateful for her help and encouragement,' she recalled in 2008. Mary Brind died on 22 October 1972. Madoline studied medicine at UCC and graduated as a doctor in 1939. She visited her stepmother, Edith, in Toronto and was very warmly received. Madoline liked Canada and applied for a medical position there. But she decided to return to Europe just before the outbreak of the Second World War. She worked in a hospital in London throughout and survived the blitz. In 1941, she married St John O'Connell, and after the war returned to Cork. The couple had three children, John, Kate and Michael. Her son, John, died when he was fifty-four.[60] Her husband died in 1996.

What fate befell Windle's youngest daughter, Nora? After leaving home during the First World War, she had worked in London. Her father wrote to Sr Monica on 6 July 1923: 'It is possible that I may have my daughter over here for a year as she has got engaged to be married – No, not very satisfactory. In my opinion except with very young people no man has a right to ask a woman to marry her unless he can follow up his request to the words "How soon"? This man has nothing to marry on, and she seems to want to wait like a fool, as I think, at her age for she is 34. However you can do nothing with women and as I have no mind to go on financing her in London and she is incapable of making an income she must e'en come over here I suppose tho' she is not the sort that conduces to a happy home. It is many years since I came to the conclusion that children are no catch but all do not seem to think so.'

Nora came to Toronto to stay with the Windles in early 1924. Windle wrote to Sr Monica on 31 March 1924 that she was going back to marry her fiancé, named Thomas, from Guernsey, who was 'no great match but he seems a decent chap and is a convert'. At Nora's wedding in 1925, Madoline, then aged ten, was a bridesmaid. The couple had two sons, Paul and Alan. The marriage was not a success. In a letter to Sr Monica, in December 1927, Windle wrote: 'I am of course in considerable anxiety about my daughter Nora for, though (as an experienced teacher of girls you will know how often this happens) she never has got anything like as close to me as other young women of whom I have written to you, of course she is my only surviving child. She seems to have had no sort of luck all her life and tho' contrary to my own fears, she insisted on marrying her husband I doubt if she is really happy tho' she is too loyal to say she isn't. Of course she was over thirty and ought to have known what she was doing and when I discovered that she was set on the affair I did all I could for her but always with a feeling that it was a mistake as I still feel that it was.'[61] Windle was correct in the latter surmise. Her husband left her to raise their two sons on her own. Nora lived in Guernsey until the outbreak of the Second World War, narrowly escaping the German invasion of the island in June 1940. She moved with her children to London, and saw Madoline frequently throughout the war years. They became good friends. Madoline had the height of regard for her and for the manner in which she coped with having to raise a family as a single parent. Nora died in 1983. She was ninety-six.

Windle's Final Years

Just over half a year after Mary's death, Windle made his final return trip to England in summer 1921. On 15 June, he wrote to Sr Monica: 'My foot is on my native heath, and shall not finally leave it, D.V. until it has been planted on Scottish soil in Glasgow.' This may appear to be in contradiction to earlier portrayals of himself as being an Irishman. In reality, he was exuberantly expressing to a close friend his immediate emotion at landing in England, his 'native heath'. While he was not eschewing his Irish identity, he had had a significant rethink about his life since moving to Canada. Ireland, in his view, had been the wasteland years. It was surprising, however, that he did not travel to Cork to meet his recently widowed son-in-law and his three grandchildren. He did not make the journey and there is no evidence that they travelled to meet him in London. However, he did express his enthusiasm to visit Glasgow as soon as his foot was on dry land. He wrote to Sr Monica: 'I write at once to assure you that I *am* in England and intend D.V. eventually to be in Scotland. I still hope to sail from Glasgow but any way I shall be there and reserve all news until we meet.'[62] Confirming his intention to see Sr Monica, he wrote on 20 June that the visit would enable him 'to introduce my wife to you and I want you to know the best and dearest woman God ever made'. Windle wrote again on 5 July that he had gone to Lourdes with Canon Roche. There he had 'a most interesting and beneficial time and prayed frequently for you.'[63] Sr Monica wrote in the biography that the shrine had not, possibly because of the crowds, impressed him that much, and that he did not find the atmosphere conducive to prayer: 'And he could not close his eyes to the irritating fact that Jews had commercialized the place.'[64]

Upon his return from France, Windle stayed a few days at Oscott with his friend Mgr Parkinson. The Windles met the Humphreys, went to Harrogate to relax and saw other friends and then travelled to Dowanhill where Edith at last got to meet Sr Monica. Nothing is recorded of the meeting. The couple sailed from Glasgow on the *Cassandra*, accompanied by Dr Stenhouse, his friend and medical adviser. Upon his return to Toronto, Windle wrote to Sr Monica on 8 September: 'I admit that, though I like Toronto and the people are most kind, it is a bit of a wrench to leave England. However my job is very obviously here for the present and must be stuck to.' Windle never returned to England. However, he had at least one opportunity to do so permanently in 1924 when he was invited by his old friend Cardinal Bourne to become the general secretary of the Catholic Truth Society (CTS) of England. 'Did you know that Cardinal Bourne invited me quite lately,' he wrote to Sr Anne Hardman on 10 June 1924, 'to come over and take charge of it [CTS England].[65] I refused with due gratitude for a variety of reasons.'[66] But he had taken over the presidency of the Catholic Truth Society of Canada for a time and had been very active on its behalf. He was also vice chairman of the board of St Michael's Hospital, a professor in the university and one of the most sought after lecturers on Catholic subjects in North America.[67]

Despite his busy schedule, Windle could not entirely shake off his interest in Ireland. As the country moved towards civil war in spring 1922, he wrote on 15 April to Parkinson: 'Bp. Kelly of Ross (one of the few respectable clerics in Ireland) told a cousin of mine a short time ago that he felt sure that things would go from bad to worse in Ireland until both sides asked England for the love of God to come in and restore peace. From the moment that Lloyd George took the line he did I felt sure that this was his policy and whatever now happens he has the whole civilised world with him.' Windle quoted a US newspaper which stated that Ireland had killed the 'noble amongst nations' idea. He felt that it was a bad thing for the Church 'which is being made responsible for most of this and tho' I would not breathe it to the enemy is for once not unjustly accused'. In his opinion, 'but this is strictly *entre nous* Maynooth will have to be extirpated to make Ireland Christian not to say Catholic and I have heard Irish priests say much the same'. Windle, in the same letter, expressed the wish 'and tho' I would much rather be in England, I can't help feeling that when every door there remained closed no matter how hard I knocked this one [Toronto] flew wide open without a word'.[68]

On 11 June 1922, he sent another letter to Parkinson: 'A cousin of mine sent me a letter (they dare not post them in Ireland now) through an English source in which she tells me that in the next parish but one to that in which I lived – both of us know it intimately – the murder gang brought a few months ago a man to the C.C. (a rabid republican like most of these young wild asses) made him hear his confession and give him absolution and then shot their victim under the priest's nose. He is said to have lost his mind but I expect never had much. Only *sub sigillo* would I reveal it to you and the few I can trust but have long believed that if Maynooth continues it is all up with the Church [in] Ireland. It is a sorry story and is doing untold harm here and no doubt everywhere.'[69]

The emergence of the Irish Free State in 1922 – home rule by another guise – did not please Windle greatly if the following is anything to judge by; writing to Sr Monica on 10 February 1923, he said: 'I do at times grizzle when I think that I have worked hard at education for all my life yet am as poor as a rat and if my health broke down and the vile reptiles now running Ireland refused to pay my pension which, seeing what they are, is always on the cards there would be nothing for me but the chilliest kind of penury.'[70]

Thankfully for Windle's peace of mind, his pension continued to be paid and the troubles in Ireland ceased to play a central part in his daily life. His surviving correspondence with Mgr Henry Parkinson – which might be taken as an example – contained no further references to Ireland. In July 1924, Windle was devastated by the news that his friend of

over forty years, Mgr Parkinson, had died suddenly, cruelly having heard
that he was in the best of health a week before. He had sung High Mass
on Corpus Christi, and carried the Blessed Sacrament in the procession.
The following day, he was taken into hospital and operated upon for his
appendix. Windle wrote to Sr Monica on 20 July: 'Heart failure (he was
74) carried him off in a couple of days, and with him goes almost the last
of my real old friends. I shed bitter tears over his death for it takes away
the last priest to whom I could write with perfect freedom and who was
always willing (and how able!) to help me with a philosophical
problem.'[71] He returned to his sense of loss in another letter on 10 August:
'Parkinson's death was a heavy blow, he having been one of the two old
friends left to me, and curiously enough the other [John Humphreys], as I
have since heard from him, was at death's door and given up by his
doctors the very day that Parkinson died – seventy-four and double pneumonia. I cannot understand how he didn't, but *Deo gratias* he did.'[72]

In a letter to Sr Monica on 23 January 1927, Windle reflected on the
three phases of his life: 'Like *omnia Gallia* it is in *tres partes* since I took my
degree. Birmingham where I really made the University, and cannot say
that I got any great amount of gratitude for it! The Governing Body there
(*very civic*) looked on the University as a civic office, the Principal as
Permanent Head Official, and though they were always civil I do think
that they thought we professors were extra able Head Clerks. Anyway I
got the Faith there.' He developed that idea more fully in another letter to
Sr Monica on 4 May 1928: 'Birmingham with all modesty I may say, I
made, for it never would, or at least not at the time nor for long after, have
come into existence but for me, a fact which Joseph Chamberlain stated
in a public speech. All the same I never got a great deal of recognition
there and when I left they sent me a vote of thanks (literally) typed on a
half sheet of ordinary note paper. The weak point of that University was
that it was too like a Corporation Department because it was created by
men with the Birmingham Corporation spirit burnt into them. They were
always polite but the Board was the Corporation; the Principal was the
Town Clerk and the Professors were the officers like the Medical Officer
of Health and so on not altogether a pleasant position for them.'

The second phase of his life was a bitter experience: 'Cork – I often
wonder why I was sent to waste, so it seems to me, 15 years, with the
most horrible people in the world devoid of generosity, gratitude,
common honesty and ordinary decency towards one another where in
any six months I heard or heard of more and crueller detraction than in
twenty years of Birmingham. Why are there no conversions in Ireland?
How could there be? If an educated man lives there and keeps his faith,
he will never lose it elsewhere.'

The third phase, in Canada, was the most positive and fulfilled: 'Toronto from the University point of view is perfection. Instead of the low intrigues and hidden insults which made a purgatory out of Cork, genuine brotherly friendliness and real recognition of anything that one does. Why how strange that I should have to come to America, whether the States or Canada, to get real appreciation and gratitude which is a thing which I have tried myself never to forget for it is so rare and I personally have had so little of it that I value even the smallest exhibition.'[73] Windle, comparing Toronto with Cork, wrote: 'No vile intrigues and mephitic lies such as formed the Irish atmosphere and no civic patronage as in Birmingham. It is truly wonderful how my lectures continue to draw though I had fully made up my mind to a much smaller attendance this time partly on account of the subject, which I fancied would not be so attractive, and partly because this is my seventh appearance and Lo! At my third lecture last Friday not only was every seat full but no standing room and people sitting all down the steps and filling the doorways. It is really most encouraging and makes me warm all over with a kind of genial glow.'[74]

When Windle chose to talk about Cork, as he did above, he was quite unrestrained in his bitterness and resentment at the pain and loss of time his sojourn had cost him, but no more so than when he wrote to Sr Monica on 23 January 1927: 'As to Cork and N.U.I., which I helped to hatch, the less said the better. The N.U. I. was and I suppose is the most utterly detestable thing that man ever had to do with. Of course Birrell, that master of cynical opportunism, was responsible for that but I never went to any of its meetings without coming away pining for a moral carbolic bath. I had one happy moment in connection with that fifteen years – it was the last when I stepped on the steamer and said good-bye to the whole abominable, concatenation. Then Toronto – well, a prophet – if I may venture so far – not without honour save in his own country and here I have had nothing but kindness and generous appreciation from the moment I started work down to this day.'[75] Windle's experiences in Ireland coloured his attitude towards Catholicism in North America. Referring to the public reaction to one of his articles in *Commonweal*, he wrote to Sr Anne Hardman on 8 August 1927 about Irish-American Catholics: '*Entre nous* you can have little idea of the venom of the Irish American – a large slice of Catholic America. They denounce the paper because I wrote for it being known to be anti-Republican *qua* Ireland. A generation will have to die out and wilt in Purgatory before this vile spirit begins to be laid. But mark! Much of it is due to the fact that these vile creatures live by the viler rags which they write to stir up bitterness. That they are – in name at least – Catholics make them worse. But enough of these pestilent beasts!'[76]

For all his sophistication, Windle was a British Empire man at heart;
he found it difficult to live in an egalitarian, multi-ethnic Canadian
democracy. It was not only Irish-Americans Windle found to be unac-
ceptable. Windle exhibited strong ethnic and religious bias against Jews.
On 4 May 1928, he told Sr Monica of his trip to Mt Clemens: 'As a place
it is the dullest and beastliest I have ever been in and the country round
flat as possible and utterly uninteresting. But the Sanitorium run by
Sisters of St Joseph of Cincinnati in conjunction with the city hospital is
all that could possibly be desired. Clean, quiet, well-managed, excellent
baths and massage, good well cooked food and *no filthy Jews* the bane of
most spas over here. Incidentally did it ever occur to you that when
Christus humiliavit seipus admortem autem crucis he had for us the additional humiliation of being a Jew? I have known nice Jews but if you
could see the things which collect at Saratoga and such like places and
who throng New York you would pine as I have often done for the clean
civilised negro in preference. Truly as now experienced a vile race.'[77]
Windle's attitude to Irish-Americans and to Jews demonstrated that, no
matter how widely read he was, he lacked tolerance and respect for political and religious diversity, living as he did in a closed, confessional world
of Catholic triumphalism.

Windle suffered a stroke in June 1928 which forced him to reduce
his professional commitments. Although he made a good recovery, and
regained his speech and his mobility, it was necessary for the couple to
move closer to the college. The Basilian order came to the couple's
rescue; they were given the use of an apartment, adjacent to St
Michael's, at 5 Elmsley Place. Fr Carr invited the Windles to occupy the
accommodation, at a rent they could afford, and for the remainder of
their respective lives: 'Why is it that I have never met that kind of thing
east of the Atlantic,' he asked.[78] On 14 September 1928, he wrote that
the new house was ideally suited for somebody who had had a stroke.
He merely had to cross the road to get into the church and go through
it to get to the college. In three minutes, he was in Queen's Park, 'a
lovely spot with trees and flowers and seats, so that my "times" are laid
in pleasant places, and here I can stay, even if, which please God is, I
hope, unlikely, incapacitated'.[79]

Writing on 26 October 1928 to a young relative, Geoffrey Cullwick,
who was working as an academic in Vancouver, Windle revealed what
he most missed having to live in Toronto: 'And we very much like the
house – a little too spacious but full of comfort and conveniences. What
I chiefly envy you is your proximity to the sea which as an inlander
perhaps does not mean much to you, but as we were brought up by it
for 25 years I simply pine for it and here I am fixed more than a

thousand miles from it and in no way comforted by a preposterous mud hole of a lake pretending to be what it isn't.'[80] On 6 February 1929, Windle wrote what appears to have been his last letter to Sr Monica, telling her that he had made 'a wonderful recovery'. But he had little or no appetite. He continued to walk and to keep up his weight. His wife had also got over a recent fall.[81] However, Windle took ill on Sunday 9 February 1929, dying on the 14th. Having left specific instructions for his funeral service, it was announced at the requiem Mass on the 16th that, in accordance with his wishes, there were to be prayers but no words of praise at the service. At his further request, he was buried in the habit of the Franciscan Third Order of which he had been a member since 1883. Six students from St Michael's were his pallbearers. He was buried in Mount Hope cemetery.

When news of Windle's death reached Ireland, resolutions of con-dolence and votes of sympathy to Lady Windle were passed by university bodies, the NUI Senate and many organisations on which the late president had served as a committee member. Bishop Cohalan of Cork presided at a Solemn High Requiem Mass in the Honan Chapel. John J. Horgan and children were in the congregation together with the architect of the Honan, J.F. McMullen. President Merriman attended as did the registrar, Alfred O'Rahilly, other members of the academic staff and a large body of students dressed in academicals. D.P. Fitzgerald, who succeeded Windle to the professorship of Anatomy in 1909, wrote in an appreciation in the Cork Examiner: 'A good Catholic, an efficient administrator, and a strict disciplinarian, Sir Bertram possessed an innate courtesy and refinement of manner never altogether forgotten even on occasions when some lapse might be human and pardonable; while a highly cultured and fluent writer he was a lucid and forcible exponent of his favourite theories and studies.'[82]

Fitzgerald argued that Windle had transformed University College Cork: 'During his 15 years here many salutary changes took place. Our gates have been flung wide open to everyone; the whole atmosphere has grown more congenial; and one feels that the College is at last our very own. Sir Bertram took a big share in this good work, and so his Presidency of University College, Cork, will be an abiding annal in its history.'[83] Writing as a colleague, Fitzgerald said: 'To those who had close relations with Sir Bertram, he showed himself a man of method and of system. Never markedly demonstrative in display of friendship, and at times somewhat cold, abrupt, and hasty in manner, yet he had always a sympathetic ear towards anything tending to the advance-ment of the College. Well versed in the rules of academic discipline, he carried them out to the very letter in discharging the many duties of his post. To some people the wall of Presidential authority around him appeared a little too formidable, but as long as humanity is what it is, there must be such.'[84]

Fitzgerald did not allow the opportunity to pass without mentioning the impact on him of the rise in militant nationalism: 'The advent of militant political activities in this country seemed to have a disturbing influence on a temperament essentially constitutional and academic; and the onset of warring elements, we feel sure, antedated his retirement from the Presidency by some years.'[85]

Perhaps the last words of this study are best left to Edith. After her husband's death, she wrote to Sr Monica on 5 November: 'Bertie had frequently spoken of retiring or seeking some other work – anything to get away from the hotbed of mistrust, opposition and powerlessness to get anything done in Cork. The last few years there were a bitter trial – intrigue after intrigue – every good intention and effort to make the University a success and prosperous was frustrated . . . and the rising party of Sin [sic] Féiners with all their political intrigue and rebellion helped to make matters worse.'[86]

In defence of Windle's political ideas, Edith further explained how nationalistic her late husband had been as a young man: 'First a young man in the early days of the Nationalist party – full of ideals of what Ireland might become if properly governed. All the years he was in Birmingham he worked and strove to help the cause of Ireland – an ardent Home Ruler – keenly interested in Gaelic and always ready to champion the cause of the down-trodden Ireland.'[87]

She then spoke of the years of striving to build up 'a University in Cork at the same time keeping by all the means in his power to make the country prosperous from its Industrial and commercial sides. I know better than anyone how hard he worked and how little he talked compared with the average Irish enthusiast. He would probably have been a happier man if he had, like his predecessor, Sir Roland Blennerhassett – accepted his position as President of the College and let it rest at that.'[88] In other words, do little or nothing as Sir Roland did so stylishly.

Edith, with brutal frankness, gave her assessment of the shattered hopes of her late husband: 'You are not Irish Sister Monica so I can say what I feel to you – my husband was too honest a man to succeed in Ireland – because he was so honest he was mistrusted on all sides – all his bright hopes were shattered and as far as Ireland was concerned his heart was broken. He lost all interest in the country after he left it and rarely spoke of Ireland. Like Jerusalem she always stones her prophets – most of her great leaders I fancy had their hearts broke.'[89] Windle carried that hurt and sadness to his grave.[90]

Notwithstanding the huge obstacles that he encountered in his fifteen years in Ireland, Sir Bertram Coghill Alan Windle made a very significant contribution to the development of university education at a local and national level. His role in the building up of UCC was unique, and his record of achievement, some might argue, has yet to be surpassed.

Notes and References

1   Ann Keogh, 'A Study in Philanthropy: Sir Bertram Windle, Sir John O'Connell, Isabella Honan and the Building of the Honan Chapel, University College Cork', unpublished MA thesis, University College Cork, 2004. My original focus studied the building of the Honan Chapel and the ideas that inspired the venture. I was very interested at first in the history of the stained glass windows of Harry Clarke and the making of the chapel's other artefacts. Professor M.J. O'Kelly's *The Honan Chapel, University College Cork* (Cork University Press, 1966 [revised edition] [1946]) is an invaluable source, as is also Sir John O'Connell's *Collegiate Chapel, Cork: Some Notes on the Building and on the Ideals which Inspired It* (Dublin: Guy, 1916; republished Cork University Press, 1932. I read more generally in order to discover the artistic, craft and architectural side of the development of Queen's College/UCC under Sir Bertram Windle, the president of the college from 1904 to 1919. Very often I read works by art historians, an approach that appeared to me to lack a broader historical context. The emphasis in that material was on the history of the arts and crafts movement and the Irish cultural revival of the late nineteenth and early twentieth centuries. My academic search led to Isabella Honan, the last surviving member of a wealthy Cork merchant family and to Sir John O'Connell, her solicitor and executor. Together with Sir Bertram Windle, each played a vital role in the provision of the Honan Scholarships (awarded on a non-denominational basis) and scientific buildings, the foundation and upkeep of the Honan Hostel and the construction and furnishing of the collegiate chapel of St Finn Barr. All three were strong Catholics. The chapel was built to replace a small oratory in the former St Anthony's Hall and to provide a suitable and fitting place of worship for the Catholic students and staff of UCC. They had a shared interest in the provision of equality of access to third-level education for Catholic students. The Honan Hostel provided subsidised accommodation for students from that religious background.

2   Professor John A. Murphy's *The College: A History of Queen's/University College Cork* (Cork University Press) was not published until 1995. Frederick O'Dwyer's *The Architecture of Deane and Woodward* (Cork University Press) appeared in 1997.

3   O'Connell, *Collegiate Chapel, Cork*.

4   Kelly, *The Honan Chapel*; this invaluable booklet has gone through a number of editions.

5   Paul Larmour, *The Arts and Crafts Movement in Ireland* (Belfast: Friar's Bush Press, 1992); see also a much earlier work: Robert Elliott, *Art and Ireland* (Dublin: Sealy, Bryers & Walker, 1911) [with preface by Edward Martyn].

6   Virginia Teehan and Elizabeth Wincott Heckett (eds), *The Honan Chapel: A Golden Vision* (Cork University Press, 2004).

7   John J. Horgan, *Parnell to Pearse* was first published in 1949. It was republished in 2009 together with a most helpful biographical sketch by his nephew, the journalist and academic, John Horgan. See his 'John J. Horgan: Biographical Introduction', in the new edition published by University College Dublin (UCD) Press, pp. vii–xxxv.

8   We are very grateful to Ms Clare Walsh, Archivist, British Province, Sisters of Notre Dame, England and Wales, for supplying us with biographical information on Sr Monica.

9   Clare Walsh also supplied a copy of the relevant pages in Sr Dorothy Gillies, *A Pioneer of Catholic Teacher-Training in Scotland: Sister Mary of St Wilfrid (Mary Adela Lescher, 1846–1926)* (Carmelite Monastery, Quidenham, Norfolk, 1978), pp. 53–4.

10 Sr Jean Bunn, Sister of Notre Dame, 266 Woolton Road, Liverpool, to Dermot Keogh, 29 December 2004. She also included a note written by Sr Monica. It read: 'Many letters from distinguished people came to me when Glasgow University awarded me the degree of DSc in 1917. Sr Mary of St Wilfrid told me to keep such letters. Their number increased when I received the LLD of Glasgow and the Neill Medal of the Royal Society of Edinburgh. My work on Amoeba was responsible for yet more. It became impossible to find accommodation. I cut out the autographs and pasted them into this book.' Sr Jean Bunn commented in her letter: 'It isn't wise to speculate without some evidence, but mindful of some of the strictures in religious life up to the Second Vatican Council in the early sixties, I have to say I get a goose pimple or two at "it became impossible to find accommodation".' Sr Jean Bunn kindly sent me two pages of the pages on which Sr Monica pasted on the signatures of those people who had written to her. Among the signatures are those of Bertram C. Windle, dated 1929 and a second signature dated 1919. She also has the signature of 'Edith Mary Windle, commonly known as just – "Ma Edith"'.

11 Sr Monica Taylor, *Sir Bertram Windle: A Memoir* (London: Longman, Green & Co., 1932), pp. 227–8; see also diary entry, 24 March 1913, Box 2, Bertram Windle Papers, Special Collections, Birmingham University (hereafter BWP).

12 See file of letters from Sr Monica to Windle and second file of letters from Windle to Sr Monica, Windle's Personal Correspondence, Box 9, BWP.

13 Windle to Sr Monica , 7 March 1923, Windle's Personal Correspondence, Box 9, BWP.

14 Windle to Sr Monica , 31 March 1923, Windle's Personal Correspondence, Box 9, BWP.

15 Sr Monica note, 20 July 1923, Windle's Personal Correspondence, Box 9, BWP.

16 Ibid.

17 John Humphreys (1850–1937) was secretary of the Birmingham Dental School from the 1880s. He helped set up theDental Students' Society. Together with Windle, he was one of the founders of Birmingham University. He was the father of Professor Humphrey Francis Humphreys, a vice-chancellor of Birmingham University. John Humphreys shared Windle's deep interest in history and wrote on Catholic martyrs in the sixteenth century.

18 We are grateful to Philippa Bassett, Senior Archivist, Special Collections, Birmingham University for providing us with this information. Ms Bassett also provided me with information on the John Humphreys collection.

19 The UCC Archives contain the minute books of the Honan Hostel, correspondence of Sir Bertram Windle, books of newspaper cuttings, annual presidential reports and related files. The UCC chaplaincy has the Honan Book of Seals and attendance book of the governors of the Honan Hostel. The Secretary's Office located early files on the Honan scholarships which continue to be awarded annually. There is also material in the National Archives of Ireland (NAI), in the files of the Chief Secretary's Office. Wills relevant to the study were also located in the NAI. The archives of the Irish Franciscans had correspondence with Windle and other material relevant to the purchase and running of St Anthony's Hall/Honan Hostel. Windle letters were also

located in the William Walsh Papers, Dublin Archdiocesan Archives. The records of the Joshua Clarke Studios were made available by the Abbey Stained Glass Studio. The Harry Clarke and Thomas Bodkin Papers in Trinity College Dublin were also consulted. There was also primary source material of relevance in the University of Birmingham and in the Westminster Archdiocesan Archives. The other primary sources consulted are listed in the bibliography.

1. THE EARLY YEARS, 1858–1904

1   See Reginald Jocelyn correspondence, Published Memoir and Associated Materials, Box 13, BWP.
2   See Taylor, *Windle*, p. 1.
3   Ibid., p. 8.
4   Edith Windle to Sr Monica, 5 November 1929, Published Memoir and Associated Materials, Box 13, BWP.
5   On 23 April 1930, Reginald Windle wrote to Sr Monica, setting out part of the family history: 'When the Admiral retired 1820? he settled in Cheltenham (his family Estate Coghill Hall, Knaresboro, had been sold by his bachelor elder brother whom he succeeded) whence he died his eldest son (my mother's brother) Joselyn retired from the 59th Foot, collected up. 7 or 8 sisters and removed them to Castle Townshend, Co. Cork. This was at the time of the potato famine 1847? My mother returned to England and married in 1854 the Revd. S.A.W. [indle] Vicar of Mayfield Staffs where we were both born. Sir Jocelyn married his cousin, the Hon Katherine Plunket (whose mother was a Miss Bushe) had a family of 6 born in Ireland, he Sir J. lived 50 years and died in Ireland. His successor, Sir Egerton married his cousin an Irish girl and had a family who were born and lived all their lives in Ireland. But my mother and her brothers and sisters were [born] English – *voila tout.*'
6   Windle's mother was also descended from Colonel Tobias Cramer from Lower Germany. In 1609, he entered the service of King James I and was sent to Ireland where he settled. A descendant, Hester Cramer, married Sir John Coghill, from a prominent Yorkshire family, who had settled in Ireland and held 'many eminent legal situations'. They had four children, two boys and two girls. James and Marmaduke had distinguished lives. The latter represented the University of Dublin in parliament for more than thirty years. Coghill became Chancellor of the Irish Exchequer. Hester, sister of Marmaduke and James, married Oliver Cramer (a cousin). Their son, John Balthasar, became heir to the Marmaduke estates. The other daughter married twice but had no children. In those circumstances, the Cramers received the title of James Coghill's estates on condition that they took the name Coghill. Taylor, *Windle*, pp. 3–5.
7   The admiral had married the sister of his daughter's husband, Charles Bushe. The latter was the rector of Castlehaven. Taylor, *Windle*, p. 5.
8   She was the 'aunt of the famous Sir Philip Sydney', and 'therefore tenth in descent from Lord Burghley'. Taylor, *Windle*, p. 2.
9   Gifford Lewis, *Edith Somerville: A Biography* (Dublin: Four Courts Press, 2005), pp. 22–4.
10 Taylor, *Windle*, p. 2.
11 See Reginald Jocelyn correspondence, 3 March 1930, Published Memoir and Associated Materials, Box 13, BWP.
12 Baptismal Certificate, 4 June 1858, Personal and Family Material of Windle, Box 11, BWP.
13 Ibid.
14 Taylor, *Windle*, p. 1.
15 See document recording details of the births and baptisms of Windle children, Personal and Family Material of Windle, Box 11, BWP; see also Taylor, *Windle*, pp. 6–7.
16 See Reginald Jocelyn correspondence, Published Memoir and Associated Materials, Box 13, BWP.
17 Taylor, *Windle*, p. 6.

18   Edith Windle to Sr Monica, 11 May 1930, Published Memoir and Associated Materials, Box 13, BWP.

19   Edith Windle to Sr Monica, 1 May 1931, Published Memoir and Associated Materials, Box 13, BWP.

20   Edith Windle to Sr Monica, 11 May 1930, Published Memoir and Associated Materials, Box 13, BWP.

21   See Reginald Jocelyn correspondence, 4 April 1930, Published Memoir and Associated Materials, Box 13, BWP. R.J. Windle wrote that 'surviving brother' refers to a brother 'Wilfred Theodore' born in 1866 at Kingstown and died there aged six months in an epidemic of cholera.

22   See Reginald Jocelyn correspondence, 20 September 1930, Published Memoir and Associated Materials, Box 13, BWP.

23   Ibid. On 1 April 1932, he wrote to Sr Monica apologising for not having been in contact for such a long time. He said that they had been away for an extra long time in the summer and 'there has been a lot of sickness and a great deal of worry – A grateful country which I served for 35 years, being drastically cut down the pension which I had earned during those years – for me that was sheer robbery, reduced any one in the future as much as you like, or can, but, when one has been earning a pension since 1886 to reduce it by nearly £100 a year with 4 days' notice of the intention to do so is not a fair deal. If they had asked me to help and suggest what I could give up I should have done my best – but this other method appears to differ very slightly from the behaviour of Bandits – then the £1 fell from Frs. 124 to Frs. 80 and stayed about there for 5 months – *Hinc illae lachrymae* and so did not write – Pardon me for inflicting my troubles on you and please send me a line to say what has happened to the Biography of my late brother, with kind regards, yours sincerely, R.J. Windle.

24   Taylor, *Windle*, p. 6.

25   See Reginald Jocelyn correspondence, Published Memoir and Associated Materials, Box 13, BWP.

26   Ibid.

27   Ibid.

28   Reginald Jocelyn Windle to Sr Monica, 24 October 1929, Published Memoir and Associated Materials, Box 13, BWP. Gives the dates for moving to Liverpool as 1873 or 1874 and to Market Rasen as 1877 or 1878.

29   Ibid.

30   Ibid.

31   Taylor, *Windle*, pp. 15–18.

32   See Reginald Jocelyn correspondence, Published Memoir and Associated Materials, Box 13, BWP.

33   Ibid.

34   Ibid.

35   Taylor, *Windle*, pp. 18–19.

36   John J. Horgan, 'Sir Bertram Windle', *Studies*, vol. xxi (1932), pp. 611–12.

37   See Reginald Jocelyn correspondence, Published Memoir and Associated Materials, Box 13, BWP.

38   Taylor, *Windle*, pp. 21–2.

39   See Reginald Jocelyn correspondence, Published Memoir and Associated Materials, Box 13, BWP.

40   Registrar, School of Physics, TCD, to Sr Monica, 1 April 1930, Personal and Family Material of Windle, Box 11, BWP.

41   Taylor, *Windle*, p. 21.

42   See Reginald Jocelyn correspondence, Published Memoir and Associated Materials, Box 13, BWP.

43   Ibid.

44   Ibid.

The Commissioners who drew up the statutes for the National University of Ireland (NUI) and its colleges. They also made the first appointments: (*back row from left*) Stephen Gwynn, John P. Boland, Alexander Anderson, Bertram Windle, Denis J. Coffey; (*front row from left*) Gen. Sir William F. Butler, the Archbishop of Dublin, William J. Walsh, Rt. Hon. Christopher Palles, Sir John Rhys, Henry Jackson.

Professor Eoin MacNeill: Windle was highly critical of his political judgment.

'Lacaduv', home of Mary (Windle) and John Horgan, Lee Road, Cork.

Douglas Hyde.

Vincent McNamara in his Ireland rugby shirt. In 1911, he began his engineering studies in UCC, and was a member of the college rugby team which won the Charity, Dudley, Munster cups and the League Shield.
He played on the Munster and on the Irish teams in 1914, becoming the first Munster half to play on the Irish team. Enlisting in the Royal Engineers, he died 29 November 1915 at Gallipoli.

Patrick Roche wearing his Olympic shirt. Graduating in engineering from UCC in 1910, he was Irish 100 yard champion 1907, 1908 & 1909. He took part in the 1908 Olympics where he won his heat but lost in the final. He enlisted in the Royal Engineers, in 1914 and was awarded the MC. He died on 25 August 1917 in Baghdad of enteric fever.

Mary Horgan née Windle who died suddenly in 1920.

45   John J. Horgan, 'Sir Bertram Windle: An Appreciation', *University College Cork Session Lists*, 1928–9, pp. 119–20.

46   See Reginald Jocelyn correspondence, Published Memoir and Associated Materials, Box 13, BWP.

47   Ibid.

48   Notes on Sir Bertram Windle. The typed script states that the document had been prepared for an exhibition at Oscott Museum in which Windle was being commemorated. The extensive typescript is based substantially on Sr Monica's biography, according to the Preface. A minute at the top of the Preface page states: 'these papers etc. have been kindly given by Sister Anne Hardman'. See pp. 2–3, Obituary and Appreciation, Published Memoir and Associated Materials, Box 13, BWP.

49   Henry Carr CSB, 'Sir Bertram Windle: The Man and His Work', *Catholic World* 129 (No. 770, May 1929), p. 169, Published Memoir and Associated Materials, Box 11, BWP. See also Henry Carr CSB, book review of Monica Taylor's *Sir Bertram Windle*, in the *Catholic World*, 136 (No. 813, December 1932), pp. 371–2.

50   Edith Windle to Sr Monica, 11 May 1930, Published Memoir and Associated Materials, Box 13, BWP.

51   Carr, 'Sir Bertram Windle', p. 169; offprint with minute From Lady Windle, 13 May 1929, Published Memoir and Associated Materials, Box 13, BWP.

52   Taylor, *Windle*, p. 23.

53   Bertram Windle, *Who's Who of the Oxford Movement* (New York and London: The Century Company, 1926), pp. 44–5. This volume is dedicated to Sr Monica.

54   That is very evident from the work he did to promote the cause of home rule when he returned to Birmingham in the early 1880s. His biographer writes: 'It would be impossible to enumerate, still less to give any adequate account of, the various addresses delivered by Dr Windle on Home Rule and in defence of the Irish National League and the Plan of Campaign.' He was never tired of pointing out the 'profound ignorance of the true causes of Irish discontent shown by Lord Salisbury's government, nor did he cease to urge upon his audiences the desirability of taking Mr Gladstone's advice to study the history of the Irish people'. Taylor, *Windle*, p. 31 ff.

55   Ibid.

56   Edith Windle to Sr Monica, 31 December 1929, Published Memoir and Associated Materials, Box 13, BWP.

57   Taylor, *Windle*, pp. 32–3.

58   Ibid., p. 29.

59   Ibid., pp. 27–8. Very little is known about Madoline Hudson, apart from the fact that she came from Birmingham. Her schoolgirl diary survives in the possession of her granddaughter, Madoline O'Connell. Dating from 1873 when she was about twelve years of age, it continues through some of her early teenage years. It paints a portrait of a precocious, high-spirited, highly intelligent young girl, good at language and with a passion for music. Madoline came from a relatively prosperous and devout family. In the early entries, she appeared to be quite scrupulous and troubled about not having said her morning prayers. She reproaches herself for being disobedient and bold. She confessed on 13 August to being 'o naughty in singing class this afternoon. I did not want to sing seconds and mother said I was to. And then I pulled faces and didn't sing my best. I can't sing alto, nearly so well as Suprano [*sic*]. I am very sorry now, I have been so unkind to mother.'

     While Victorian in tone and highly moralistic, the diary also reveals that Madoline was not without ambition: 'Dear old Diary don't tell anyone but I will be a great singer when I grow up. I must be somebody great' ['You may be a great <u>ass</u>, nothing else', is written at a later date.] She is increasingly conscious of her good looks and, in particular, about her attractive thick hair. She reproaches herself, asking 'God to give me a humble contrite spirit'. ['O you little donkey!' was added at a later date following that entry.] On 11 October she explains that she has been very busy at her boarding school and has neglected filling in her diary. The following day, she said she had finished reading *Lorna Doone* – 'it is a splendid novel – well worth reading'. On 13 October, she wrote: 'Mrs Gibson came to tea today. I danced in the afternoon and had to wear my grey and cerise silk dress. I was so pleased to see Mrs. G. I am going to her house on Friday, her portrait is promised to us!' On 14 October she wrote of the death of 'poor little Fred Whitfield: it is very sad. Archie[?] Chamberlain came after school to see mother, he is grown very tall and his voice is cracking, but I think he looks the same. Mrs Gibson's portrait came this afternoon, it is beautiful. I love her very much, she is very pretty, blue eyes, and lovely hair, she is rather stout, very clever, sings well and has a great talent for drawing and painting, she used to teach it here but as she is now married she can't.' Madoline went to visit Mrs Gibson where she enjoyed herself greatly and saw 'a quantity of beautiful photos and also views of Paris'. Madoline also wrote of going to a lovely party at the Chamberlains: 'I danced a lot with Harry Chamberlain, Meggie, Laura, . . . and Archie once (he isn't bad and awfully tall). Mr Chamberlain spoke to me, and Mr Anderton began singing "I dream of thee, Sweet Madoline".' It is not clear whether the Chamberlains in question were related to Joseph Chamberlain.

Madoline was ever conscious of her growth to womanhood: 'I am getting very vain dear diary isn't it sad. I like to look in the glass at my hair and my face because I perhaps am getting rather good looking. [Then there is an entry from a later date: 'I'm not, I am very middling.'] Now I must and will conquer this, I will put down how many times I look in the glass, and then I shall feel so ashamed if it is a good many times that I shall leave off looking, God helping me.' But she found she could not count the number of times, her conscience always reproaching her. She would place her trust in God's help.

In school, she appeared to do well, writing on 15 October [1873] of having to do the Cambridge exam at Christmas: 'I am afraid I can't pass,' she wrote. She took the examination and passed. Madoline also wrote of studying 'Philosophe'. On 14 February 1874 she wrote of how she was getting on 'very nicely' at school. She was studying French and English, and had begun to learn German which she found 'very difficult'.

She also speaks of the beginnings of her emotional interest in boys. But she also referred to a friend who committed suicide because he had been working too hard for his Oxford examinations. As the diary progresses, one witnesses the emergence of a young, sophisticated woman. She played the piano at a concert at which Harry Chamberlain was present: 'I gave him a nod from the platform.' A few lines further on in the same entry, she continues: 'It is extremely likely that we are all descended from monkeys. It is the Darwinian Theory. Papa does not believe it but I do.'

Unfortunately, the diary, apart from a few fragments, does not continue into adulthood. She records on the last two pages the death of her father in 1881.

60 John Humphreys to Sr Monica, 5 September 1930, Published Memoir and Associated Materials, Box 13, BWP: 'I met Sir Bertram first in 1883 and our friendship remained unbroken until the time of his death. We never had a jar, or the slightest quarrel though we differed somewhat in our religious views. Our connection was one unbroken record of the happiest association.'

61 Taylor, *Windle*, pp. 133–5.
62 Ibid., p. 135 ff.
63 Edith Windle to Sr Monica, 1 May 1931, Published Memoir and Associated Materials, Box 13, BWP.
64 Edith Windle to Sr Monica, 11 May 1930, Published Memoir and Associated Materials, Box 13, BWP.
65 Horgan, 'Sir Bertram Windle: An Appreciation', p. 121.
66 Notes on Sir Bertram Windle, Obituary and Appreciation, Published Memoir and Associated Materials, Box 13, BWP.

67 Francis Gasquet was born on 5 October 1846. He joined the Order of St Benedict and was ordained a priest on 19 December 1871. He became a cardinal on 25 May 1914. He was Vatican archivist and Vatican librarian from 9 May 1919. He was a close friend of Windle's from the time they met in Newcastle. The date is not recorded, but it was probably about 1900. The first letter in the correspondence is 22 February 1902. Gasquet wrote to Windle on 9 June 1906, thanking him for a copy of his recent book: 'but more glad to think that though we don't often meet now we have not forgotten each other – for I can answer for my side.' On 27 August 1903, Gasquet had written to Windle: 'I reciprocate and more than reciprocate all you say. Of the great pleasure your friendship has given me I can truthfully say that there is no one, above acquaintances I have made during many years past, that is more to me in every way than you.'

68 Bertram Windle and Catholic Truth Society of Ireland, *Catholics and Evolution* (Catholic Truth Society of Ireland, 1900). In 1917 his publication *The Church and Science* was awarded the Gunning Prize of the Victoria Institute. In 1919 it was awarded the best book published in support of revealed religion.

69 Mivart, a distinguished biologist, attended King's College, London, from which he intended to go to Oxford. He converted to Catholicism in 1844, being received into the Church by Dr Moore, afterwards president of St Mary's, Oscott. Mivart was automatically denied access to Oxford because he was not an Anglican. He studied at St Mary's, Oscott and at Lincoln's Inn. He was called to the Bar in 1851. He chose a career in the sciences. He lectured at the medical school of St Mary's Hospital, Birmingham, between 1862 and 1884. In 1874, he was appointed Professor of Biology at the (Catholic) University College, Kensington. He was made a member of the Royal Institution in 1849 and of the Royal Society in 1867. Mivart wrote an important reply to Darwin in 1871. He received the degree of Doctor of Philosophy from Pius IX in 1876, and Doctor of Medicine from Louvain in 1884. He was also a member of the Linnean Society and of the Zoological Society. He supported the concept of evolution while minimising the contribution of natural selection, according to his entry in the *Encyclopaedia Britannica*. He referred to individuation, an innate plastic power which produced new species. He did not accept the evolution of human intellect. That was conferred by divine power. He sought to reconcile his evolutionism with the Catholic faith. His publications alienated him from Darwin and Huxley. He also fell out of favour with the Catholic Church. He was a Professor of the Philosophy of Natural History at the Catholic University of Leuven from 1890 to '93. There, he published a series of papers which appeared to come into conflict with Church teaching. The publication of 'The Continuity of Catholicism' in 1900 and 'Some Recent Apologists' brought his orthodoxy under serious suspicion. The offending articles were placed on the Vatican's index. He was excommunicated by Cardinal Vaughan in 1900, dying that year in London on 1 April. He was buried without the last rites and his remains were not placed in a Catholic graveyard. After a petition, Mivart was buried in Kensal Green Catholic cemetery on 18 January 1904. Entry for Saint George Jackson Mivart, *Encyclopaedia Britannica*, http://www.britannica.com/EBchecked/topic/386372/Saint–George–Jackson–Mivart (accessed 4 March 2010) and see also entry for St George Jackson Mivart, *Catholic Encyclopaedia*, http://www.newadvent.org/cathen/10407b.htm (accessed 4 March 2010).

70 To view complete published works of Windle see bibliography.

71 Windle, *Life in Early Britain*; and *Remains of the Prehistoric Age in England*.

72 Bertram Windle, *Chester: A Historical and Topographical Account of the City* (London: Methuen, 1904); Windle and John Murray (Firm), *A Handbook for Residents and Travellers in Wilts and Dorset*, 5th edn (London: John Murray, 1899); Windle and John Murray (Firm), *A Handbook for Travellers in Somerset*, 5th edn (London: John Murray, 1899).

73 Windle, *Shakespeare's Country* (London: Methuen, 1899); *The Wessex of Thomas Hardy* (London: John Lane, 1902).

74 Dr R. Allan Bennett (Talcahuno, Chile), 'Sir Bertram Windle', *The British Medical Journal*, 27 April 1929, p. 792.

75 Horgan, 'Sir Bertram Windle: An Appreciation', p. 127.

76 Ibid.

77 Ibid., p. 121.

78 See Reginald Jocelyn correspondence, Published Memoir and Associated Materials, Box 13, BWP.

79 Carr, 'Sir Bertram Windle', p. 169; offprint with minute From Lady Windle, 13 May 1929, Published Memoir and Associated Materials, Box 13, BWP.

80 Horgan, 'Sir Bertram Windle: An Appreciation', p. 120.

81 Notes on Sir Bertram Windle, Obituary and Appreciation, Published Memoir and Associated Materials, Box 13, BWP.

82 J.W. Mackail and Guy Wyndham (eds), *Life and Letters of George Wyndham* (London: Hutchinson, n.d.), vol. ii, p. 408.

83 Denis Gwynn, 'Sir Bertram Windle, 1858–1929: A Centenary Tribute', *University Record*, vols 2, 3 and 4 (1958), p. 52.

84 Wyndham to Oliver Lodge, undated, Bertram Windle's Personal Correspondence, Box 9, BWP.

85 Horgan, 'Sir Bertram Windle', p. 615; Horgan was a strong Parnellite, a political activist, a solicitor, a prominent figure in Cork public life and a journalist of distinction. He was the Irish correspondent of *The Round Table* for many years where he showed himself to be an acerbic student of Irish politics. His father, Michael Joseph, was a close friend of Charles Stewart Parnell, and a distinguished member of professional Cork society. John J. Horgan's mother, Mary Bowring, was from Dorset; see also Murphy, *The College*, p. 413.

86 Horgan, 'Sir Bertram Windle', pp. 614–15.

87 Ibid.

88 Murphy, *The College*, p. 154.

89 Horgan, *Parnell to Pearse*, pp. 140–1.

90 Horgan, 'Sir Bertram Windle', pp. 614–15.

91 Douglas Hyde to Windle, 14 October 1904, Windle's Personal Correspondence, Box 9, BWP.

92 Letter in file, Degrees, Certificates, Licences, Personal and Family Material of Windle, Box 11, BWP.

93 Horgan, *Parnell to Pearse*, pp. 140–2.

94 Taylor, *Windle*, p. 144.

95 Ibid.

96 Percy Faraday Frankland to Windle, 25 October 1904, Windle Miscellaneous Correspondence, 1901–1928, Box 9, BWP.

97 George Henry Morley, Secretary, 3 November 1904, to Windle, Windle's Personal Correspondence, Box 9, BWP.

98 Taylor, *Windle*, p. 145.

99 Ibid., p. 146 ff.

100 Ibid.

101 Windle's Personal Correspondence, Box 9, BWP.

102 Taylor, *Windle*, p. 150 ff.

103 Horgan, 'Sir Bertram Windle: An Appreciation', pp. 119–20.

104 Windle to Sr Monica, 23 January 1927, Windle's Personal Correspondence, Box 9, BWP.

105 Wyndham felt obliged to resign following the controversy which surrounded the publication of the Dunraven proposals for devolution. He had been on holidays in September. His under-secretary, Sir Antony MacDonnell, claimed that he had kept his superior informed about the progress of the proposal. The Irish attorney general, Sir Edward Carson, described the proposal as 'a gross betrayal'. Michael Davitt called it a 'wooden horse stratagem' while John Dillon viewed it as the culmination

of a campaign to kill home rule with kindness. John Redmond viewed the initiative much more positively. Wyndham, his health on the point of collapse, resigned in March 1905 'not because of health, not because of MacDonnell, but because my policy – which is *not* the policy of the Reform Association – cannot proceed now'. See Denis Gwynn, *The Life of John Redmond* (London: George G. Harrap, 1932).

106   Taylor, *Windle*, p. 170.
107   Bertram Windle's Personal Correspondence, Box 9, BWP; see also Taylor, *Windle*, pp. 172–3.
108   Taylor, *Windle*, p. 236.
109   Gwynn, 'Sir Bertram Windle, 1858–1929: A Centenary Tribute', p. 50.
110   Horgan, 'Sir Bertram Windle', p. 615.
111   Murphy, *The College*, p. 187.
112   D.P. Fitzgerald, 'Late Sir Bertram Windle: Appreciation by Former Colleague', *Cork Examiner*, 19 February 1929; see Cuttings Book, no. 27, College Archives, UCC.

2.   THE 'UNIVERSITY OF MUNSTER' AND THE FOUNDING OF THE NATIONAL UNIVERSITY OF IRELAND

1   Fr Fergal McGrath SJ: see 'The University Question', in Patrick J. Corish (ed.), *A History of the Catholic Church. Vol. 5: The Church since Emancipation* (Dublin: Gill & Macmillan, 1971), p. 125.
2   There had been two significant personal initiatives shortly before the setting up of the new commission. W.J.M. Starkie had been president of Queen's College, Galway, between 1895 and 1897. He was then appointed resident commissioner of national education. He proposed that Dublin University and the Royal University were to remain unchanged. A new university was to be set up for Catholics and for Presbyterians if they so desired it. A council of university education would guarantee uniformity of standards. That proposal won support from the Archbishop of Dublin, William Walsh. John H. Pigot, a graduate of Trinity College, made a more radical proposal; he sought to make Trinity equally acceptable to both Protestants and Catholics. To that end, he proposed the placing of the Divinity School off campus, the opening of a Catholic church in the university grounds, the introduction of chaplains of the major religions, and the establishment of a chair of Catholic Philosophy, then known as mental and moral science. The above is based on the lucid account of the evolution of the university question by the late Fr Fergal McGrath SJ, 'The University Question', pp. 123–4.
3   Susan M. Parkes, 'Higher Education, 1793–1908', in W.E. Vaughan (ed.), *A New History of Ireland: Ireland under the Union, 1870–1921*, vol. VI (Oxford: Oxford University Press, 2010, pp. 564–5).
4   McGrath, 'The University Question', p. 125.
5   Parkes, 'Higher Education, 1793–1908', pp. 568–70.
6   McGrath, 'The University Question', p. 127.
7   Mackail and Wyndham, *Life and Letters of George Wyndham*, p. 541.
8   Windle to Wyndham, 27 January 1906, MS 24,948 (11), National Library of Ireland (hereafter NLI).
9   Windle to O'Brien, 17 January 1905, UC/WOB/PP/AO/147, CA, UCC.
10   Windle to William O'Brien, 20 January 1906, UC/WOB/PP/AO/150/, CA, UCC.
11   Taylor, *Windle*, p. 179.
12   Windle to William O'Brien, 11 February 1906, UC/WOB/AO/160 (1–2), CA, UCC.
13   Ibid.
14   Ibid.
15   Windle to William O'Brien, 15 March 1906, UC/WOB/AO/174/, CA, UCC.
16   Ibid.
17   Windle to William O'Brien, 29 March 1906, UC/WOB/PP/AO/181 (1–3), CA, UCC.
18   Windle to William O'Brien, 10 May 1906, UC/WOB/PP/AO/196 (1–2), CA, UCC.

19   William O'Brien to Windle, 11 May 1906, UC/WOB/PP/AO/197 (1–6), CA, UCC.
20   Windle to William O'Brien, 15 September 1906, UC/WOB/PP/AO/213, CA, UCC.
21   William O'Brien to Windle, 17 September 1906, UC/WOB/PP/AO/218 (1–3), CA, UCC.
22   Taylor, *Windle*, pp. 182–3.
23   Thomas J. Morrissey, SJ, *Towards a National University: William Delany, SJ (1835–1924). An Era of Initiative in Irish Education* (Dublin: Wolfhound Press, 1983), pp. 228–9.
24   The scheme consisted in making Trinity College one of five constituent colleges for a new University of Dublin, together with a new Queen's College Dublin and the existing colleges in Galway, Cork and Belfast.
25   Morrissey, *Towards a National University*, p. 229.
26   Windle to William O'Brien, 28 October 1906, UC/WOB/PP/AO234 (1–2), CA, UCC.
27   Morrissey, *Towards a National University*, p. 230.
28   Windle to William O'Brien, 28 October 1906, UC/WOB/PP/AO234 (1–2), CA, UCC.
29   *Cork Examiner*, 19 November 1906.
30   Ibid.
31   Ibid.
32   Ibid.
33   Ibid.
34   Ibid.
35   Windle to O'Brien, 28 October 1906, UC/WOB//PP/AO/P10/234(1), CA, UCC.
36   Windle to O'Brien, 28 October 1906, UC/WOB//PP/AO/P10/234(2), CA, UCC.
37   Windle to O'Brien, 30 November 1906, UC/WOB/PP/AO/247/, CA, UCC.
38   Taylor, *Windle*, p. 187.
39   Morrissey, *Towards a National University*, p. 230.
40   Ibid., pp. 231–2.
41   Taylor, *Windle*, p. 186.
42   Section reproduced in Taylor, *Windle*, p. 187; but the transcription is not verbatim. I have checked text against diary and rendered it faithful to the original.
43   The Fry Commission was made up of Lord Chief Baron Palles, Sir Thomas Raleigh, Sir Arthur W. Rucker, Professor Henry Jackson, S.H. Butcher, Dr Hyde, Dr Coffey and Mr Kellaher.
44   Parkes, 'Higher Education, 1793–1908', p. 565.
45   Sir Edward Fry, *Sir Edward Fry: An Autobiography* (London: Oxford University Press, 1921), pp. 138–9.
46   Parkes, 'Higher Education, 1793–1908', p. 566.
47   Morrissey, *Towards a National University*, pp. 232–3.
48   Quoted in Taylor, *Windle*, pp. 186–7.
49   Windle to William O'Brien, 14 February 1907, UC/WOB/PP/AP/, CA, UCC.
50   Ibid.
51   Windle to William O'Brien, 15 February 1907, UC/WOB/PP/AP/22/, CA, UCC.
52   Ibid.
53   Ibid.
54   Taylor, *Windle*, p. 188; my transcription of the diary differs slightly to that of Sr Monica.
55   Windle to William O'Brien, 4 August 1907, UC/WOB/PP/AP/66 (1–2), CA, UCC.
56   Windle to William O'Brien, 3 September 1907, UC/WOB/PP/AP/90/, CA, UCC.
57   Ibid.
58   Ibid.
59   Windle to William O'Brien, 7 October 1907, UC/WOB/PP/AP/112/, CA, UCC.
60   Windle to William O'Brien, 10 October 1907, UC/WOB/PP/AP/117/, CA, UCC.
61   Taylor, *Windle*, p. 190.
62   Ibid., pp. 190–1.
63   F.S.L. Lyons, 'The Developing Crisis, 1907–1914', in Vaughan (ed.), *A New History of Ireland*, pp. 123–4.
64   Windle to William O'Brien, 13 March 1908, UC/WOB/PP/AQ/33 (1–2), CA, UCC.
65   Ibid.

66 Ibid.
67 Ibid.
68 *Statement of the Governing Body in Support of the Claim for the Establishment of a Separate University for Munster, Cork, 1918,* p. 11, Personal and Family Material of Windle, Box 11, BWP.
69 Windle to William O'Brien, 1 April 1908, UC/WOB/PP/AQ/38/, CA, UCC.
70 Taylor, *Windle,* p. 192.
71 Ibid., p. 193.
72 Political leaders and mayors of the region were represented on the new NUI governing body. Protestant and Catholic bishops of the Munster region also served as governors. See Donal McCartney, *The National University of Ireland and Éamon de Valera* (Dublin: The University Press of Ireland, 1983), p. 9.
73 John Privilege, *Michael Logue and the Catholic Church in Ireland, 1879–1925* (Manchester University Press, 2009), p. 48.
74 McCartney, *The National University,* p. 9.
75 John Coolahan, 'From Royal University to National University, 1879–1908', in Tom Dunne (ed.) and co-eds John Coolahan, Maurice Manning and Gearóid Ó Tuathaigh, *The National University of Ireland 2008: Centenary Essays* (Dublin: University College Dublin Press, 2008), p. 17.
76 The work of the commissioners was completed by 31 July 1911, thus giving their full power to the governing bodies of the three constituents together with the NUI Senate.
77 Coolahan, 'From Royal University to National University', p. 17.
78 The Royal University was dissolved on 31 October 1909. The Jesuits ended their control of University College in 1909.
79 Parkes, 'Higher Education, 1793–1908', pp. 568–70.
80 Coolahan, 'From Royal University to National University', p. 17.
81 *Statement of the Governing Body in Support of the Claim for the Establishment of a Separate University for Munster, Cork, 1918,* p. 9, Personal and Family Material of Windle, Box 11, BWP.
82 Ibid., p. 28, Personal and Family Material of Windle, Box 11, BWP.
83 Windle to Sr Monica, 23 January 1927, Windle's Personal Correspondence, Box 9, BWP.

3. The Modernisation of QCC/UCC, 1905–1913

1   To view complete published works of Windle see bibliography.
2   Taylor, *Windle,* p. 163.
3   See Donal McCartney, *UCD: A National Idea: The History of University College Dublin* (Dublin: Gill & Macmillan, 1999); Patrick Corish, *Maynooth College, 1795–1995* (Dublin: Gill & Macmillan, 1995); and R.B. McDowell and B.A. Webb, *Trinity College Dublin* (Dublin: Trinity College Dublin Press, 2004).
4   Windle to McGrath, 26 November 1913, NUI, Windle file 1910–11, Box 31 [All references to NUI files were kindly supplied by Dr Paul Loftus].
5   Windle to McGrath, 6 May 1914, NUI, UCC file 1908–19, Box 1.
6   Windle to McGrath, 13 June 1912, NUI, UCC file 1908–19, Box 1.
7   Windle to McGrath, 13 October 1912, NUI, UCC file 1908–19, Box 1.
8   Windle to McGrath, 3 December 1913, NUI, UCC file 1908–19, Box 1.
9   Windle to McGrath, 5 December 1913, NUI, UCC file, 1908–19, Box 1.
10 Windle to McGrath, 12 January 1913, NUI, UCC file, 1908–19, Box 1.
11 Attracta Halpin, "The NUI, 49 Merrion Square," in Tom Dunne (ed.), *The National University of Ireland 1908 – 2008 – Centenary Essays* (UCD Press, Dublin, 2008), pp 291–2.
12 *Statement of the Governing Body in Support of the Claim for the Establishment of a Separate University for Munster, Cork, 1918,* p. 11, Personal and Family Material of Windle, Box 11, BWP.

13   See Murphy, *The College*, p. 369.

14   *Cork University Record*, 1944, pp. 11–12.

15   Denis Gwynn, 'Sir Bertram Windle and Endowments', manuscript compiled in 1959 on the fiftieth anniversary of Windle's death; UC/DG/U52/5ff, p. 12.

16   Ibid., pp. 12–15.

17   Ibid.

18   Ibid., p. 12.

19   Murphy, *The College*, p. 129 ff.

20   As mentioned earlier, the chair of Anatomy and Physiology was held by J.J. Charles until his retirement in 1907. It was split that year, Windle holding Anatomy and D.T. Barry was appointed to Physiology. Windle was succeeded in Anatomy in 1909 by D.P. Fitzgerald. See Professor J.C. Sperrin-Johnson, 'Recollections of Queen's College, Cork', *Cork University Record*, no. 6 (Easter 1946), p. 15; Professor Charles was described in the article as a 'typical Victorian'. He was 'a tall and stately person, with piercing grey eyes. He retained closely-trimmed side-whiskers, and was habitually sheathed in the cylindrical frock-coat of the period which reached to the knees, and with which was associated a silk hat. In the laboratory and dissecting room he wore a sort of smoking-cap', p. 16.

21   Wyndham to Windle, 18 November 1905, Wyndham folder, Windle's Personal Correspondence, Box 9, BWP.

22   Wyndham to Windle, 25 November 1905, Windle's Personal Correspondence, Box 9, BWP.

23   Wyndham to Windle, 25 January 1906, Windle's Personal Correspondence, Box 9, BWP.

24   Wyndham to Windle, 27 January 1906, MS 24,948 (11), NLI.

25   Ibid.

26   Wyndham to Windle, 4 March 1907, Windle's Personal Correspondence, Box 9, BWP.

27   Gwynn, 'Sir Bertram Windle, 1858–1929: A Centenary Tribute', p. 52.

28   Denis J. O'Sullivan, *The Cork School of Medicine: A History* (University College Cork, 2007), p. 36.

29   Marcus Hartog, 'Presentation to Sir Bertram C.A. Windle', *Official Gazette*, vii, 27, Hilary term (January 1920), p. 263.

30   O'Sullivan, *The Cork School of Medicine*, p. 38.

31   Ibid.

32   I am grateful to Catriona Mulcahy, UCC Archivist, for bringing this appointment to my attention. Further details have been added from Joseph P. Cunningham and Ruth Fleischmann, *Aloys Flieschmann (1880–1964), Immigrant Musician in Ireland* (Cork University Press, Cork, Cork, 2010), see pp 86, 87, 104, 108, 113, 119 and 372–3

33   Murphy, *The College*, p. 130.

34   Mary Ryan, 'Random Recollections', *Cork University Record*, no. 5 (1945), pp. 15–19.

35   Mary Tierney Downes and Adelaine M. Stuart were the first women to be admitted to the college in the session 1885–6.

36   Y.S., 'Professor Mary Ryan, MA', *Cork University Record*, no. 6 (Easter 1946), pp. 17–18.

37   Professor J.C. Sperrin-Johnson, 'Professor Marcus M. Hartog', *Cork University Record*, no. 7 (Summer 1946), pp. 14–16.

38   Professor T. Dillon, 'Further Reminiscences', *Cork University Record*, no. 3 (Easter 1945), pp. 27–30.

39   Gwynn, 'Sir Bertram Windle, 1858–1929: A Centenary Tribute', p. 53.

40   Ibid., p. 150.

41   Windle to Sr Monica, 16 January 1929, Windle's Personal Correspondence, Box 9, BWP.

42   See MS 17,999, NLI. In the same letter, Windle wrote about the change in chief secretary from Wyndham to Bryce. 'Bryce at any way seems to be sound on the language question. Isn't this the queerest country in its government. Here you have one Chief Sec. fining people for putting their names on carts in Irish and within a few weeks another is in office who receives a Gaelic League deputation and addresses them in

Irish himself! Gilbert and Sullivan were the only true philosophers after all so far as Ireland is concerned.'

43 We are grateful to Professor Seán Ó Coileáin for helping me locate sources on Fr Henebry; see Dr Cornelius Buttimer, 'Celtic and Irish College, 1849–1944', *Journal of the Cork Historical and Archaeological Society*, xciv, 253 (January–December 1989), pp. 88–112; see appreciation by Rev. Michael Sheehan, 'The Reverend Dr Henebry: Some Stray Recollections', *Catholic Record of Waterford and Lismore*, vol. iv (May–October 1916), pp. 46–86; see also Obituary, *University College Cork Official Gazette*, vi, 18 (June 1916), pp. 174–5.

44 Buttimer, 'Celtic and Irish College, 1849–1944', p. 97.

45 'Patrick Joseph Merriman Obituary', *Cork University Record*, no. 1,, Summer 1944, p. 11. Merriman became registrar of UCC in 1915 and succeeded Windle as president in 1920; he died in office on 13 September 1943.

46 *Statement of the Governing Body in Support of the Claim for the Establishment of a Separate University for Munster, Cork, 1918*, pp. 15–16, Personal and Family Material of Windle, Box 11, BWP.

47 Taylor, *Windle*, pp. 206–7; taken from *Statement of the Governing Body in Support of the Claim for the Establishment of a Separate University for Munster, Cork, 1918*, pp. 15–16, Personal and Family Material of Windle, Box 11, BWP.

48 *Statement of the Governing Body in Support of the Claim for the Establishment of a Separate University for Munster, Cork, 1918*, pp. 20–4, Personal and Family Material of Windle, Box 11, BWP.

49 Lewis, *Edith Somerville*, p. 222.

50 Ibid., p. 346.

51 Edith to Sr Monica, 5 November 1929, Published Memoir and Associated Materials, BWP.

52 Ibid.

53 Lewis, *Edith Somerville*, p. 61.

54 Ibid., p. 395.

55 Windle had, on his mother's side, other strong family connections with Castletownshend. Edith Windle explained the details of that relationship to Sr Monica in a frank letter in 1929: 'Adjoining that estate is Glen Barrahane, sometimes spelt Glenbarrahane: always pronounced as one word, the property for three generations of the Coghills. First Sir Jocelyn, secondly Sir Egerton, husband of Hildegarde who still lives there. The present baronet, Sir Patrick, who must be aged about 35 is unmarried and I believe lives somewhere near London. Colonel Kendal Coghill: brother to Sir Jocelyn lived in Castletownshend at The Point, now known as Cosheen (its old name a very charming home with beautiful garden facing Castletownshend Harbour. He is buried in Castletownshend Protestant Church along with all the other Coghills. Cosheen is now owned and inhabited by Admiral Boyle Somerville: the cousin with whom Bertie had so much in common over prehistoric interests. Uncle Kendal lived at Cosheen when I first met him after we went to live in Ireland: he was an old man then (a very peppery one) I don't know whether he lived there before he retired from the Army. He never married but kept a bachelor's establishment.' Edith Windle to Sr Monica, 31 December 1929, Published Memoir and Associated Materials, Box 13, BWP.

56 See Vice-Admiral Boyle Somerville, *The Chart-Makers* (Edinburgh: William Blackwood & Sons, 1928).

57 Edith Windle to Sr Monica, 31 December 1929, Published Memoir and Associated Materials, Box 13, BWP.

58 Boyle T. Somerville, '"The Fort" on Knock Drum, West Carbery, County Cork', *The Journal of the Royal Society of Antiquaries of Ireland*, vol. 1, no. 1, Seventh Series (30 June 1931), pp. 1–14; 'Ancient Stone Monuments near Lough Swilly, County Donegal,' *The Journal of the Royal Society of Antiquaries of Ireland*, vol. 19, no. 2, Sixth Series, (31 December 1929), pp. 149–75; 'Prehistoric Monuments in the Outer

Hebrides, and their Astronomical Significance', *The Journal of the Royal Anthropological Institute of Great Britain and Ireland*, 42 (June 1912), pp. 23–52; '77. Remarks on Mr. Stone's Paper on the Date of Stonehenge, and on the Dating of Megalithic Structures by Astronomical Means Generally', *Man*, 22 (September 1922), pp. 133–7; 'Account of a Visit to Niuafou, South Pacific', *The Geographical Journal*, vol. 7, no. 1 (January 1896), pp. 65–71; 'Ethnographical Notes in New Georgia, Solomon Islands', *The Journal of the Anthropological Institute of Great Britain and Ireland*, 26 (1897), pp. 357–412; 'Ethnological Notes on New Hebrides', *The Journal of the Anthropological Institute of Great Britain and Ireland*, 23 (1894), pp. 363–93; 'Notes on Some Islands of the New Hebrides', *The Journal of the Anthropological Institute of Great Britain and Ireland*, 23 (1894), pp. 2–21; *Commodore Anson's Voyage into the South seas and around the World* (London and Toronto: W. Heinemann, 1934); *The Chart-Makers* (Edinburgh and London: W. Blackwood & Sons, 1928); *Will Mariner a True Record of Adventure* (London: Faber & Faber, 1936); Sidney H. Ray, 'Songs and Specimens of the Language of New Georgia, Solomon Islands', *The Journal of the Anthropological Institute of Great Britain and Ireland*, 26 (1897), pp. 436–53; *Ocean Passages for the World: Winds and Currents* (London: HMSO, 1923); *Ocean Passages for the World: Winds and Currents* (London: Hydrographic Dept. Admiralty, printed by HMSO, 1950); *Report on Sounding Cruise of HMS* Egeria *(Commander Morris H. Smyth) on the Proposed Pacific Cable Route: N. Pacific Ocean, 1899* (London: Hydrographic Dept. Admiralty, 1900).

59   Somerville, *The Chart-Makers*, pp. 5–9.

60   Ibid.

61   Ibid.

62   Ibid., p. 394.

63   Windle kept a diary for most of the years that he was at UCC. It is a rich source of information about his professional and family life. It shows him to be a man of routine; each entry records whether he attended Mass, comments on the weather and then sets out his activities during each particular day. The source is much more than a desk diary. The entries are sometimes quite detailed and extensive. But the diaries are difficult to read. Windle wrote in an abbreviated style, joining his words and sometimes only using initials to indicate to whom he had spoken.

64   Ruth Dudley Edwards, *Patrick Pearse: The Triumph of Failure* (London: Faber & Faber, 1977), pp. 111–51; and Elaine Sisson, *Pearse's Patriots: St Enda's and the Cult of Boyhood* (Cork University Press, 2004).

65   Patrick Pearse to Windle, 15 May 1910, Windle's Personal Correspondence, Box 9, BWP.

66   Pearse to Windle, 23 November 1910, Windle's Personal Correspondence, Box 9, BWP.

67   Pearse to Windle, 20 December 1910, Windle's Personal Correspondence, Box 9, BWP.

68   Joyce Padbury, 'A Young Schoolmaster of Great Literary Talent', Mary Hayden's friend, Patrick Pearse', in Roisín Higgins and Regina Uí Chollatáin (eds), *The Life and After-Life of P.H. Pearse* (Dublin: Irish Academic Press, 2009), pp. 33–44.

69   We are grateful to Anne-Marie Ryan, researcher/exhibition assistant, Pearse Museum, for locating this document for us. The reference is 03.0948a-c and is dated 15 October 1912. There is an earlier document, reference 03.1016, which lists Windle as a member of an 'Educational Council': it is dated 22 January 1912.

70   Declan Kiberd, 'Patrick Pearse: Irish Modernist', in Higgins and Uí Chollatáin (eds), *The Life and After-Life of P.H. Pearse*, p. 80.

71   For a very good overview of Pearse's life, see Joe Lee, 'Patrick Henry Pearse (1879–1916)', *Dictionary of Irish Biography* (Dublin: Royal Irish Academy, 2009), vol. 8, pp. 19–28.

72   Kevin Girvin, *Seán O'Hegarty: O/C First Cork Brigade, Irish Republican Army* (Cork: Aubane Historical Society, 2007), see Chapters 1 and 2.

73   See Traolach Ó Ríordáin, *Conradh na Gaeilge i gCorcaigh, 1894–1910* (Baile Átha Cliath: Cois Life Teoranta, 2000); Máire Ní Síocháin, 'Idir Dhá Ré Conradh na Gaeilge i gCorcaigh, 1910–1922', Cuid a hAon, *Journal of the Cork Historical and Archaeological*

Society, vol. 109 (2004), pp. 67–200; and Gerry White and Brendan O'Shea, '*Baptised in Blood': The Formation of the Cork Brigade of the Irish Volunteers, 1913–1916* (Cork: Mercier Press, 2005), pp. 16–17.

74 *Report of the President to the Governing Body for 1910–1911*, p. 10; letter signed by Windle, J.P. Molohan, registrar, and H.C. Clifton, secretary, CA, UCC.

75 Taylor, *Windle*, p. 215.

76 Ibid.

77 Lady Aberdeen to Windle, 22 August 1911, Lady Aberdeen's visit file, College Archives, UCC. She had sent him a handwritten letter on 21 July 1911 expressing delight at being able to see Windle on his next trip to Dublin. She was also grateful for having been 'entrusted such a mission. I do thank you from my heart for promoting this cause so vital to the homes of Ireland [?] or to the women students themselves.' They were going to Belfast the following day but would be back in Dublin and would remain there all August. (There are no details to explain the references in Aberdeen's letter but it is likely to have been part of a shared interest in the promotion of public health.)

78 Windle, at the time of the Aberdeen visit, was very worried about his wife's health: 'Oh God spare me Edith. The operation going on as I write this.' On 7 November, he noted: 'Edith going on well DG.' The doctor spent a good deal of the night with Edith on the 10th and Windle slept for only two hours. On 12 November, there was still anxiety about her recovery: 'dearest darling ever of my heart what should I do without her.' The following day, according to his diary, Edith was a good deal better: 'still no solid food. Slept well in night and read and was cheerful during day.' On 15 November, she was 'going on slowly but progressing'.

79 Windle Diary, 25 December 1911, Box 1, BWP.

80 At the end of 1911, Windle had begun to take an interest in buying a motor car. On 11 January 1912, he recorded: 'Beautiful day: Mass. Went out in morning and bought a MOTOR-CAR! And made arrangements with Bank: also got a better coat.' He was mastering trying to drive his new car. He went out in it on the 17th, driving it down the Western Road and up to his own door: 'felt more confidence and began to understand thing better.' He derived much pleasure from his new purchase. On 11 March 1912, he wrote: 'After breakfast took Edith and Nora in Car (with driver) and off to Macroom: Drove whole way there and back and feel much more confidence. Market day in Macroom and drove right through it which is far worse than Patrick Street. Well satisfied with this day's work.' On 16 March, Saturday, he drove his car through Patrick Street and up into a garage: 'a direful job in the rain.' Windle took to the road for the first time by himself, without any chauffeur, on Sunday 17 March 1912. He was with Edith and John O'Connell: 'great job getting it to start: away via Coachford to Macroom: and then intended to Inchigheela but road more than awful . . . and home again. Quite successful but awfully tired.' On Sunday, 24 March, Windle, growing in confidence, went out with Edith and Nora in the car. They drove to Bandon and nearly to Ballineen: 'a good many showers and mostly very wet.' On 1 April, Windle drove to an archaeological site with D. O'Donoghue. He got a pot and what bones he could and took them home. He also visited a dolmen and resolved to measure it again. He was back home by 4.45. He was on the road again on 4 April when he and his wife went to Fermoy and Mitchelstown, both of which had markets. He drove on to Cahir and Cashel. They visited the castle and on the way down from the site, Windle missed the road and had an awful time trying to turn. He ran 'into a wall: smashed wind-screen: bent mud-guard' and came to a stop: 'heaps of gibbering people round about making remarks and offering holy water.' They made it to Clonmel. The following day, he had an accident, crashing into a cow and smashing the lamp glass. Despite the mishaps he made it to Waterford where it was 'no joke along quays'. He got the car repaired. Returning to Cork on the 6th he ran into another cow which jumped out and bent the mudguard. Windle concluded: 'Nothing to do but stop when cows are about.'

When he got to the city, he noted: 'Traffic in Cork awful.' He had yet another scare when 'an old shawled female fool in South Mall . . . jumped backwards under the car. Home and bathed.' On 9 April, Windle drove to Holycross, County Tipperary. He visited a historical ruin the following day, spending 'the entire day measuring it'. He visited another site on 11 March, and took in yet another on his way back on 13 April. Windle set out on another car journey at 12.00 on 21 April 1912, going to Macroom, Millstreet and Banteer. He drove on a terrible road and in terrible weather. 'Not to be tried again,' he noted, reaching home at 6.30. On Sunday 12 May, he went as far as Rathmore and Banteer, 91.3 miles, he noted, and on 'a splendid day all through'. On 16 May, he drove to the north-west of the county: 'Then on lying advice turned up to Lacadris. Got to an awful hill had to turn back. Then at [an acute bend] ran into wall and bent steering gear . . . had to get a horse and tow the thing six miles into Macroom: a horrid and difficult job.' He vowed after that experience: 'Nothing but highways in future.' He returned on 20 May to Macroon: 'man showed me how, by a piece of faulty construction, this accident and the other one occurred – a perfect death-trap. ' He 'took car home' with difficulty to the Johnson and Perrot garage in Cork, showed them what was wrong and told them to put it right. He was 'very tired and worn by anxiety of all this'.

81   UC-MB-GB-7, 5 February 1912, pp. 524–5.
82   Windle Diary, 6 March 1912, Box 1, BWP.
83   Taylor, *Windle*, pp. 219–20; she is quoting a letter from Humphreys which is not dated.
84   Gasquet to Windle, 3 June 1912, Windle's Personal Correspondence, Box 9, BWP.
85   Taylor, *Windle*, pp. 222–3.
86   Ibid., p. 222.
87   Windle Diary, 19 July 1912, Box 1, BWP.
88   Taylor, *Windle*, pp. 222–3.
89   Ibid., p. 225.
90   In 1913, Windle conducted a strong lobby to bring a school of dentistry to Cork. When Lady Aberdeen visited in the early part of the year, for a 'Health Week Conference', he used the occasion to give a lecture entitled 'Teeth'.
91   Taylor, *Windle*, p. 132.
92   John Humphreys to Sr Monica Windle, 4 November 1929, Published Memoir and Associated Materials, Box 13, BWP.
93   Taylor, *Windle*, p. 132.
94   Horgan, *Parnell to Pearse*, pp. 149–50.
95   Ibid.
96   Ibid.
97   Ibid.
98   Ibid.
99   Taylor, *Windle*, p. 181.
100 Ibid.
101 Ibid., p. 198.
102 Horgan, 'Biographical Introduction', pp. vii–xxxv; Bridget Hourican, 'John J. Horgan', in *Dictionary of Irish Biography*, vol. 4, pp. 792–4; and see '*Lusitania* Coroner Dies in Cork', *Irish Independent*, 22 July 1967.
103 Windle Diary, 20 March 1908, Box 1, BWP.
104 Windle Diary, 15 September 1908, Box 1, BWP.
105 Windle Diary, 16 September 1908, Box 1, BWP.
106 *Cork Examiner*, 17 September 1908; I am grateful to Mr Kieran Burke, Executive Librarian Local Studies, Central Library, Cork, for locating this report for me.
107 Windle to William O'Brien, 21 September 1908, UC/WOB/PP/AQ/75.
108 Ibid.
109 Ibid.
110 Horgan, *Parnell to Pearse*, p. 161.

111   The hurt caused by Windle to Michael Joseph Horgan and particularly to his wife was quite unforgivable. Besides John J's 'sin' of falling in love with Mary, it is difficult to understand what fuelled Windle's dislike of the 'Horgan gang'. Perhaps, and this is speculation on our part, Windle did not like Horgan's Parnellite politics. Parnell had been best man at Michael Joseph's wedding. The latter had been his election agent through thick and thin. Is that what fuelled Windle's lingering resentment? We think it most doubtful but it cannot be ruled out completely as a partial explanation.

112   Photographic album in possession of Madoline O'Connell, Cork.

113   Madoline O'Connell, 'A Life Well Lived', *UCC Graduate* (September 2008), p. 32.

114   Horgan, *Parnell to Pearse*, p. 160.

115   Windle Diary, 15 April 1912.

116   O'Connell, 'A Life Well Lived', p. 35.

117   Windle's personal health was not helped by the move to Cork. He suffered and would continue to do so throughout his life – very badly – from hay fever. That illness rendered him unable to leave a darkened room at certain points of the year. He also confronted other problems. His childhood and early upbringing had given him exposure to a gloomy theology of Calvinism. He found it very hard to replace the negativity and gloom of that outlook with compensating ideas from Catholicism. But there may also have been a problem which was more related to his mental health. Windle's father suffered from clinical depression. It is probable that his son also faced recurring cycles of that illness.

118   A.T.Q. Stewart, *Edward Carson* (Belfast: Blackstaff Press, 1981); pp. 133–4.

119   On 26 August 1913, a tramway strike had begun in Dublin. This was the culmination of nearly three years of agitation for better working conditions and for the recognition of the newly formed Irish Transport and General Workers' Union. Led by James Larkin and James Connolly, the labour conflict escalated over the following weeks, precipitated by a general lockout led by the former nationalist MP, William Martin Murphy, who was the proprietor of the Dublin Tramways and of the *Irish Independent*. On 27 October, Larkin was sentenced to seven months' imprisonment for seditious language. On 19 November 1913, James Connolly, Larkin's main lieutenant, set up the Irish Citizen Army. Windle was no admirer of the 'Larkin gang'. Ireland faced the prospect of widespread social unrest and a form of politics that was spilling over into violence.

120   NUI, UCC file, 1908-19, Box 1.

121   Windle to McGrath, 27 March 1913, NUI, Windle file 1912–14, Box 84.

122   Windle to McGrath, 3 April 1913, NUI, UCC file 1908–19, Box 1.

123   Chair of Mathematical Physics, Secretary's File 211, College Archives, UCC.

124   Ibid.

125   Horgan, *Parnell to Pearse*, pp. 246–7.

126   Papers sent to Senate from 20 June 1913 to 12 December 1913, NUI.

127   I am grateful to Ms Ann Milner, NUI, for helping me identify the above de Valera correspondence in Volume 81 of NUI correspondence records.

128   Papers sent to Senate from 20 June 1913 to 12 December 1913, NUI.

129   Ibid.

130   UC/MB/AC, 6 June 1913, pp. 31–5.

131   Ibid.

132   UC/MB/AC, 6 June 1913, pp. 291–4.

133   Ibid.

134   UC/MB/GB, 13 June 1913, pp. 31–4.

135   Ibid.

136   Ibid.

137   Ibid.

138   Minutes of the NUI Senate, vol. 111, 4 July 1913, pp. 139–40, NUI.

139   See Volume 81 of NUI correspondence records, NUI; see also Donal McCartney, *The National University of Ireland and Eamon de Valera* (University Press of Ireland, 1983),

p. 17 ff; see also Owen Dudley Edwards, *Éamon de Valera* (GPC Books, London, 1987), p. 42.

140   Hilary Richardson, 'Robert Alexander Stewart Macalister', in James McGuire and James Quinn (eds), *Dictionary of Irish Biography*, (Dublin: Royal Irish Academy, 2009), vol. 5, pp. 686–7.

141   Philip G. Lee, 'Notes on the Ogham Chamber at Knock-shana-wee', *Journal of the Cork Historical and Archaeological Society*, vol. XVII (1911), pp. 58–62.

142   'Letter to the Editor: Rath at Cnoc Sean a Mhaithe', *Cork Examiner*, 27 November 1910.

143   Here we are relying on the narrative of Murphy, *The College*, p. 184.

144   See R.A.S. Macalister, 'On Some Recently Discovered Ogham Inscriptions', *Proceedings of the Royal Irish Academy, Section C: Archaeology, Celtic Studies, History, Linguistics, Literature*, vol. 32 (1914–16), pp. 138–46.

145   On 16 October 1913, Windle was back in Dublin. He noted in his diary: 'Coffey looking very well and put on two stone weight. [Christopher] Nixon [pro-vice-chancellor] more incredibly ignorant and asinine than ever.' On 17 October 1913, still bruised over the de Valera case, he commented on the meeting of the UCC governing body: 'quite peaceful but little more than a quorum because NO JOB ON', an obvious reference to the sensitive question of the controversial professorship of Mathematical Physics.

146   Windle was back to Dublin again on the 22nd where he stayed in Killiney with the O'Connells. He attended a long meeting of convocation. He was at a Senate meeting on the 24th at which [Michael F.] Cox [MD], according to Windle, gave an 'extraordinary exhibition of bad taste'. Back in Cork, he continued with a round of meetings.

147   Murphy, *The College*, p. 184.

148   Despite Windle's membership of the Gaelic League going back to the 1880s, he was perceived to be a West Briton. Yet he was very sound, as far as that organisation should have been aware, on the question of compulsory Irish for matriculation in the National University of Ireland. He had at first opposed such a policy but later defended it with great conviction. On 23 April 1919, in the year Windle left UCC, he wrote a memorandum for the chief secretary which came down firmly on the side of compulsory Irish. However, his support for that controversial policy did not save him from the sustained criticism throughout his time in Cork from those cultural nationalists who perceived him to be 'unsympathetic' and Anglophile. He remained a much misunderstood man and a sign of contradiction.

149   Windle went to Dublin on 18 November and stopped overnight in his club. He attended a meeting with the Department of Education and also a meeting of the Senate of the NUI.

150   'The Rath-Cave at Cnoc Sean-Mhaighe', *Cork Examiner*, 18 November 1913.

151   Ibid.

152   Macalister contested the dimensions given in the paragraph in *Sinn Féin*: 'It was nothing of the kind. The measurements are wrong. The roof consisted of lintels, some of which were sandstone. The sides were not supported by sandstone slabs, whatever that may mean. It was a small insignificant, awkward and filthy hole in the ground: beyond all comparison the most uncomfortable cave I have ever examined. It had very little interest in comparison with the inscriptions, which were cut on the building stones, which the builders had pillaged from an adjacent cemetery.' He thought that 'righteous anger' would be justified if the rath had been destroyed to supply stones for fences or were sold for commercial gain to a dealer. He could conceive of no language strong enough to characterise such acts. He supposed what might have happened if either of the above had occurred since the beginning of the century. 'The Rath-Cave at Cnoc Sean-Mhaighe', *Cork Examiner*, 18 November 1913.

153   Ibid.

154   Ibid.

155 'Ancient Irish Monuments: The Recent Discovery of Knockshanawee', Eoin MacNeill letter, *Cork Examiner*, 19 November 1913.
156 Murphy, *The College*, p. 184.
157 'The Removal of Ogham Stones' [letter to the editor], *Cork Examiner*, 22 November 1913; we are grateful to Dr Niall Keogh for locating this letter.
158 'Letter to the Editor' [Windle], *Cork Examiner*, 22 November 1913.
159 See *Cork Examiner*, 25 November 1913.
160 Windle was referring to a future distinguished author and senior Irish civil servant, Patrick Sarsfield Ó hÉigeartaigh.

4. THE CATHOLIC CHURCH AND THE HONAN BEQUEST

1 See support for this thesis in Fergus Campbell, *The Irish Establishment, 1879–1914* (Oxford: Oxford University Press, 2009).
2 Gillian M. Doherty and Tomás O'Riordan, 'The Synod of Thurles', *Multitext*, UCC, http://multitext.ucc.ie/d/The_Synod_of_Thurles_1850 (accessed 4 March 2010).
3 Morrissey, *Towards a National University*, pp. 315–16.
4 Taylor, *Windle*, p. 195.
5 Ibid., p. 164.
6 Ibid.
7 Ibid., p. 167.
8 Ibid., p. 169.
9 Ibid., p. 170.
10 Canon Sheehan to Windle, 20 October 1905, Miscellaneous Correspondence, Box 9, BWP.
11 Ibid.
12 Taylor, *Windle*, p. 178.
13 Windle to Douglas Hyde, 12 April 1906, MS 17,999, NLI.
14 Taylor, *Windle*, p. 184.
15 Ibid., p. 187.
16 Ibid., p. 189.
17 Ibid., p. 196.
18 Murphy, *The College*, p. 197.
19 Presidential Reports, University College Archive, UCC.
20 Bartholomew Egan OFM, 'The Friars Minor and the Honan Hostel, University College, Cork', *Archivum Franciscanum Historicum*, An. 73 (1980), Collegio S. Bonaventura, Colle S. Antonio 00046, Grottaferrata, Rome, p. 7.
21 Taylor, *Windle*, p. 198.
22 Jeremy Williams, *Architecture in Ireland, 1837–1921* (Dublin: Irish Academic Press, 1994), p. 61.
23 Sir Bertram Windle to Fr Francis Maher, 24 November 1908, St Anthony's Hall, Folder 226, Doc. No. E56.6, Franciscan Archive, Dun Mhuire, Killiney; see also Egan, 'The Friars Minor and the Honan Hostel', p. 7.
24 Taylor, *Windle*, p. 199.
25 Sir Bertram Windle to Fr Francis Maher, 16 January 1909, St Anthony's Hall, Folder 226, Doc. No. 56.27; Franciscan Archive; see also Egan, 'The Friars Minor and the Honan Hostel', p. 6.
26 Egan, 'The Friars Minor and the Honan Hostel', pp. 6–7.
27 Ibid., p. 7; and Taylor, *Windle*, p. 200.
28 Egan, 'The Friars Minor and the Honan Hostel', p. 10.
29 Ibid., p. 11.
30 Cardinal Secretary of State, Merry del Val to Fr Benignus Gannon, 16 September 1909, St Anthony's Hall, Folder 226, Doc. No. E56.39, Franciscan Archives; see also Egan, 'The Friars Minor and the Honan Hostel', pp. 10–11.
31 Anon., 'Irish Franciscans and the University', *The Tablet*, 16 October 1909, pp. 602–3;

St Anthony's Hall Folder 226, Doc. No. E56.45, Franciscan Archives; quoted in Egan, 'The Friars Minor and the Honan', pp. 14–15.

32 Taylor, *Windle*, p. 204.

33 See *Cork Examiner*, 7 October 1909; Windle was deeply honoured to receive the knighthood of St Gregory. He believed it to be the work of his friend, Fr Maher. However, other Catholic friends including the Archbishop of Birmingham and Cardinal Gasquet may also have been pressing for the award.

34 Archbishop Walsh to Windle, 16 July 1909, UC/OFFICERS/8/72, College Archives, UCC.

35 Egan, 'The Friars Minor and the Honan Hostel', p. 13.

36 Sir Bertram Windle to Fr Francis Maher, 20 February 1910, St Anthony's Hall, Folder 227, Doc. No. E56.59, Franciscan Archives; see also Egan, 'The Friars Minor and the Honan Hostel', p. 16.

37 Cuttings book, no number, College Archives, UCC.

38 Windle to Archbishop William Walsh, 24 March 1912, NUI Files, William Walsh Papers, Dublin Archdiocesan Archives [henceforth DAA] Dublin.

39 Windle to Archbishop William Walsh, 24 March 1912, NUI Files, William Walsh Papers, DAA.

40 Windle to the Bishop of Limerick, Edward Thomas O'Dwyer, undated memorandum (probably January or February 1914) from Episcopal Archives, Limerick, St Anthony's Hall, Folder 227, Doc. No. E56.73, Franciscan Archives; see also Egan, 'The Friars Minor and the Honan Hostel', pp. 27–8.

41 Article from *The Tablet*, reprinted in the *Cork Examiner*, 14 August 1912; from Cuttings book, no. 20, College Archives, UCC.

42 Ibid.

43 Ibid.

44 Ibid.

45 Here Fr Bartholomew Egan quotes from a fragment by the Friar Peter Begley: see Egan, 'The Friars Minor and the Honan Hostel', p. 22.

46 Ibid.

47 Ibid., p. 24.

48 Windle to the Bishop of Limerick, Edward Thomas O'Dwyer, undated memorandum (probably January or February 1914) from Episcopal Archives, Limerick, St Anthony's Hall, Folder 227, Doc. No. E56.73, Franciscan Archives; see also Egan, 'The Friars Minor and the Honan Hostel', p. 27.

49 Windle to the Bishop of Limerick, Edward Thomas O'Dwyer, undated memorandum (probably January or February 1914) from Episcopal Archives, Limerick, St Anthony's Hall, Folder 227, Doc. No. E56.73, Franciscan Archives; see also Egan, 'The Friars Minor and the Honan Hostel', p. 29.

50 Windle to the Bishop of Limerick, Edward Thomas O'Dwyer, undated memorandum (probably January or February 1914) from Episcopal Archives, Limerick, St Anthony's Hall, Folder 227, Doc. No. E56.73, Franciscan Archives; see also Egan, 'The Friars Minor and the Honan Hostel', pp. 29–30.

51 John Humphreys, Windle's friend, had studied this period extensively and written on the subject. It is little wonder that the martyred priest was of great personal interest to both men. On 24 August 1930, Humphreys wrote to Sr Monica: 'For the last month I have been *very busy*. In connection with the ceremony of honouring Father John Wall O.S.F. the last man who was martyred for his faith in England in the reign of Charles II. During my life I have written a good deal about his sufferings and the noble way he faced a most cruel death at Worcester in 1679. Being a Worcestershire man his heroism appealed to me, and I contributed to the Birm. Archaeological Society a paper dealing with the 'Titus Oates Plot' and its effect on my country: The paper was written early in the century. Yesterday there was an enormous gathering at the Harrington Church, representing *all shades* of religious opinions who had assembled to pay honour to the memory of the great martyr and to pay homage at his shrine in Harrington Catholic

Churchyard. There, engraved on his white marble cross is the record of his life and doings. I think you would have been touched if you had seen the sight yesterday. All were animated by the same spirit of love and devotion to the memory of the Saint. I will tell you when we meet how I have been working for to save the venerable Harrington Hall where Fr Wall served as chaplain to Lady Mary Yate, and, thank God, the present Archbishop of Birmingham has raised a large sum for its restoration and I bought on behalf of my friend Mrs Ferris, a rich Birmingham Lady, the old hall for a centre of Catholic activity. The Bishop is a fine man, and his action has stimulated everybody. Restoring the hall effectually and yesterday I had the honour of giving an address, the first since the hall was completed.' John Humphreys to Sr Monica, 24 August 1930, Published Memoir and Associated Materials, Box 13, BWP.

52 *Limerick Leader*, 9 January 1911.
53 Ibid.
54 *Cork Constitution* (undated), Cuttings Book, no. 21, College Archives, UCC.
55 Ibid.
56 See Windle to *The Irish Times*, 21 April 1913, Cuttings Book, no. 21, College Archives, UCC.
57 See Tristram to *The Irish Times*, 22 April 1913, Cuttings Book, no. 21, College Archives, UCC.
58 See Windle to *The Irish Times*, 23 April 1913, Cuttings Book, no. 21, College Archives, UCC.
59 See Tristram to *The Irish Times*, 24 April 1913, Cuttings Book, no. 21, College Archives, UCC.
60 See Windle to *The Irish Times*, 25 April 1913, Cuttings Book, no. 21, College Archives, UCC.
61 See Tristram to *The Irish Times*, 26 April 1913, Cuttings Book, no. 21, College Archives, UCC.
62 Taylor, *Windle*, p. 205.
63 Obituary, The Rev. Sir John R. O'Connell, *Irish Times*, 30 December 1943.
64 Ibid.
65 See Sir John O'Connell, *Thom's Directory*, 1921; this entry gives the date when he qualified as a solicitor as 1889.
66 Obituary, The Rev. Sir John R. O'Connell, *Irish Times*, 30 December 1943.
67 See Sir John O'Connell, *Thom's Directory*, 1921; this entry gives his wife's name as Mary.
68 Obituary, The Rev. Sir John R. O'Connell, *Irish Times*, 30 December 1943.
69 Ibid.
70 Ibid.
71 Ibid.
72 In London, O'Connell was a member of the Reform and National Liberal clubs and in Dublin he was a member of the Stephen's Green and Royal Automobile clubs. See Sir John O'Connell, *Thom's Directory*, 1921.
73 Richard I. Henchion, 'The Remarkable Honan Family: Their Parsimony and their Charity', *Evening Echo*, 22 April 1976.
74 'Death of Miss Honan', *Cork Examiner*, 18 August 1913.
75 The report continued: 'Indeed, all such institutions and kindred organisations had in the late Miss Honan a patron and benefactress to whom they can never measure their indebtedness. To recount the endless chain of charitable actions in the deceased lady's long life would be impossible, for the knowledge of much of her noble work was denied to the public by her unostentatious methods of making her presents. She was never wishful to have her donations trumpeted, her reward was in the self possession of the fact that she had done good and helped to add glory to the House of God, and facilities to institutions caring for sickness and disease. She was a philanthropist, an honour and credit to her native city, in which her death is sincerely regretted. Her life work of zeal for church, and ambition to provide infirmaries with

adequate equipment are mirrored in St Patrick's Church and the North Infirmary, in which she caused to be erected a handsome operating theatre. These are only two incidents. There are many others not less munificent, all which speak the desires which shaped and guided the acts of a great Catholic lady, whose last gift was to the church from which her remains were interred: namely, the gift of a pulpit. Her lamented death has removed a personality and a benefactress which helped to illumine the reputation of Cork for generosity of spirit and kindness of heart.' 'Funeral of Miss Honan', *Cork Examiner*, 20 August 1913.

76   Will of Isabella Honan, 16 August 1913, National Archives of Ireland (NAI), Bishop Street, Cork.

77   Taylor, *Windle*, p. 226.

78   As a way of comparing what £40,000 stood for in 1913 terms, an entry in the Honan Hostel Minute Book recorded the following wages for 1918: '5 servants @ 7 shillings per week for thirty two weeks = £55. 4 staff [Honan Hostel] at 12s 6d per week for 32 weeks = £70.' The warden of the Honan Hostel was paid £50 a year. Honan Minute Book, loose page inserted at 1918, p. 48, College Archives, UCC.

79   *Cork Examiner*, 28 October 1913, Cuttings Book, no. 21, College Archives, UCC.

80   Ibid.

81   O'Connell to Windle, reprinted in the *Cork Examiner*, 6 April 1914, Cuttings Book, no. 21, College Archives, UCC.

82   Ibid.

83   Ibid.

84   Ibid.

85   Windle to O'Connell, 5 April 1914, reprinted in the *Cork Examiner*, 6 April 1914, Cuttings Book, no. 21, College Archives, UCC.

86   Cuttings Book, no. 21, College Archives, UCC.

87   Taylor, *Windle*, p. 228.

88   The following governors were present: Sir Bertram Windle (chair), Archbishop of Cashel, John M. Harty, the Bishop of Cork, T.A. O'Callaghan, Bishop of Cloyne, Robert Brown, the Dean of Cork, Mgr Shinkwin, Archdeacon O'Leary PP, Fr Hugh M.G. Evans CSSP, Sir John Robert O'Connell, Sir Stanley Harrington, J.P. Molohan, Patrick Thomas O'Sullivan MD and W.J. Dunlea. Minute Book of the Honan Hostel, Cork, 26 January 1915, College Archives, UCC.

89   Minute Book of the Honan Hostel, Cork, 26 January 1915, College Archives, UCC.

90   A further sum of money left by Isabella Honan to Mrs Mary Murphy (amounting to £6,000 in shares) would revert to the Honan Trust upon her death. Japanese government bonds were to be lodged to the governors of the Bank of Ireland, South Mall, Cork, with the dividends to accrue to the Honan Hostel account. A sum of £220 was to be set aside for the annual payment of the chaplains. The Bank of Ireland, South Mall, was named as the bank for the Honan Trust. Minute Book of the Honan Hostel, Cork, 26 January 1915, College Archives, UCC.

91   Minute Book of the Honan Hostel, Cork, 26 January 1915, College Archives, UCC.

92   Ibid.

93   O'Connell to Windle, reprinted in the *Cork Examiner*, 6 April 1914, Cuttings Book, no. 21, College Archives, UCC.

94   Windle to O'Connell, 5 April 1914, reprinted in the *Cork Examiner*, 6 April 1914, Cuttings Book, no. 21, College Archives, UCC.

95   Editorial, *Cork Examiner*, 6 April 1914, Cuttings Book, no. 21, College Archives, UCC.

96   The first meeting of the governors of the Honan Hostel, Cork, had been held at the Honan Hostel on Tuesday 26 January 1915 at 10.30 a.m. The following governors were present: Sir Bertram C.A. Windle FRS, KSG, MD in the chair; Most Rev. John M. Harty DD, Archbishop of Cashel; Very Rev. T.A. O'Callaghan DD, Bishop of Cork; Very Rev. Robert Brown DD, Bishop of Cloyne; Right Rev. Monsignor Shinkwin, Dean of Cork; Very Rev. Archdeacon O'Leary PP; Very Rev. Hugh M.G. Evans, CSSP; Sir John Robert O'Connell; Sir Stanley Harrington; J.P. Molohan MA; Patrick Thomas

O'Sullivan MD; and W.J. Dunlea Esq., LLD. Professor Smiddy, registrar and secretary of the governors, was in attendance.

97   Minute Book of the Honan Hostel, Cork, 18 May 1915, College Archives, UCC.

98   *Cork Examiner,* 19 May 1915.

99   *University College Cork Official Gazette,* Trinity Term (1916), pp. 187–8.

100 The evidence is very strong in support of that view. The governors of the Honan Hostel passed a resolution of sympathy following her untimely death in 1925. O'Connell replied to the warden, Mr Joseph Downey, on 6 July 1925: 'I am very grateful for and very much touched by your letter of 27th conveying to me the resolution passed at the meeting of the Governors of the Honan Hostel on 25th June, of sympathy with me in the great bereavement that I have suffered in the loss of my dear wife. The resolution which refers to the deep interest my dear wife took not alone in the initial work in the establishment of the Hostel and building of the Chapel and furnishing of same but also her continued interest in its welfare, touches me very much, because it reminds me of the fact that were it not for her constant sympathy and deep interest in this work, it would not have been possible for me to have carried it out as successfully as it has been. She took a very deep interest in the furnishing of the Hostel and in every detail in the building of the Chapel and its decoration, and also in the magnificent stained glass windows of Mr Harry Clarke, and the unique set of vestments, the gold set of which was designed by her sister who died some years ago.' Minutes of the Honan Hostel, 25 June 1925, College Archives, UCC.

101 Paul Larmour, *The Arts and Crafts,* p. 134; see also Elizabeth Wincott Heckett, 'The Embroidered Cloths of Heaven: The Textiles', in Teehan and Wincott Heckett (eds), *The Honan Chapel,* p. 136.

102 Nicola Gordon Bowe, *Harry Clarke.* Cited in Nicola Gordon Bowe monograph *The Life and Work of Harry Clarke* (Irish Academic Press, Dublin, 1989) (a monograph and catalogue of the Harry Clarke exhibition, Douglas Hyde Gallery, Trinity College, Dublin, 12 November to 8 December 1979), p. 11.

103 Dr Gordon Bowe writes: 'In the remaining four decades of his life [from 1881] he accumulated considerable wealth and a notorious reputation for lavish entertaining at his sumptuously furnished and book-lined house overlooking Killiney Bay. His guests at dinner included the cream of the artistic, legal and literary world of the time.' Waldron joined the Dublin Stock Exchange in 1881. He was, as indicated by Dr Gordon Bowe, very successful in that career. He was a nationalist MP, a privy councillor, governor of the National Gallery of Ireland, a senator of the National University and a member of the Royal Irish Yacht Club. He died, aged sixty-six, on 27 December 1923. Bowe, *Harry Clarke,* pp. 13–17.

104 By 1912, Clarke was a regular visitor at the Waldron *salon* in Killiney. There he met Sir John O'Connell, Sir Bertram Windle and the art critic Sir Thomas Bodkin. All four – Waldron, O'Connell, Windle and Bodkin – would be critical to his career. He won a travelling scholarship from the Department of Agriculture and Technical Instruction in Dublin, which he supplemented by securing commissions for drawings from the London publisher, George Harrap, who recognised his genius and originality. He had many rebuffs from other London publishers. That commission for forty full-page illustrations, sixteen in colour, for Hans Andersen's selected fairytales enabled him to travel widely in France from January 1914. In gratitude for his part in helping him secure the travelling scholarship, Clarke designed a decorative lantern for Waldron. The young artist made a memorable visit to the continent where among the many highlights was his trip to Chartres Cathedral. There he was fortunate to meet the cathedral guardian, Etienne Houvet, who was making a photographic record of the stained glass and permitted Clarke to climb the scaffolding and study the medieval stained glass at close quarters. Clarke's health deteriorated and he was forced to return to London where he recuperated and worked hard on the drawings for the Harrap book. His second trip to Paris in

May 1914 brought him back to Chartres. He visited the Sainte Chapelle, the Beaux Arts and Versailles. In the Louvre, he would have seen his own Saint Patrick panel on exhibition as part of a travelling international exhibition of British arts and crafts. Clarke spent much of his time in the Trocadero Museum at Chaillot: a virtual museum of the history of stained glass making. He also visited the museum at Cluny, housing an excellent collection of medallions. Some believe those to be part of the original glass of the Sainte Chapelle. After a number of weeks in Paris, he visited many of the most important cathedrals of France, including those in Rouen, Amiens and Fecamp. He returned in July to Dublin and holidayed on the Aran Islands with friends and fellow artists, among them Seán Keating and Harry's future wife, Margaret Crilly, a very talented portrait painter. Bowe, *Harry Clarke*, pp. 12–21.

105   Taylor, *Windle*, p. 230. This connection was first made by Dr Gordon Bowe; see *Harry Clarke*, pp. 40, 258.

106   Bowe, *Harry Clarke*, footnote 54, p. 258.

107   Taylor, *Windle*, p. 251.

108   Joshua Clarke Studio Order Book, supplied by Mr Ken Ryan, The Abbey Stained Glass Studio, 18 Old Kilmainham Road, Kilmainham, Dublin 8. This is part of a submission made by Ken Ryan and Abbey Stained Glass in the 1990s to the then dean of the Honan, Fr Gearoid O'Sullivan CM.

109   Cutting likely to be from the *Cork Examiner*, 5 July 1916; see Cuttings Book, No. 22, College Archives, UCC.

110   Ibid.

111   See article entitled 'Saint Finn Barr's Collegiate Chapel: Impressive Opening Ceremony', *Cork Examiner*, 6 November 1916; newspaper consulted together with the clippings in Cuttings Book, No. 22, College Archives, UCC.

112   Ibid.

113   Ibid.

114   Ibid.

115   Ibid.

116   Ibid.

117   Ibid.

118   Ibid.

119   Ibid.

120   Ibid.

121   See unmarked cutting, possibly the *Evening Echo*, 8 November 1916. See also 'Saint Finn Barr's Collegiate Chapel: Impressive Opening Ceremony', *Cork Examiner*, 6 November 1916; newspaper consulted together with the clippings in Cuttings Book, No. 22, p. 24, College Archives, UCC.

122   Ibid.

123   J.J.H. reviewing O'Connell, *Collegiate Chapel Cork Studies*, vol. 5 (December 1916), pp. 612–14.

124   The reviewer complimented the quality of the book and felt it was 'a pioneer in Irish publishing; for it is both beautiful and austere'. It was further felt that it might become a model for other books. The reviewer referred to the great work done by the English Catholic middle class. It was felt that the Honan family were to the fore in providing the inspiration for others with wealth and means to be philanthropic. The review concluded: 'Cork, ever renowned for its gallantry, has set the happy fashion.' Unsigned review, *The Dublin Review* (April 1917), pp. 297–9.

5.   RADICAL POLITICS, THE FIRST WORLD WAR AND THE 1916 RISING

1   White and O'Shea, *'Baptised in Blood'*, p. 16 ff.

2   Ibid.

3   For a full account of this incident, see Horgan, *Parnell to Pearse*, p. 226 ff and Michael

Tierney, *Eoin MacNeill: Scholar and Man of Action, 1867–1945*, edited by F.X. Martin (Oxford: Clarendon Press, 1980), p. 124 ff.

4   *Irish Times*, 15 and 20 December 1913.

5   See MacNeill and Casement letters in *The Irish Times*, 17 December 1913; see also editorial, 'Volunteers and Policies', to which MacNeill referred, *The Irish Times*, 16 December 1913.

6   On that occasion, Windle may have been annoyed by what he thought was a reversal in the position of John O'Connell over the funding of his Honan projects. On 2 December 1913, O'Connell was 'backing out. He [O'Connell] wants to give much less than he promised. Is there one dependable man in this damned land?' On 3 December, he felt upset by developments in college and stated: 'Well – observe this ends my doing anything more than I *must*.'

7   White and O'Shea, *'Baptised in Blood'*, pp. 27–30.

8   Taylor, *Windle*, pp. 227–8. See also diary entry, 24 March 1913, Box 2, BWP.

9   On a personal level, Windle was delighted to receive the following news from Gasquet. The latter wrote on 8 May: 'Yes the news is true and on the 28th I am to receive the "Hat". But I hope and am sure that this will not make the least change in our friendship which I prize so much . . . It will be now [?] be an additional reason for your finding your way to Rome now, for I have an excellent place for my workers or shall have when the changes are complete and I hope I shall always be able to put you up.' Gasquet to Windle, 8 May 1914, Windle's Personal Correspondence, Box 9, BWP.

10   Domestic life was less than perfect; he was having trouble with his daughter Nora. He wrote in his diary on 31 July: 'somewhat of an upset with Nora who says she is miserable though she doesn't say why. Wants to go to Ramsay [?] to which I agree if her aunt can arrange it.' There is no explanation for the rows, but Nora was twenty-five and may have found it a strain to live in such a buttoned-down household. On 1 August, his diary reveals: 'After breakfast had it out with Nora explaining how ungrateful her conduct had been and how ungracious in face of all that had been done for her. Not a word did she say but had a good deal of talk afterwards to Edith.' The following day, 2 August, Windle entered in his diary: 'After breakfast Nora off her own bat told me she was sorry she had been such a beast and I told her she had often given me a sore heart as god knows she has: Perhaps things may be better.' On 5 August, Windle's diary referred to 'seeing about getting Nora off to-morrow'. The following day, he wrote: 'Saw Nora off by train to Birmingham. She preferring I[sle] of Man to our society. Perhaps better so as things are . . .' On 8 August, having returned to Ireland, he recorded that he had had no news from Nora.

11   Taylor, *Windle*, p. 237.

12   Gwynn, *John Redmond*, p. 356.

13   Taylor, *Windle*, p. 238.

14   Ibid., p. 237.

15   On Sunday 16 August, Windle had a visit from Bishop Amigo of Southwark and Canons Murnane and Roche. He showed them around the college. Windle was fortunate not to have been caught up in the war on the continent. He was a member of a group of intellectuals who had represented the British Churches at a peace conference in Germany. Another meeting was scheduled to open in Liège, Belgium, on 9 August. Windle took the very unusual step of writing in red ink part of the diary entry for that day: 'I was aghast frankly that I had a notice that the Conference was "postponed": what a state of affairs.' But by the time the president of UCC had written that entry, the bishop of that city had been imprisoned by the invading German forces. His palace, where the conference was to have taken place over two days, had been occupied.

16   Taylor, *Windle*, pp. 238–9.

17   John J. Horgan, 'Precepts and Practice in Ireland, 1914–1919,' *Studies*, 8, 30 (June 1919), pp. 210–26.

18   Taylor, *Windle*, p. 238.

19   Herbert H. Asquith, *Memories and Reflections, 1852–1927* (London: Cassell & Co., 1928), pp. 2–33.

20   On 20 September, Redmond spoke at Woodenbridge, County Wicklow: 'I am glad to see such magnificent material for soldiers around me, and I say to you, 'Go on drilling and make yourselves efficient for the work, and then account yourselves as men, not only in Ireland itself, but wherever the firing-line extends, in defence of right, of freedom, and of religion in this war.' Gwynn, *John Redmond*, pp. 391–2.

21   But the war had its less than glorious side. On 18 September, Windle walked into the city centre where he observed much drunkenness: 'drinking dreadful . . . The corner boys waylay the women who get money from relief funds and entice them to spend it on drinks – meantime the children starve.'

22   *Cork Examiner,* 4 October 1919.

23   *Statement of the Governing Body in Support of the Claim for the Establishment of a Separate University for Munster, Cork, 1918,* p. 21, Personal and Family Material of Windle, Box 11, BWP.

24   He was the youngest son of Patrick Joseph and Margaret McNamara (née O'Connell), of 'Analore', Castle Road, Blackrock, Cork. He had three older brothers. McNamara attended Christians, in Cork, where he distinguished himself as a scholar and a rugby player. we found this reference to the 1911 census http://www.census.nationalarchives.i.../nai001895441/ (access date 27 May 2010) and another on the First World War Talk http://ww1talk.co.uk/forums/showthread.-php?p=4947.

25   His Professor of Civil Engineering, C.W.L. Alexander, wrote in appreciation following his death: 'When College were hard pressed and in sore straits, you could be sure that Macky was in the thick of the tussle, and that if relief could be brought, he would do it. And no one was quicker to seize an opening or more subtle in luring the enemy to destruction. Any thought of personal distinction never entered his head. The success of the team was his goal, and he cared nothing for scoring tries himself.' Alexander, who was reaching the end of his playing career, played on the college team with him during some of that time. One year UCC won the Charity, Dudley and Munster cups, and the League Shield. McNamara played with Harry Jack for Munster and at half back for Ireland in 1914 in three internationals. Alexander continued: 'When the call came for men for King and Country, Vincent McNamara felt it his duty to offer himself. Perhaps you will say it was love of adventure and a desire to see the outer world. In some degree it was. But let me say, as perhaps the one best qualified to judge, that a high sense of duty was the determining cause in his enlisting in the Royal Engineers. He went off to Chatham in February with his old friend and leader, John Linehan, after receiving a substantial token of his fellow students' good will.' His professor, who kept in touch with him by letter, followed his short-lived military career: 'In his military training he acquitted himself singularly well, and was drafted to the Dardanelles in June. The writer had several letters from him, all breathing the familiar spirit of banter and pleasantry so peculiarly his own. How he met his death on 29th Nov. we do not know, beyond that it was due to some gas explosion.' Alexander concluded: 'Good-bye, dear Macky. That mortal frame we loved to look upon is laid to rest on the rugged shore of Gallipoli, but we believe that Death is swallowed up in Victory, and that the Light that shone out upon us through those clear eyes entered that fuller Life beyond.' C.W.L. Alexander, 'Vincent McNamara', *Annual Journal of the Engineering Society, University College Cork* (January 1916), pp. 6–9.

26   We are grateful to Neil Shuttleworth, 16 New Street, Broadbottom, Hyde, SK14 6AN, UK, who prepared a study on Patrick Roche in 2007.

27   *Report of the President to the Governing Body for 1914–1915,* p. 10; letter signed by Windle, J.P. Molohan, registrar and H.C. Clifton, secretary, College Archives, UCC.

28   Windle to Sr Monica, 7 May 1915, Windle's Personal Correspondence, Box 13, BWP.

29   As this chapter draws heavily on Windle's personal diary, no citation is given other than the date. See Windle's diaries, Boxes 1 and 2, BWP.

30   Gwynn, *John Redmond*, pp. 423–4.
31   F.S.L. Lyons, *John Dillon: A Biography* (London: Routledge & Kegan Paul, 1968), p. 364.
32   Horgan, *Parnell to Pearse*, pp. 272–6.
33   Senia Pašeta's revealing study, *Before the Revolution: Nationalism, Social Change and Ireland's Catholic Élite, 1879–1922* (Cork University Press, 1999).
34   See Campbell, *The Irish Establishment*, pp. 297–320.
35   There is need for a study of UCC graduates and political affiliation.
36   Lawrence W. McBride, *The Greening of Dublin Castle: The Transformation of Bureaucratic and Judicial Personnel in Ireland, 1892–1922* (Washington, DC: Catholic University Press, 1991), pp. 155–6, 190.
37   Taylor, *Windle*, p. 250.
38   Marcus Hartog, address on presentation to Sir Bertram and Lady Windle, 15 October 1919; see *University College Cork Official Gazette*, vii, 27 (January 1920), p. 265.
39   Anon., *War Record of University College Cork, 1914–1919* (University College Cork, n.d.), pp. 1–20.
40   Taylor, *Windle*, pp. 246–7.
41   Gasquet to Windle, 12 September 1915, Windle's Personal Correspondence, Box 9, BWP.
42   He added one final thought: 'I ought to add, with great thankfulness the end of a critical period which Edith passed through with much less physical and psychical disturbance than might have been feared and in all ways a thing to be profoundly grateful for.'
43   Bertram Windle, *What is Life? A Study of Vitalism and Neo-Vitalism* (London: Sands, 1908), pp. 133–43.
44   There is one letter, dated 3 September 1884, from the well-known evolutionist Jack Mivert in Windle's Personal Correspondence, Box 9, BWP.
45   Sir Bertram Windle, *Twelve Catholic Men of Science* (London: Catholic Truth Society, 1912), p. v.
46   Those chosen by Windle were as follows: Thomas Linacre (1460–1524); Andreas Versalius (1514–64); Nicolaus Stensen (1638–87); Aloisio Galvani (1737–98); René Théodore Laennec (1781–1826); Johannes Müller (1801–26); Sir Dominic Corrigan (1802–80); Angelo Secchi SJ (1818–78); Johann Gregor Mendel (1822–44); Louis Pasteur (1822–95); Albert de Lapparent (1839–1908); and Thomas Dwight (1843–1911). Ibid., p. vi.
47   He raised at the end of the piece a reference to the 'Darwinian bias' or 'Darwinian dogmatism'. He called for a fair hearing for Dwight's book, and not an attack based on the ancient legal advice: 'No case; abuse the plaintiff's attorney.' He added: 'Fire the accusation that he is "reactionary" against your opponent, and go your way satisfied that you have destroyed him and his opinions for ever.' He returned to the defence of Dwight against charges of having 'reactionary motives'. That was what was said about him, as it was said 'about any attempt to criticize the popular scientific idol of the day'. Windle wanted his subject's book to be given 'a fair hearing'. He did not wish to see him consigned to condemnation without an objective reading by those who chose the old Ephesian method of crying: 'Great is Diana of the Ephesians.' Windle, *Twelve Catholic Men of Science*, pp. 22–3.
48   Sir Bertram Windle, *A Century of Scientific Thought and Other Essays* (London: Burns & Oates, 1915).
49   Windle made an analogy between religion and science on the first page of his leading article which had the same name as the collection of essays. He referred to a lovely mountain tarn in Kerry: 'High up, embosomed in the mountains, for the most part of the year it is even unfishable, because its sheltered position leaves its surface too glassy for the trout to be deceived by the fly. When, however, the wind blows from the right quarter, what a change in the lake! Its mirror-like surface is torn with waves, miniature water-spouts and spindrift rage and tear over its face. It is hardly recognizable as the peaceful thing it was, and will be again. For when the wind dies down,

once more the pool returns to its peaceful state; once more puts on its glassy surface. Yet, no doubt, profound changes have taken place in the disposition of its waters: they are not as they were. The depths of the pool have been stirred, all cannot be as it was before the storm raged. The pool is the same, though a profound reconstruction of its constituent parts may have taken place.'

50   Windle, *A Century of Scientific Thought*, p. 18.
51   Ibid., p. 20.
52   Ibid., p. 32.
53   Ibid., p. 56.
54   Ibid., p. 105.
55   Ibid., p. 157.
56   Ibid., p. 195.
57   Sir Bertram Windle, *The Church and Science* (London: Catholic Truth Society, 1920)
58   Ibid., p. 2.
59   Ibid., p. 11.
60   Ibid., p. 404.
61   Ibid., p. 408.
62   Gwynn, *John Redmond*, p. 464.
63   On 31 January, Windle noted: 'Had to give Smiddy a good going over, he having written a most impertinent letter (as I told him) saying that he had not expected me to "interfere" in the details of his conferences. Finding his head a good deal swollen I punctured it and he left me a good deal smaller.'
64   Michael MacDonagh, *The Life of William O'Brien, the Irish Nationalist: A Biographical Study of Irish Nationalism, Constitutional and Revolutionary* (London: Ernest Benn, 1928), pp. 207–8.
65   Horgan, *Parnell to Pearse*, p. 287.
66   Ibid., pp. 285–7.
67   Horgan, 'Biographical Introduction', pp. xii–xiii.
68   P.S. O'Hegarty, *The Victory of Sinn Féin: How it Won it and How it Used it* (Dublin: Talbot Press, 1924), p. 5.
69   In his diary for 21 August 1918, Windle wrote a historical footnote: 'J.M. Plunkett brought to Germany in a submarine. Nobody knew [?] him. Huns abandoned their promise of 2 [?] subs. Sent Casement in submarine. Broke down. [?] to Heligoland. Put on another and dropped in Kerry . . . and MacNeill did his best to stop rebellion knowing it to be hopeless.'
70   McIntyre was the editor of a newspaper called *Searchlight* and Dickson of *The Eye-Opener*. Both men had been arrested by Bowen-Colthurst when he sacked a tobacconist shop. He took them prisoner together with the owner. Both men were unionist in sympathies and loyal supporters of the British Empire. Sheehy Skeffington had been taken out with the raiding party as a hostage. He had protested at the shooting dead by Bowen-Colthurst of a seventeen-year-old boy. The following morning all three were taken out into the courtyard where they were shot by a firing squad. Sheehy Skeffington was seen to move on the ground. Bowen-Colthurst ordered a second firing party to finish him off. His body was then put in a sack and buried in the barracks. His wife was never informed of his arrest, murder or clandestine burial. See Margaret Ward, *Hanna Sheehy Skeffington: A Life* (Cork University Press, 1997), pp. 156–7.
71   The entry for Friday 28th also stated: 'Examiner article splendid and wrote and told Crosbie [editor of *Cork Examiner*] so.'
72   Horgan, *Parnell to Pearse*, pp. 291–2.
73   The governing body was obliged to advertise the vacancies in the professorships and lectureships in the college caused by 'the expiration of seven years from the date of the dissolution of the Royal University of Ireland and having applications for the same from the persons whose names are set down below have submitted these names to the Academic Council who, after having obtained reports from the

various faculties, have unanimously recommended to the governing body the election of these candidates.' The motion recommended the election of those candidates. There were twenty professors and eleven lecturers listed. The motion was passed. UC-MB-GB-8, Governing Body Minutes, 3 May 1916, pp. 147–8, College Archives, UCC.

74   UC-MB-GB-8, Governing Body Minutes, 3 May 1916, p. 147, College Archives, UCC.

75   James Walsh was born near Bandon, County Cork. He worked for the postal service and was active in the Gaelic Athletic Association. In the 1916 rising, he was in the Hibernian Rifles and served under James Connolly in the GPO. He was arrested and sentenced to death. The sentence was commuted to life imprisonment and he was released in 1917 in a general amnesty.

76   Lyons, *John Dillon*, p. 380.

77   *1916 Rebellion Handbook* (Introduction by Declan Kiberd) (Dublin: The Mourne River Press, 1998 [1916]), p. 62.

78   Horgan, *Parnell to Pearse*, p. 291.

79   Lyons, *John Dillon*, pp. 380–2.

80   See Dermot Keogh, 'The Catholic Church, the Holy See and the 1916 Rising', in Gabriel Doherty and Dermot Keogh (eds), *1916: The Long Revolution* (Cork: Mercier Press, 2007), pp. 250–309.

81   On 29 May, he worked in his office and walked in the college grounds. His terse entry is as follows: 'Miss Danaher to be married next week which is what comes of having young women as professors. Another bad [abbreviation which may mean bad] appointment.'

82   Born in Holy Cross, County Tipperary, in 1842, he studied at Maynooth where he became friendly with a seminarian two years ahead of him, William J. Walsh, who became Archbishop of Dublin in 1885. O'Dwyer became Bishop of Limerick in 1886 and went on to play a prominent role in the political life of Ireland until his death in 1917. He was a man of fiercely independent views – views which he defended with vigour and polemical skill. Because of his opposition to the Plan of Campaign in the 1880s, he earned the unenviable reputation of being a 'Castle' bishop – a defender of British rule in Ireland. Thomas J. Morrissey SJ, *Bishop Thomas O'Dwyer of Limerick, 1842–1917* (Dublin: Four Courts Press, 2003).

83   Morrissey, *Bishop Thomas O'Dwyer*, p. 376.

84   The general added that they would have been placed under arrest if they had been laymen, and he would be pleased the bishop would move both men to employment where they would not have contact with the people. The letter struck the wrong chord with O'Dwyer, who told Maxwell bluntly in a letter which he dictated on 9 May: 'Whatever may be the rights of the military under martial law, a bishop in the exercise of his authority has to follow the rules of ecclesiastical procedure.' That barb was aimed at Maxwell's own use of his military powers which had resulted in summary executions of the leaders of the rising. O'Dwyer also made use of an episode in Maxwell's own life which further undermined his moral authority to conduct executions. He referred in his letter to the general's participation in the Jamestown raid of December 1895. On that occasion, Maxwell was one of a number of adventurers – led by L. Storr Jameson – who entered the Transvaal intending to take Johannesburg and depose Paul Kruger. The raid failed and Maxwell was jailed. O'Dwyer, picking up the changing mood of the people, shared the growing anger over the executions, the deportations and the mistreatment of the public. The letter, the publication of which was delayed by the censor until the end of May, was incendiary in content, tone and attitude towards British military authority. O'Dwyer referred to Maxwell as a 'military dictator'. The bishop, refusing to act against the two priests, said he could have no part in proceedings 'which I regard as wantonly cruel and oppressive'. Referring to the aforementioned raid: 'You remember the Jameson Raid, when a number of buccaneers invaded a friendly state and fought the forces of the lawful government. If ever men deserved the supreme punishment it was they.

But officially and unofficially the influence of the British government was used to save them, and it succeeded. You took care that no plea for mercy should interpose on behalf of the young fellows who surrendered to you in Dublin. The first information which we got of their fate was the announcement that they had been shot in cold blood.' The bishop accused Maxwell of showing no mercy to pleas for clemency after the rising: 'Personally I regard your action with horror, and I believe that it has outraged the conscience of the country.' He wrote that the deporting of hundreds without trial was 'one of the worst and the blackest chapter in the history of the misgovernment of this country'.

85   Keogh, 'The Catholic Church, the Holy See and the 1916 Rising', p. 288.

86   *1916 Rebellion Handbook*, p. 248.

87   Governing Body Minutes, 14 June 1916, p. 150.

88   For studies of Walsh, see Thomas Morrissey, *William Walsh, Archbishop of Dublin, 1841–1921* (Dublin: Four Courts Press, 2000) and Jérôme aan de Wiel, *The Catholic Church in Ireland, 1914–1918* (Dublin: Irish Academic Press, 2003).

89   The Archbishop of Dublin did not agree with the draconian reaction of the British government to the uprising. But it might be kept in mind that he had, despite being seriously ill at the time, done everything possible to stop it. On 11 May 1916, Walsh replied to a letter from Sir John Maxwell using a form of language which was both mockingly deferential and antagonistic. Asked to furnish the general with the names of priests who had distinguished themselves during the rising, Walsh refused to identify anyone, even those who had been in the thick of the action, like the clergy of the parish of Marlboro' Street and the Capuchins of Church Street. Walsh felt it would be 'invidious to treat those cases as if they were exceptional'. The archbishop had subscribed to the relief fund set up by the Lord Mayor of Dublin and had petitioned for a fair trial for Alderman Thomas Kelly, one of the many swept up by the British authorities in the aftermath of the rising. See Sheila Carden, *The Alderman: Alderman Tom Kelly (1868–1942) and Dublin Corporation* (Dublin City Council, 2007), pp. 96–112.

90   Keogh, 'The Catholic Church, the Holy See and the 1916 Rising', pp. 285–6.

91   Windle had a particular love of dogs. In helping Sr Monica write her biography, Edith wrote: 'Bertie loved all dogs. We had so many; about such one I could tell endless stories. At one time in Cork we had as many as three dachshunds in the house. Peter (she was mine) and a son of theirs Fighe. Felcter had a family of five. Long before that Bertie had a dachs called Solomon – Solly for short – he came over from England in a box and nearly died on the way – a very tiny puppy that Bertie used to carry about in his coat pocket. I forget how many were the years of his little life but he died of double pneumonia after distemper. I sat up those nights with the poor dear. There was also a Sally – a year or more before we left Cork. Dorothy (my sister, sometimes called 'Bove') brought her over from London – a tiny puppy – given to her by Lord Dawson the King's physician. Sally came to an untimely end at Listarkin. Someone in the village had put poison about to kill barking dogs that were an annoyance at night and the poor little harmless creature was the first to fall a victim when Dorothy took her to the village post office. Sally dropped dead in the road while she was inside buying stamps. I could only decide whether the dog you speak of was Sally or Solly by the year. In both cases we had another dog from England – Peggy followed Sally and was left with Colonel Somerville at Drisane when we came to Canada. She has long since been gathered to her fathers.'

92   On 15 September, he wrote: 'That scoundrel of Limerick [Bishop O'Dwyer] once more spits . . . at Freedom. How can a country get on with prelates such as he and W.J.W. [Archbishop of Dublin].'

93   Governing Body Minutes, 11 October 1916, p. 165.

94   Ibid., p. 166.

95   Ibid., p. 168.

96   Joseph V. O'Brien, *William O'Brien and the Course of Irish Politics, 1881–1918* (Berkeley, CA: University of California Press, 1976), p. 229.

97   On 7 November, Windle reviewed the numbers entering UCC. That year the numbers attending were 143 (ninety-six medicals). The figure had been ninety-six the previous year and forty-five when he had first come to Cork. That was significant progress.

98   McBride, *The Greening of Dublin Castle*, pp. 219–21.

99   Ibid.

100   Windle wrote to Sr Monica on 21 December 1916 to mention a prize-winning student, Dr Bridget O'Connor, who had got a job there as a medical officer of health, 'an excellent job for a girl of 23. I should like her to meet S. Anne if there'. In another letter, on 18 January 1917, Windle thanked Sr Monica for putting Dr O'Connor into contact with her community. Windle to Sr Monica, 17 January 1917, Windle's Personal Correspondence, Box 9, BWP.

101   Gasquet to Windle, 20 December 1916, Windle's Personal Correspondence, Box 9, BWP.

6. THE RISE OF SINN FÉIN AND THE IRISH CONVENTION

1   For a lucid examination of British opinion for the period, see George Boyce, 'British Opinion, Ireland and the War, 1916–1918', *Historical Journal*, 17, 3 (1974), pp. 575–93; see also T. Hennessy, *Dividing Ireland: World War I and Partition* (London: Routledge, 1998); Alvin Jackson, *Ireland, 1798–1998: Politics and War* (Oxford: Blackwell Publishers, 1999).

2   He reported on 1 February that there had been 'an indescribable squabble between women on Herb-growing [project] – all incompetent and all must be got out if the thing is to go.' He noted on 3 February 1917: 'America breaks off diplomatic negotiations to Germany. A great wonder! Will they now act determinedly.' On 9 February, he wrote: 'British making small but useful advances. America still on brink. What a lily-livered loon Wilson is!' He wrote on 14 February that he had gone to stay with the O'Connells. He discussed with his hosts the pressing issue of military chaplains, and showed little sympathy for the exclusion of Irish clergy, stating: 'yet heaps of lazy curates about here'. On 15 February, he attended a meeting of the Royal Irish Academy where Mahaffy of Trinity 'behaved as usual like arrogant buffoon – However beat him by the skin of the teeth.'

3   Terence Denman, *A Lonely Grave: The Life and Death of William Redmond* (Dublin: Irish Academic Press, 1995), p. 102.

4   Ibid., p. 104.

5   He refers to the outbreak of revolution in Russia on 16 March: 'Revolution in Russia. Duma asserts itself and the king. (D.G. another of them gone.) The Rasputin business must have sickened all decent people and even Russia doesn't want a James I with his peculiar sexual ideas.'

6   Denman, *A Lonely Grave*, p. 108 ff.

7   Gasquet to Windle, 28 March 1917, Windle's Personal Correspondence, Box 9, BWP.

8   Taylor, *Windle*, p. 256.

9   Bernadette Whelan, *United States Foreign Policy and Ireland: From Empire to Independence, 1913–1929* (Dublin: Four Courts Press, 2006).

10   There was a strong international response to his death. His wife, Eleanor, and brother, John, received over 400 messages of condolence.

11   Denman, *A Lonely Grave*, pp. 127–9.

12   Horgan, *Parnell to Pearse*, p. 303.

13   Taylor, *Windle*, p. 256.

14   Word is indistinct. The meaning however is clear. Expecting her to be chaste is out anyway.

15   Gasquet informed him that the presentation copy for the pope of *Religion and Science* had never arrived. The cardinal regarded the work as 'most excellent and just the book we have been looking for. It will do great good I am sure.' Gasquet, who had

loaned it to a theologian who knew English well, wrote: 'He was enthusiastic about it and said that it was just the book that was wanted at the present time.' Gasquet had read Windle's circular regarding military chaplains. There was nothing in it that was not known in Rome from other sources: 'I believe that the basis of the difficulty is that touched on by Card. Logue – that the disposition of the chaplains remains in the hands of the archbishop of Westminster and the Irish bishops and clergy do not want to have any English Bishop in the position. I can, to a certain extent, understand their objection in this regard but it is sad that the spiritual needs of the Irish soldiers should suffer.' Gasquet to Windle, 30 June 1917, Windle's Personal Correspondence, Box 9, BWP.

16   On 4 June 1917, Windle wrote: 'That damned ass [Count] Plunkett making a worse snorter of himself than ever. My God what a country which tolerates such scurf. But with the Bishops it has [,] lice are bound to breed.' On 12 June, Windle wrote: 'but things have got very bad including that Sinn Féin evidently are anxious to avoid disturbance and seem to want a constitutional movement for a Republic – an impossible dream. May I get speedily out of this country. Yes – but where.'

17   See Fidelma McDonnell, 'Riches of Clare: 1917 Rising of an Irish Political Colossus', *Clare Champion*, 26 September 2003, http://www.clarelibrary.ie/eolas/claremuseum/news_events/1917_rising.htm (accessed on 27 May 2010).

18   Horgan, *Parnell to Pearse*, p. 304.

19   Windle kept a close eye on the statements of Bishop O'Dwyer of Limerick. On 18 July, he wrote: 'Bishop of Limerick writes a letter which would disgrace a devil from hell – containing a lie which he either knows or could know was a lie. If not mad, he deserves any death that could be inflicted on him.'

20   Horgan, *Parnell to Pearse*, p. 304.

21   Windle noted that Nora, his daughter, had left Cork to go back to the WO (War Office); see Taylor, *Windle*, pp. 256–7.

22   Windle to Sr Monica, 22 July 1917, Windle's Personal Correspondence, Box 9, BWP.

23   Privilege, *Michael Logue*, p. 119.

24   R.B. McDowell, *The Irish Convention, 1917–18* (London: Routledge & Kegan Paul, 1970), pp. 99–100.

25   Horgan, *Parnell to Pearse*, p. 303.

26   See Andrew Scholes, *The Church of Ireland and the Third Home Rule Bill* (Dublin: Irish Academic Press, 2010) for an excellent treatment of the role of the Church of Ireland bishops in the convention, pp. 132–47.

27   Most of this quotation was reproduced in Taylor, *Windle*, pp. 268–9; however, his biographer did not include Windle's swingeing comments on the Irish Catholic bishops. We have added this and made other inclusions to be faithful to the original.

28   Gasquet to Windle, 28 July 1917, Windle's Personal Correspondence, Box 9, BWP.

29   Later that evening, he wrote upon hearing of the death of Bishop O'Dwyer of Limerick: 'a pestilent prelate but a kind-hearted man'.

30   Horgan, *Parnell to Pearse*, p. 309.

31   Windle's Personal Correspondence, Box 9, BWP.

32   Dorothy Macardle, *The Irish Republic* (Dublin: Wolfhound Press, 1999), pp. 228–9.

33   Frank Callanan, *T.M. Healy* (Cork University Press, 1996), pp. 529, 719.

34   C.J. Woods and William Murphy, 'Thomas Ashe', *Dictionary of Irish Biography*, vol. 1, (Dublin: Royal Irish Academy, 2009), pp. 176–7.

35   Plunkett to Leslie, 3 October 1917, Box 27, Folder 55, Shane Leslie Papers, Special Collections, Georgetown University, Washington DC.

36   Gwynn, *John Redmond*, pp. 567–8.

37   Gasquet also told him that he had at last had the pleasure of having presented his book to the pope and explained to him its merits. The pope sent Windle his photograph and had written on it his thanks and a blessing to you and yours.

38   Windle to Sr Monica, 4 November 1917, Windle's Personal Correspondence, Box 9, BWP.

39 Plunkett to Leslie, 2 November 1917, Box 27, Folder 55, Shane Leslie Papers, Special Collections, Georgetown University, Washington, DC.

40 Gwynn, *John Redmond*, pp. 570–1.

41 On 15 December 1917, Windle told Sr Monica: 'I never made a real friendship – and I am pleased to think I have done so with you – almost entirely by letter for I can scarcely convince myself that we have only had one brief interview otherwise than on paper . . . However I suppose one must do the work that comes to hand as well as one can.' Windle to Sr Monica, 15 December 1917, Windle's Personal Correspondence, Box 9, BWP.

42 Turning to the war, Maher wrote: 'The death toll, too, is mounting. A few days ago since Fr Monteith, ordained about three years ago, probably our most brilliant mathematician, was killed at the Front, though so far we [Jesuit chaplains] have been fortunate. For the men themselves it is of course one of the most glorious deaths a Jesuit can die – a martyr of charity – and one idly in his room envies these lucky fellows – but from a poor Father Provincial's point of view, and the needs of the future, tis different. The whole flower of our province is out – intellectually as well as in any other way, I am glad to say. The stories one hears from them are often terribly sad, the most piteous being the occasional nerve breakdowns of young officers – mere boys.' Taylor, *Windle*, p. 259.

43 Gwynn, *John Redmond*, p. 574.

44 Ibid., pp. 565–6.

45 Ibid.

46 Taylor, *Windle*, p. 260.

47 Gwynn, *John Redmond*, p. 580 ff.

48 Taylor, *Windle*, p. 261.

49 Amid the unrelenting gloom of the convention, Windle arranged to meet Sir John O'Connell on the evening of 15 January 1918. The latter promised Windle a sum of between £3,000 and £4,000 to build a new bridge in front of the new entrance to the college, the old bridge having been washed away in heavy floods. Taylor, *Windle*, p. 261.

50 C.S. (Todd) Andrews, *Dublin Made Me: An Autobiography* (Cork: Mercier Press, 1979), p. 102.

51 Lord Midleton to Lord Edmund Talbot, 19 December 1920. This letter was sent to Lady Leslie; see Shane Leslie Papers, Folder 4, Box 27, special collections, Georgetown University, Washington, DC.

52 *Irish Times*, 22 January 1918; see also editorial in *The Irish Times*, 23 January 1918.

53 Plunkett told Windle in February that it was a 'dead certainty' that he 'should be nominated to Senate in new Parliament in order to look after Education!' 'That's a thing that would need a lot of consideration,' Windle commented.

54 Cardinal Logue to Mr O'Connor, 1 March 1918, Ireland File, 1918–1932, Bourne Papers, Westminster Archdiocesan Archive.

55 He then gave her news about recent religious events in the college: 'We have had two splendid retreats – boys one week, girls next, finished to-day. I think every Catholic student boy or girl had been to his or her duties. That is something. We had an excellent retreat a CSsR and most of the best men for boys (and, my wife says, girls) we have ever had. I cannot tell you how good the girls are here nor how they edify me – about 100 went to the General communion yesterday together in the women's club here. You can imagine what a Babel it was (at breakfast).'

56 'John Redmond Dies; Many Pay Tribute', *New York Times*, 7 March 1917.

57 Lyons, *John Dillon*, p. 432.

58 Ibid., p. 431.

59 Horgan, *Parnell to Pearse*, pp. 320–1.

60 Lyons, *John Dillon*, p. 432.

61 Taylor, *Windle*, pp. 263–5.

62 On 24 March, Windle wrote: 'Back to town [Cork] and will bring up the PIG I have won in a raffle!'

63   *Report of the Proceedings of the Irish Convention*, Cd 9019, 1918, p. 4, British Parliamentary Papers.

64   The *Report of the Proceedings of the Irish Convention* explained why delegates had not opted for a majority report 'in the sense of a reasoned statement in favour of the conclusions upon which the majority are agreed, but is left to gather from the narrative of proceedings what the contents of such a report would have been'. It added: 'On the other hand, both the Ulster Unionists and a minority of the Nationalists have presented Minority Reports covering the whole field of the Convention's enquiry. The result of this procedure is to minimise the agreement reached, and to emphasise the disagreement.' This was an admission of failure. In the end, there were independent reports from the delegations of the Ulster unionists, from a majority of the nationalist members, from the Labour representatives, and notes by the provost of Trinity College and the Archbishop of Armagh, the Earl of Dunraven and the southern unionists. Windle sided in the end with the nationalist majority. The note read that 'we do not at this moment desire to press our objection to the fiscal proposals contained in the Prime Minister's letter, as we hold it to be of paramount importance that an Irish Parliament with an Executive responsible thereto should be immediately established . . .' It spoke about fiscal autonomy only being postponed. In that context, 'according to all precedents in the British Empire, an Irish Parliament is entitled, and ought to become the sole taxing authority for Ireland, unless and until, in the general interest it sees fit to part with some portion of its financial independence.' A free trade agreement between Great Britain and Ireland was considered desirable. It was not considered acceptable to have any other city than Dublin as the capital and administrative centre.

65   Windle's diary for 10 April 1918 reads in part: 'Foch said to be perfectly confident and 250,000 dead Germans said to be lying on ground which they had taken. This may be so but what a world in which such things can be done to please the arrogance of one man!'

7.   THE CONSCRIPTION CRISIS AND THE 'GERMAN PLOT'

1   Horace Plunkett to Shane Leslie, 6 May 1918, Box 27, Folder 56, Shane Leslie Papers, Special Collections, Georgetown University, Washington, DC.

2   Sir Arthur Conan Doyle to the *Freeman's Journal*, 4 April 1918; reproduced in *The Irish Times*, 5 April 1918.

3   'Special Extra – The Irish Problem', *The Irish Times*, 8 April 1918.

4   Plunkett to Leslie, 6 May 1918, Box 27, Folder 56, Shane Leslie Papers, Special Collections, Georgetown University, Washington, DC.

5   Ibid.

6   'North King's County Election', *The Irish Times*, 8 April 1918.

7   Horgan, *Parnell to Pearse*, p. 327.

8   Plunkett to Leslie, 6 May 1918, Box 27, Folder 56, Shane Leslie Papers, Special Collections, Georgetown University, Washington, DC.

9   On 16 April, Windle received a reply to a letter he had sent to Midleton with whom he had become quite friendly during the convention. The leader of the southern unionists was pessimistic about developments but appreciative of the support that he had received from Windle: 'Your letter is far too kind, to make it possible for me not to answer it, and tell you how much we appreciated your independent support throughout the Convention. Things have gone strangely amiss. The Catholic Church has disappointed us; so had Ulster; the "backbenchers" showed the lack of training . . . and the Government are taking action at the worst moment. But something has been done if the spirit of possible co-operation for a settlement has been established, and your letter is an encouragement. The co-operation regarding conscription of Dillon and de Valera bodes very ill for our hopes. It seems as if, much as we must sacrifice, the official Nationalists must receive only and not give?'

10   Lyons, *John Dillon*, pp. 433–4.

11 'The Archbishops'Appeal', *Irish Times*, 18 April 1918.
12 'Meeting of Parliamentary Party', *Irish Times*, 22 April 1918.
13 Aan de Wiel, *The Catholic Church in Ireland*, p. 220 ff.
14 'Ireland and Conscription', *Irish Times*, 22 April 1918.
15 Ibid.
16 Horgan, *Parnell to Pearse*, p. 327.
17 Shortt was MP for Newcastle. His father had been born in Tyrone and had gone to university in Trinity College Dublin. He later moved to Newcastle where he married. Lord French, who succeeded Wimborne, was – according to *The Irish Times* – a popular and distinguished Irishman with a home in Ireland. In the case of the latter, the cabinet overcame the difficulty posed by the fact that French was a soldier. See aan de Wiel, *The Catholic Church in Ireland*, pp. 209–10; See also 'New Chief Secretary for Ireland', *Irish Times*, 4 May 1918.
18 'Letter from Sir Horace Plunkett', *Irish Times*, 6 May 1918.
19 A.W. Samuels, attorney general, memorandum, 10 May 1918, Ireland file, 1918–1932, Cardinal Bourne Papers, Westminster Archdiocesan Archive.
20 Ibid.
21 Ibid. He said that there was 'abundant evidence of hostile association with the German enemy forthcoming, and there should be no more delay in banishing these enemies of the State from Ireland. They are day by day organising effectively and concocting rebellion'. He also wanted the seditious press 'rigorously suppressed and their printing works seized and type confiscated, and the seditious literature with which the newsvendors'shops are crammed cleared out of them and pulped'. Samuels wanted the government to move against 'the refugees from military service who flocked in thousands to Ireland from Great Britain since the commencement of the war, and who are a most undesirable and unpopular element amongst the Irish population, engaged in betting and whippet-racing, who the police could at once identify and round up'. He considered that that would be 'quite a popular application of conscription in Ireland to begin with. An announcement that any person identified in the future as taking part in illegal drilling would be deemed fit for military service and conscripted would also have a very useful effect.'
22 Ibid.
23 Walter Long to Cardinal Bourne, 11 May 1918, Ireland file, 1918–1932, Cardinal Bourne Papers, Westminster Archdiocesan Archive.
24 'Discovery of a German Plot in Ireland', *Irish Times*, 25 May 1918.
25 Ibid.
26 Aan de Wiel, *The Catholic Church in Ireland*, p. 220 ff.
27 On 13 April 1919, Brigadier-General Reginald Dyer opened fire on unarmed men, women and children during a protest in the Jallianwala Bagh Garden in the northern Indian city of Amritsar. The casualties were 1,100 wounded and 379 dead. The numbers may have been higher.
28 'Discovery of a German Plot in Ireland', *Irish Times*, 25 May 1918.
29 'Mr Dillon and Sinn Féin', *Irish Times*, 27 May 1918.
30 'The German Plot', *Irish Times*, 31 May 1918.
31 'The German Plot', *Irish Times*, 21 June 1918.
32 'Smashing reply to Mr Dillon', *Irish Times*, 30 July 1918.
33 Windle to Sr Monica, 18 July 1918, Windle's Personal Correspondence, Box 9, BWP.
34 Ibid.
35 On 27 July, he wrote: 'Irish members making asses of themselves and vulgar little Devlin trying to be funny and only succeeding in being emetic.'On 30 July, Windle walked with Edith to the city centre and enjoyed it heartily. However, he found that his wife was 'tired suddenly at end'. He wrote: 'No doubt this menopause is pure hell and now *four years* of it. Who would be a woman.' He tried to be understanding but his grasp of what she was experiencing was more clinical than

emotional. He described her symptoms rather than empathised with her. On 4 August, Sunday, he wrote from Listarkin: 'Mass (D.G. no sermon from Daly) and short week with Edith. Feeling better and she a bit better too I hope.'

36 Windle then went on to talk about the Roger Casement affair. He spoke of Casement's pleas to Irish prisoners to form a band of officers to return to Ireland to lead Sinn Féin troops. None of them knew or had heard of him (save one man who had seen him . . . in Cork). Windle then referred to Joseph Mary Plunkett in the most unflattering terms. 'He had been brought to Germany in a submarine. Nobody knew him Huns abandoned their promise of two submarines. Casement was sent in a submarine which broke down near to Heligoland. He was put on another and dropped in Kerry. Then he was seized by government and MacNeill did his best to stop rebellion knowing it to be hopeless'(Diary, 21 August 1918).

37 Ireland file, 1918–1932, Cardinal Bourne Papers, Westminster Archdiocesan Archive. We are grateful to Dr Niall Keogh for undertaking this research on our behalf.

38 Ibid.

39 Ibid.

40 In 1913, Alice Borthwick succeeded her dead husband as editor of the *Morning Post*.

41 Bowe, *Harry Clarke*, pp. 82–6.

42 'Mail Boat Sunk', *Irish Times*, 11 October 1918.

43 Gasquet to Windle, 23 October 1918, Windle's Personal Correspondence, Box 9, BWP.

44 On 12 November, he wrote: 'Lloyd George (lying impostor) in his glory.'

45 Horgan, *Parnell to Pearse*, p. 327 ff.

46 Brian Walker, *Parliamentary Election Results in Ireland, 1801–1922* (Dublin: Royal Irish Academy, 1978), p. 5.

47 Windle was convinced, in a note written on 28 January, that the majority of Sinn Féin deputies would not abide by their abstentionist policy. He wrote on 28 January: 'Most of them will seize the first excuse – it will not be hard to find one – to go into Parliament and grab the £400 p. a. which is what they want.'

48 Lyons, *Dillon*, pp. 454–5.

49 Professor Stockley was a TD for the NUI from 1921 to 1923. He was an alderman from 1920 to 1925. He took the anti-Treaty side in the civil war. Prof. Alfred O'Rahilly was elected to Cork Corporation after the 1916 rising. He was arrested in 1921 and spent a number of months on Spike Island. He was elected to Dáil Éireann in 1923, serving until his resignation in 1924. He took the Treaty side and served the government in a number of capacities. He changed sides and voted for de Valera's Fianna Fáil in 1932.

50 Windle's Personal Correspondence, Box 9, BWP.

51 Ibid.

52 Ibid.

53 On 12 November, he wrote disapprovingly of the Professor of English: 'Stockley mad ape prancing round country to make Sinn Féin speeches. Shows how hard up they are for a man.'

8. The University of Munster – Windle's Last Hurrah

1 O'Connell to Windle, 12 July 1917, Munster University Box, College Archives, UCC.

2 Ibid.

3 See Murphy, *The College*, p. 267 ff; see also the multi-volume work by J. Anthony Gaughan, in particular, *Alfred O'Rahilly: Academic* (Dublin: Kingdom Books, 1986), vol. 1 , pp. 34–161.

4 Born in Listowel, County Kerry, he was educated at Blackrock College before attending the Royal University, graduating with a first in Mathematical Physics and Experimental Physics in 1907 . Afterwards, he entered the Jesuit order at Stonyhurst, Lancashire, to study for the priesthood. He left in 1914.

5 UC/MB/GB/8, Meeting of the University Committee, 22 February 1918, College Archives, UCC.

6   Windle to George H. Morley, University of Birmingham, 11 February 1918, Munster University Box, College Archives, UCC.
7   Windle to Morley, 18 April 1918, Munster University Box, College Archives, UCC.
8   Windle to George Crosbie, 13 February 1918, Munster University Box, College Archives, UCC.
9   Gaughan, *Alfred O'Rahilly: Academic*, p. 67.
10   'A Munster University', *Irish Times*, 30 March 1918.
11   The governing body, at the same meeting, passed a resolution of condolence upon the death of John Redmond: 'That We the Governing Body of University College Cork put on record the expression of our sincere sorrow and deep regret at the death – all too early – of Mr J.E. Redmond, a distinguished Irishman, justly esteemed and respected by men of every shade of politics and a great statesman who was largely instrumental in bringing about the establishment of the National University and the reconstruction of the College. That we tender our heartfelt sympathy to his sorrowing widow and family. That the Secretary be directed to forward copy of this resolution to Mrs Redmond, Mrs Max Green and Capt. W. Redmond MP', UC/MB/GB/8, Governing Body meeting, 9 March 1918, College Archives, UCC.
12   *Statement of the Governing Body in Support of the Claim for the Establishment of a Separate University for Munster* (Cork, 1918), Personal and Family Material of Windle, Box 11, BWP.
13   Downey to Windle, 29 March 1918, Munster University Box, College Archives, UCC.
14   Munster University Box, College Archives, UCC.
15   *University College Cork Official Gazette*, no. 24, Trinity term (July 1918), pp. 231–3.
16   Windle to Walter Long, 10 June 1918, Munster University Box, College Archives, UCC.
17   He also gave examples of press reaction to the petition for an independent university. *The Irish Times* wrote: 'It is said with great truth that a Federal University can never be a real success . . . But considering the importance of efficient education in the great struggle after the war, it is essential that a College like that in Cork should immediately be elevated to the status of an independent University.' The *Educational Supplement* of the London *Times* wrote: 'it is sincerely to be hoped that the College, which possesses a magnificent educational record, will be allowed a free hand in working out its own destiny and giving full self-expression to a city which is itself and no other.' In conclusion, Windle asked that a deputation from Munster might be received by the lord lieutenant.
18   UC/MB/GB/8, Governing Body meeting, 30 October 1918, College Archives, UCC.
19   Windle returned to criticising the Irish bishops and clergy on 11 January: 'But the ecclesiastics of this country are the most powerful emetics in the world. Even to think of them [causes] nausea.'
20   The spelling of MacMahon varies. O'Connell uses McMahon in his letter quoted above.
21   O'Connell to Windle, 11 January 1919, Munster University Box, College Archives, UCC.
22   On the 13th he was told that the pre-war government 'for economy did away with military transport'. Hence . . . took all munitions to magazine in Park and put them away. When rebellion broke out these men went to magazine – killed sentry and took off just the things they wanted. Hence rebels had plenty of stuff [and army none] till it could be sent from other centres. What a set of muddles.'
23   On 8 March 1919, Windle received a letter from Dublin Castle saying that the 'Chief Secretary had been considering the statement of needs which you submitted to his predecessor, Mr Shortt, at the deputation received by him in January. As you will understand, it is impossible for Mr Macpherson to make a definite statement as to the amount of additional grants which the Government propose to provide until the Estimates have been finally approved by the Treasury and presented to Parliament but, in the meanwhile, he is anxious to lose no time in doing what he can to help the Irish Colleges to deal with their most urgent and immediate needs.

He has, accordingly, asked Sir William McCormick to take an early opportunity of entering into a confidential discussion with you, or with some other representative of your college, and he would be glad if you would put yourself into direct communication with Sir William.'A meeting was suggested in the Department of Scientific and Industrial Research in London.

24 Munster University Box, College Archives, UCC.
25 Samuels to Windle, 3 February 1919, Munster University Box, College Archives, UCC.
26 UC/MB/GB/8, Governing Body meeting, 6 February 1919, pp. 316–17, College Archives, UCC.
27 Gasquet to Windle, 9 February 1919, Windle's Personal Correspondence, Box 9, BWP.
28 Munster University Box, College Archives, UCC.
29 Ibid.
30 Ibid.
31 UC/MB/GB, 15 February 1919, p. 329, College Archives, UCC.
32 Munster University Box, College Archives, UCC.
33 Samuels to Windle, 22 February 1919, Munster University Box, College Archives, UCC.
34 In the memorandum, Windle argued that the National University would lose a certain amount of its income in the shape of fees paid by Cork students for examination, 'but on the other hand they would gain more than they would lose, in my opinion, because they would not have to pay Travelling expenses for Cork representatives on the Senate which amounts to some two or three hundred pounds a year, I suppose.' The NUI would also save on external examiners and would not have to pay printing costs or for invigilators. Windle argued that there was no other way in which the NUI would suffer 'for it will be observed that the Governing Body of the College is not asking, as it might reasonably ask, for any share in the University endowment of £10,000 per annum.' That was based on the view that the NUI would still have constituent colleges in Galway and Dublin. But if 'the decision of the Government should be to set up three Universities (following the example of the disruption of the Victoria University in England), then the Governing Body would naturally expect to have its share of the University Endowment'. Windle Memorandum, 'Respecting the Munster University Proposal', Munster University Box, College Archives, UCC.
35 Munster University Box, College Archives, UCC.
36 Plunket Barton had written to Windle on 26 March 1918: 'I am in agreement with your wish for a University at Cork, and have been of that opinion for some years. I am not influenced by the consideration that the Senate is dominated by Dublin.' Munster University Box, College Archives, UCC.
37 Meeting of the Senate, National University of Ireland, 28 February 1919, NUI Senate Minutes, vol.VI, NUI Archives, Merrion Square, Dublin; I am grateful to the registrar of the NUI, Attracta Halpin, for giving me copies of this minute.
38 Munster University Box, College Archives, UCC.
39 Ibid.
40 Ibid.
41 Ibid.
42 Dixon to Windle, 5 March 1919, Munster University Box, College Archives, UCC.
43 Munster University Box, College Archives, UCC.
44 Ibid.
45 On 5 March, Windle wrote to O'Connor mentioning that if he were 'to say a word to the Attorney General Mr Samuels on the matter of an independent University for Munster it would have a great effect'. Windle continued: 'He is, I understand, in charge of this matter and, I am given to believe, is a little nervous as to what view the Irish Members may take of it. If he could learn from you that you were in favour of it and if he had the same assurance from Mr Devlin, to whom I am writing at the same time, I am convinced that the two pieces of information would have a very great effect. I venture therefore to ask you to take the opportunity of saying a word to him on the

matter.' Windle had written to Sir Maurice Dockrell MP on 17 February asking him to speak to Macpherson or Samuels and to use his influence with them regarding the setting up of a Munster University which 'commends itself to persons of all creeds and politics'. Windle said the Munster university was 'a gift which has been asked for by this locality for the past 80 years'. Munster University Box, College Archives, UCC.

46 Munster University Box, College Archives, UCC.
47 Ibid.
48 Ibid.
49 Ibid.
50 Ibid.
51 Ibid.
52 Ibid.
53 Ibid.
54 Ibid.
55 Ibid.
56 Ibid.
57 Ibid.
58 Ibid.
59 Ibid.
60 Murphy, *The College*, pp. 204–5.
61 We have been unable to find copies of either edition of the magazine in Special Collections, UCC. We have consulted a copy of the May 1919 issue.
62 Murphy, *The College*, p. 205.
63 UC/MB/GB/8, Governing Body meeting, 24 April 1919, College Archives, UCC.
64 Ibid.
65 Ibid.
66 Besides de Róiste, the statement was signed by the TDs – Piaras Béaslaí, Cathal Brugha, James A. Burke, Michael P. Colivet, Con Collins, James Crowley, John Hayes, Richard F. Hayes, Michael Collins, Thomas Hunter, David R. Kent, Finian Lyncy, Joseph MacDonagh, Terence MacSwiney, P.T. Moloney, Pádraig O'Keefe and Austin Stack.
67 UC/MB/GB/8, Governing Body meeting, 24 April 1919, College Archives, UCC.
68 'Munster University – Reply to Governing Body', *Irish Independent*, 28 April 1919.
69 *Irish Independent*, 3 May 1919.
70 Editorial, *An Mac Léighinn/The Student*, 2, 4 (May 1919), p. 335.
71 Ibid.
72 Ibid.
73 Munster University Box, College Archives, UCC.
74 Ibid.
75 Taylor, *Windle*, p. 277.
76 Munster University Box, College Archives, UCC.
77 Meeting of the Senate, National University of Ireland, 7 May 1919, NUI Senate Minutes, vol. VI, NUI Archives, Merrion Square, Dublin.
78 Windle to Waldron, 9 May 1919, Munster University Box, College Archives, UCC.
79 Gaughan, *Alfred O'Rahilly: Academic*, p. 71.
80 Ibid., pp. 71–2.
81 Munster University Box, College Archives, UCC.
82 Ibid.
83 Tadhg Foley, 'James Creed Meredith', *Dictionary of Irish Biography* (Dublin: Royal Irish Academy, 2009), vol. 6, pp. 482–4.
84 Munster University Box, College Archives, UCC.
85 Donal McCartney, 'University College Dublin', in Tom Dunne (ed.), *The National University of Ireland 1908–2008* (University College Dublin Press, 2008), pp. 92–3.
86 Meeting of the Senate, National University of Ireland, 21 May 1919, NUI Senate Minutes, Vol. VI, NUI Archives, Merrion Square, Dublin.
87 Munster University Box, College Archives, UCC.

88   Dr Cox cited Bishop Berkeley as an upholder of the single university ideal. This was challenged by Professor Timothy Corcoran SJ who would not accept any such laudation for a man who had upheld the 'villainous penal laws that ruined the education of Catholics in this country'.

89   'National University of Ireland – Sinn Féin and the Munster University – Bishop Berkeley and Roman Catholics', *Irish Times*, 7 June 1919.

90   On 8 June, he recorded that he had written an article for the *Catholic Times* and a review for *Studies* 'and told editor [of latter] I should write no more for him – because of Sinn Féin tendencies though I did not say that'.

91   UC/MB/GB/8/0202, Governing Body Minutes, 13 June 1919, pp. 345–9, College Archives, UCC.

92   Ibid.

93   Ibid. See also Munster University Box, College Archives, UCC.

94   UC/MB/GB/8/0202, Governing Body Minutes, 13 June 1919, pp. 345–9.

95   McCartney, 'University College Dublin', p. 93.

9. 'Years of Harvesting': Canada, 1920–1929

1   Windle to Mgr Henry Parkinson, Rector of Oscott College, 24 June 1919, OCA/2/9/16/5/W/58, Birmingham Archdiocesan Archives.

2   Gasquet to Windle, 29 July 1919, Windle's Personal Correspondence, BWP; he ended his letter: 'I am going to make a trip to England this year and in fact hope to start this day week (July 6) and should be in the "old country" by the middle of the month. Is there any chance of your being in England this summer and of our meeting. The safest address would be Downside Abbey.'

3   *Cork Examiner*, 4 October 1919.

4   Ibid.

5   Ibid.

6   Ibid.

7   *Cork Examiner*, 11 October 1919.

8   Ibid.

9   *Cork Examiner*, 4 October 1919.

10   Ibid.

11   Ibid.

12   Ibid.

13   On 3 November, he spent from 10.30 to 12.45 posing. Breaking for lunch, he returned to the studio and remained there from 2.45 until 4.30. On Wednesday 5 November he was back with Scully from 10.30 until 12.30. He then went to Bishop Cohalan to say goodbye. He had a farewell dinner that evening with Professor O'Sullivan. On 7 November, he sat in the morning for Scully for another two hours.

14   Taylor, *Windle*, p. 290.

15   It is our hypothesis that Gasquet may have had more to do with helping Windle secure his new position than the cardinal was prepared to admit.

16   The *replica* portrait hangs in St Michael's College, Toronto.

17   Marcus Hartog, address on presentation to Sir Bertram and Lady Windle, 15 October 1919; see *University College Cork Official Gazette*, vii, 27, Hilary term (January 1920), p. 265.

18   Windle Diary, 17 November 1919, Box 2, BWP.

19   Windle was quoting from memory from the first line of Psalm 113: 'In exitu Israel de Aegypto, domus Iacob de populo barbaro' or 'When Israel went out of Egypt, the house of Jacob from a barbarous people.'

20   Canon Roche to Windle, 6 December 1919, Windle's Personal Correspondence, Box 9, BWP.

21   Windle to Sr Monica, 23 November 1919, Windle's Personal Correspondence, Box 9, BWP.

22 Taylor, *Windle*, p. 291.

23 Sr Monica's decision not to place her letters into the archives for the years 1914–20 may have a number of explanations. The idea of such a correspondence taking place between a young nun and a distinguished married male academic may not have entirely met with the approval of her superiors. She may have been instructed to destroy the earlier correspondence. It is much more likely that Sr Monica, sensitive about the content of the letters which may have related to her struggles in religious life or her conflicts over faith and science, decided not to put them into the archives.

24 UC/MB/GB/8/0210, Governing Body Minutes, 29 November 1919, p. 370, College Archives, UCC.

25 Ibid., pp. 373–4; see also Minutes of the Senate, vol. vii, 18 July 1919–17 December 1920, pp. 99 and 138–9.

26 UC/MB/GB/8/0218, Governing Body Minutes, 18 December 1919, pp. 382–4, College Archives, UCC.

27 Merriman to Windle, 25 January 1920, Windle's Personal Correspondence, Box 9, BWP.

28 Ibid.

29 Taylor, *Windle*, pp. 298–9. (This letter is not given in full in the biography. It is not among the correspondence in the Windle archives.)

30 Stockley, a Sinn Féin alderman, was shot at by two assailants on his way home to Tivoli on St Patrick's night, 1920. The *Irish Independent* described him as having had 'a providential escape'. Despite four shots being discharged, he suffered only a cut hand and grazed temple. 'Mysterious Shooting of AF Stockley, Marvellous Escape', *Irish Independent*, 19 March 1920. The *Freeman's Journal* on 23 March 1920 reported that Stockley 'had another rather startling experience' when a British soldier lunged at him with a bayonet near his home in Tivoli. A priest friend, who accompanied him, challenged the soldier who promptly stood to attention. 'A Startling Incident', *Freeman's Journal*, 23 March 1920.

31 UC/MB/GB/8/0231, Governing Body Minutes, 19 March 1920, pp. 404–8, College Archives, UCC.

32 UC/MB/GB/8/0235, Governing Body Minutes, 18 May 1920, p. 417, College Archives, UCC; Sir John O'Connell was also welcomed to the meeting which also voted on the candidates for the chair of History: the Academic Council had voted to place Wrenne first and Hogan and O'Kane as equal second. The governing body vote was: Hogan (10); Wrenne (6) and O'Hegarty (3).

33 Windle to Sr Monica, 28 February 1920, Windle's Personal Correspondence, Box 9, BWP.

34 A few years later, in the mid-1920s, they purchased a house at 48 Roselawn Avenue where they lived for a number of years.

35 Windle to Sr Monica, 23 January 1920, Windle's Personal Correspondence, Box 9, BWP; see also Taylor, *Windle*, p. 295.

36 Windle to Sr Monica, 28 February 1920, Windle's Personal Correspondence, Box 9, BWP.

37 Windle to Sr Monica, 28 December 1919, Windle's Personal Correspondence, Box 9, BWP; Taylor, *Windle*, p. 295. He wrote on 28 January, about his accommodation: 'We have a flat of four rooms, sitting, bed, bath, kitchen, and of course no servants. Servants here get one hundred and ten pounds per annum and upwards, with board and lodging! And we have no room for one if I could afford it. Well then, at 7.a.m. a furious alarm-clock drags me from bed. I jump up, light the gas-stove in the kitchen, put the kettle on, attend to the radiators if they want it, clean the boots (never had such shininess under any servant), make tea for wife and self. In half an hour my wife gets up. When she is cooking the breakfast I devote time to the rosary and some spiritual reading. Breakfasts we could have in the café attached to the apartments, but prefer to get our own. After breakfast she cleans up, and I go to college. Two or three times a week, three if we are good, a woman comes in and

does all the rough work. Once a month or so a man comes and polishes the floors.'

38 Taylor, *Windle*, p. 380.
39 Gasquet to Windle, 9 August 1920, Windle's Personal Correspondence, Box 9, BWP.
40 Ibid.
41 Windle to Shane Leslie, 20 October 1920, Shane Leslie Papers, Box 31, Folder 20, Special Collections, Georgetown University, Washington, DC.
42 See Kevin O'Gorman, 'The Hunger-Strike of Terence MacSwiney', *Irish Theological Quarterly*, 59, 2 (1993), pp. 114–27; see Alfred O'Rahilly's encomium to Terence MacSwiney, Lord Mayor of Cork, in *Old Ireland*, 4 September 1920; and Alfred O'Rahilly, 'Some Theology about Tyranny', *Irish Theological Quarterly* (October 1920); both articles reproduced in J. Anthony Gaughan, *Alfred O'Rahilly: Public Figure*, vol. 2I (Dublin: Kingdom Books, 1989), pp. 409–30.
43 Fr Donal O'Donovan, *The Murder of Canon Magner and Tadhg O'Crowley* (Dunmanway, 2005), pp. 7–13.
44 'Deacon, Rev. Michael Carmody, CC, Dunmanway; Sub-deacon, Rev. John Ambrose, CC, Cape Clear; Master of Ceremonies, Rev. Richard J. Barrett, CC, Cathedral, Cork. His Lordship Most Rev. Dr Cohalan pronounced the final Absolution in both (interments).' Extracts from the *Cork Examiner*, Saturday 18 December 1920. 'Very Rev. Canon Thomas J. Magner, PP', Diocese of Cork and Ross website, http://www.corkandross.org/priests.jsp?priestID=714 (accessed 20 April 2010).
45 O'Donovan, *The Murder of Canon Magner and Tadhg O'Crowley*, pp. 37, 39; the Month's Mind Mass took place on 17 January 1921 in St Patrick's Church, Dunmanway. Windle's close friend, Canon Roche of Ballincollig, was present together with a very large number of clergy.
46 Windle to Mgr Henry Parkinson, 22 January 1922, OCA/2/9.16/5/W/58, Birmingham Archdiocesan Archives
47 Windle Diary, 11 November 1920, Box 2, BWP.
48 Windle to Sr Monica, 11 November 1920, Windle's Personal Correspondence, Box 9, BWP.
49 O'Connell, 'A Life Well Lived', p. 32.
50 Horgan, *Parnell to Pearse*, p. 160.
51 Windle to Sr Monica, 9 December 1920, Windle's Personal Correspondence, Box 9, BWP.
52 Windle Diary, 24 December 1920, Box 2, BWP.
53 Windle to Sr Monica, 23 September 1920, Windle's Personal Correspondence, Box 9, BWP.
54 Windle to Sr Monica, 2 February 1923, Windle's Personal Correspondence, Box 9, BWP.
55 Windle to Sr Monica, 22 March 1923, Windle's Personal Correspondence, Box 9, BWP.
56 Windle to Sr Monica, 10 May 1923, Windle's Personal Correspondence, Box 9, BWP.
57 Commenting on his country of adoption, he wrote: 'I am just starved here for want of real beauty for there is none – natural beauty I mean. That at least I had all around in Cork and it is – not an intoxicant – but a thing without which I wilt a good deal and here I am in the most humdrum uninteresting country I ever inhabited. Round Birmingham is a paradise to it. However one must put up with what one has.' Windle to Sr Monica, 2 August 1923, Windle's Personal Correspondence, Box 9, BWP.
58 Windle to Sr Monica, 6 September 1923, Windle's Personal Correspondence, Box 9, BWP.
59 Horgan, 'Biographical Introduction', pp. x–xi.
60 O'Connell, 'A Life Well-Lived', p. 32.
61 Windle to Sr Monica, 8 December 1927, Windle's Personal Correspondence, Box 9, BWP.
62 Windle described the crossing to Sr Monica on 15 June 1921: 'We had a wondrous smooth passage, a not pleasant twelve to fourteen hours of fog and icebergs (heard,

not seen) which delayed us so that we arrived twelve hours late in Liverpool yesterday at 5.30 and here 12.30 a.m. this morning.'

63 Windle to Sr Monica, 5 July 1921, Windle's Personal Correspondence, Box 9, BWP.

64 Taylor, *Windle*, p. 324.

65 Part of the reason for Windle's refusal to take the post may have been his dislike of James Britten. He wrote to Sr Monica on 6 December 1924: 'You will see that I have buried the hatchet with the dead body of James Britten. He was the most cantankerous and rudest man I ever met and we were not on writing terms for some time before his death. He deeply resented the fact that I would not take his side – or any side – in the CTS scuffle in England and after standing his abuse as long as I could I received from him a letter such as I had had from him before – in which every carefully studied insult was packed. I tore it up; put it back into its envelope; and sent it to him in another. That ended that. But he did a lot of good work which might have been multiplied by ten but for his quarrelsome nature and vile tongue and pen when annoyed. And that good work ought to be the only thing remembered about him R.I.P.' In another letter to Sr Monica on 2 February 1923, he wrote about his desire to settle an old score with an external examiner: 'Between ourselves I once had a row royal with Gregory your friend when he was examining for us and after these years I am sure he was in the wrong and I was in the right. Yet instead of apologizing he was quite distinctly rude. Since then I have had nothing to do with him and what my wicked mind still bends towards is how very nice it would be to deal him one clean smack on the jaw. I daresay I should not even if I had the chance but the prospect at this distance seems quite alluring.'

66 Windle to Sr Anne Hardman, 10 June 1924, Windle's Personal Correspondence, Box 9, BWP.

67 E.J. McCorkell CSB, 'Bertram Coghill Alan Windle, F.R.S., F.S.A., K.S.G., M.D., LL.D., Ph.D., Sc.D', *CCHA*, Report, 25 (1958), p. 58.

68 Windle to Mgr Henry Parkinson, Rector of Oscott College, 15 April 1922, OCA/2/9/16/5/W/58, Birmingham Archdiocesan Archives.

69 Windle to Mgr Henry Parkinson, Rector of Oscott College, 11 June 1922, OCA/2/9/16/5/W/58, Birmingham Archdiocesan Archives.

70 Windle continued: 'Yet I see the unrighteous who deal in tallow and coffee and such like things flourishing like green bay trees and able to go hither and thither. There wants to be another worked to balance things a bit but I wonder how it is to be done because many of those described a few lines about as unrighteous are really good pious folk without a second idea in their heads to talk to the first which is how to make money. I often think that making money is the lowest type of intelligence for the makers are such a dense stupid people. Yet I wish I had had a little of their stupidity.' Windle to Sr Monica, 10 February 1923, Windle's Personal Correspondence, Box 9, BWP.

71 Windle to Sr Monica, 20 July 1924, Windle's Personal Correspondence, Box 9, BWP.

72 Taylor, *Windle*, p. 359.

73 Windle's Personal Correspondence, Box 9, BWP.

74 Windle to Sr Monica, 23 January 1927 and 4 May 1928, Windle's Personal Correspondence, Box 9, BWP.

75 Windle to Sr Monica, 23 May 1927, Windle's Personal Correspondence, Box 9, BWP.

76 Windle to Sr Anne Hartman, 8 August 1927, Windle's Personal Correspondence, Box 9, BWP.

77 Windle to Sr Monica, 4 May 1928, Windle's Personal Correspondence, Box 9, BWP.

78 Windle's Personal Correspondence, Box 9, BWP.

79 Windle to Sr Monica, 14 September 1928, Windle's Personal Correspondence, Box 9, BWP.

80 Windle to Geoffrey Cullwick, 26 October 1926, Windle's Personal Correspondence, Box 9, BWP; Cullwick was from Wolverhampton. He was on the faculty in the

Engineering Department, University of British Columbia, Vancouver.

81   Windle, possibly prompted by Sr Monica, returned to the subject of UCC in a letter quoted earlier in the text: '*Entre nous* I never could get over Stockley's [Professor of English] disloyal actions during the war – he would have been interned but for my intervention. I told him that it was a dishonourable thing for a man holding his post under the King's warrant to behave treasonably as he did. We had little to do with one another after that and as I cannot like anyone whom I can't respect I hope never to see him again unless we meet in Heaven by which time he will have been well cleaned up. Any way he is God's own ass and perhaps that fact may intercede for him.' That was his final comment to Sr Monica about UCC and Ireland.

82   *Cork Examiner*, 19 February 1929.

83   Ibid.

84   Ibid.

85   Ibid.

86   Edith Windle to Sr Monica, 5 November 1929, Published Memoir and Associated Materials, Box 13, BWP.

87   Ibid.

88   Ibid.

89   Ibid.

90   Ibid.

Bibliography

Primary Sources

UNIVERSITY COLLEGE CORK ARCHIVE
Special Collections:
William O'Brien Papers
Alfred O'Rahilly Papers

College Archive:
Governing Body Minutes, 1904–29
Academic Council Minutes, 1904–29
Honan Hostel Minute Books
Honan Hostel Agenda Book
Newspaper Cuttings Books
Sir Bertram Windle's Correspondence
Secretary's Files
Academic Council Files
Munster University Box
The UCC Official Gazette and *The Cork University Record*

UNIVERSITY OF BIRMINGHAM SPECIAL COLLECTIONS
US73, Papers of Bertram Windle

BIRMINGHAM ARCHDIOCESAN ARCHIVES
Oscott Papers relating to Bertram Windle

TORONTO
University of St Michael's College, Toronto, John M. Kelly Library
Bertram Coghill Alan Windle, University of St Michael's College, Faculty 1919,
     W5, boxes FAS 17, FAS 18 and FAS 19

IRISH COLLEGE, ROME
Michael O'Riordan Papers
John Hagan Papers

NATIONAL ARCHIVES, BISHOP STREET, DUBLIN
Will of Isabella Honan, 16 August 1913
Will of Robert Honan, 2 November 1907
Will of Matthew Honan [destroyed in Four Courts, 1922]
Will of Rev. Sir John R. O'Connell, 28 December 1943
Chief Secretary's Office (CSO) Files

DUBLIN ARCHDIOCESAN ARCHIVES
Archbishop William Walsh Papers
[Letters from Windle to Walsh, National University of Ireland File and Laity Files]

GEORGETOWN LIBRARY, WASHINGTON, DC
Shane Leslie Papers

CORK ARCHIVES INSTITUTE
Sophie Raffalovich Papers
Corporation Minutes

NATIONAL UNIVERSITY OF IRELAND
Details of honorary doctorate conferred on Sir John O'Connell, 1930
Minutes of NUI Senate and Standing Committees 1909–19
Correspondence circulated to members of Senate
Correspondence to Senate
Windle and UCC correspondence with NUI
McGrath to Windle correspondence

IRISH FRANCISCAN ARCHIVES (Dun Mhuire, Killiney)
File on St Anthony's Hall, 1906–16, Folder Number 226/7
File of correspondence with Sir Bertram Windle, Folder Number 226/7, Document
    Number 56.53

CENTRAL CATHOLIC LIBRARY (Merrion Square, Dublin)
Documents and Journals:
The Irish Ecclesiastical Record
Studies
The Dublin Review
The Irish Monthly

NATIONAL LIBRARY OF IRELAND
John J. Horgan Papers
William O'Brien Papers
John Redmond Papers
George Wyndham Papers
The Irish Builder
The Studio

NATIONAL COLLEGE OF ART AND DESIGN
Cuttings on Harry Clarke

ABBEY STAINED GLASS STUDIOS, DUBLIN
Joshua Clarke Studio Order Book, supplied by Mr Ken Ryan

TRINITY COLLEGE DUBLIN
Harry Clarke Papers
Thomas Bodkin Papers

UNIVERSITY COLLEGE CORK, SECRETARY'S OFFICE
Files relevant to the Honan Scholarships

UNIVERSITY COLLEGE CORK, CHAPLAINCY
Book of Seals of the Honan Hostel
Assorted files relating to the Honan Chapel
Attendance Book of Governors of the Honan Hostel

CLOYNE DIOCESAN ARCHIVES
Bishop Robert Browne Papers
Cork Diocesan Archive
Files relating to Bishops Thomas A. O'Callaghan and Daniel Cohalan
The Fold

CORK CHAMBER OF COMMERCE
Minute Books

CORK CITY LIBRARY
Cork Examiner
Cork Constitution
Evening Echo
Journal of the Cork Historical and Archaeological Society
Cuttings files

CORK COUNTY LIBRARY
Cork Examiner

WESTMINSTER ARCHDIOCESAN ARCHIVES
Fr Ian Dickie to Ann Keogh, undated, circa 2002
Information taken from vicar general's card index regarding Rev. Sir John
    O'Connell
Cardinal Francis Bourne Papers

CONVENT OF MERCY (Oaklea, Tunstall Rd., Sunderland)
Sr Wilfrid to Ann Keogh, 25 July 2004

Mary Hudson School Diary fragment for part of 1870s
(In possession of Dr Madoline O'Connell, her granddaugher)

Secondary Sources: Books, Articles and Unpublished Theses

1916 Rebellion Handbook (introduction by Declan Kiberd) (Dublin: The Mourne
    River Press, 1998 [1916])
aan de Wiel, Jérôme, *The Catholic Church in Ireland, 1914–1918* (Dublin: Irish
    Academic Press, 2003)
Alexander, C.W.L., 'Vincent McNamara', *Annual Journal of the Engineering Society,
    University College Cork* (January 1916), pp. 6–9

Andrews, C.S. (Todd), *Dublin Made Me: An Autobiography* (Cork: Mercier Press, 1979)

Anon., *War Record of University College Cork, 1914–1919* (University College Cork, n.d.), pp. 1–20

Anon., 'The Stained Glass at the Chapel of the Honan Hostel Cork', *Irish Builder and Engineer* (28 April 1917), pp. 198–202; see also articles in same publication, 5 December 1914, 28 October 1916 and 31 March 1917

Anon., Obituary, The Rev. Sir John R. O'Connell, *The Irish Times*, 30 December 1943

Anon., 'Rev. Sir John O'Connell', *Cork University Record*, no. 1 (Summer 1944), pp. 14–15

Anon., 'The Franciscan Sisters of Calais', *The Fold* (May 1956), pp. 31–3

Anon., 'The Honan Home', *The Fold* (July 1957), pp. 31–5

Arnold, Bruce, *A Concise History of Irish Art* (London: Thames & Hudson, 1969)

Asquith, Herbert H., *Memories and Reflections, 1852–1927* (London: Cassell & Co., 1928), vol. 2

Bodkin, Thomas, 'The Art of Mr Harry Clarke', *The Studio* (November 1919)

Bowe, Nicola Gordon, *Harry Clarke* (a monograph and catalogue of the Harry Clarke exhibition, Douglas Hyde Gallery, Trinity College Dublin, 12 November to 8 December 1979)

Bowe, Nicola Gordon, *The Life and Work of Harry Clarke* (Dublin: Irish Academic Press, 1989)

Bowe, Nicola Gordon, 'Harry Clarke: A Poet in Stained Glass', *Intercom*, 24, 6 (July/August 1994), pp. 4–9

Bowe, Nicola Gordon, Caron, David and Wynne, Michael, *A Gazetteer of Irish Stained Glass: The Works of Harry Clarke and the Artists of an Tur Gloine, 1903–1963* (Dublin: Irish Academic Press, 1988)

Byrne, Rev. Peter, CM, 'Church Building in Ireland', *Irish Ecclesiastical Record*, vol. vii (January–June 1916), pp. 105–21

Byrne, Rev. Peter, CM, 'The Building and Decoration of Churches in Ireland', *Irish Ecclesiastical Record*, vol. ix (January–June 1917), pp. 175–95

Byrne Costigan, Ethna, *Ethna Mar Twice* (New York: Vantage Press, 1989)

Callanan, Frank, *T.M. Healy* (Cork University Press, 1996)

Campbell, Fergus, *The Irish Establishment 1879–1914* (Oxford: Oxford University Press, 2009)

Canning, Fr Bernard J., *The Bishops of Ireland, 1870–1987* (Donegal: Donegal Democrat, 1987)

Carden, Sheila, *The Alderman: Alderman Tom Kelly (1868–1942) and Dublin Corporation* (Dublin City Council, 2007)

Carr, Henry, CSB 'Sir Bertram Windle: The Man and His Work', *Catholic World*, 129 (No. 770, May 1929), pp. 165-71

Clarke, Harry, Illustrations in Charles Perrault's *Fairy Tales of Charles Perrault* (London: George G. Harrap, 1922)

Clarke, Harry, Illustrations in Hans Andersen's *Fairy Tales* (London: George G. Harrap, 1930)

Clarke, Michael Laurence, 'Some Moments with My Father', *The Stained Glass of*

Harry Clarke, 1889–1931 (London: The Fine Art Society, 1988) (no pages given)

Collins, Neil, *The Splendid Cause: The Missionary Society of St Columban, 1916–1954* (Dublin: The Columba Press, 2009)

Conlon, Patrick, OFM, 'Berkeley Hall – St Anthony's Hall – Honan Hostel, UCC', *Journal of the Cork Historical and Archaeological Society*, vol. 100 (1995), pp. 16–28

Coolahan, John, 'From Royal University to National University, 1879–1908', in Tom Dunne (ed.), *The National University of Ireland 2008: Centenary Essays* (University College Dublin Press, 2008)

Corish, Patrick J., *Maynooth College, 1795–1995* (Dublin: Gill & Macmillan, 1995)

Costello, Peter, *Dublin Churches* (Dublin: Gill & Macmillan, 1989)

Crookshank, Anne and the Knight of Glin, *The Painters of Ireland, 1660–1920* (London: Barrie & Jenkins, 1978)

Cunningham, Joseph P., and Fleischmann, Ruth, *Aloys Fleischmann 1880–1964: Immigrant Musician in Ireland* (Cork University Press, 2010)

Dalsimer, Adele M., *Visualizing Ireland: National Identity and the Pictorial Tradition* (London: Faber & Faber, 1993)

Denman, Terence, *A Lonely Grave: The Life and Death of William Redmond* (Dublin: Irish Academic Press, 1995)

Doherty, Gabriel, and Keogh, Dermot (eds), *1916: The Long Revolution* (Cork: Mercier Press, 2007)

Dowling, William J., 'Harry Clarke, Dublin Stained Glass Artist', *Dublin Historical Record*, xvii, 2 (1962), pp. 55–61

Dudley Edwards, Ruth, *Patrick Pearse: The Triumph of Failure* (London: Faber & Faber, 1977)

Dunne, Tom (ed.), *The National University of Ireland 2008: Centenary Essays* (University College Dublin Press, 2008)

Egan, Bartholomew, OFM, 'The Friars Minor and the Honan Hostel, University College, Cork', *Archivum Franciscanum Historicum*, An. 73 (1980), Collegio S. Bonaventura, Colle S. Antonio 00046, Grottaferrata, Rome

Elliott, Robert (preface by Edward Martyn), *Art in Ireland* (Dublin: Sealy, Bryers & Walker, 1911)

Farrell, Brian (ed.), *The Irish Parliamentary Tradition* (with three essays on the Treaty debate by F.S.L. Lyons) (Dublin: Gill & Macmillan, 1973)

Fitzgerald, D.P., 'Late Sir Bertram Windle: Appreciation by Former Colleague', *Cork Examiner*, 19 February 1929

Foley, Tadhg, 'James Creed Meredith', *Dictionary of Irish Biography* (Dublin: Royal Irish Academy, 2009), vol. vi

Fry, Sir Edward, *Sir Edward Fry: An Autobiography* (London: Oxford University Press, 1921)

Galloway, Peter, *The Cathedrals of Ireland* (Institute of Irish Studies, Queen's University Belfast, 1992)

Gaughan, Fr J. Anthony, *Alfred O'Rahilly: Academic* (Dublin: Kingdom Books, 1986)

Gaughan, Fr J. Anthony, *Alfred O'Rahilly: Public Figure* (Dublin: Kingdom Books, 1989)

Gillies, Sr Dorothy, *A Pioneer of Catholic Teacher-Training in Scotland: Sister Mary of St Wilfrid (Mary Adela Lescher, 1846–1926)* (Carmelite Monastery, Quidenham, Norfolk, 1978)

Girvin, Kevin, *Seán O'Hegarty, O/C First Cork Brigade, Irish Republican Army* (Cork: Aubane Historical Society, 2007)

An Ghobán Saor, 'Cheap Churches', 'Ailing Churches and Pining Parochial Houses', *The Irish Ecclesiastical Record*, vol. viii (July–December 1916), 5th series, pp. 206–17, 273–84

Griffin, Fiana, 'The Glass Master', *The Irish Times*, 17 March 2001

Gwynn, Denis, *Edward Martyn and the Irish Revival* (London: Jonathan Cape, 1930)

Gwynn, Denis, *The Life of John Redmond* (London: George G. Harrap, 1932)

Gwynn, Denis, 'The College's First Year', *Cork University Record*, no. 21 (Easter 1951)

Gwynn, Denis, 'The Origins and Growth of University College Cork', *University Record*, vols 2, 3 and 4 (1958), pp. 33–47

Gwynn, Denis, 'Sir Bertram Windle, 1858–1929: A Centenary Tribute', *University Record*, vols 2, 3 and 4 (1958), pp. 48–58

Gwynn, Stephen, *John Redmond's Last Years* (London: E. Arnold, 1919)

Gwynn, Stephen, *The Irish Situation* (London: Jonathan Cape, 1921)

Hartog, Marcus, 'Presentation to Sir Bertram C.A. Windle', *Official Gazette*, vii, 27, Hilary term (January 1920), pp. 261–6

Henchion, Richard I., 'The Remarkable Honan Family: Their Parsimony and their Charity', *Evening Echo*, 22 April 1976

Henry, Francoise, *Irish Art in the Romanesque Period, 1020–1170 AD* (Ithaca, NY: Cornell University Press, 1970)

Higgins, Roisín, and Uí Chollatáin, Regina (eds), *The Life and After-Life of P.H. Pearse* (Dublin: Irish Academic Press, 2009)

J.J.H. (probably Horgan, John J.), reviewing Rev. Sir John R. O'Connell, *The Collegiate Chapel Cork: Some Notes on the Building and on the Ideals which Inspired It* (Dublin: Guy, 1916; republished Cork University Press, 1932), *Studies*, vol. 5 (December 1916), pp. 612–14

Horgan, John J., 'Sir Bertram Windle: An Appreciation', *University College Cork Session Lists*, 1928–9, pp. 119–20

Horgan, John J., 'Sir Bertram Windle', *Studies*, vol. xxi (1932), pp. 611–26

Horgan, John J., *Parnell to Pearse* (Dublin: Browne & Nolan, 1949; republished by University College Dublin Press, 2009)

Horgan, John, 'John J. Horgan Biographical Introduction', in John J. Horgan, *Parnell to Pearse* (Dublin: Browne & Nolan, 1949; republished University College Dublin Press, 2009), pp. vii–xxxv

Hort, G.M., 'A Chapter on Church Windows', *Irish Monthly*, vol. 44 (August 1916), pp. 477–93

Hourican, Bridget, 'John J. Horgan', in *Dictionary of Irish Biography* (Dublin: Royal Irish Academy, 2009), vol. 4, pp. 792–4

Hurley, Richard, and Cantwell, Wilfrid, *Contemporary Irish Church Architecture* (Dublin: Gill & Macmillan, 1985)

Kelly, Michael J., *The Honan Chapel, University College Cork* (Cork University Press, 1946)

Kennedy, S.B., *Irish Art and Modernism* (Dublin: Hugh Lane Gallery and Belfast Institute of Irish Studies, Queen's University Belfast, 1991)

Kennedy, Thomas P., 'Church Building', in Patrick J. Corish (ed.), *A History of the Catholic Church. Vol. 5: The Church since Emancipation* (Dublin: Gill & Macmillan, 1970), no. viii, pp. 1–36

Keogh, Ann, 'A Study in Philanthropy: Sir Bertram Windle, Sir John O'Connell, Isabella Honan and the Building of the Honan Chapel, University College Cork', unpublished MA thesis, University College Cork, 2004

Keogh, Dermot, *The Rise of the Irish Working Class: The Dublin Trade Union Movement and Labour Leadership 1890–1914* (Belfast: Appletree Press, 1982)

Keogh, Dermot, *The Vatican, the Bishops and Irish Politics* (Cambridge University Press, 1986) (reissued 2005)

Keogh, Dermot, *Ireland and Europe, 1919–1948* (Dublin: Gill & Macmillan, 1988), pp. 256; published in paperback: *Ireland and Europe 1919–1989* (Cork and Dublin: Hibernian University Press, 1989)

Keogh, Dermot, 'Episcopal Decision-making in Ireland', in Maurice O'Connell (ed.), *Education Church and State: Proceedings of the Second Daniel O'Connell School* (Dublin: IPA, 1992)

Keogh, Dermot, *Twentieth Century Ireland: Nation and State* (Dublin: Gill & Macmillan, 1994), pp. 504 (reissued 2005 with extra chapter covering the period between 1980s and 2005)

Keogh, Dermot, *Ireland and the Vatican: The Politics and Diplomacy of Church and State, 1922–1960* (Cork University Press, 1995)

Keogh, Dermot, with O'Driscoll, Finín, 'Ireland', in Tom Buchanan and Martin Conway (eds), *Popular Catholicism in Europe 1918–1965* (Oxford: Clarendon Press, 1996)

Keogh, Dermot, 'Catholics and the "Godless" Colleges, 1845–1995', in Pádraig Corkery and Fiachra Long (eds), *Theology in the University – The Irish Context* (Dublin: Dominican Publications, 1997)

Keogh, Dermot, *Jews in Twentieth Century Ireland: Refugees, Anti-Semitism and the Holocaust* (Cork University Press, 1998), pp. 336 (awarded the 1999 James S. Donnelly, Snr. Prize by the American Conference for Irish Studies in the History/Social Science Category). Reprinted in 2002 and 2006

Keogh, Dermot, 'The Catholic Church, the Holy See and the 1916 Rising', in Gabriel Doherty and Dermot Keogh (eds), *1916: The Long Revolution* (Cork: Mercier Press, 2007)

Keogh, Dermot, 'The Catholic Church in Ireland since the 1950s', in Leslie Woodcock Tentler (ed.), *The Church Confronts Modernity – Catholicism since 1950 in the United States, Ireland and Quebec* (Washington, DC: The Catholic University Press of America, 2007)

Keogh, Dermot, *The Making of the Irish Constitution 1937* (with Andrew McCarthy,

PRTLI1 project) (Cork and Dublin: Mercier Press, 2007)

Keogh, Dermot,'The Resilience of Catholic Devotionalism', in E. Grollet, N. Keogh and E. Keogh (eds), *Collective Memory in Ireland and Russia* (All-Russia State Library for Foreign Literature, Moscow, 2007)

Keogh, Dermot, *Jack Lynch – A Biography* (Dublin: Gill & Macmillan, 2008), pp. 550

Kiberd, Declan, 'Patrick Pearse: Irish Modernist', in Roisín Higgins and Regina Uí Chollatáin (eds), *The Life and After-Life of P.H. Pearse* (Dublin: Irish Academic Press, 2009)

Larmour, Paul, *The Arts and Crafts Movement in Ireland* (Belfast: Friar's Bush Press, 1992)

Leask, Harold G., *Irish Churches and Monastic Buildings* (Dundalk: Dungalgan Press, 1987 and 1990), vols 1 and 2

Lee, Joe, 'Patrick Henry Pearse (1879–1916)', *Dictionary of Irish Biography* (Dublin: Royal Irish Academy, 2009), vol. 8, pp. 19–28

Lee, Philip G., 'Notes on the Ogham Chamber at Knock-shan-a-wee', with notes by Mr Cremin, *Journal of the Cork Historical and Archaeological Society*, vol. xvii (1911), pp. 58–62

Lewis, Gifford, *Edith Somerville: A Biography* (Dublin: Four Courts Press, 2005)

Lyons, F.S.L., *The Fall of Parnell, 1890–91* (London: Routledge & Kegan Paul, 1960)

Lyons, F.S.L., *John Dillon: A Biography* (London: Routledge & Kegan Paul, 1968)

Lyons, F.S.L., *Ireland since the Famine* (London: Weidenfeld & Nicolson, 1971)

Lyons, F.S.L., *Studies in Irish History: The Irish Parliamentary Party, 1890–1910* (Westport, CT: Greenwood, 1975)

Lyons, F.S.L., *Charles Stewart Parnell* (London: Collins, 1977)

Lyons, F.S.L., *The Burden of our History: The W.B. Rankin Memorial Lecture Delivered before the Queen's University of Belfast on 4 December 1970* (Queen's University Belfast, 1979)

Lyons, F.S.L., *Culture and Anarchy in Ireland, 1890–1939: The Ford Lectures Delivered in the University of Oxford, 1978* (New York: Doubleday, 1979)

Lyons, F.S.L., (with R.A.J. Hawkins), *Ireland under the Union: Varieties or Tension. Essays in Honour of T.W. Moody* (Oxford: Oxford University Press, 1980)

Lyons, F.S.L. (ed.), *Bank of Ireland, 1783–1983: Bicentenary Essays* (Dublin: Gill & Macmillan, 1983)

Lyons, F.S.L., 'The Developing Crisis, 1907–1914', in W.E. Vaughan (ed.), *A New History of Ireland: Ireland under the Union, 1870–1921* (Oxford: Oxford University Press, 2010), vol. vi, pp. 123–44

Macalister, R.A.S., 'On Some Recently Discovered Ogham Inscriptions', *Proceedings of the Royal Irish Academy, Section C: Archaeology, Celtic Studies, History, Linguistics, Literature*, vol. 32 (1914–16), pp. 138–46

Macardle, Dorothy, *The Irish Republic* (Dublin: Wolfhound Press, 1999)

McBride, Lawrence W., *The Greening of Dublin Castle: The Transformation of Bureaucratic and Judicial Personnel in Ireland, 1892–1922* (Washington, DC: Catholic University Press, 1991)

MacCarthy, Fiona, *Eric Gill* (London: Faber & Faber, 1989)

McCartney, Donal, *The National University of Ireland and Éamon de Valera* (Dublin: The University Press of Ireland, 1983)

McCartney, Donal, *UCD: A National Idea. The History of University College Dublin* (Dublin: Gill & Macmillan, 1999)

McCartney, Donal, 'University College Dublin', in Tom Dunne (ed.), *The National University of Ireland 1908–2008* (University College Dublin Press, 2008)

McCorkell, E.J., CSB, 'Bertram Coghill Alan Windle, F.R.S., F.S.A., K.S.G., M.D., LL.D., Ph.D., Sc.D.', *CCHA*, Report, 25 (1958), pp. 53–8

MacDonagh, Michael, *The Life of William O'Brien, the Irish Nationalist: A Biographical Study of Irish Nationalism, Constitutional and Revolutionary* (London: Ernest Benn, 1928)

McDowell, R.B., *The Irish Convention 1917–18* (London: Routledge & Kegan Paul, 1970)

McDowell, R.B., and Webb, B.A., *Trinity College Dublin* (Trinity College Dublin Press, 2004)

McGrath, Fr Fergal, SJ, 'The University Question', in Patrick J. Corish (ed.), *A History of the Catholic Church* (Dublin: Gill & Macmillan, 1971), vol. 5, *The Church since Emancipation*, vi, pp. 84–142

Mac Greevy, Thomas, 'St Brendan's Cathedral, Loughrea, 1897–1947', *Capuchin Annual, 1946–7*, pp. 353–73

Mac Greevy, Thomas, *'Life That is Exile': Daniel Corkery (1878–1964) and the Search for Irish Ireland* (Queen's University Belfast: Institute of Irish Studies, 1993)

Mackail, J.W., and Wyndham, Guy (eds.), *Life and Letters of George Wyndham* (London: Hutchinson, n.d.), vols i and ii

Martin, Francis X., and Byrne, Francis J., *The Scholar Revolutionary: Eoin MacNeill, 1867–1945, and the Making of the New Ireland* (Shannon: Irish University Press, 1973)

Maume, Patrick, *D.P. Moran* (Dundalk: Published for the Historical Association of Ireland by Dundalgan Press, 1995)

Miller, David W., *Church, State and Nation in Ireland, 1898–1921* (Dublin: Gill & Macmillan, 1973)

McManus, Damian, *Ogham Stones at University College Cork* (Cork University Press, 2004)

Morrissey, Fr Thomas J., SJ, *Towards a National University: William Delany, SJ (1835–1924). An Era of Initiative in Irish Education* (Dublin: Wolfhound Press, 1983)

Morrissey, Fr Thomas J., SJ, *William Walsh, Archbishop of Dublin, 1841–1921* (Dublin: Four Courts Press, 2000)

Morrissey, Fr Thomas J., SJ, *Bishop Thomas O'Dwyer of Limerick, 1842–1917* (Dublin: Four Courts Press, 2003)

Murphy, John A., *The College: A History of Queen's/University College Cork* (Cork University Press, 1995)

Ní Síocháin, Máire, 'Idir Dhá Ré Conradh na Gaeilge i gCorcaigh, 1910–1922', Cuid a hAon, *Journal of the Cork Historical and Archaeological Society*, vol. 109 (2004), pp. 67–200

O'Brien, Joseph V., *William O'Brien and the Course of Irish Politics, 1881–1918* (Berkeley, CA: University of California Press, 1976)

O'Connell, Sir John, *The Crib of the Nativity: Its Origin and Its History* (London: Catholic Truth Society, n.d.)

O'Connell, Sir John, *Glendalough: Its Story and Its Ruins* (Dublin: Catholic Truth Society, n.d.)

O'Connell, Sir John, *Collegiate Chapel, Cork: Some Notes on the Building and on the Ideals which Inspired It* (Dublin: Guy, 1916; republished Cork University Press, 1932)

O'Connell, Sir John, *Blessed Joan of Arc: Maid of Orleans* (Dublin: Catholic Truth Society, 1920)

O'Connell, Sir John, 'Great Scientist and Catholic: Sir Bertram Windle and his Work', *The Universe*, 2 December 1932

O'Connell, Sir John, 'The Crib of the Nativity: Its Origin and Its History', *The Irish Ecclesiastical Record*, vol. xliv (July–December 1934), pp. 602–13

O'Connell, Sir John, *Lyra Martyrum: The Poetry of the English Martyrs, 1503–1681* (London: Burns, Oates & Washbourne, 1934)

O'Connell, Sir John, *Saint Thomas More* (London: Duckworth, 1935)

O'Connell, Madoline, 'A Life Well Lived', *UCC Graduate* (September 2008)

O'Donovan, Fr Donal, *The Murder of Canon Magner and Tadhg O'Crowley* (Dunmanway, 2005)

O'Dwyer, Frederick, *The Architecture of Deane and Woodward* (Cork University Press, 1997)

O'Gorman, Kevin, 'The Hunger-Strike of Terence MacSwiney', *Irish Theological Quarterly*, 59, 2 (1993), pp. 114–27

O'Halpin, Eunan, *The Decline of the Union: British Government in Ireland, 1892–1920* (Dublin: Gill & Macmillan, 1987)

O'Hegarty, P.S., *The Victory of Sinn Féin: How it Won it and How it Used it* (Dublin: Talbot Press, 1924)

O'Kelly, M.J., *The Honan Chapel, University College Cork* (Cork University Press, 1966 [revised edn] [1946])

O'Rahilly, Alfred, 'Some Theology about Tyranny', *Irish Theological Quarterly* (October 1920)

O'Reilly, Seán D., *Irish Churches and Monasteries: An Historical and Architectural Guide* (Cork: The Collins Press, 1997)

O'Riordan, Rev. M., *Catholicity and Progress in Ireland* (London: Kegan Paul, Trench, Trubner, 1906)

Ó Ríordáin, Traolach, *Conradh na Gaeilge i gCorcaigh, 1894–1910* (Baile Átha Cliath: Cois Life Teoranta, 2000)

O'Sullivan, Denis J., *The Cork School of Medicine: A History* (University College Cork, 2007)

Padbury, Joyce, '"A Young Schoolmaster of Great Literary Talent", Mary Hayden's Friend, Patrick Pearse', in Roisín Higgins, and Regina Uí Chollatáin (eds), *The Life and After-Life of P.H. Pearse* (Dublin: Irish Academic Press, 2009)

Parkes, Susan M., 'Higher Education, 1793–1908', in W.E. Vaughan (ed.), *A New*

History of Ireland: Ireland under the Union, 1870–1921 (Oxford: Oxford University Press, 2010), vol. vi, pp. 539–70

Pašeta, Senia, *Before the Revolution: Nationalism, Social Change and Ireland's Catholic Élite, 1879–1922* (Cork University Press, 1999)

Plunkett, Count, KCHS, FSA, 'Decoration', *The Irish Monthly*, vol. 39 (1911), pp. 315–24

Plunkett, Horace Curzon, *Ireland in the New Century* (Dublin: Irish Academic Press, 1982)

Power, Rev. Prof., *The Chapel of St Finnbar, University College Cork: Its History Architecture and Symbolism* (University College Cork, n.d.)

Privilege, John, *Michael Logue and the Catholic Church in Ireland, 1879–1925* (Manchester University Press, 2009)

Pyle, Hilary, *Jack B. Yeats* (London: Andre Deutsch, 1989)

Raguin, Virginia Chieffo, *The History of Stained Glass: The Art of Light Medieval to Contemporary* (London: Thames and Hudson, 2003)

Richardson, Hilary, 'Robert Alexander Stewart Macalister', in James McGuire and James Quinn (eds), *Dictionary of Irish Biography* (Dublin: Royal Irish Academy, 2009), vol. 5, pp. 686–7

Ryan, Mary, 'Random Recollections', *Cork University Record*, no. 5 (1945), pp. 15–19

Scholes, Andrew, *The Church of Ireland and the Third Home Rule Bill* (Dublin: Irish Academic Press, 2010)

Sisson, Elaine, *Pearse's Patriots: St Enda's and the Cult of Boyhood* (Cork University Press, 2004)

Somerville, Vice-Admiral Boyle, *The Chart-Makers* (Edinburgh: William Blackwood & Sons, 1928)

Stewart, A.T.Q., *Edward Carson* (Belfast: Blackstaff Press, 1981)

Taylor, Sr Monica, *Sir Bertram Windle: A Memoir* (London: Longman, Green & Co., 1932)

Teehan, Virginia, and Wincott Heckett, Elizabeth (eds), *The Honan Chapel: A Golden Vision* (Cork University Press, 2004)

Tierney, Michael, *Eoin MacNeill: Scholar and Man of Action, 1867–1945*, edited by F.X. Martin (Oxford: Clarendon Press, 1980)

Walker, Brian, *Parliamentary Election Results in Ireland, 1801–1922* (Dublin: Royal Irish Academy, 1978)

Walsh, Patrick J., *William J. Walsh, Archbishop of Dublin* (Dublin: Talbot Press, 1928)

Ward, Margaret, *Hanna Sheehy Skeffington: A Life* (Cork University Press, 1997)

West, Trevor, *Horace Plunkett: Co-operation and Politics* (Gerrards Cross: Colin Smythe, 1986)

Whelan, Bernadette, *United States Foreign Policy and Ireland: From Empire to Independence, 1913–1929* (Dublin: Four Courts Press, 2006)

White, Gerry, and O'Shea, Brendan, *'Baptised in Blood': The Formation of the Cork Brigade of the Irish Volunteers, 1913–1916* (Cork: Mercier Press, 2005)

White, James, 'Introduction' to catalogue, *The Stained Glass of Harry Clarke, 1889–1931* (The Fine Art Society, London, 1988), no pages given

Whyte, John Henry, *A History of Irish Catholicism* (Dublin: Gill, 1967)

Whyte, John Henry, *Catholics in Western Democracies: A Study in Political Behaviour* (Dublin: Gill & Macmillan, 1981)

Whyte, John Henry, *Interpreting Northern Ireland* (Oxford: Clarendon Press, 1990)

Williams, Jeremy, *Architecture in Ireland, 1837–1921* (Dublin: Irish Academic Press, 1994)

Wincott Heckett, Elizabeth, 'The Embroidered Cloths of Heaven: The Textiles', in Virginia Teehan and Elizabeth Wincott Heckett (eds), *The Honan Chapel: A Golden Vision* (Cork University Press, 2004)

Windle, *Catholics and Evolution* (Ireland: Catholic Truth Society of Ireland, 1900)

Woods, C.J., and Murphy, William, 'Thomas Ashe', *Dictionary of Irish Biography*, (Dublin: Royal Irish Academy, 2009), vol. 1, pp. 176–7

Websites

Doherty, Gillian M. and O'Riordan, Tomás, 'The Synod of Thurles', *Multitext*, UCC, http://multitext.ucc.ie/d/The_Synod_of_Thurles_1850 (accessed 4 March 2010)

Entry for St George Jackson Mivart, *Catholic Encyclopedia*, http://www.newadvent.org/cathen/10407b.htm (accessed 4 March 2010)

Entry for Saint George Jackson Mivart, *Encyclopaedia Britannica*, http://www.britannica.com/EBchecked/topic/386372/Saint-George-Jackson-Mivart (accessed 4 March 2010)

Entry for Vincent McNamara, 1911 Census, *National Archives of Ireland* http://www.census.nationalarchives.i.../nai001895441/ (accessed 5 March 2010)

Entry for Vincent McNamara, *World War I Talk*, http://ww1talk.co.uk/forums/showthread.php?p=4947 (accessed 4 March 2010)

Sir Bertram Coghill Alan Windle: Select Bibliography

BOOKS AND PAMPHLETE

A Handbook of Surface Anatomy and Landmarks (London: Lewis, 1888)

The Proportions of the Human Body (London: Baillière, Tindall and Cox, 1892) (The frontispiece is a facsimile of a drawing by Michelangelo Buonarrotti, 1475–1564)

(introduction treating of pigmy races and fairy tales), in Edward Tyson, *A Philological Essay Concerning the Pygmies of the Ancients*/now edited (London: D. Nutt, 1894)

Life in Early Britain: being an account of the early inhabitants of this island and the memorials which they have left behind them (London: D. Nutt, 1897)

Shakespeare's Country (London: Methuen & Co., 1899)

Catholics and Evolution (Catholic Truth Society of Ireland, 1900)

The Malvern Country (London: Methuen & Co., 1901)

The Wessex of Thomas Hardy (New York: J. Lane; The Bodley Head, , 1902)

Chester: a historical and topographical account of the city (illustrated by Edmund H. New) (London: Methuen, 1903)

Remains of the Prehistoric Age in England, illustrated by Edith Mary Windle (London: Methuen, 1904)

A School History of Warwickshire (London: Methuen, 1906)

What is Life? a study of Vitalism and Neo-Vitalism (London: Sands & Co., 1908)

Facts and Theories: being a consideration of some biological conceptions of to-day (London: Catholic Truth Society, 1912)

Twelve Catholic Men of Science (London: Catholic Truth Society, 1912)

A Century of Scientific Thought & Other Essays (London: Burns & Oates, 1915)

Science and Morals and Other Essays (London: Burns & Oates, 1919)

The Church and Science (London: Catholic Truth Society, 1920)

Vitalism and Scholasticism (London and Edinburgh: Sands & Co., 1920)

The Romans in Britain (London: Methuen & Co. 1923)

On Miracles and Some Other Matters (London: Burns, Oates and Washbourne, 1924)

Evolution and Catholicity (New York: The Paulist Press, 1925)

Who's Who of the Oxford Movement: prefaced by a brief history of that movement (New York and London: Century, 1926)

The Catholic Church and its Reactions with Science (London: Burns, Oates and Washbourne; New York: The Macmillan Company, 1927)

The Evolutionary Problem as it is Today (New York: J.F. Wagner; London: B. Herder, 1927)

Religions Past and Present: an elementary account of comparative religion (London: Williams & Norgate, 1927)

ARTICLES

'On the Embryology of the Mammalian Muscular System. No. I: The Short Muscles of the Human Hand (With Plates III and IV)', *The Transactions of the Royal Irish Academy,* 28 (1880), pp. 211–40

'Reports and Analyses and Descriptions of New Inventions in Medicine, Surgery, Dietetics, and the Allied Sciences', *The British Medical Journal,* 1, no. 1201 (5 January 1884), p. 18

'The Pectoral Group of Muscles', *The Transactions of the Royal Irish Academy,* 29 (1887), pp. 345–78.

'Medical Examinations', *The British Medical Journal,* 1, no. 1414 (4 February 1888), p. 271

'The Pectoral Group of Muscles [Abstract]', *Proceedings of the Royal Society of London,* 45 (1888), pp. 99–101

'Monsters and Teratology', *The British Medical Journal,* 2, no. 1603 (19 September 1891) p. 669

'The Scientific Standard of a Medical Degree in the New University for London', *The British Medical Journal,* 1, no. 1626 (27 February 1892), p. 469

'University of Birmingham, The Birmingham Medical School: Its Needs, Aspirations, and Ideals', *The British Medical Journal,* 2, no. 2075 (6 October 1900), pp. 988–90

'74. An Excavation in Kemerton Camp, Bredon Hill', *Man,* 5 (1905), pp. 133–5

'A Note on Some Kitchen-Middens in the North of Ireland', *The Journal of the*

Royal Society of Antiquaries of Ireland, 1, no. 1, Sixth Series (31 March 1911), pp. 1–4

'A Note on Two Megalithic Structures near Gallarus', *Kerry Archaeological Magazine*, 1, no. 6 (April 1911), pp. 339–41

'On Certain Megalithic Remains Immediately Surrounding Lough Gur, County Limerick', *Proceedings of the Royal Irish Academy, Section C: Archaeology, Celtic Studies, History, Linguistics, Literature*, 30 (1912), pp. 283–306

'A Note on an Early Interment near Macroom', *The Journal of the Royal Society of Antiquaries of Ireland*, 2, no. 2, Sixth Series (30 June 1912), pp. 169–72

'Some Recent Works on the Antiquity of Man', *Studies: An Irish Quarterly Review*, 3, no. 11 (September 1914), pp. 215–35

'The Latest Gospel of Science', *Studies: An Irish Quarterly Review*, 4, no. 13 (March 1915), pp. 49–60

'A Note on Two Objects on the North Slope of Mushera Beg, Co. Cork,' *The Journal of the Royal Society of Antiquaries of Ireland*, 5, no. 4, Sixth Series (31 December 1915), pp. 316–17

'Science and the War', *The Dublin Review* (July 1917), pp. 127–40

'The Travail of Ireland; [II] The Convention – A Member's Afterthoughts', *The Dublin Review* (July/August/September 1918), pp. 12–19

Barling, Gilbert, and Windle Bertram C. A., 'British Medical Association. Fifty-Eighth Annual Meeting', *The British Medical Journal*, 1, no. 1533 (17 May 1890), pp. 1164–5

Windle, Bertram C. A., and Hussey, Charlotte, 'Notes & Queries', *Kerry Archaeological Magazine*, 1, no. 6 (April 1911), pp. 376–9

Windle, Bertram C. A., and Shore, T. W., 'Proposed Reconstitution of the University of London', *The British Medical Journal*, 1, no. 1582 (25 April 1891), pp. 933–4

PAMPHLETS AND LECTURES NOT PUBLISHED OR PUBLISHED WITHOUT A DATE

On the Brain in a Case of Motor Aphasia with Deafness (n.p.)
On the Ferric Chloride Reaction in Urine (n.p.)
The Morbid Anatomy of Diabetes Mellitus (Dublin)
Account of a Teratoma Springing from the Sphenoid of a Calf, with the Results Produced by the Tumour (n.p.)
Exophthalmic Goitre (Dublin)
Occasional Report on Anatomy (Birmingham)
[A Collection of Archaeological Pamphlets on Roman Remains Formed by Sir B.C.A. Windle and Relating Principally to Great Britain]
Recent Developments in the Queen's College (n.p.)
On Anthropometric Work in Large Schools (London)
The Occurrence of an Additional Phalanx in the Human Pollex (London)
Primary Sarcoma of the Kidney (n.p.)
Teratological Evidence as the Heredity of Acquired Conditions (London)
Windle, Bertram C. A., and Catholic Truth Society, *The Catholic Aspect of the Education Question* (London: Catholic Truth Society)

Index